D0217317

Personal Security

A Guide for International Travelers

Personal Security

A Guide for International Travelers

Tanya Spencer

CRC Press
Taylor & Francis Group
Boca Raton   London   New York

CRC Press is an imprint of the
Taylor & Francis Group, an **informa** business

CRC Press
Taylor & Francis Group
6000 Broken Sound Parkway NW, Suite 300
Boca Raton, FL 33487-2742

© 2014 by Taylor & Francis Group, LLC
CRC Press is an imprint of Taylor & Francis Group, an Informa business

No claim to original U.S. Government works

Printed on acid-free paper
Version Date: 20130524

International Standard Book Number-13: 978-1-4665-5944-8 (Paperback)

Visit the Taylor & Francis Web site at
http://www.taylorandfrancis.com

and the CRC Press Web site at
http://www.crcpress.com

Praise for the Book

"**Personal Security: A Guide for International Travelers** provides the perfect mix of lessons-learned, tools, and recommendations from experts so that readers can personalize their own approach to managing travel risks. If followed, the information provided will allow readers to get out and experience the local culture while still traveling safely."

—Bernie Sullivan, Director Global Security, Hanesbrands Inc.

"This book is a must-have for any traveler. Having worked in South and Southeast Asia, I know the advice provided in the book holds the key to keeping safe, avoiding dangerous situations, and managing threats when they occur. The book's methodological framework, combined with the author's extensive experience and hands-on knowledge, provide very practical and useful advice."

—Kathrine Alexandrowiz, Independent consultant at Kathalyst, former coordinator for the "Regional Risk Management Project for NGOs in Asia Pacific" (ECHO)

"**Personal Security: A Guide for International Travelers** is a go-to guide for all travelers irrespective of mission or purpose. An excellent piece of work."

—Major Avtar Singh, CPP, CFE, CAS, Chairman, ASIS International New Delhi, India, Chapter # 207

"This is a must-read book and an invaluable resource for global corporations and international business travelers—those concerned with security and safety issues while working and living abroad. Personal stories from experienced travelers, combined with Spencer's expert advice, highlight a broad range of critical issues, particularly ways to avoid risk and danger during worldwide travels."

—Christina Fuglsbjerg, Global Mobility Specialist, AS3 Companies

"Each of us have individual reasons that compel us to travel—for recreation, for passion, or for our work. Travel security awareness is critical and something that should be ever-present, though that is not always the case. The author provides the reader with an original, easy-to-read book that makes the perils of travel, and how to manage them, understandable even to non-security experts. Happy reading and safe travels!"

—**Federico Bernasconi, Head of Security, Prysmian Group**

"In today's uncertain world, **Personal Security: A Guide for International Travelers** is essential reading for business and leisure travelers the world over. Using her wealth of experience and knowledge, Spencer delivers a highly informative and invaluable guide, presenting personal safeguards and precautions—both pre- and post-departure—that can be taken. A highly recommended read."

—**Adrian Shaw, Founder of Expatcompare and Head of Medical & Travel—AAIB; specialist in Iraq, Libya, Afghanistan, and frontier markets**

Contents

Acknowledgments

Writing this book has been an incredible journey for me, so there are many people I want to thank for their part in its development. After I coauthored *Travel Wisely: A Personal Security Guide for Women Travelers* (available in Danish as *Rejs Sikkert: Guide Til Personlig Sikkerhed For Kvinder, Der Rejser* [self published]) with Chris Poole in 2008, a seedling idea to write a book for a global audience was formed. The idea blossomed when *Rejs Sikkert* was updated and reprinted in 2011. That book's success had much to do with the insights we gained from a workshop we conducted and the feedback from previews that we sent to our networks.

The timing was perfect when, in connection with my presentation "Communicating Security: What You Need to Know, to Tell Others" at the ASIS International Conference in Orlando in 2011, Mark Listewnik from CRC Press asked me to submit a book proposal about travel security. Here was my chance to fulfill a dream.

Creating this book with the support of the many respondents to market surveys who sent in their wish lists of topics and travel stories, 62 contributors who lent their expertise on current travel risks, and the many others who simply sent their encouragement has been a fantastic experience. After the book was drafted, I needed "fresh eyes" on it, and in that regard I owe great thanks to Michael Koefoed, Beth Rehman, Johanne Duus Hornemann, and most of all Carrie Clinton for their editorial advice.

My deepest gratitude goes to my near and dear family, who supported me throughout this journey. Dreams do come true.

Tanya Spencer

Introduction

Guised as a visa problem, the police called me into the station, but my human rights work in Kosovo was the real reason. That, and their suspicions about my activities and workshops for inter-ethnic/religious dialogue during a time when war raged in the rest of Yugoslavia and Kosovo was a power-keg ready to be ignited. The "information conversation," as the five Serbian secret and regular police called it, was actually an interrogation lasting several hours. Throughout, I secretly hoped that my colleague was able to reach my embassy or organization: I knew what they were capable of if they decided to take me to the cellar.

But international sanctions meant many things did not function properly, so he was not able to make the call before the police collected him and searched the team office/apartment. Afterwards, I was furious with my sending agency for not preparing me for such a situation given my job and the consequences for all the people I was associated with (even my neighbors were subsequently interrogated). But, at the time, not much thought was put into security—doing the job was the important thing.

The police probably did not deport me, as they had threatened to do, because I was scheduled to leave in two days to report to my organization's general assembly, and, belatedly, attend my preparation course. I ended up being a resource person at that workshop when I assisted the trainers with adding a security component. They invited me to be a trainer at the next workshop. Ever since then, my professional journey has led me to write this travel security book.

My intention with this book is to help international travelers prevent security incidents and react in life-saving ways during a crisis. Just as food and culture vary from one location to the next, the security situation differs from place to place. So, let the realities of your destination be the decisive factors in determining how much time, effort, and resources you will use on managing travel risks. It is all about being realistically prepared for the situations that you might face. Whether heading for Ankara, Buenos Aires, or Cape Town, you can feel and be safer.

A central theme throughout this book is that your interaction with your environment involves a unique and dynamic set of circumstances. Accordingly, the book focuses on providing practical and flexible frameworks, models, and tools, as well as suggestions from experts, lessons-learnt stories from travelers, and literature for further reading so that you can customize your approach to managing travel risks. The key message here is: *Your security is personal.*

To best explain what this book has to offer you, a description of its development should help highlight the key benefits. In 2012, I used my professional networks to survey travelers and managers responsible for traveling staff. I relied substantially upon various LinkedIn groups focused on travel, security, culture, business, NGO, and duty of care. Essentially, they were asked what was needed in *the* travel security book that they would buy for themselves and/or recommend to their traveling staff. A wealth of responses came in, from "wish lists" of topics that they would like covered to favorite travel tips and advice. Expert contributors and industry "thought-leaders" were then actively sought with the aim of having different "voices" from around the world discussing current travel risks and trends to be aware of. As all of these inputs came together, the book became a cross between travel stories and an encyclopedia of "best practice."

I would like to take this opportunity to thank all the survey respondents and the many people who simply sent messages of encouragement. And to the 62 contributors who crafted original text or gave this book license to modify previously published materials, thank you again for your time and efforts to provide the book's readers with best practice advice and tips.

Throughout the process, I aimed to ensure that the book:

- Is geared specifically for a global audience, traveling wherever and however.
- Is relevant and user-friendly.
- Is comprehensive both in terms of covering travel risks and current trends, but also recognizing the "human factor" in the security equation.
- Applies travel risk management concepts to reality, and in the process demonstrates the flexibility and benefits of a proactive approach. And it identifies any limitations.
- Provides basic tips, facts, and definitions. Moreover, it should be well supplemented with "golden nuggets" of information and insights.
- Emphasizes preventative measures, but also cover reactive options to fully prepare readers for various situations.
- Helps empower readers to proactively manage travel risks so that they gain peace of mind and improve their ability to make the most out of the opportunities that travel brings.

An invaluable metaphor I like to use for travel security is to think of it as the headlights of a vehicle: You turn on your headlights to illuminate not only what is in front of you but also to alert to you any potential dangers that could affect your ability to reach your goal—that could be establishing a market presence in Pretoria or vacationing in Phnom Penh. This book aims to help you determine when and to what extent your security headlights need to be turned on to illuminate the way.

Wherever and however you travel, I wish you safe journeys!

UTILIZING THIS BOOK

The book was written so that it can be read cover to cover if, say, you are responsible for the security of traveling staff, or only called upon as a quick reference guide, in which you dip into certain subjects to confirm what you already know and add to what you want to know in order to continuously be a safe and aware traveler. Though the book's primary audience is business and NGO travelers, it is for anyone who works or plays in potentially risky destinations.

Throughout the book, relevant sections are cross-referenced. For instance, in the **Information Security: Identity Theft and Industrial Espionage** section (**see Section 1.11**), the subject of credit card skimming is cross-referenced to the mitigating advice in the **Crime and Corruption** section **(see Section 2.16)**. Cross-referencing is extensively employed to aid you with painting a complete picture of the circumstances that you may face, and security measures that you might opt for.

External articles and resources are also widely referred to. Often, there is an explanation of what you can expect from them. References are collectively issued at the end of each chapter. Every effort was made to supply further reading suggestions that are available on the Internet. The **Further Reading and Resources** index at the end of the book categorizes all the referenced materials into subject areas. This index also notes whether it is a recommended text. Inevitably, the cited facts, statistics, and perhaps some of the issues will become outdated. But the book's flexible approach to proactively managing travel risks will still be relevant.

The main tools woven throughout the book are the **Risk Management Framework (RMF)** and the Knowledge, Skills, Attitude, and Behaviors model. The five steps of the **RMF**, as described in the next section, are the backbone for managing travel risks proactively. You can use it to make informed decisions and choose the best actions. All readers are recommended to read the **RMF** section to get the most out of the book. The Knowledge, Skills, Attitude, and Behaviors model, as described in the **Building Situational Awareness** section **(see Section 1.3)**, can be used as part of your preparations and throughout your trip.

All the tools and models in the book are illustrated using real cases and likely scenarios. Throughout the book, many questions are posed for your individual reflection so that you can modify the advice to suit your travel realities.

RISK MANAGEMENT FRAMEWORK

Because the world is dynamic and every situation is different, this book demonstrates how you can practically apply the **Risk Management Framework (RMF)** in order to feel and be safer while traveling. The **RMF** entails five stages:

RMF 1 Being informed of the threats and the likelihood of meeting those threats.

RMF 2 Understanding your vulnerabilities and strengths from the local perspective and in the situational context. And being aware of the extent to which you are potentially exposed to a threat.

RMF 3 Creating options for yourself that reduce the likelihood and impact of a threat.

RMF 4 Continuously monitoring and adjusting to the situation.

RMF 5 Having confidence in your security precautions and reactions.

You can apply the five risk management steps regardless of whether you are visiting your company's new operation in Tel Aviv, heading to Tbilisi to monitor an NGO project, or planning to enjoy Tokyo's sights and sounds. Through expert advice and real examples from travelers, the book spotlights how you can think about and implement the **RMF** to improve your security. Even though this book focuses on human-made threats, you can apply the framework to other types of risks. References to the framework will, for example, be cited as **(RMF 1)**.

FIGURE I.1   Courtesy of Peter Steudtner/www.panphotos.org.

Putting aside the question of whether the world is becoming a more dangerous place or not, it is still a great place to travel and enjoy the variety of flavors and cultures (Figure I.1). The flexibility of the **RMF** allows you apply it wherever and however you travel. The framework is demonstrated thoroughly to illustrate its practical application to a variety of situations.

Author

When **Tanya Spencer** was 18 years old, Rigoberta Menchu, a Guatemalan human rights activist, personally thanked her for helping save countless lives because Tanya ran an alert network that involved writing to U.S. politicians about urgent cases. Rigoberta Menchu, many years later, was the first indigenous woman to be awarded the Nobel Peace Prize. Tanya's professional career, spanning over 25 years, has focused on supporting people's ability to work and live with a "peace of mind."

She owns TrainingSolutions, a provider of travel security and crisis management courses, consultations, and coaching for global organizations. Tanya has trained thousands of people (the United Nations, governments, business people, engineers, journalists, refugees, aid workers, rural people, amongst others) for an A–Z range of destinations, literally Albania to Zimbabwe and most countries in between. She has traveled to more than 40 countries, most of them "hot spots." Tanya's approach to travel security is based on insights gained from her intercultural, interreligious, and international experiences.

Internationally published, Tanya has written about travel security, peace education and conflict resolution, security management, international policy, and leadership skills for security professionals. She is active in ASIS International, the world's largest security network, as an Assistant Regional Vice President, the European representative for Women in Security, and a member of the Crisis Management and Business Continuity Council. She served four years as a board member of the ASIS Denmark chapter and was named the Danish chapter's Member of the Year, 2009.

Her educational credentials include an MSc in social policy and planning in developing countries from the London School of Economics, a BA in peace and conflict studies and a diploma in conservation and resource studies from the University of California, Berkeley, and management certificates from Wharton/ASIS International and the University of London.

Contributors

The travelers who shared their lessons learnt and the thought-leaders who proffered their expert advice are:[*]

Syed Ali: Major (Retired) Pakistan Army and INGO security officer **(see Section 1.12.2)**.

"Anita": International business traveler **(see Section 2.15)**.

Fazal Bahardeen: Chief executive officer, Crescentrating **(see Section 1.2.8)**.

Adam Bates: Vice president, Insurance Services of America **(see Section 1.9)**.

Dan Belai: Security consultant, ATC Systems and ASIS International Romania Chapter Chair **(see Section 2.4)**.

Dorthe Borum: Business traveler, textile industry **(see Section 1.2)**.

Dr. Donald Bosch: Director of clinical services, Headington Institute **(see Section 1.17)**.

David Brient: Executive coach, DB Coaching Ltd. **(see Section 2.3)**.

Dmitry Budanov: ASIS International Russia Chapter chair **(see Section 2.16.8)**.

Gabor Bunth: Director of loss prevention, St. Pancras Renaissance Hotel London, Marriott International **(see Sections 1.15 and 2.15)**.

CBM International: Modified excerpts from 2011 "Safety and Security Factsheets" **(see Sections 1.2.4 and 2.2.4)**.

Jack Chu: President, RA Consultants Ltd. **(see Sections 1.4, 2.2.1, and 2.4)**.

Darrell Clifton: Author of *Hospitality Security* (CRC Press, 2012) and director of security, Circus Circus Hotel and Casino **(see Sections 1.15 and 2.15)**.

Brittany Damora: Political risk analyst **(see Sections 1.1.2, 1.6, and 2.4)**.

Major (Retired) Paul Devassy, CPP: ASIS International India Chapter member. Regional security manager in an MNC in India **(see Sections 2.10.3, 2.12.1, and 2.12.2)**.

"Frank": Former business traveler, entertainment industry **(see Section 1.4)**.

Rudy Friederich: Chief inspector (retired) U.S. Marshals Service **(see Section 2.3)**.

"Geanie": Educationalist **(see Section 2.15)**.

Tom Givens: Owner and chief instructor, Rangemaster. Author of more than 100 magazine articles and five textbooks including *Fighting Smarter* (Rangemaster,

---

[*] Contributors chose how their names ("alias," full name, or first name only) and descriptions would appear.

2000). He is an expert witness in cases involving firearms and firearms training **(see Section 2.3)**.

Vivi Hannibal: Business director, Special Contingency Risks **(see Section 3.3.4)**.

Ali Hayat: Security consultant **(see Section 2.2)**.

Anthony Hegarty: Managing director, Discreet Risk & Security Management Services **(see Section 2.5)**.

Jytte Hollender: Director and owner, hollender.dk ApS **(see Section 2.15)**.

Major Eliud Muita Ikua: Head of security, Communications Commission of Kenya **(see Section 2.15)**.

Ken Nygaard Jensen: Security adviser, Ministry of Foreign Affairs of Denmark **(see Sections 1.11.2, 2.11.2, and 2.16.8)**.

Jerome: Frequent business traveler and diver. Retail, manufacturing, and customer goods industry **(see Sections 2.10.2 and 3.6)**.

"John": Chief security officer, energy sector **(see Section 2.11.2)**.

Mark Johnson: Security and fraud control specialist in telecom and online crime investigations and management, social media, and online games risks, TRMG **(see Section 1.11.1)**.

Bruno Kalhoj: Regional security advisor, Control Risks **(see Section 1.4)**.

Patrick Kane: Senior director of security with a global aviation services provider **(see Sections 1.13 and 2.13)**.

Sian Kelly: Health, safety, and well-being consultant and executive coach. Director, Calm-Consulting **(see Section 2.17)**.

Lena Lauridsen: Intercultural consultant and author, Itim International **(see Section 1.7)**.

"Lisa": Frequent business and family traveler **(see Section 2.16.1)**.

Fritz Lorenzen: Global physical security manager, climate and energy manufacturing sector **(see Section 1.9)**.

Abigail Lucas Maia: IT computer forensic and security specialist. Owner and chief executive officer, Secluded IT Aid **(see Sections 1.12.1 and 2.12)**.

Neil Mackinnon: Security consultant and duty of care specialist, G2X Consulting Ltd., Travel Safety & Security Consulting **(see Section 1.9)**.

Sarah Martin: Consultant and specialist on prevention and response to gender-based violence **(see Section 3.4)**.

Chris E. McGoey: Security consultant, McGoey Security Consulting **(see Section 1.16)**.

Kirsten Mols: IT director **(see Section 1.2.6)**.

Birgitte Bang Nielsen: Board member, Transparency International, Denmark **(see Section 2.16.8)**.

Leanne Olson: Charge nurse in the pediatric emergency department at the Children's Hospital of Eastern Ontario and a former nurse with international aid organizations **(see Sections 1.8 and 2.8)**.

James Otigbah: Security and executive protection specialist, Excel Security Solutions AG **(see Section 1.3)**.

Fernando Lanzer Pereira de Souza: Management consultant, executive coach, and international trainer in cross-cultural management **(see Sections 2.2, 2.7, and 2.16.6)**.

Steve Phelps: Owner, Security & Intelligence Solutions Ltd. **(see Section 2.14.6)**.

Phil: Security management trainer, humanitarian sector **(see Section 2.15)**.

Catherine Plumridge: Director, Humanitrain. Former nurse (critical care and tropical medicine), former British Army Officer, and has worked for several NGOs, ICRC, and the UN **(see Section 3.8)**.

Chris Poole: Author, trainer, and consultant in violence prevention, especially for women and girls. Director, Violence Prevention in Practice (Voldsforebyggelse I Praksis) **(see Section 2.2.3)**.

Andreas Poppius: Security consultant, adventure traveler, and former senior security officer/Swedish Embassy, Kabul, Afghanistan **(see Sections 1.1.3, 2.8, 2.14.3, and 3.1.1)**.

"Raquel": Safety and security manager for rapid response teams, humanitarian sector **(see Section 1.17)**.

Tony Ridley: Consultant, speaker, author, and advisor, Travel Risk Management Solutions **(see Section 1.12.2)**.

Jochen Riegg: Protection officer, human rights monitoring NGO **(see Section 3.6)**.

Robert: Educational project facilitator **(see Section 2.7)**.

Abhimanyu Singh: Head of risk advisory, RECON-Risk Evasion & Control. Lead on APAC and MENA regions for the International Protect and Prepare Security Office (IPPSO) based in Delhi, India. He is an author, speaker, and consultant **(see Sections 2.6 and 2.14)**.

Prakash Sivasankaran: Senior security architect, telecom solution provider **(see Section 1.4)**.

Mark Snelling: Psychodynamic counselor and training consultant, InterHealth **(see Section 1.17)**.

Solène: Humanitarian aid worker **(see Section 2.3)**.

Richard Stevens: Managing director, CAT-UXO Ltd. **(see Section 1.4)**.

John J. Strauchs: Security design consultant at Strauchs, LLC who has worked in Saudi Arabia, Kuwait, Jordan, Singapore, Hong Kong, Vietnam, Greece, Venezuela, and Colombia amongst others **(see Sections 1.15, 2.15, and 3.9.1)**.

Andrew Taylor-Gammon: International security and crisis management specialist **(see Section 3.9.2)**.

Scott A. Watson: Security management consultant **(see Section 2.2.8)**.

Pablo Weisz: Regional security manager (the Americas), Travel Security Services, a joint venture between Control Risks and International SOS **(see Section 2.5)**.

Tim Williams: Director of political and security risk, Stirling Assynt **(see Section 1.6)**.

1 Before You Go

To support your pre-trip preparations, this chapter maps out expert advice and lessons learnt from real life cases to give you insights into such questions as:

- What tools are needed to flexibly manage travel risks **(see Section 1.1)**?
- Which of your personal characteristics are strengths or weaknesses in a given context **(see Section 1.2)**?
- What knowledge, skills, attitudes, and behaviors are needed to be a safer traveler **(see Section 1.3)**?
- What should be on your pre-trip checklist **(see Section 1.4)**?
- What are your organization's responsibilities to you and what are your responsibilities **(see Section 1.5)**?
- How much time, effort, and resources should you invest in understanding a destination's politics **(see Section 1.6)**?
- How does your cultural background influence your interactions with different cultures **(see Section 1.7)**?
- What is needed to be a healthy traveler **(see Section 1.8)**?
- Why should you double-check your insurance coverage **(see Section 1.9)**?
- What are some useful, lightweight security gadgets worth packing **(see Section 1.10)**?
- To what extent is your personal and organizational information exposed to threats **(see Section 1.11)**?
- Which communication equipment and procedures do you really need **(see Section 1.12)**?
- What can you do to make air travel safer and more pleasant **(see Section 1.13)**?
- How can you map out safer transportation options **(see Section 1.14)**?
- Which security criteria should you employ when selecting your accommodation **(see Section 1.15)**?
- What steps can you take to protect your home while you are away **(see Section 1.16)**?
- How can you better recognize real and perceived fears **(see Section 1.17)**?
- What are the key points you should keep in mind before you go **(see Section 1.18)**?

The security measures you need in Denver will be different than those for Dhaka. Your decision to adopt one security measure over another will depend on the unique interplay between you and your environment. Accordingly, this chapter provides flexible frameworks, models, and tools, as well as suggestions for further reading so that you can customize your approach to managing travel risks, wherever you travel. The aim is to boost your security awareness knowledge, skills, attitudes, and behaviors so you can rely upon the "best available options" throughout your journeys.

"Prevention is better than the cure" as the old saying goes. The emphasis of this chapter is on proactively mitigating risks, and it should be highlighted that many of the tips can also often help you reduce the impact of security incidents.

1.1 PROACTIVELY ANALYZING THE RISKS

To be honest, you probably do not want to think about security more than you have to: Let the realities of your destination be the decisive factors in determining how much time, effort, and resources you will use on analyzing a location. That said, even doing basic research before your trip and asking questions while in the country will improve your security awareness.

Threat, contextual, and situational analyses are tools that you can apply to your travel situation as required. The more you integrate them into your travel regime, the greater the chances will be that you will know how to prevent security incidents and to react in worst-case scenarios.

Before moving on to the various analysis tools, it is important to define risk: Two typical definitions of risk are "the potential for damage or loss of an asset" and/or "the likelihood and impact of encountering a threat." Risk can be described with words, visualized with graphs, and even represented in LEGO models, but in the end its formulation is limited by the fact that it cannot truly calculate for life's dynamism and complexities. Therefore, there are many ways to represent risk: Some experts draw risk at the center of concentric circles of threats, assets, and vulnerabilities so when these three factors overlap a risk exists. Others use the mathematical equation: Risk = Impact × Probability, where impact is the asset's value and probability is the likelihood of a threat meeting a vulnerability. Whichever model you use, the key issue is that you can mitigate risks by reducing the assets (e.g., not wearing expensive jewelry) and/or vulnerabilities (e.g., using a reliable taxi service at night) that are exposed to a threat. In some cases, you can reduce the threat, but in general, the manifestation of a threat is outside of your control. In other words, you can make yourself and your belongings a less tempting and/or easy target.

To see risk as it relates to traveling, it is the pain, suffering, embarrassment, and costs of repairing/recovering from the situation, and it occurs when something you value, including you, is exposed to a likely threat. In "Padmaj's" story that **Paul Devassy** describes in his contribution **"Recounting a Friend's Story: 'International Financial Analysis Firm Employee Loses Laptop from a Shopping Mall Parking Lot—Eeeek!'"** (see Section 2.12), his company had to bear the costs of the lost laptop and contingency efforts against any possible data or system breaches. In this case, the organization had information technology (IT) security measures in place, but any company in that situation will still have to invest in damage control. As for "Padmaj," he felt the incident's immediate and lasting consequences because it affected the next day's important business meeting, he suffered embarrassment once his colleagues found out, and it was clear that his bosses had a negative view of the episode. The threat existed in the parking lot environment, perpetrated by either an opportunistic passerby or a criminal waiting to rob tempting goodies left in vehicles.

For "Padmaj," the worst part of the ordeal was that he had made it easy for the perpetrator to take advantage of the laptop bag's being exposed on his front seat, as he hurriedly focused on running an errand squeezed into an already busy schedule. In other words, all those problems were quite preventable.

Life is full of risks, but opportunities come to those who manage them. Proactive risk management, in its most simplified but still most effective form, entails continuously implementing these three steps:

1. Gather information.
2. Analyze the risk.
3. Develop options.

Accordingly, the following three sections on threat, context, and situational analyses and the vulnerability analysis (see Section 1.2) in the subsequent section are discussed in detail so that you know what information to gather, how to analyze risks, and which decisive criteria you need to employ when developing the best options to act upon. The examples and cases presented in the book can further aid you with understanding the key components needed to wield the **Risk Management Framework (RMF)** effectively.

1.1.1 Threat Assessment

A threat is someone or something that intends to cause harm or loss of an asset. When you are the asset that will be harmed, threats to you could include kidnapping, sexual violence, stabbing, and so forth. Threats against your belongings could include laptop theft due to industrial espionage, loss of your passport and wallet due to street crime, or valuables taken during a house burglary while you are abroad.

To further your understanding of threats, for each type of threat consider when, where, who (perpetrator and target), how, which local details, and what is the perpetrator's end goal.

- When does the threat most often occur?
- Where are the typical locations?
- Who are the likely perpetrators?
- Who are the preferred targets (see Section 1.2)?
- How do the perpetrators execute their threat?
- Which local details and specifics do you need to be aware of?
- What is the perpetrator's end goal?

Even though every situation is unique, you can flexibly apply these types of questions when assessing threats. The more critical a threat is, the more effort you want to put into testing any assumptions and gaps. This assists you with being realistically prepared and focused on the real dangers: Overall, this process usually frees up your time and energy (Figure 1.1).

If you get the opportunity to understand the intention, capacity, and history of the perpetrator(s), then you will have a better chance of weighing the likelihood of a

FIGURE 1.1   Courtesy of Beth Rehman.

threat occurring. Behind a perpetrator's intention is a motivation—these are needs and wants that he or she is trying to satisfy. A street criminal might be motivated because he needs a drug fix and you happen to be there, talking on your mobile phone and looking distracted **(see Section 2.16)**. Tribesmen who kidnap you are doing it to get cash by selling you to a terrorist network. That network, with its political-religious agenda and sophisticated understanding of the international media, might eradicate you because they need their recruitment numbers to go up **(see Section 3.3)**. Capacity or capability is linked to the perpetrator's methods and his ability to achieve his goals. High-level cyber criminals have the skills to influence markets **(see Section 1.11)**. A seductress involved in social engineering will be charming, beautiful, and perhaps equipped with a sleeping drug to put in your drink **(see Section 2.11)**. The perpetrator's history with prior attempts and successful executions is another key factor in determining the probability of an incident occurring. If your home has been broken into, there is a greater chance that the perpetrators will try again, so if you have the attitude of "why lock the barn door after the horse has run out," then you are vulnerable to another burglary **(see Section 1.16)**.

Weighing the likelihood of a threat helps you in many ways: Mainly, it allows you to realistically adjust your security measures to match the threats, saving you mental energy and resource expenditures. Essentially, you can be a more effective traveler because you are appropriately using your time, resources, and efforts on managing your security. For example, take the threat of kidnapping. There is no need for you to attend a course on it if your business mainly shuttles you between northern Norway and southern Sweden. But, it should be your top priority if you are relocating to Mexico and will travel throughout Latin America. There is a greater probability that you might encounter kidnapping in Latin America than in Scandinavia because there are criminals who intend to make money from your capture, have the network to pull it off, and have enough experience to do it as a routine matter.

Having insights into the probability of an incident occurring can also assist you when you are trying to decide if a rumor is fact or fiction. What do you know about the perpetrators' intention, capacity, and history? Why would they want to pull something like this off? Can they do it? Have their announcements been accurate in the past? Even with these insights, there are no guarantees that all your decisions will be 100% perfect, but you are aiming to make well-informed decisions.

You can also use other models to assess threats: Examples in this book include the six W's **(see Section 2.2.2)** and the ability, opportunity, intention triangle **(see Section 2.16)**. Use whichever model or create your own mix of relevant components that suits you and your realities.

Specifically regarding threat levels as often used by governments, organizations, and risk analysis services, these are often illustrated using a color-coded system: red represents high/extreme risk, orange is for medium/high risk, yellow indicates moderate/low risk, and blue or green is for minimum risk. During the research phase of this book, several respondents who are travelers themselves and/or have security management responsibilities for travelers asked for advice on how to interpret and utilize these. As for interpreting these, far too much depends on the reliability, agenda, and interests of the source to give generic advice, except to say be aware of these factors and think about how they might influence the provided information **(see Section 1.1.2)**.

Regarding utilizing this information as a tool to help safeguard you, you can directly link each level with actions you should be taking. Let's say your next destination has a yellow threat level, but a general election will soon commence, which is worrying since the last elections resulted in massive bloodletting. On the other hand, tensions have gotten better in the past three years. As you prepare for your trip, you might wager that nothing will happen during your stay. But, be forewarned, it is a common mistake to assume there is a linear, step-by-step progression up the levels. Real life does not work that way and situations can quickly escalate if the right triggers are introduced **(see Sections 1.1.3 and 3.2)**. Therefore, in a set of circumstances such as this one already at the yellow phase, you probably should have your personal documents and essential valuables packed in a secure and accessible location. And you should have an exit strategy that is realistic enough to cope with "what ifs." If you go through the process of creating a personalized list of actions linked to the various threat levels, then remember to keep it simple and easy to follow. For example, you could create a matrix with a column for the threat level and one for your actions. If you feel it could be useful, you can add columns for indicators that a threat is increasing and/or actions you can expect from your organization. Needless to say, the actions on your list will depend on the types of threats and circumstances of your destination.

1.1.2 CONTEXT ASSESSMENT

A country's general background is the context, entailing its history, politics, culture, demographics, climate, infrastructure, economy, and so forth. While all this information is interesting, it is very time consuming and therefore impractical for most people, especially for frequent flyers. The extent you bother to understand the overall context will depend on several factors. For example, if you are the managing director of a new multimillion-dollar operation in Morocco, then it is worth your effort to thoroughly read up on and continuously ask questions about the context. Needless to say, if you are on a five-day bird-watching safari in Malaysia, the most you might do is skim over your guidebook on the airplane and listen to your guide's stories and answers to questions. In these two examples, the different factors of return-on-investment, the length of the visit, the threat levels, and the need to relax while on vacation or be a successful manager will determine the time, effort, and resources you put into gaining knowledge about the context.

For most travelers, having a basic understanding of the context better enables you to assess your environment and your interaction with it. As a British person, you may be alarmed when some local persons are treating you poorly, but it may help to understand that in some countries people still resent colonial Britain. In another context you may get the same treatment, but this time it is because the local people assume all British are disorderly drunks. How you deal with either potentially threatening situation should, ideally, be informed by your knowledge of the context.

You might read something like the next contribution, **"Briefing on Indonesia,"** when you gather information from:

- Open sources: http://www.wikitravel.org, http://www.worldtravelwatch. com, and http://www.ihatetaxis.com.
- Paid-for services providing country reports and briefings: http://www. riskline.com, http://www.controlrisks.com, and http://www.asigroup.com.
- Government websites: http://www.smartraveller.gov.au, http://www.voyage. gc.ca, and http://www.fco.gov.uk.
- International news: http://www.aljazeera.com, http://www.cnn.com, and http://www.bbc.co.uk.

To customize any information contained in a briefing (verbal or written) to you, you can to ask yourself the basic questions of "What, who, when, how, where, which local details?" Then assess the information in light of how it might affect you and your itinerary. For example, while reading the **"Briefing on Indonesia,"** you could ask "For the cities I will be traveling to, where specifically is crime a problem? Which situations and methods do the criminals prefer?" Similarly, you could consider earthquakes and terrorism. Your aim is to draw a picture of your destination's situation and how it might affect you. You are then in a good position to take the right security precautions and measures.

BRIEFING ON INDONESIA: A CONTEXT ANALYSIS EXAMPLE

BRITTANY DAMORA
POLITICAL RISK ANALYST

The security environment across the archipelago has improved notably in recent years. However, the threat from terrorism persists and should not be ignored. Typical targets include tourist areas such as Bali as well as Western-associated and commercially or politically viable assets in Jakarta. For travelers, ethnic or communal violence and civil unrest continue to pose a notable security risk in certain parts of the archipelago.

That said, crime is the most likely security risk to foreign businesses and individuals. Western visitors and expatriates can be victims of petty crime due to their perceived wealth. This is more of an issue in urban areas where wealth discrepancies are highly visible.

Indonesia is particularly vulnerable to natural disasters and climate change. Situated on the volatile seismic area of the "Ring of Fire," Indonesia is in an active volcanic and earthquake region. Strong earthquakes are possible anywhere in the country, but are less likely in Kalimantan and southwest Sulawesi. In 2010, there were more than 200 earthquakes measuring 5 or more on the Richter scale across Indonesia.

Remember that the politics of information are often at play when you gather information about a destination's threats and situation. Let's say you come from a small country and you check your government's website about various countries, you might assume that you are getting information from a good source. Unbeknownst to you, the website is filled with edited text from a larger Western government's country briefings. And it just so happens, for the country you will be going to, bilateral economic relations heavily influence the source of the information. Or, in another example, you rely on the country reports your company receives from a paid-for service. However, note the concern **Ken Nygaard Jensen** raises in **"Avoiding Espionage: The Extreme Examples of Russia and China but Applicable for All Business Travels" (see Section 1.11.2)** that these services might be fearful of mentioning something that will get them kicked out of the country. Even news sources may edit the story about your destination to more suit their conservative, liberal, or governmental slant than to provide you with unbiased information. In other words, the quality of information you can get depends upon factors outside of your control.

Within your control, however, is to collect information from a variety of sources ranging from the traditional ones (TV news, government website) to newer ones available through social media (Twitter, blogs, local podcasts). In some cases, it is worth the effort to consider the political, financial, social, and so forth backgrounds of your sources. This will help you to better understand their possible agendas, which in turn will help you determine how you will use a particular source.

If you are heading toward a very risky destination, you probably will spend more time on going over the information and put greater emphasis on establishing at least three trusted sources on each of the global, national, and local levels. Just because you might be going on vacation does not necessarily mean you can relax on gathering information. It is the interface between the threats in the environment and who you are, what you do, and how you do it that should be the decisive factors. If you and your old school mates are planning a boating holiday, filled with beers and remembrances, off the Kenyan coast, it is highly advisable that you are well-informed about Somali pirate activities before you go and especially through your captain's local contacts once you are there (and, because everybody at sea in such a location needs to see themselves as part of information chain, you should probably not allow yourself to get so exceedingly bleary-eyed from alcohol or laughs that it decreases your situational awareness).

Another important thing to remember while you are in the country is that some sociocultural-political-economic subjects can be highly sensitive because, amongst other reasons, they are essential to the identity of people and a place. Asking a demographics question out of innocent curiosity could make your client feel cornered into telling why a particular ethnic group has left the area, so instead he gives you an angry, evasive response. Carrying documents with this type of information can also cause you problems with certain customs officials or police (**see Section 1.13**). It would be terribly ironic if in your attempts to be more security aware, you inadvertently triggered a security incident.

1.1.3 SITUATIONAL ANALYSIS

Situational analysis entails the same components as the contextual analysis but it is focused on the current and ongoing circumstances. To illustrate the difference between the two, think of the context as the climate and the situation as the weather. Even though you live in a semi-arid climate, it might be raining right now. Within a certain context, such as a semi-arid climate, a new situational factor can result in a stronger chain reaction than would normally be expected, such as flooding. How the overall system copes with a new factor will depend on other contextual factors such as infrastructure. To relate this to the security situation of location, then the context could be an ethnic conflict that devastates parts of the country but leaves the rest peaceful enough to have a good tourism industry and external investments in the economy, as was the case in Sri Lanka for many years. During the war, a bag left at a bus station would cause the authorities to evacuate a wide area and call in the bomb squad. Before the war, station officials would have simply dealt with the bag. In the tense period after the war, a smaller area would be evacuated and the bomb experts would be used.

When you analyze a situation, you should be aware of how external factors might have security consequences for you: This is known as the "butterfly effect"—when a butterfly flaps its wings and the chain reaction results in a major storm on the other side of the world. If you are visiting a country and your government puts that country on the terror watch list or accuses it of currency manipulation, for example, then you might suddenly witness boisterous demonstrations against your country or hostility against you. The following contribution illustrates the interconnectedness of the world and the implications for your security.

THE MOHAMMAD CARICATURES IN YEMEN: PROTECTED BY RELATIONSHIPS

ANDREAS POPPIUS

SECURITY CONSULTANT, ADVENTURE TRAVELER, AND FORMER SENIOR SECURITY OFFICER/SWEDISH EMBASSY, KABUL, AFGHANISTAN (HTTP://WWW.U3KOMPETENS.SE)

I lived, traveled, and studied in Yemen for about six months in 2005 to 2006. During this time, the caricatures of Mohammad were published and the situation for Westerners in the country became more complicated.

One Sunday (weekends are from Friday to Saturday) as I arrived to my language class, I met my teacher, who was extremely agitated and a bit sinister. He explained about the publishing of the caricatures in the Danish press and that all Danes preferably should be considered the enemy of Islam. He further told me that he got it all from the mosque last Friday, where the mullah convinced the masses that it was a deliberate attack against their faith.

Since I had spent the weekend traveling in the countryside, I had at that moment no clue about what actually going on and to what extent. He soon filled me in, also claiming that I had to be careful on the streets of Sana'a. Because he knew me, he was very concerned about my safety and suggested that I should claim to be Italian if confronted (I am completely blond, with blue eyes and a semi-red beard). Anyway, we ended up having a three-hour discussion about freedom of speech, of which he in this case had little understanding. We both agreed on my being cautious and that he and his friend would keep me up to date about what was going on in the city. This resulted in my avoiding different protests, harassments, and other troubles—the only thing that happened to me as an effect of this was a short skirmish at the market where a few young Yemenis behind me spoke badly about Danes. When I answered them in their language and explained that I was Swedish, I immediately was accepted and the strain decreased.

When traveling in countries with a constant underlying tension, make sure to:

- Keep track of the world's news, and remember that you could be affected by events taking place in countries far away—news has no geographical boundaries.
- Develop and maintain a good relationship with the inhabitants of the country you are visiting—this could give you life-long friends and in many contexts this is also vital to your safety and security.

- Don't be afraid of discussions about religion, politics, and cultural differences. But make sure that you are speaking to people you trust. If you may get very critical, then it is important that you trust them a lot and that they might not be made insecure by having critical discussions with you.
- Always show your respect to the country's religion and culture—even if you don't agree with all the customs.
- If possible, learn the language or at least a few key words.

For your situational analysis of a country, you want to pay particular attention to relationships and trigger points. Relationships are the dynamic interplay within a country, in the region, and further afield. In **Andreas Poppius's** Yemen example, there was the relationship between faraway Denmark and large parts of the Muslim world. While on the microlevel, there were his relationships (and the time, effort, and resources he put into those before the threatening situation arose) with his local contacts.

During your research into a country's contextual background, you probably noticed certain issues or trigger points that either in the past and/or potentially in the near future could ignite underlying tensions. Typical trigger points include:

- Politics: elections, transitions
- Economics: devaluation of the currency, a major corruption case
- Societal issues: death of a leader, religious ceremonies
- Historical: anniversary of a lost battle, ethnic conflict, or suppression
- Legal: sensitive court case, jailing of lawyers
- Interrelations: regional tit-for-tat skirmishes, burning of religious artifacts in another part of the world
- Climatic: poor governmental response to a massive over-flooding, food prices soar due to a major harvest drying out
- Infrastructure: collapse of a kindergarten because of poor maintenance, insufficient affordable housing for the very poor resulting in vulnerable slum areas
- Cultural: foreigners wearing inappropriate clothing, government bans a traditional custom

This list only gives a small sliver of the wide spectrum of possible trigger points. But you can use it as a good starting point for when you need to develop your own situational analysis that highlights key relationships and potential trigger points. You can also refer to the Political, Economic, Societal, and Technology (PEST) model applied in the **Political Considerations** sections **(see Sections 1.6 and 2.6)** to help you identify possible trigger points.

1.1.4 Life Is Full of Risks, but Opportunities Come to Those Who Manage Them

The purpose of conducting threat, contextual, and situational analyses is to better understand your environment and your interaction with it **(RMF 1)**. Together with your personal considerations **(RMF 2)**, the aim is to give you insights and options

FIGURE 1.2   Courtesy of Peter Steudtner/www.panphotos.org.

that work for you (**RMF 3, 4, and 5**). Even a cursory analysis can help you be a more effective traveler because you will know when you can cruise without concern or when to "turn up your security lights" and steer clear of preventable security incidents (Figure 1.2).

With that aim, a highly recommended resource available at Red 24's website is the "Threat Forecast 2013." It provides practical analysis of the threats, useful visuals with explanations, and, in particular, the calendar of potentially risky dates for 2012 gives an overview that any traveler can draw upon.[1] Another interesting resource is the "Interactive Charts" available on Lloyd's website, which provide pictorial overviews of worldwide risks.[2] The "Heat Map" and the other pages covering trends, victims, and so forth on the Aid Worker Security Database website is particularly useful for NGO workers.[3]

1.2   PERSONAL CONSIDERATIONS AND VULNERABILITY ANALYSIS

How will you be perceived at your destination? Who you are, what you do, and how you do it will affect your security while traveling. Will you be seen as a busy business-man who has the time neither to properly attend to his belongings nor follow up on a police report? As a "do-good" NGO employee who talks about helping the people yet drives around in a 4-wheel-drive car? As a meek woman who would not dare repel a sexual advancement? How would you rather be perceived? Hopefully as a traveler who is confident in his or her security measures and ability to react appropriately if an incident arises.

As human beings, we bring in all kinds of considerations when assessing another person, especially in the initial encounters, including job title, skin color, nationality, clothes, language, possessions, viewpoints, and cultural sensitivity—the list is almost endless. When you travel, you need to see yourself through the local "glasses" of those with potentially good, neutral, or ill intent. Take the following contribution as an example.

MY SKIN HAS A DIFFERENT COLOR FOR EACH DESTINATION

TANYA SPENCER

*GLOBAL TRAVEL SECURITY AND CRISIS MANAGEMENT SPECIALIST,
TRAININGSOLUTIONS (HTTP://WWW.TRAININGSOLUTIONS.DK)*

In Kosovo I was black and in Kenya I was white. My color is closer to "coffee with milk" as they called me in Latin America. The context sees me through its filters. In many countries, as diverse as Pakistan, Ethiopia, and Guatemala, I "blend in," which definitely gives security advantages. Personal factors such as my skin color affect my interactions with people. The key for me, as an international traveler, is to be aware when these factors positively or negatively affect my security.

Figure 1.3 shows one way to visualize the interplay between you and your environment. To apply the model, let's say you are visiting Brazil for the first time, and while your spouse is in meetings all day, you would rather venture out, as in the contribution **"Inconspicuous in São Paulo" (see Section 2.2)**. What can you do to reduce your vulnerabilities? At the organizational level, you may consider the attitudes of the local community toward your company if there have been recent disputes **(see Section 1.2.2)**. For the layer involving your immediate environment, you could be on your third trip to Libya, but it is the first time you have been invited to see some beautiful vistas about 40 minutes away from the plant. What landmine awareness questions should you be asking your business partner before and during the trip **(see Section 1.4)**? And an example of

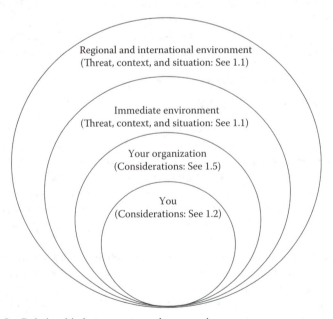

FIGURE 1.3   Relationship between you and your environment.

how international and regional politics and economics can increase your vulnerabilities while traveling could be that you are fair haired and blue eyed and visiting a Muslim country when demonstrations against the Mohammed drawings break out: What options should you have if you have been there for a longer period **(see Section 1.1.3)**, and what choices do you have if you are just a visitor **(see Section 3.6)**? You should always ask: What about your characteristics should be included in your vulnerability analysis?

The process of analyzing the threats, context, and current situation **(RMF 1)** will give you insights about your personal situation, characteristics, or activities that will increase or decrease your vulnerabilities in a particular location **(RMF 2)**. To customize your individual vulnerability analysis, you could ask yourself questions such as:

- What are the strengths and weaknesses of my personal characteristics, particularly as seen from the local perspective?
- What threats and opportunities come with the tasks I intend to accomplish on this trip?
- Where am I potentially exposed to the threats?
- How will the cultural, economic, political, and so forth situation in the country and with my country affect the way in which the people interact with me?
- Which aspects (e.g., taking off my watch, learning a few words and gestures) do I have control over?

You can reflect inwardly and consider the assumptions, attitudes, and actions that you may have toward the people you will meet during your journeys, and outwardly in terms of any new characteristics you might gain while in a country. For instance, if you are traveling to a hierarchical society (and 90% of the world is), then it could be to your advantage to act with authority and highlight important relations when dealing with officials, all the while being respectful **(see Section 2.7)**. Clothing is one characteristic that is within your control and greatly influences the attitudes toward you. Your choice of clothing broadcasts various messages to other people, so the key is to be aware of both the positive and negative signals you might be sending, as in **Dorthe Borum's** contribution.

WHAT YOU WEAR ISN'T JUST A FASHION STATEMENT

DORTHE BORUM
BUSINESS TRAVELER, TEXTILE INDUSTRY

Before I travel, I always think about what I will wear. Not because I'm in the design industry but because through my clothes I can signal respect for the country and culture I will be visiting; at the same time, requiring respect for me from my hosts. As a businesswoman, I've often experienced that appropriate clothing has significant meaning which impacts upon the results of my business transactions and affects the relationship I have with my business partners.

The website Journeywoman.com provides advice from fellow travelers about culturally, socially, and in some cases legally acceptable clothing for female travelers.[4] The RealMenRealStyle website has an ebook and links to videos, some of which are relevant for male travelers.[5] The REI website is geared toward adventure travelers but the proffered advice can apply to most travelers.[6]

Before you decide to change something, such as not wear a religious symbol, you can ask yourself if the change is worth it for you. The choice is yours. As an aware traveler, you should be clear about the potential consequences and have a plan for how to deal with them. You may choose to wear your religious symbol but decide to be cautious about discussing religious and spiritual matters (see Section 2.2.8). From a security perspective, good questions to ask are: For the situations that you may find yourself in, what modifications are absolutely required? And are you willing to make them?

Throughout this book there are several examples in which personal characteristics play a decisive role in the situation. Take the two contributions about the demonstrations against the Mohammed cartoons. In the story of a passing demonstration in Sri Lanka, skin color made a difference in the options available to the contributor compared with those of his wife (see Section 3.6). As a frequent traveler, he understood this and made sure that his Danish-looking wife and young daughter were hidden away from the mob while he and the shopkeeper, both with brown skin and wearing the local outfit of a t-shirt and a sarong, stood at the front door. In an example from Yemen, the contributor's personal characteristic of building good relations before the insecure period resulted in his being protected and cared for by his local contacts—this was despite his looking quite Nordic (see Section 1.1.3). While reading the examples from the book and other ones you know, consider how your personal characteristics could play out in the same situation. Given the historical, cultural, political, and so forth contexts of your destination, how could they be a factor in your upcoming travels?

Having insights into your vulnerabilities stemming from who you are, what you do, and how you do it will help you mitigate potential problems because these give you the opportunity to apply appropriate security measures. You might be proud of your new position as chief financial officer, but in numerous destinations in the world it is best to carry neutral business cards, preferably in a secondary "OK to rob" wallet. If there is street crime in a place where kidnapping is also a threat, then losing the secondary wallet with $100 (or whatever the normal rate is for that location) and one credit card is better than potentially revealing that you are a high-value commodity that petty criminals can cash in on. The annoyance of being robbed in a foreign country could escalate into a ghastly ordeal for you, your family, and your colleagues. Instead, at the point where your vulnerabilities might interface with a threat in a real situation, you should have mitigating measures in place, like carrying a secondary wallet.

The preceding sections cover specific aspects of personal considerations that might apply to you. While reading the relevant sections, consider the mitigating measures you can potentially put in place. It could be talking with your airline company about your mobility limitations if you are a disabled or elderly traveler. As with all the advice, stories, and examples in this book, you need to customize these lessons learnt to suit the unique interplay between you and your environment while traveling or working abroad.

1.2.1 BUSINESS TRAVELERS

"Act global, think local" is a twist on a common phrase that applies to your travel risk management. While being a global business traveler, having insights into the local nuances, customs, and threats will help you develop a risk assessment that can support your business dealings. To draw a picture of your destination's situation, you can refer to, for example, **"Doing Business in a Changing Middle East by Understanding Political Islam" (see Section 1.6)**, **"Words of Advice for Travelers to Papua New Guinea" (see Section 2.4)**, **"Ensuring Your Organization's Duty of Care: Lessons from Mexico on Threat Analysis and Robust Response" (see Section 2.5)**, **"India's Unique Business Risks" (see Section 2.6)**, **"Corruption and International Business in Russia: A Prediction Based on In-Depth Analysis" (see Section 2.16)**, and **"China's Special Risks for Business Travelers" (see Section 2.2.1)**.

Localized insights are part of the picture **(RMF 1)**: You also need to understand your particular vulnerabilities because of who you are, what you do, and how you do it **(RMF 2)** so that you can take proactive steps to manage potential insecurities **(RMF 3, 4, and 5)**. You can mitigate vulnerabilities while traveling, for example, by applying security measures to prevent industrial espionage **(see Sections 1.11, 1.12, 2.11, and 2.12)** if you are destined for either China or Russia. As business travelers are this book's primary audience, all the advice in this is book is designed for you to flexibly apply to your travel needs and to appropriately address your travel realities.

As a security-aware business traveler, you might want to also review the **Organizational Considerations** section **(see Section 1.5)**, which covers duty of care and duty of loyalty issues as they affect your safety and security when you represent your company abroad. Most companies care for the security of their employees to some extent. At issue is the simple, critical question: Is it enough? It could be worth your time and effort to test assumptions about and, at the same time, gain reassurances from your company.

For further reading, the Internet is awash with resources. Many international news agencies have websites dedicated to business travelers: CNN Business Traveller and The Economist Gulliver Business Travel are two examples.[7] Online magazines such as Executive Travel and Business Traveller are good sources for information.[8] Also, it is fairly common for travel-related service providers to post articles, videos, apps, and blogs on their websites: A full spectrum is available from fun perks typically chronicled in articles such as "James Bond as Business Traveler: Hotels Worthy of 007" on the Orbitz blog[9] to analyzing threat trends like the video "5 Business Travel Threats for 2013" on the **Tony Ridley** website.[10] Government agencies often provide preventative advice to business travelers. A particularly comprehensive, yet concise, example is the "Safety and Security for the Business Professional Traveling Abroad" brochure by the U.S. Federal Bureau of Investigation (FBI).[11]

These are in addition to the multitude of resources listed throughout this book. For example, any of the "standard bearers" listed in the **Nongovernmental**

Organization (NGO) Travelers section (**see Section 1.2.2**) could be a valuable resource for business travelers, especially those working for companies who have yet to develop appropriate security measures, say a small company that is just branching out in Latin America. This is because these highly recommended resources give easy-to-use guidelines that are applicable to most travelers. The only exception is *Staying Alive* by the International Committee of the Red Cross, which is geared toward conflict risks.

1.2.2   NONGOVERNMENTAL ORGANIZATION (NGO) TRAVELERS

Nongovernmental organization (NGO) is a broad term encompassing the development and humanitarian sectors. As a staff member of an NGO, you could have very different types of assignments abroad. For your new job as a human resources manager, you could be about to transfer from Tanzania to the New York headquarters. Or you could be an experienced French surgeon about to do your first assignment for a medical NGO working in the Syrian refugee camps based in Turkey. Amongst the various jobs and locations, it is not surprising that aid workers who work in conflict zones, natural disasters, and "complex emergencies" (emergencies involving multiple problems and threats) have a particularly dangerous job. While humanitarian organizations often prefer to see themselves as neutral agents who serve the needs of beneficiaries, there are several reasons why, unfortunately, both international and local workers face additional risks due to aid being a socioeconomic and media commodity that is, to varying degrees, often manipulated politically. Who you work for, what you will be doing, where and when you will be doing it, and similar factors will play a significant role in how dangerous the assignment might be and which repercussions you might experience.

Citing a United Nations study and interview with Jan Egeland, chief UN humanitarian coordinator from 2003 until 2006 through the height of the Iraq war, the AFP news bureau article "Attacks and Interference Heighten Humanitarian Risks" sheds light on the wider context in which NGOs operate.[12] To summarize the article in terms of the **Risk Management Framework (RMF)**:

RMF 1: Threat analysis (**see Section 1.1.1**)
  • NGOs work in high-risk countries such as Afghanistan and Sudan where they can be direct or indirect targets.
RMF 1: Context assessment (**see Section 1.1.2**)
  • A "militarization and politicization of humanitarian work" in which governments and militants use various levers to gain influence over humanitarian operations. According to Egeland, this has "compromised both access to victims in conflicts and compromised security for aid workers."
RMF 2: Increased vulnerability (**see Section 1.2**)
  • The NGO sector is a growth industry with development and relief (conflict zones and natural disasters) operations in a multitude of countries.

The April 2011 AFP article noted that for each of the past four years there have been about 40 kidnappings of NGO staff. Sadly, about 100 aid workers die each year. The death toll has tripled over the past decade. Hence, there are many who call on governments and militants to allow the humanitarian space to be "impartial, neutral, independent and go after the needs and not serve an agenda."

As a security-aware NGO worker, you can apply the **RMF** to any job situation, from complex emergencies to stable development projects.

- **RMF 1:** Threat analysis—which threats are you likely to encounter and where?
- **RMF 1:** Context assessment—how is your agency funded and how is this perceived by the various key actors?
- **RMF 1:** Situational analysis—which current or upcoming local, regional, or international events could trigger insecurity?
- **RMF 2:** Vulnerability analysis—how could the lack of security measures by other NGOs negatively and positively affect your agency's security?
- **RMF 3:** Analysis of options—what is needed to implement various plans?
- **RMF 4:** Continuously monitoring and adjusting—is your agency sharing security updates with other NGOs and partners? And are updates reaching the right staff?
- **RMF 5:** Confidence in your security precautions and reactions—what security precautions does your agency have in place and do these sufficiently address the risks?

Development and, especially, emergency jobs require flexibility. Accordingly, you can adjust the **RMF** questions as needed. Working for an NGO does not require that you unnecessarily risk yourself. Therefore, you can draw upon the **RMF** to help you be safer. Good security enables good programs.

If you want to read up on your organization's responsibilities to you and the equivalent responsibilities that you bear to safeguard your security, then see the duty of care and duty of loyalty prescriptions in the **Organizational Considerations** section **(see Section 1.5)**—though written primarily for business travelers, the same rights and obligations apply to NGOs and all their staff.

As for further reading, the "standard bearers" are still the best resources that provide generic security management guidelines for both managers and travelers to safeguard against the various threats that staff might encounter.

- *Good Practice Review 8: Operational Security Management in Violent Environments*—this resource by the Humanitarian Practice Network of the Overseas Development Institute is also commonly known as GPR 8. The original version from 2000 is widely used within the NGO sector. The December 2010 version is even more practical while retaining the conceptual overviews.[13]
- *Safety First: A Safety and Security Handbook for Aid Workers*—this classic from 1995 was recommended by several respondents of the surveyed LinkedIn groups. The revised version from 2010 by the International Save the Children Alliance is written in a straightforward manner.[14]
- *Generic Security Guide for Humanitarian Organizations*—the 2004 version by ECHO (European Commission's Directorate-General for Humanitarian Aid & Civil Protection) has not been revised recently, but it is still a good resource, especially the annexes.[15]

- *Staying Alive: Safety and Security Guidelines for Humanitarian Volunteers in Conflict Areas*—written by the International Committee of the Red Cross, it shows its colors in that it is geared toward conflict risks like mines and aerial bombing. The well-known 1999 version was updated in 2006.[16]

A well-known resource is *To Stay and Deliver: Good Practice for Humanitarians in Complex Security Environments* by the Office for the Coordination of Humanitarian Affairs (OCHA). However, its strategic orientation means it is mainly just useful to NGO managers.[17] An excellent resource, even though it is not so well known, is the *New Protection Manual for Human Rights Defenders* by Protection International.[18] It offers the same risk management components as the other resources, but it has a different angle of appealing mainly to grassroots organizations. Actually, the manual's explanations of concepts, visual aids, and models and user-friendly attributes make it a recommended resource to NGO managers in general and particularly if you work with partner organizations.

As an aid worker, you should be aware of two more highly recommended resources: At http://www.allindiary.org, you can download a calendar that also has NGO-specific information such as the humanitarian principles, protection of beneficiaries, and security advice. At http://www.aidworkers.net, there are blogs, advice, and a forum—as they write, "Tired of re-inventing the wheel? We are.... Aid Workers Network is a free service set up to enable aid workers to share practical advice and resources with each other." Both can be used as part of your preparations and throughout your assignment.

1.2.3 WOMEN TRAVELERS

Women are a significant and growing segment of travelers. In the United States, for example, the average adventure traveler is a 47-year-old female.[19] In 2012, International SOS announced they noticed a trend in which companies were not properly preparing their staff for the extra safety and security issues facing women travelers, who make up 45% of business travelers.[20] In one of their surveys of women working for international businesses in the Asia Pacific region, 75% of respondents noted that their organization could do more to address the specific needs of their traveling female staff. In particular, the women felt female-specific medical and security concerns could be better addressed.

In this book, the **Medical Considerations** sections **(see Sections 1.8 and 2.8)** cover general recommendations and some specific advice for female travelers. Regarding security issues, woven throughout this book is advice specifically for women travelers. To give a few examples, in the **Personal Belongings and Documents** sections **(see Sections 1.10 and 2.10)** there are suggestions for protecting your purse and wallet. In the **Transportation (see Section 2.14)** and **Accommodations (see Section 2.15)** sections, you'll find supplementary advice for female travelers.

Regarding gender-based threats, while men nearly exclusively face the threat of "honey traps" **(see Section 2.11)**, women are disproportionately targeted for sexual assault and violence. To help you mitigate sexually oriented threats, the contribution **"Psychological Techniques That Prevent Violence" (see Section 2.2.3)** provides practical advice in the form of seven elements from trusting your intuition to taking action. Actually, it is advisable to review that contribution before you travel because you may want to consider, practice, and implement some of the suggestions prior to your departure. Similarly, though not focused on threats against women, the contribution **"States of Awareness: The Cooper Color Codes" (see Section 2.3)** is useful for identifying and reacting to the build-up of a potentially dangerous situation. The contribution **"Sexual Assault: Preventing and Responding as an International Traveler" (see Section 3.4)** covers a range of places and situations in which female travelers are particularly vulnerable and offers concrete advice on how to prevent and respond to sexual violence.

For further reading, one of the most comprehensive and highly recommended sites is the Journeywoman website. It covers an array of information (i.e., cultural, medical, safety) for different types of trips (i.e., solo, business, family) in probably every country.[21] The website Gutsy Traveler is filled with practical advice for all types of trips.[22] The About.com and the Streetdirectory Singapore Guide are websites that offer a diverse selection of topics, and once you start following links, a wide range of resources is accessible.[23] A comprehensive and recommended resource that you can download is the PDF "Her Own Way: A Woman's Safe-Travel Guide."[24] It has also medical advice and links to further reading.

1.2.4 TRAVELERS WITH DISABILITIES

If you are either a person with disabilities or his or her travel companion, then there are a few special considerations and actions you should review before you go abroad, as the following contribution summarizes.

**SCENARIO THINKING: PLANNING FOR
TRAVELING WITH DISABILITIES**

CBM INTERNATIONAL

*MODIFIED EXCERPTS FROM 2011 "SAFETY AND SECURITY FACTSHEETS"
(HTTP://WWW.CBM.ORG). REPRINTING AND MODIFICATIONS MADE
BY PERMISSION. COPYRIGHT © 2011 CBM INTERNATIONAL.*

Much of the advice in this book will be the same for persons with disabilities. However, due to mobility and communication challenges, certain issues will need to be specifically highlighted if you yourself are a person with a disability or when you work or travel with persons with disabilities.

- In advance and on arrival carefully consider the accessibility challenges you might face regarding accommodation, transport, visits, and so forth.
- Similarly, before you travel, assess your requirements for specific devices you might need and while traveling. Be aware of the assistance you might need if confronted with a crisis scenario.
- Ensure that people are informed of your needs.

When reading this book, imagine yourself or the persons you are traveling with in the various situations covered and consider what can be done or planned beforehand to ensure your safety and security while traveling.

Specifically regarding air travel, the article entitled "Air Travel with Mobility Devices or Mobility Aids: Airlines and Wheelchairs, Walkers, Canes" by About. com Air Travel advises:

- Wheelchairs and walkers can be gate checked or sometimes used up to the door. However, owners of wet battery cell wheelchairs should be informed that these could cause delays so it is suggested that you call the airline beforehand.
- Wheelchair and cane users can request that airport screeners assist them and perform a manual pat-down. As with all travelers, you can ask for a same-sex screener.
- Some airports provide passes so that your own escort can follow you to the gate.
- Prepare your chair for gate checking by doing things such as making sure your bag is ready for the security check and is easily accessible.
- Ensure that you inform your airline of your mobility limitations. This is the best way to make sure that you get the assistance you require.
- Ask beforehand when, where, and how your mobility aid will be returned to you if you needed to check it in.
- Make sure that both you and your airline document your requirements.
- Try to pre-board the plane. Generally, aisle seats allow greater maneuverability while in-flight.
- Ask for assistance from the airline staff and any airport staff in the airport in which you have to disembark.
- Some airlines give highly discounted rates for travel companions.[25]

In addition to this list, the article "Travelling with Disability" on the website Streetdirectory Singapore Guide recommends that you should check with your doctor about how to be safely screened if you have a medical implant.[26] Your ability to easily navigate air travel can affect your safety and security, so equipping yourself with the right assistance is highly advisable. And, at the very least, having the right support for your requirements makes for a more enjoyable trip.

In the corresponding section in **Chapter 2 (see Section 2.2.4)**, there is additional advice for your time abroad. On the Internet, a good resource is the "Disabled Travelers" article available on the United Kingdom's Foreign and Commonwealth Office website.[27]

For further reading, extensive resources can be found on the websites http://www. able-travel.com, http://www.disabledtravelersguide.com, and http://www.e-bility. com. On Lonely Planet's website, you can find their forum dedicated to disabled travelers.[28]

1.2.5 ELDERLY TRAVELERS

The article "Older People Looking to Achieve Travel Dreams" on the Street-directory Singapore Guide website reports on a study by Bradford and Bingley which found more than one third of all journeys by Britons were done by people over 50 years old,[29] and 48% of seniors over age 55 wished they had traveled more. To quote the study: "There's no stopping globetrotting grandparents or restless retirees."

As a senior traveler or a travel companion, there are a few extra considerations you should keep in mind before you head for a destination. These mainly revolve around medical and mobility issues. Regarding medical issues, ideally you should arrange for a doctor's consultation six to eight weeks before your trip, though attending to this at the spur of the moment is better than nothing. You should be checked for your personal condition and your destination's conditions in terms of vaccinations, hygiene, and so forth **(see Section 1.8)**. The article "Safe and Healthy Travels for Senior Citizens" gives a good overview of the pre-trip medical considerations and is available on the U.S. Centers for Disease Control and Prevention website.[30] If you use medicines, you should review the **Personal Belongings and Documents** section **(see Section 1.10)** for the considerations that you need to keep in mind for transporting medicines, such as the fact that some countries do not permit certain medicines.

Once you have taken care of the preventative issues, you can look at your contingency measures. One of the most important is to have sufficient travel insurance **(see Section 1.9)**. You will be asked detailed questions, which you will have to answer honestly and completely, in order for the insurer to assess the risks. Simply because you are over 50 years old in many cases means that you will probably pay a higher premium. If you have any preexisting medical conditions, that will also be a factor. But, at the end of this process, what you will gain is proper coverage and a way to deal with life's surprises. A good overview article on the Travel Insurance Guide website is "Over 65's Travel Insurance."[31]

The About.com Air Travel article "Seniors—Air Travel Tips and Advice" has some practical advice:

- Ask if discounts for seniors and companions are available.
- Consider your seating options in terms of boarding and restrooms.
- If you need assistance with your luggage, find out which service personnel to contact.
- If you are carrying medications, be informed of airport security regulations.
- Ask for any assistance that you may require.
- Your carry-on bags should be light, especially if you may need assistance.
- Avoid booking the last flight of the day if you need wheelchair assistance because there tends to be fewer available staff. This can cause delays, which can be particularly problematic if you have a connecting flight.[32]

Regarding mobility, tips and advice are covered in the **Travelers with Disabilities** section **(see Section 1.2.4)**.

As for further reading, the website About.com Senior Travel is filled with practical advice.[33] The "Travelling Seniors" PDF as part of the Australian government's "Smart

Traveller" materials is a recommended resource.[34] The website 50 Plus Info Bus: Senior Travel also has some good resources worth reviewing.[35] There are numerous websites, such as Canadian Senior Years that are portals of information with lots of links.[36]

1.2.6 HOMOSEXUAL, BISEXUAL, AND TRANSGENDER TRAVELERS

For gay, lesbian, bisexual, and transgender travelers, many of the special considerations you might want to take revolve around your destination's cultural and societal acceptance of you. Where there is a lack of acceptance, you can potentially run into security problems. In many countries, it is illegal to be a homosexual. In others, you have legal rights but they are ignored. The subsequent contribution lists practical advice for you to keep in mind.

SPECIAL CONSIDERATIONS FOR A TRANSGENDER TRAVELER

KIRSTEN MOLS
IT DIRECTOR

Some of the considerations I need to have and actions that I need to take as a transgender person who travels extensively are:

- What is the legislation in the part of the world I will visit—including places en route. Is it legal to be LGBT?
- Can I be open? Transpersons are visible. Gays, lesbians, and bisexuals are not. Still, I visit the LGBT websites in the country I will visit to gain knowledge of the general climate for LGBT persons. I try to find out how the police treat LGBT persons and places to go, if I need help.

If I travel as my preferred gender, and not the one I was born as, I might encounter special security issues:

- Passport photo versus current appearance.
- Should bodily checks at airport security be done by male or female? As a frequent traveler who is a transgender person, I have to take extra precautions to ensure my safety.

Specialized travel agents and websites can help you be a well-informed traveler—for example, the Gays On Tour website has general security tips and specific advice for various regions. This is supplemented with other resources.[37] Similarly, the Queer Trip website has a travel tips page.[38] The International Lesbian, Gay, Trans, and Intersex Association homepage has a world map, with which you can quickly overview such issues as hate crimes and legal restrictions.[39] There are also resources provided by governments like "LGBT Travellers" by the United Kingdom's Foreign and Commonwealth Office[40] or the "Homosexual, Bisexual, and Transgender Travel—FAQ" by the Foreign Affairs and International Trade Canada.[41]

1.2.7 TRAVELING FAMILIES

When you book your ticket, look for or ask about services available to traveling families. For example, on some international flights, you can reserve a bassinet for infants up to 9 months old, and infant food is available but must be reserved at least 24 hours before your departure. Be forewarned that if you are planning to carry more than 3 liquid ounces, then the items may be tested for explosives **(see Section 1.13)**.

If you are planning to travel alone with your children, know that some countries require a parental consent letter from the other parent: These rules are to help protect children against international parental custodial disputes and illegal trafficking. The "Child Travel Consent" article on the LawDepot.com website provides a sample you can use,[42] or you can check the governmental website of your destination to see if they have a form that you should use. Additional requirements could include birth certificates, baby passports, and so forth. The "Travelling with Children" PDF produced by the Canadian government is a recommended resource for its overview of the legal issues.[43]

For traveling families, the Internet has plenty of resources. On the Parents website the article "Traveling Abroad with Kids" is a practical resource.[44] Another practical article is "6 Safety Tips for Traveling Abroad with Kids" on the Flipkey Blog.[45] The first article looks at ticket and jet lag issues, whereas the second one focuses on advice you can use while in transit or at events. The Streetdirectory Singapore Guide website has several relevant articles: "Single Parent Travel" is one example.[46] The About.com Air Travel article "Documents, Info, Policies and Advice" is highly recommended because it has a well-indexed family travel section with links to a multitude of articles.[47] The "Flying with Children" article on a blog by a flight attendant of 13 years and mother for 11 years is insightful and very comprehensive but, on the flipside, it is quite long.[48] The "Children and Flying Fears" PDF by the Children's National Medical Center lays out easy-to-follow advice for each step of air travel.[49]

Particularly if your family will be living abroad, you should explain (using role play, drawing, or whatever is most appropriate) how things might be different. For example, it is typical for Danes to say their name when they answer the phone—an insecure habit that could lead to a watershed of leaked private information. When you live abroad, your child should not give out any private information without your permission.

Security does not have to be scary—make it a "what would you do if ..." game. Role plays and games are easier for your child to remember. Even with children who are three years or older, you can talk about what they should do in certain situations, while avoiding talking about the consequences.[50] You do not want to put your fear in them but you do want them to know what to do if a stranger offers them a ride to school, for example. Teach your child to say "No" to potentially dangerous situations, and occasionally revisit the game and point out examples from daily life to remind your children how to be safe abroad and at home. The article "Child Safety Tips" on the How Stuff Works website is part of a series of articles about child safety: Because it comes from 2006, a few statistics are not current but it does offer a lot of practical advice such as telling your children not to go off with anyone they have not met with you.[51] To help you identify schools, programs, and activities that are child safe, the PDF "Choose with Care: A Parent's Guide to Choosing Child Safe Organisations" is a good starting point.[52]

1.2.8 Religious Travelers

In this and the corresponding section in **Chapter 2**, the contributors deal with two different aspects of traveling as a person of faith. **Scott Watson's** contribution as a Christian missionary and a security expert raises security issues related to talking about your religious beliefs or activities in public **(see Section 2.2.8)**, whereas the following contribution by **Fazal Bahardeen** outlines how Muslim travelers can adhere to prayer prescriptions during their journeys.

While this piece does not directly pertain to travel security, it does relate to a traveler's overall well-being: Preserving balance and attachment are key components needed for the skills that your security management abilities rely upon, including maintaining perspective and clarity **(see Sections 1.17 and 2.17)**. This is particularly the case if you are a frequent flyer or live abroad for extended periods in situations in which you have not built up good social networks, healthy habits, or a sense of "normality." Regardless of whether you practice a faith or not, you can ask yourself: How can I draw upon my spiritual beliefs and values to aid my well-being while traveling? As part of my pre-trip activities, do I need any supporting materials, such as a prayer rug, bible, incense, or apps on my smartphone?

KNOWING WHAT TO DO AND BRING BEFORE TRAVELING TO OBSERVE MUSLIM PRAYER WHILE ABROAD

FAZAL BAHARDEEN

CHIEF EXECUTIVE OFFICER, CRESCENTRATING (HTTP://WWW. CRESCENTRATING.COM). REPRINTING AND MODIFICATIONS MADE BY PERMISSION. COPYRIGHT © 2012 CRESCENTRATING. FOR THE ORIGINAL ARTICLE, SEE "12+1 TIPS TO SAFEGUARD YOUR SALAATH WHILE TRAVELING," UPDATED VERSION, NOVEMBER 25, 2012; HTTP://WWW. CRESCENTRATING.COM/EN/MUSLIM-GUIDES/TRAVEL-TIPS-ETIQUETTES/ ITEM/1859-SAFEGUARD-SALAATH-PRAYERS-WHILE-TRAVELING.HTML.

Knowing the rules related to Salaath and Wudhu and having a few things in the travel bag will go a long way for a Muslim traveler to ensure that he or she does not miss Salaath while traveling.

KNOW THE RULES

There are number of concessions for travelers when it comes to Wudhu and Salaath. Knowing those rules will greatly ease the performance of Salaath on time while traveling. There are minor differences of opinion among the scholars on some of these rules; as such, it is best that you consult a trusted scholar to get a full understanding. The most important of the rules that a traveler needs to know are:

- Conditions pertaining to shortening and combining of prayers. This is probably the most important knowledge to have as a traveler.
- Rules regarding the requirement to face the Qiblah direction while on a moving train, plane, and so forth. This is very important, especially if you are traveling by plane and need to perform your Salaath while on board.
- Rules regarding the performance of Qiyam (standing position), while "seated" for obligatory Salaath. Same rules for non-obligatory prayers such as Witr.
- Dispensations regarding Wudhu for travelers. Especially the conditions for Al Masah (wiping over leather socks and shoes) and how to perform it.
- Rules of wiping over the turban or hijab during Wudhu.
- Conditions that allow for praying with your shoes on.
- Conditions for performing dry ablution (Tayammum) and how to perform it. Although the chances of one doing this are low, it is good to know.

BRING A TRAVEL KIT

The following few things will not take much space in a travel bag, but will go a long way to ease the performance of Salaath outside of your home.

- A travel prayer mat. Now you can get them in sizes that allow you to carry them inside your trouser pockets or handbags. Having one will come in very handy.
- Prayer timetable. You can download a prayer time calculator on most mobile phones, smartphones, tablets, and notebooks/PCs. Downloading one of them in all your digital devices is a good idea.
- Qiblah compass. You can either carry a physical compass or download a digital one (if your digital device has the functionality). However, the accuracy of both the digital and the physical compasses in closed environments, like hotel rooms, cannot be fully relied on. If you have Internet access, then you can check the Qiblah direction and prayer times tool on the Crescentrating website.
- Wear footwear that will allow you to perform Wudhu without much hassle.
- For prayer times and Qiblah direction for your flights, you can use the Crescentrating "Air Travel Prayer Times Calculator" and get a printout and/or email the prayer times and Qiblah directions before boarding the plane.

Where there are no proper Wudhu facilities, you need to have some balancing skills to wash your legs! Practicing some gymnastic skills will help!

Knowing the above rules and having the minimum in your Salaath travel kit will make it easier to perform Salaath no matter where you are. As for the rules themselves, since there are minor differences among scholars regarding the application of some of those rules, it is best to learn the rulings from a scholar whom you prefer/trust/have access to.

It is worth mentioning that the Crescentrating website has various practical articles, guides, and blogs for Muslim travelers.[53] The website Safe Travel Solutions has articles and training materials for Christian missionaries: The article "Defining Faith-Focused Security," for example, argues that security enables missionaries to fulfill their calling.[54] The website Flyertalk.com has a forum for all religious travelers.[55] The website IndependentTraveler.com, which is an offshoot of TripAdvisor, has a forum and articles for religious and spiritual travelers.[56]

1.3 BUILDING SITUATIONAL AWARENESS

Situational awareness is highly relevant to travel risk management because it is about "maintaining the big picture and thinking ahead." The Wikipedia description in the "Situation Awareness" article states:

Situational awareness involves being aware of what is happening in the vicinity to understand how information, events, and one's own actions will impact goals and objectives, both immediately and in the near future. Lacking or inadequate situational awareness has been identified as one of the primary factors in accidents attributed to human error. Thus, situational awareness is especially important in work domains where the information flow can be quite high and poor decisions may lead to serious consequences (e.g., piloting an airplane, functioning as a soldier, or treating critically ill or injured patients).[57]

Of course, this book adds "being a security aware traveler" to the list of domains where situational awareness plays a critical role.

The Wikipedia article also notes "Situation awareness often describes the ability to see objects in time and/or space through multiple perspectives and interpretations." Situational awareness involves three levels:

- Level 1: Perception of elements in current situation.
- Level 2: Comprehension of current situation.
- Level 3: Projection of future status.

The article includes a flowchart diagram in which there is a continuous flow between the environment and you (i.e., your situational awareness, decisions, and actions). In the diagram, the individual factors that influence your situational awareness, decisions, and actions include "goals and objectives," "preconceptions," "information processing mechanisms," "abilities," "experience," and "training."

There are many ways and levels to build up your security awareness. One way to act and be more security aware is to consider the knowledge, skills, attitudes, and behaviors (KSAB) that are necessary to be a safer traveler. To take a few examples:

- Knowledge: Understanding key relationships in the national politics, reading the threat assessment provided by your company.
- Skills: Attending a culture and travel security workshop, practicing using Coopers Colors **(see Section 2.3)** before you travel.
- Attitudes: Wanting to avoid security incidents, showing respect for local customs.
- Behaviors: Following your organization's security advice, reporting suspicious activities near your hotel and office.

On another level, you can work on expanding your awareness of your immediate surroundings by practicing a few situational awareness exercises. For instance, you could notice one thing about the people, places, vehicles, or a mix in your vicinity: You can do this any time—walking, sitting in traffic, or dining at a restaurant (Figure 1.4).

FIGURE 1.4   Courtesy of Carrie Clinton.

Another exercise is while you are out of a room you are familiar with, have a family member or colleague put up pieces of masking tape (so it will not ruin any surfaces) with colored dots on them around the room. Or make some other small changes (you should not know what to expect). How many do you spot within 15, 30, 60 seconds of coming into the room? For another exercise, ask someone to put out 10 items on a table and cover them. Give yourself 20 seconds to look at the items before re-covering them. How many can you name one minute later? Or the next day? If you know any military personnel, former or present, then they might be a good source for additional exercises. These types of exercises boost your situational awareness skills because you become more alert to your surroundings. In our daily lives, our brains absorb a great deal of information and put a lot of it into a big box, so these exercises help our brains to file information. The benefit of doing these types of exercises is they help you to be conscious of which information you need to act on to be a safer traveler.

As the subsequent contribution points out, taking personal responsibility for your own security is essential to being an aware traveler. The contributor also lists having security measures that appropriately address the threats and maintaining constant awareness. Regarding how to conduct a threat analysis, refer to the **Threat Assessment** section **(see Section 1.1.1)**, and specific threats are addressed throughout this book.

BEING YOUR OWN BODYGUARD

JAMES OTIGBAH

SECURITY AND EXECUTIVE PROTECTION SPECIALIST, EXCEL SECURITY SOLUTIONS AG (HTTP://WWW. EXCELSECURITYSOLUTIONS.CH)

Most large organizations that have an executive protection program provide bodyguards as a last resort to protect their most vulnerable employees, once it has been determined that there is a possible threat against those persons. To protect a person around the clock can be very expensive, especially for large organizations that have several employees operating in high-risk zones. Due to financial reasons, engaging a bodyguard is not a valid option for the individual traveler or organizations with a limited security budget.

This leads to the question: What can one do to stay safe when traveling or when staying in regions where the risk of kidnapping is high, without employing the services of a bodyguard? In order to answer that question, it makes sense to understand the role of a bodyguard and the three principles of personal security.

One of the main reasons for using a bodyguard can be summed up in one word: convenience. Bodyguards help facilitate the travel and safety of the protectee, freeing him from some major tasks and concerns of personal security. For anyone traveling to a new environment, it is very convenient to have all your travel and security arrangements taken care of by a professional, in order to concentrate on the main tasks to be accomplished at the destination. The reverse side of the coin is that it can be perceived as inconvenient to be constantly in the company of bodyguards. It can be rather stressful for the protectee to always be told what best to do and what not by the bodyguard, even though the latter only has the protectee's welfare at heart. During most assignments, the protectee will also make decisions or take actions that are counter to the bodyguard's advice. It is then expected from a bodyguard to be flexible and adapt his security program to the new situation.

At the start of developing an executive protection program for our client, we have to weigh the threat faced by the individuals concerned by conducting a threat assessment. The threat assessment enables us to determine what possible threat can occur in a given environment, the likelihood of an occurrence, and the appropriate protective measures to be established to counter the threat. It also enables us to identify any potential threats against an individual's work and living environment. Particular attention is placed on traveling between locations, as this is often the most dangerous time, where the protectee is most vulnerable. The threat assessment also takes into consideration the private activities of the protectee.

A threat assessment is not necessarily a written document and is subject to constant changes and updates. With some training and knowledge, most people can conduct one. In reality, most people are constantly assessing the threats to themselves without realizing it. One of the most important aspects of an executive protection program is the advance procedure. It involves visiting every location the protectee intends to visit and coordinating all the necessary security arrangements before, during, and after the visit. The advance work aims to minimize the occurrence of negative surprises.

Once the bodyguard is actually out in the field with the protectee, any threat indicators missed during the advance procedure or any new ones may be detected during this stage of the assignment and reacted upon. If an attack or an unfortunate incident occurs, the bodyguard has to switch instinctively to a reactive mode, utilizing all the training, experience, and knowledge gained during the advance procedures to minimize the damage. For example: If the protectee was to require emergency medical attention, the bodyguard would already know the closest and most suitable medical facility to deal with such an emergency due to his advance procedure.

The three principles of personal security, as defined by James Brown in his book *The Bodyguard's Bible: The Definitive Guide to Close Protection*[*]:

1. Everyone is responsible for his or her own security.
2. Security should be commensurate with the threat.
3. Constant awareness is the basis of good security.

James Brown, BEM, talks about these three principles and that they form the basis of anyone's personal security, whether they work as a bodyguard or not. These three principles should be lived by every person, regardless of the place they live and work, be it the safest environment possible or the most challenging one.

One of the fundamental principles we convey during the pre-assignment briefing to our client is that the protectee is ultimately responsible for his/her own personal security and safety. For the client who is about to pay out a considerable amount of money to someone whom he expects to look after him, this statement often comes as a surprise. A misleading concept among many clients who use the services of bodyguards is that they can discharge all responsibility for personal security to the bodyguard. However, if given an explanation for the statement, the client generally does understand and consent to it. If the bodyguard was to take on the full responsibility of the protectee's safety and security, the bodyguard would have to dictate every single one of the protectee's actions and movements.

This does not diminish the role and importance of a bodyguard in any way, but emphasizes to the protectees that they are quite capable of contributing to their own safety and security by making sensible choices and the right decisions.

The second principle deals with the proportionality of security in relation to the threat. The right balance has to be found in order to achieve the desired goal for both the client and the protector. Many factors come into play from the security provider's perspective as well as the client's.

In many instances, when in extreme locations that have just experienced war, for example, it makes sense to use armed local protection and bulletproof vests and to drive in protected convoys from location to location. Such measures will, however, be out of place in many other parts of the world, where discretion and keeping a low profile may be the better option. By not drawing attention to oneself, moving from one location to another in a low-key vehicle, and by applying the principles of personal protection, the desired level of security can be achieved.

The most difficult one of the three principles to put into practice is constant awareness. Constant awareness is a basic human survival skill that we

---

[*] James Brown, *The Bodyguard's Bible: The Definitive Guide to Close Protection*. Bible Publications, 2007.

have lost over time, due to a hectic lifestyle and advancement in technology. Awareness has often been equated to the sixth sense; with women it is generally referred to as intuition, with men as instinct. Some people are born with a heightened sense of awareness; however, it can also be acquired through learning and experience.

I would certainly recommend using a bodyguard for high-risk countries and regions with politically volatile situations. For relatively safe and stable countries, I would feel comfortable not recommending a bodyguard, if I felt the protectee knows and applies the three principles of personal security as stated above. To learn or enhance the application of these three principles and foremost to increase the personal security and safety awareness, I would strongly recommend attending a travel security or a hostile environment course. In addition to the three principles, these courses give the participants the opportunity to acquire cultural awareness and other country-specific knowledge.

For further reading, the Wikipedia article "Situation Awareness" is a recommended starting point.[58] The article "Got Situational Awareness?" on the PeakMind blog applies the three levels (perception, comprehension, projection) to trekking: Even though it has a narrow subject, the way the article explains situational awareness can be read by anyone interested in honing the skills needed to make better real-time decisions and actions.[59] In the forum entitled "Situational Awareness Exercises," there are many good exercises that people suggest; however, it should be noted that because it is hosted on the Defensive Carry website, some of the inputs are military orientated.[60] The highly recommended article "Pyramid for Personal Safety" on the No Nonsense Self Defense website makes the case that awareness is a hybrid of knowledge and habits.[61] In the corresponding section in **Chapter 2 (see Section 2.3)**, additional resources are listed.

1.4   PLANNING AND PREPARING

Travel checklists are useful resources. The "Travellers Checklist" by the Canadian government is one example.[62] Or, if you are moving abroad, the list of considerations in the Streetdirectory Singapore Guide articles "5 Tips for Those Who Are Considering Becoming an Expatriate"[63] and "Moving Tips: 12 Amazing Tips to Facilitate Relocation"[64] could come in handy. The About.com Air Travel article "Documents, Info, Policies and Advice" is highly recommended for all air passengers: For the listed pre-trip considerations, from bereavement travel to customer service issues, it has links to a multitude of articles.[65]

For all your trips, you can consider using the "Travel Wise Checklist," which corresponds with the advice in this book and is available on the TrainingSolutions website.[66] It is organized into three columns—"aware," "secure," and "world" travelers—that are color coded yellow, orange, and red. Items in the "aware" column apply to all travelers—it includes reminders for passports and visas, hard and electronic copies of contact list, to charge equipment before departure, and so forth. Where appropriate, the "secure" traveler column builds on the "aware" items. For example, it is generally advisable for all travelers to have a communication back-up plan, whereas a traveler going to a medium-risk (orange) destination should specifically consider taking a satellite phone in some circumstances. This also applies to travelers to high-risk (red) locations. There are few items in the "world" traveler column because, if you have taken care of the items in the first two columns, then most of your preparations are done.

Blank spaces on the template allow you to customize the form. By taking what you know about the threats in the environment (**RMF 1**) and your vulnerabilities to them (**RMF 2**), you can add items that are uniquely part of your planning and preparations. To address a particular threat (**see Section 1.1.1**), you might include packing a security chain and lock for your laptop, for example, if the university where you will be a guest lecturer has had a problem with laptop theft. As for vulnerabilities (**see Section 1.4**) you might list emailing the hotel to make sure they have good wheelchair accessibility even for the emergency exits. Of course, the amount of time, effort, and resources you put into security planning will depend on whether you are traveling to Timbuktu or Tahoe City.

Even though written specifically about China, **Jack Chu's** contribution is a good example of considerations you can take when preparing for a trip abroad. He recommends that you make a travel plan of your itinerary, accommodations, and domestic travel. You can download a "Travel Plan" template from http://www.trainingsolutions.dk to create a single document of this type of information for each of your journeys.[67] The **Preparedness** section (**see Section 2.4**) provides additional considerations by drawing on cases of Romania, Papua New Guinea, and China. As you read these and the other cases, stories, and expert advice in this book, you can add points to your travel checklist that are specific to you and your destination.

PLANNING TRAVELS TO CHINA

JACK CHU

PRESIDENT, RA CONSULTANTS LTD. (HTTP://WWW.RA.COM.HK)

China is a safe country for Chinese as well as foreign travelers. Most of your planning and preparing for traveling to and within China will be the same as you would take for other countries where crime can happen.

ANALYZE YOUR RISKS FIRST

- Go online and use different Chinese search engines, such as http://www.baidu.com or http://www.sina.com. Both of these are very popular and used by local Chinese.
- One resource you can use is a country report, which is publicly accessible by visiting the website of U.S. Department of State, Bureau of Diplomatic Security, http://www.osac.gov, and looking at

the China country report that can tell you about the safety issues for business travelers and tourists.

- Since China is a huge country, understand your risk level for the location you are going to travel to. In general, the crime ratio is still very low, even in the big cities. But due to the economic crisis, especially in the coastal region, crime can happen.
- And be aware of the local culture and customs, especially for areas with minority nationalities.

MAKE YOUR TRAVEL PLAN

- Make your travel plan of where you will visit, where you will stay, and what transportation you need for domestic travel. Make your travel arrangements well in advance.
- Try to make pre-arrangements for the hotel to provide you with a pickup service from the airport. They are safe and convenient.
- Try to find a good local contact, especially one who knows about travel security. Contact him or her and ask questions whenever you are not clear.
- Keep in mind that, when there are national long holidays or a student's holiday, it can be very difficult to make temporary bookings whether for air, train, or hotel.

BOOK YOUR TICKETS AND HOTELS THROUGH YOUR TRAVEL AGENCY OR IN CHINA

- Book your international tickets, domestic tickets, and hotels before traveling to China, if possible. Chinese airlines and train services do meet international standards. You can book domestic travel tickets in China if you cannot book them before arrival. There are a lot of online booking agencies, and hotel business centers can be helpful with this.
- You can book the air tickets or hotel accommodations online by one of the popular traveling agents Ctrip.com (http://www.english. ctrip.com). This agency has 16 branch offices throughout China and currently employees over 12,000 people.

BUY YOUR TRAVEL INSURANCE

- Try to buy an insurance policy for life insurance and luggage lost or delay policies.
- Some multinational companies have bought kidnapping policies for traveling executives. In case of any incidents, they can contact the insurance company for support.

Specifically regarding money matters, for some destinations, you may want to also consider how money is best handled (local or international currency, credit or travel cards). What are the exchange rates? When and where can you first access money—does this fit in your plans? Let's say you will be arriving at six in the evening: Should you get some local currency before your arrival so that you can take a taxi? What is the price of not arranging for money matters beforehand? It all depends on the destination, as in the following contribution.

EXIT DREAM, ENTER REALITY: HOW NOT EXCHANGING MONEY BEFOREHAND CHANGED MY FIRST DAY AS AN ADOPTIVE DAD (AND WHY I'LL NEVER MAKE THAT MISTAKE AGAIN)

"FRANK"
FORMER BUSINESS TRAVELER, ENTERTAINMENT INDUSTRY

A couple of years ago, we went to Ethiopia to pick up our newly adopted son. My wife had been to Addis Ababa a few times for work, and we had talked with another adoptive couple, so we felt prepared. But, the thing is, we didn't think about exchanging money, and what a headache that turned out to be!

We thought we had some hours until the anticipated drive out to him, so we went to lunch and had planned to go to the bank afterwards. Instead, I got the call in the middle of my first bite. We roughly threw some food in the direction of our mouths and hastily paid the bill before the organizer's transportation to the orphanage arrived. For the return ride, the driver had to depart immediately, so we opted to stay longer to give all the staff and children the donated gifts we had brought with us (needless to say 70 kilograms of stuffed animals and 2 kilograms of lady stockings did cause the custom officials to ask a few questions at the airport!).

When we were ready to go, we simply asked a taxi driver to take us to a bank. But the bank did not service credit cards. Oh no. Back to the taxi and my family. The same scene at the next bank, and I had a creeping sense that our first day together was not going to look anything like the dreams I had had for all those years. Our driver kindly offered to take us to our accommodation and arrange for payment later. Whew. But, we were still hungry, "in debt," and generally in need of cash.

Our bed and breakfast let us borrow a stroller and we proceeded to walk from bank to bank in fairly warm temperatures. In the end, my wife and son stayed in one bank and I kept up the ritual until I could get some money. It was a bad time to learn that lesson! But, it's a lesson we'll never forget.

For additional advice about money matters, refer to the "secret stash" discussion in the **Personal Belongings and Documents** section **(see Section 1.10)** and the ATM issues in the **Crime and Corruption** section **(see Section 2.16)**. Speaking with your bank advisor before a trip can also be a good resource. You can also browse the Internet for advice: For instance, the Compare Prepaid website, though for the United Kingdom, provides explanations, customer reviews, and of course, comparisons between various prepaid, travel money, and credit cards.[68]

While most of your preparations will focus on you, it is "best practice" to also check the support you hope to get from external parties like your organization or government. Especially for high-risk destinations, but also in general, it is good to test your assumptions and expectations. For example, governments provide less financial support than many think, usually none. Your embassy/consular service may help you make contact with your family or company, explain local requirements, and sometimes recommend local services, but any costs will be borne by you or your next of kin in the event of your death or severe injury.

If you will be traveling for your organization, you might be offered a verbal briefing, as in **Bruno Kalhoj's** contribution or you might be given a written update like in **Prakash Sivasankaran's** contribution. Both cases illustrate the benefits gained by the travelers.

BRIEFING FOR BANGLADESH: "BECAUSE YOU TOLD ME THAT IT WOULD BE LIKE THAT, I FELT COMFORTABLE ABOUT IT AND TOTALLY AT EASE"

BRUNO KALHOJ
REGIONAL SECURITY ADVISOR, CONTROL RISKS

One of my own favorite examples was a young woman I briefed before she had to travel to Bangladesh. In addition to all the usual travel security stuff, I told her that the private sphere of a Bangladeshi is about 10 centimeters (4 inches). While I was telling her that I had my face ten centimeters from hers. When she came back she told me that after she landed in Dhaka, she went out of the plane and there were thousands of Bangladeshi men all around staring at her *very close*, "but because you told me that it would be like that, I felt comfortable about it and totally at ease."

ARRANGE TO GET WEEKLY AND DAILY REPORTS WHEN TRAVELING TO RISKY AREAS

PRAKASH SIVASANKARAN
SENIOR SECURITY ARCHITECT, TELECOM SOLUTION PROVIDER

We have a lot of staff traveling throughout India and Asia. It has been extremely useful to provide precautionary advice to our business travelers planning their visits to risky or sensitive regions. This includes daily travel alerts on the latest events and weekly regional security forecasts. When travelers are aware of the latest security risks, this helps them reschedule their travel to another time or to a different location. Regional and global forecasts highlight any unforeseen risks on a wider scale but still might have local repercussions.

Also, with the traveler, we go over potential localized disruptions, namely, transport strikes, riots, and so forth. The detailed travel advice pertaining to a location/region gives comfort to the travelers visiting sensitive areas. Along with advice, it is important that the traveler is well prepared with adequate precautionary measures.

Even though it is your organization's responsibility to ensure that you will be safe during your work trips, you still have a responsibility to seek out support and advice based on your personal risk analysis of the threats and your vulnerabilities (**RMF 1 and 2**). What sort of external support will you need before your departure, during a trip, and in the event of a security incident? Does your organization offer a travel security course that is appropriate for your travel realities? Does your insurance cover a potential spontaneous diving trip? Does your company pay your family your salary in the event that you are kidnapped? Resources, equipment, and "to do's" that can help you mitigate any gaps in support should go on your personalized travel checklist.

One consideration that many travelers probably have not thought about is landmine awareness. But, as opportunities (both work and fun) open up in countries formerly plagued by conflict, this is an issue that you may want to consider. In **Richard Stevens'** contribution, he makes the case that because 80% of the world's countries have landmines, many more travelers need to be aware of the risks. Even if a country has landmines, it does not mean that your destination will be dangerous, but the point is you have to find out if where you will be, what you will be doing, and how you will do it might be risky. If landmines do show up when you do a context assessment (**see Section 1.1.2**), then you should put mitigating measures in place.

WHEN SHOULD YOU HAVE MINES AWARENESS ON YOUR TRAVEL CHECKLIST?

RICHARD STEVENS

MANAGING DIRECTOR, CAT-UXO LTD. (HTTP://WWW.CAT-UXO.COM)

Read the country briefing ... check. Have appropriate communication procedures and equipment ... check. Packed a first aid kit ... check. Know how to avoid minefields ... ??? If you are traveling to the Middle East, Southeast Asia, and many parts of Africa, your travel checklist needs to include mines awareness. OK, maybe it isn't on a checklist for the average package holiday tourist, or something even backpackers need to be concerned with unless they like going off the beaten track, but let's say you are a business development consultant thinking of moving into postconflict regions such as Iraq, Libya, and central Africa. You will want to take note. Imagine all the planning you have to consider when entering into a new business venture in say, Tripoli. Your head is a blur with financial projections, productivity charts, and import/ export restrictions, and mines awareness doesn't even register. You could easily and unwittingly be in danger when visiting a facility because it was a contested property, was in a conflict zone, or the road you are about to venture out on was a heavily bombed front line—you don't know unless you are aware of the potential risks and ask your local contact. The United Nations has done assessments, and as illustrated by Handicap International (see Figure 1.5) there are currently over 80 countries affected by landmines. Many of them are emerging markets that businesses are rushing to and development and emergency NGOs are working in. "What is mine awareness" and "why mine awareness" are two questions that should be asked by travelers to these parts of the world.

The establishment of a new United Kingdom parliamentary committee on landmines highlights the growing concern on the continued use of landmines throughout the world. The public impression and well-publicized media campaigns by such celebrities as Angelina Jolie give the public the

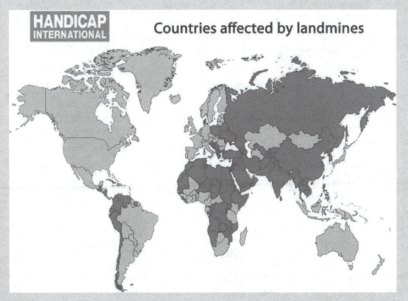

FIGURE 1.5 Handicap International's map of countries affected by landmines.

idea that this is a legacy issue and not a continuing concern for developing countries or emerging markets. However, a recent United Nations survey concluded that the use of antipersonnel mines in 2011 was the highest in over seven years. Landmines not only kill and injure people, but they also prevent economic growth and development. In Iraq, many contracts have been issued and commenced only to be stopped because of the unconsidered threat of landmines.

Previously, mine awareness training concentrated on the technical details of the mines and their explosive content. However, if you are within visual contact of a landmine, then your mine awareness training has failed to help you to avoid the minefield in the first place. Mine awareness should concentrate on four main areas:

1. An introduction to mine awareness. This should give you an incentive to consider the landmine threat. It should not be lengthy and detailed, but it should highlight that your failure to consider or understand what mine awareness is can result in severe injury or death.
2. A basic input about landmines. Knowing how a landmine functions allows individuals to better identify what type of mines are available, but this section should avoid any technical details on individual mines.
3. Emphasize preventative measures. A section on preventative measures, such as knowing typical places where minefields could be deployed, will help individuals avoid them. The signs and markings that are often missed by the unaware can many times be seen well before entering any dangerous area. The local population has probably been living with the landmine threat for some time and may have well-established local marking systems. Having a better understanding of how to observe these indicators often helps you to prevent encountering landmines.
4. Advice on how to react. In the unfortunate event that you find yourself in a minefield, what actions should you take? Sometimes doing nothing and awaiting possible rescue is the best option. Another is to retrace your steps; however, this is extremely dangerous because you are in a minefield. It is now that you wish you had taken a course in mine awareness!

If you are traveling to any of the 80 countries listed on the map and your activities might put you within harm's way, you should seriously consider getting appropriate training. At a minimum, it's worth remembering some basic mine awareness rules, as listed in Figure 1.6. Mines awareness is something to have in place should you ever need it, but hopefully you never will.

FIGURE 1.6   Extracts from Mines Awareness App, CAT-UXO.

For more details on mine awareness, how landmines function, and what to do in a minefield, you can download the free "Landmine Awareness" app by CAT-UXO available from iTunes.[69] Regarding other apps that could be useful to have as an international traveler, the NBC News Travel Kit article "Best Apps and Websites for Travelers" is a good place to start.[70]

1.5   ORGANIZATIONAL CONSIDERATIONS

For those of you who travel in a work capacity, the focus of this section is on organizational responsibility ("duty of care") and traveler responsibility ("duty of loyalty") issues that are needed to safeguard you. The corresponding section in **Chapter 2 (see Section 2.5)** illustrates some of the issues using case studies from South Korea and Mexico. While the statistics and examples provided here derive from the business world, it is important to emphasize that the same organizational and personal responsibilities apply for NGOs and their staff.

Duty of care are the legal, economic, and moral obligations borne by companies to take reasonable steps to protect their employees (and their dependents) from risks associated with their work activities. It encompasses various aspects such as safety, security, health, and staff's well-being. These aspects unfold into a set of practical activities, such as providing sufficient resources for travel risk management (e.g., equipment, training), utilizing a range of methods (e.g., pre- and postdeployment briefings, blogs, events) to promote security awareness, and purchasing the right insurance coverage (e.g., kidnapping, medical evacuation, risky location). Duty of care involves the organization's responsibility to:

- Keep abreast of travel risks and ensure traveling employees are informed of these.
- Provide resources, mainly money and time, so that managers with travel security responsibilities and traveling staff have the skill set they need to prevent security incidents and react appropriately if an event should arise.
- Create a culture of security awareness, which is supported throughout all levels of the company and evidenced by the right amount of "carrots"

(positive incentives such as 24-hour support, access to relevant resources, ability to opt out of a risky assignment) and "sticks" (negative consequences for not following security policies and procedures, namely, disciplinary measures). Such a culture also involves prioritizing security in such a way that allows employees to adapt to situations "in real time"—for example, a staff member informs his in-line manager in headquarters that his situational analysis indicates there are rising tensions in an area that his trip to the processing center will pass through. The tinderbox of religious strife has resulted in the road being closed down, sometimes for days at a time. If it turns out that nothing happened, then senior managers should not berate the missed opportunity.

- Monitor implementation of travel risk measures because, without behaviors and actions driven by security awareness, these measures are simply a façade and probably only serves as a "tick in the box" exercise.

It is in the interest of the organization to take its duty of care seriously because security events can adversely affect its brand, reputation, and staff morale and can incur legal actions against the company and drops in stock prices, to name a few costly repercussions.

Essentially, duty of loyalty refers to your obligations and responsibilities as a traveler to be security aware and to follow guidelines that safeguard the company's assets, which of course includes you. You have the right to require that your organization meets its duty of care obligations, while at the same time, you have a responsibility to comply with travel risk management efforts.

1.5.1 DUTY OF CARE

In mid-2012, International SOS conducted a set of webinars to benchmark health and security duty of care issues in the BRIC countries (Brazil, Russia, India, and China): 59% of respondents chose "preparation before travel" as a key factor to mitigate risks to corporate travelers and expatriates.[71] This ranked above other areas such as cultural and situational awareness. The webinars were part of a series of benchmarking studies starting in 2009. All are available on the International SOS website.[72]

Perhaps the emphasis on proper preparation is related to the fact that companies are branching out into riskier locations, as studies by International SOS are proving: In one study from 2011 of 4,700 international business travelers, 60% claimed that they traveled to risky locations at least once a year and 16% do so five or more times a year.[73] The 2011 "Duty of Care and Travel Risk Management Global Benchmark Study" surveyed 628 companies of various sizes with headquarters in 50 countries and found that 95% of respondents had operations in high-risk locations with 74% of local staff working in such areas and 70% of international assignees doing so.[74]

Given where companies operate, it is reassuring that the benchmark study shows that companies are making positive gains when it comes to managing the travel risks employees face:

- 81% make employees aware of the 24-hour advice and assistance number to call
- 64% brief employees about risks prior to travel
- 64% prescribe specific travel behaviors to employees
- 61% inform employees of changing risk conditions when traveling
- 55% provide pre-trip information in writing to employees[75]

However, when these figures are compared with key indicators, it is clear that more can be done to ensure that employees are safe and secure while working for their international companies.

- 43% have mandatory briefings prior to employee travel to high-risk locations
- 36% have the ability to show that employees read and reviewed travel policies and procedures
- 32% conduct person–location risk assessments prior to expatriate assignments
- 20% require employees to sign that they understand travel risk[76]

These low figures could be part of the reason why 40% of Global 500 enterprises replied that staff had experienced terrorism **(see Section 3.9)**, 47% violent crime **(see Section 2.16)**, 49% political upheaval **(see Section 3.6)**, and 74% illness while on assignment **(see Sections 1.8 and 2.8)**—the sections in this book covering these topics are listed here to help you avoid joining such statistics. As the report states:

> Companies seem to have a certain level of awareness regarding the need to plan their Duty of Care responsibilities. They are, however, much less aware of how to implement Duty of Care, especially in regard to the vital importance of communication, education and training, and auditing through management control and analysis to ensure that Duty of Care obligations are being met.[77]

Organizations need to make sure that traveling personnel are not only informed about the risks but also understand how to mitigate them.

A 2009 white paper "C'est La Vie? A Step-By-Step Guide to Building a Travel Risk Management Program" by Advito explains the challenges to implementing successful travel risk management:

- Underestimation by the employer—there is a tendency for organizations to not prioritize travel risk management until an incident affects a staff member.
- Underestimation by the employee—lack of awareness and complacency help invite hazards into the lives of travelers.
- Distorted perspective—the focus on major incidents like kidnapping and terrorism often means less sensational but more probable threats are overseen.
- Fragmentation of responsibility—gaps exist because organizations need to create the appropriate structures and processes to coordinate the

involvement of various departments (e.g., human resources, security, medical, and legal).

- Status of travel management—managers with security responsibilities for traveling staff need to "speak" the language of business, and senior-level managers and directors need to "hear" legitimate security considerations.
- Staying up to date—follow and understand the dynamics of the destinations.[78]

To understand how these challenges influence the implementation of travel risk management, take the example of Mexico topping the list of perceived most dangerous locations (see Section 2.1): The article "2011 'Extremely Turbulent' for Business Travelers" on the Risk and Insurance website cites **Pablo Weisz**, who is a risk management expert focusing on the Americas and a contributor in this book (see Section 2.5): "The No. 1 placement of Mexico at that list is probably a reflection of "the CNN effect"—when media outlets over-report incidents in one country versus another—and is not a reflection of its security risks vis-à-vis other countries in Latin and Central America."[79] Distorted perspectives can then result in over-resourced yet unnecessary security protocols and restrictions in locations where they are not needed, which inevitably take resources away from other places where they might be more wisely used. Referring to the underprioritized areas of "political, criminal, and security" threats, "environmental and health" risks, and "natural hazards" in their global survey of more than 500 companies, the "Lloyd's Risk Index, 2011" asks the provocative question:

> In focusing so much on the most visible and regularly encountered types of risk, are businesses making themselves more vulnerable to statistically rarer but, potentially, more dangerous risk? Some of these low probability, high impact events are the ones which actually have the power to devastate businesses, but their lower frequency means businesses may be less likely to focus on them.[80]

And for each one of the challenges, numerous examples can be found to illustrate the difficulties with implementing a strategy for safer international travels.

One way forward is for your company to follow the key findings from the Advito white paper, namely, for organizations to:

- Assign management responsibility—involve a select group of key stakeholders who drive the proactive management of risks and coordinate with relevant departments.
- Determine risk types—map out specific risks to staff, perhaps drawing up a risk matrix.
- Assess risk exposure—chart exposure and check the organization's ability to manage risks effectively.
- Mitigate or manage—apply a range of tools including tracking systems, training, and clear policies.
- Communicate—ensure that travelers are aware of organizational and personal responsibilities.
- Audit—monitor and adapt to situations.[81]

1.5.2 DUTY OF LOYALTY

If your organization has security policies and procedures in place, then it is your responsibility to follow them, while, of course, adding a dose of common sense to mitigate "real time" situations. However, it can be wise to check that your organization is able to and does take its duty of your care seriously. Sample questions you can ask include:

- Has your organization properly conducted a risk analysis including threat, contextual, situational, and vulnerability assessments, and addressed the implications for your traveling realities?
- Does it have appropriate travel security policies and guidelines? Have these been clearly communicated to staff? Are they appropriate and updated?
- Has your organization properly trained you in personal security? For your upcoming trips, are there any new issues that you need training or briefing in?
- Does your organization provide regular updates and briefings?
- What contingency measures are in place and what information do you need to reduce the impact of any eventual security incident?
- Is there an atmosphere in which security, your security, is taken seriously?

Whether you work for a giant corporate enterprise or a small humanitarian agency, both you and your organization share the responsibility to protect you and your assets throughout the duration of your trip abroad. Safeguarding you and your belongings does not necessarily require huge outlays of cash, but it does demand reasonable inputs of time and effort. The world is full of risks, but opportunities come to those who proactively manage them.

For further reading about duty of care and duty of loyalty issues, International SOS's Dialogues on Duty of Care website is useful for keeping abreast of the latest reports and issues.[82] The Travel Risk Management Solutions website has numerous articles, presentations, and videos that cover basic to advanced duty of care issues.[83]

1.6 POLITICAL CONSIDERATIONS

Politics is essentially about moving a critical mass of ideas, people, influence, and resources in a certain direction. As such, any associated political considerations on your part can be weighty yet nebulous things. To get a grasp on political dimensions, it may be helpful to review the context and situational analysis sections (see Section 1.1), simply because "context is the arena for action," to borrow a quote from the research paper "Mapping Political Context: A Toolkit for Civil Society Organizations."[84] The next contribution underscores how political considerations can impinge upon where you maneuver in Thailand. While the sociopolitical situation is complex, the mitigating measures available to you are rather easy to implement.

WHEN POLITICAL TENSIONS KICK OFF IN THAILAND, WHERE NOT TO BE

BRITTANY DAMORA
POLITICAL RISK ANALYST

Given the ongoing political tensions in Thailand, especially during election periods and contentious dates/events, it is critical that business travelers are aware that official buildings within the capital are most likely to be targeted, whereas tourist destinations tend not to be. Particularly during periods of heightened tensions, it is important to review the location of your meetings or conference and its proximity to government offices prior to arrival. This prior planning gives you more options to manage the situation. Moreover, unlike other antigovernment groups, Red Shirt demonstrations are typically announced by the group in advance and are reported by local news agencies. Your task, or one that you delegate, is to keep abreast of this information to avoid areas where protests would take place.

Politics is important because it shapes positions, perspectives, progress, and people. Accordingly, "best practice" recommends that *all* travelers should have at least a cursory understanding of the politics in their destination. However, in reality, political considerations are usually not at the top of the agenda for most package-deal tourists, nor for many frequent flyers, to be honest. A general guideline for determining how deeply you should consider politics is: The more you have at stake, the more resources, efforts, and time you should invest in this. Similarly, this applies if you will be heading to locations in which politics could potentially affect you. In such cases, you need to pay closer attention to the discourse, interplay, nuances, and so forth, of the key stakeholders (both visible and lesser so) as well as regional and international aspects of these factors and others. It is complex. There is no doubt that political considerations, as a subject, are expansive and dynamic. And that is before you add the possible interactions between you and your environment when, say, you will be negotiating an important deal, whether sealing an agreement with an internationally renowned museum as a struggling artist, gaining access through rebel-held territories as an NGO worker, or establishing the prospects of a multimillion-dollar contract with an interim government who is operating without even a finalized constitution.

To assist with understanding the dynamics of politics and its implications for you, you can utilize various models. Anything that can fit on A4 paper cannot possibly reflect the true dynamism of life, so models have their limitations, but they can help you gain insights that better enable you to have a safe and successful trip. The PEST (political, economic, sociocultural, technological) model can be flexibly applied to most situations:

- Political: Which political alliances and oppositions exist, and which ones do the people you will be interacting with belong to? If you get involved in this scene, how will people try to "play" you for their political gain?
- Economic: What is the structure of the economy and who gains/loses? How could your resources potentially support or interfere with the winners and losers?

- Sociocultural: What are the facts about the population (i.e., ethnicities, religions, health, education) and how trustworthy is the source of information? In what ways could the different groups interpret your presence?
- Technological: How is technology applied for progress or suppression, and who uses which technology in what ways? Do any stakeholders have enough motivation and capacity to use technological means to monitor you?

Similarly, you can supplement the PEST model with additional categories such as media, legal, international, infrastructure, and environmental. For example, questions for "Environmental" issues could be: How likely is it that the government will impose an embargo or breach their contract with your company as part of their tactics to reclaim natural resources? Who are the economic winners and losers of, say, a mining operation? Is there a risk that the police might open fire on striking workers, potentially triggering a destabilizing set of events?

Whichever model, theory, or concept you choose, the key criteria for its utility are: Does it make sense to you? Can you easily apply it? Does it address the realities of the destination—what are the limitations and benefits?

Tim Williams's contribution explains some of the political considerations involved if you want to successfully operate in the Middle East as a business. His piece exemplifies how you can expand upon the political factors when conducting your PEST analysis. Of course, if you are heading there or anywhere else, you should similarly apply the other factors in the PEST model. Remember to ask questions about and to get answers related to the interface among the factors. For example, how did the previous regime's economic winners and losers fare during the recent political upheavals? Reflect over how any potential situation will affect you and your activities (Figure 1.7). If your situation warrants it, the greater the time, effort, and resources you invest in understanding politics and its implications for you, the greater the dividends. In other words, proactive risk management does protect investments and assets.

FIGURE 1.7   Courtesy of Peter Steudtner/www.panphotos.org.

DOING BUSINESS IN A CHANGING MIDDLE EAST BY UNDERSTANDING POLITICAL ISLAM

TIM WILLIAMS

DIRECTOR OF POLITICAL AND SECURITY RISK, STIRLING ASSYNT (HTTP://WWW.STIRLINGASSYNT.COM)

The uprisings that began at the end of 2010 have swept away the old orders in Tunisia, Libya, and Egypt. Elements of the regime have been replaced in Yemen, and Syria has long passed the point of no return for President Assad. Developments in Bahrain and Syria have also had a significant impact on sectarian relations throughout the Middle East.

RISE OF POLITICAL ISLAM

One of the most significant changes to occur is the rise of political Islam. Islamists are now in the lead in Tunisia and Egypt, have gained momentum in Morocco and Jordan, and an Islamist leader is in an influential position in Libya.

The Muslim Brotherhood is the most established and influential political Islamist movement. The majority of Western governments and businesses have not dealt directly with political Islamists and they are not well understood.

The Brotherhood is a comprehensive organization with political, social, and religious dimensions. It has Salafist roots (a literalist interpretation of Islam that considers the Prophet's early followers to be the true believers) but has moderated in the course of its extensive political engagement. The Brotherhood has not been involved in militancy for decades, nor is it in league with jihadists—who also subscribe to Salafism. While the Brotherhood aims for the restoration of the Caliphate—a goal it shares with al-Qaeda and other Salafists—it has no practical plan for achieving this, unlike the jihadists.

POLITICAL ISLAM IS NOT A BARRIER TO FOREIGN BUSINESSES

Sudden seismic shifts in business environments are unlikely to occur under new Islamist administrations as they are likely to pursue a pragmatic agenda. In Egypt, the Brotherhood's priority will be the economy, which will demand that the movement demonstrate a competent and even-handed approach to the international community. Indeed, the Brotherhood has gone to pains to exhibit moderation and has stated that "beer and bikinis" (issues of real significance to Salafists) matter little compared with the economy.

Anticorruption is another key priority for Islamists and so operating with integrity, and being seen to do so, will be critical for companies wishing to do business in countries where political Islam is now a force. Avoiding partnerships with those tainted by graft associated with former regimes will also be important.

Meanwhile, regional sectarian relations are now so poor that there are risks to doing business with companies run by Shia, including in countries where political Islam has not made gains. It is imperative that firms understand these implications and know the background of those with whom they are doing business. Prominent dealings with Israel could also prove to be a major barrier to business in countries where political Islam is now a force.

Finally, other religious minorities and women's rights are unlikely to prosper under Islamists and companies may therefore need to consider revisions to their marketing strategies.

AL-QAEDA REMAINS A THREAT

Al-Qaeda's leadership came under pressure to demonstrate its continued relevance when the Arab uprisings first began. Since then, the group's leadership has directed militants not to carry out attacks in those countries where peaceful protests have led to political change, while giving support to militancy in areas where armed uprisings have already begun. As a result the movement has faced some limitations in countries where peaceful demonstrations have gained ground and is effectively barred from carrying out attacks in Tunisia and Morocco, at least for now.

However, al-Qaeda was aggressively pursued by some of the regimes that have now collapsed and is now benefitting from a more benevolent environment in the region. This is enabling it to spread ideology, recruit, and fundraise. It will also seek to take advantage of heightened sectarian tensions by striking Shia targets in Syria and Iraq in order to galvanize Sunni support and ensure a flow of funds and recruits.

Al-Qaeda has long sought involvement in the Palestinian struggle and the deterioration in the security environment in the Sinai and Syria will enable it to better strike Israel. The group's expansion in southern Yemen means that it poses a greater threat to shipping in the Gulf of Aden, while a developing capability in the Red Sea area will allow it better access to the Bab el-Mandab strait. Al-Qaeda has exploited the unrest in Libya and the porous borders in North Africa to expand in the Sahel region and acquire greater weaponry. This has given it a new foothold in northern Mali and increased the kidnapping threat to Westerners in the region. The risk of kidnapping has also increased in Nigeria where al-Qaeda has begun to cooperate with local militants.

While the changing political environment across the region is likely to be one that is navigable for companies seeking to do business in countries where Islamists are part of the political landscape, firms may face increased risks as jihadists seek to exploit the instability in the Middle East.

If your circumstances justify a deeper understanding of the political circumstances of your destination, then you could critically assess the situation by using the World Bank's governance indicators:

- Voice and accountability
- Political stability
- Government effectiveness
- Regulatory quality
- Rule of law
- Control of corruption[85]

Because "governance consists of the traditions and institutions by which authority in a country is exercised"[86] these indicators can be used to assess the political space within and direction of a country.

As an international traveler, the trick is to see these indicators in light of how they potentially relate to you and your activities. If you are an adoptive parent, then government effectiveness directly relates to how long you have to eagerly wait to bring your child home. There is not much you can do about it, but knowing this might help you be cognitive about the bureaucratic delays. If you work for an NGO, all of these issues are at play: To what extent do you need to be aware of these to effectively reach your intended beneficiaries? Donors? Media audience? What about internally: Do local staff have a voice, and is the organization accountable to them, too? If you are a businessperson, the regulatory burden may be an issue that consumes your energy, but if you plan to "set up shop" in a country, it is worth arranging for an internal or external assessment of all the governance indicators or similar indicators. That said, if your company has a corporate social responsibility (CSR) strategy and active plan, then these issues should already be addressed (the NGO equivalents are Do Not Harm and Sphere projects). But you can still find out what you need to fulfill your role. Regardless of whether your company has joined the CSR bandwagon or not, you can booster your personal maneuverability in the political landscape by being aware of the key issues, planning accordingly, and reacting appropriately.

For further reading about the components of the PEST model, you can refer to the Mind Tools and Quick MBA websites to find articles entitled "PEST Analysis."[87]

1.7   CULTURAL CONSIDERATIONS

Have you ever experienced a cultural clash while traveling or even in your home country? Why did people behave as they did? What about your contribution to the situation? How can you, in the future, avoid cultural misunderstandings? To understand foreign cultures, you first need to reflect upon your own according to culture experts **Lena Lauridsen** (in this section) and **Fernando Lanzer Pereira de Souza** **(see Section 2.7)**. How do your society's beliefs shape your values, attitudes, and biases? What tone of voice is used during exchanges? Which forms of physical contact are allowed in public spaces? Understanding your own culture and that of your host country is a process that starts before you go and continues throughout your trip.

In **Lena Lauridsen's** contribution, she advises travelers to use a conceptual framework that can help them to recognize the structural patterns that define the values of a culture. Being aware of the culture's values better enables you to understand the do's and don'ts of that society. These insights can better enable you to steer clear of potential fault-lines and head toward smooth intercultural relations. A cultural misstep that deteriorates into a security incident could result in your getting a black eye and bloody nose, for example. But more often, cultural misunderstandings surface in our daily interactions with people, potentially affecting relationships or goals.

You can create the conditions for smooth intercultural exchanges, by being particularly observant about such key areas as:

- Beliefs and religion—in Thailand, people believe that kind spirits live below doorsills so they never walk directly on one.[88]
- Customs—in Asia and the Middle East people do not open gifts in front of each other.[89]
- Dress codes—in Latin American countries, it is acceptable for men to wear a guayabera (a lightweight, open-neck shirt with two breast pockets) as business attire.[90]
- Greetings—in China, people bow slightly when they meet or shake hands, and they use full titles in introductions.[91]
- Permissible forms of physical contact—in sub-Saharan Africa, it is common to see people holdings hands while they talk on the street.[92]
- Body language—in Brazil, it is very offensive to use the American "OK" sign with the thumb and forefinger touching, thus creating a circle while the other fingers point upward.[93]
- Language—in France, people use language to fence and jostle with one another and expect counter sparring.[94]
- Protocol—in many Asian countries, if you are given the seat facing the door, you should not pay the restaurant bill.[95]
- Food—in Muslim countries, you do not touch food with your left hand.[96]
- Personal space—in most of Turkey, there can be about one meter (3 feet) between speakers, whereas in coastal region, people are more tactile but this is confined to the same gender.[97]
- Time—in Mexico, life's daily interactions are not pinned to a linear timeline.[98]

If you are working abroad, then you should also keep in mind other areas such as leadership, listening, and meeting styles.

All that said, often smooth cultural relations are less about your specific knowledge of gift giving or language skills and more about your general attitude of being open toward others and showing mutual respect.

MEETING THE CULTURAL CHALLENGES
OF THE GLOBAL WORKPLACE

LENA LAURIDSEN

INTERCULTURAL CONSULTANT AND AUTHOR,
ITIM INTERNATIONAL (HTTP://WWW.ITIM.ORG)

Business in the twenty-first century has become a worldwide enterprise. The global workplace is challenging, as people from different cultures travel around the globe in order to work, collaborate, negotiate, or simply enjoy. Whether Brazilian or Bosnian, many increasingly recognize the importance of cultural knowledge when we interact and do business across the global. Moreover, cultural understanding is also a very efficient tool to reduce feeling unsafe when we travel.

As a global traveler, you need broad knowledge and concepts you can apply everywhere. If you only travel to one or two countries, you will benefit from country-specific knowledge. In both cases, you can attend a culture and security workshop on this before you travel. The rest you can read up on in the many travel resources that are available. However, training will give you more in-depth and accurate knowledge than you can find in books.

Your pre-departure preparations can start with considering the differences between your culture and the countries you will travel to in terms of values/attitudes/beliefs, motivation, and communication. For example, imagine you are traveling in Russia and Eastern Europe and you hear people speaking to one another. You may get the feeling that they are arguing or are on unfriendly terms. In fact, this is just the tone of voice used and there is no unfriendliness connected with it. However, the tone of voice can easily be misinterpreted, resulting in your giving off a nervous demeanor. Such a situation could digress into an insecure episode. Instead, envision yourself as someone who is culturally aware about key areas like body language, tone of voice, permissible forms of physical contact, and so forth.

Knowing the do's and don'ts involves understanding the structural patterns that define the values of a culture. Once you master this knowledge, you can start identifying the "why" behind different behaviors. To embark on this process, you first need to be reflective about yourself and your culture. This will help you to identify why you react as you do. This better enables you to compare your own cultural values with those of your hosts in a neutral way. Consider points that could lead to stereotyping, prejudices, and conflicts. How you manage these cultural differences is critical to your success as a global traveler and worker. Furthermore, having insights into these will certainly affect the degree to which you feel safe while traveling.

Next, it is useful to have a general conceptual framework that can help you to understand how, generally speaking, people from different nations view and solve basic problems. Geert Hofstede, Professor Emeritus in Organizational Anthropology and International Management at the University of Limburg, conducted one of the most comprehensive studies of culture ever done. Today he is still recognized as the "father" of cultural studies, and his research is used worldwide and his work is developed and kept updated.

Hofstede identified five dimensions of national cultures. These dimensions represent elements of common structure in the cultural systems of the countries. They are based on very fundamental issues in human societies to which every society has to find its particular answers. Hofstede's five dimensions of national cultures are:

1. Power distance index (PDI)
2. Individualism versus collectivism (IDV)
3. Masculinity versus femininity (MAS)
4. Uncertainty avoidance index (UAI)
5. Long-term orientation (LTO)[*]

These dimensions are the cornerstones for identifying the values of a culture. They can tell us a lot about people's behavior in all kinds of potential interactions. Knowing about them and how they influence human behavior can help us be more culturally aware travelers. What is important to remember is that the spectrums given below are just differences, one culture isn't better than another. We all have our preferred ways of doing things that are developed though centuries and shaped by our surroundings.

1. HIGH VERSUS LOW POWER DISTANCE INDEX (PDI)

Power distance is the extent to which the members of a society accept that power in institutions and organizations is distributed unequally (see Table 1.1). Examples of low PDI cultures are the Anglo-Saxon and Nordic countries, whereas most of Africa, South America, Asia, the Middle East, and the southern part of Europe are high PDI cultures.

TABLE 1.1
High versus Low Power Distance Index (PDI)

High	Low
• High dependence needs	• Low dependence needs
• Inequality accepted	• Inequality minimized
• Hierarchy needed	• Hierarchy for convenience
• Change by revolution	• Change by evolution

---

[*] Geert Hofstede, Gert Jan Hofstede, and Michael Minkov, *Cultures and Organizations: Software of the Mind*, 3rd ed., McGraw-Hill, 2010.

2. INDIVIDUALISM VERSUS COLLECTIVISM (IDV)

The fundamental issue addressed by this dimension is the degree of inter-dependence a society maintains among individuals (see Table 1.2). It relates to people's self-concept, "I" or "we." Individualism, where individuals take care of themselves and their immediate families only, can be found in most of Europe and the Anglo-Saxon world. With collectivism, people belong to groups (relatives, clan, or other in-groups) who look after them in exchange for loyalty. It is typically found in South America, Africa, Asia, and the Middle East.

3. MASCULINITY VERSUS FEMININITY (MAS)

The fundamental issue addressed by this dimension is how we are moti-vated as individuals (see Table 1.3). People in tender, feminine cultures (MAS−) tend to consider modesty, caring for others, and the quality of life very important. Tough, masculine cultures (MAS+) place more value on assertiveness, achievement, and success. Typical traits for feminine cul-tures are the trust in others and belief that no one would want to harm oth-ers deliberately. Scandinavian countries are very strong feminine cultures, but so are countries such as the Netherlands, Spain, France, many cultures in Africa, and a few in Asia as well. The Anglo-Saxon world is on the masculine side.

TABLE 1.2
Individualism versus Collectivism (IDV)

Individualism	Collectivism
• "I" conscious	• "We" conscious
• Private opinions	• Relationships over tasks
• Fulfill obligations to self	• Fulfill obligations to group
• Loss of self-respect, guilt	• Loss of "face," shame

TABLE 1.3
Masculinity versus Femininity (MAS)

Masculine	Feminine
• Ambitious and need to excel	• Quality of life—serving others
• Tendency to polarize	• Striving for consensus
• Big and fast are beautiful	• Small and slow are beautiful
• Admiration for the achiever	• Sympathy for the unfortunate
• Decisiveness	• Intuition

4. STRONG VERSUS WEAK UNCERTAINTY AVOIDANCE INDEX (UAI)

This dimension explains the degree to which the members of a society feel uncomfortable with uncertainty and ambiguity, plus the extent to which they try to avoid such situations (see Table 1.4). Scandinavia, the Anglo-Saxon world, and to some degree India and Chinese-influenced Asia are weak in uncertainty avoidance. They do not require detailed instructions, they believe in "gut feelings," and their need for rules and regulations is lower. People with weaker uncertainty avoidance can seem very controlled, alert, and focused on "doing something." Because they have to be constantly prepared for changes, they tend to control their emotions.

The opposite is true for cultures that have strong uncertainty avoidance. Here, rules and regulations are seen as "need to have." People from these cultures can become frustrated if they feel rules are lacking. Germans, for example, are typically known for their *ordnung muss sein* and are very keen on rules, standards, and safety. It is no coincidence that German engineering is often recognized as having world-class standards. In a culture with stronger uncertainty avoidance, it is socially acceptable to show emotions.

5. LONG-TERM ORIENTATION VERSUS SHORT-TERM ORIENTATION (LTO)

This dimension deals with how much a society has a more pragmatic future-oriented perspective rather than a conventional historic or short-term point of view (see Table 1.5). China and Chinese-influenced Asia are all long-term orientated, while the rest of the world is comparably short-term focused. Culturally speaking, that makes these countries unique.

TABLE 1.4
Strong versus Weak Uncertainty Avoidance Index (UAI)

Weak	Strong
• Relaxed, lower stress	• Anxiety, higher stress
• Emotions not shown	• Showing emotions accepted
• Acceptance of dissent	• Need for agreement
• There should be few rules	• Need for law and rules

TABLE 1.5
Long-Term Orientation versus Short-Term Orientation (LTO)

Long-Term Orientation	Short-Term Orientation
• Many truths (time, context)	• Absolute truth
• Pragmatic	• Conventional/traditional
• Acceptance of change	• Concern for stability

As a global traveler, it is of great help to know these dimensions and how they interact: Where does your culture stand on each of these dimensions? How do these dimensions shape society's values/attitudes/beliefs, motivation, and communication? When you consider these in relation to your host country's dimensions, what are the similarities and dissimilarities? You can use the five dimensions as a general conceptual framework to help you understand the values of each culture. This, in turn, helps you recognize the "why" behind different behaviors.

The writer Anaïs Nin once said, "We do not see the world as it is, we see it as we are." There is much truth to this. We all have a cultural filter that colors our way of looking at the world and others. Cultural understanding is about opening our eyes to our cultural filters and becoming conscious about what is *really* going on instead of assuming what is. When traveling, this can mean the difference between enjoying the trip by being alert when needed, instead of being unsure about how to interpret daily interactions.

Working and traveling internationally are complicated issues, requiring a lot more than a list of do's and don'ts. Being culturally aware implies a deeper understanding of culture and how it impacts our character and the way we interact with others. When we are traveling, cultural filters will also affect how others view us. Before we start to analyze other cultures, we need to first examine our own "cultural programming" and how it impacts us—consciously and unconsciously.

Cultural understanding incorporates recognizing the beauty of our own culture and noting what might be counterproductive. We only become truly culturally aware when we raise our consciousness about our own culture and reflect upon its implications. Being aware of our own cultural preferences before we travel can help us better interpret the situations that we face while traveling or in our global workplace.

To read more about cultural dimensions so that you can better maneuver in intercultural settings, http://www.geert-hofstede.com has several resources you can draw upon. The MindTools website has a detailed and practical article entitled "Hofstede's Cultural Dimensions: Understanding Workplace Values around the World."[99] Recommended books include *Cultures and Organizations* (as cited in **Lena Lauridsen's** contribution), *Understanding Global Cultures*,[100] and *Do's and Taboos around the World*.[101] The corresponding section in **Chapter 2 (see Section 2.7)** lists additional resources.

1.8   MEDICAL CONSIDERATIONS

During the research phase of this book, several professional networks and LinkedIn groups were asked which topics they wanted covered: Many respondents requested a "one stop" book that also included medical advice. Staying healthy throughout a trip makes the experience more effective and enjoyable. Moreover, when you are healthy, you are better positioned to manage all the aspects of your adventure, including your security.

Accordingly, this section and the corresponding one in **Chapter 2 (see Section 2.8)** address the medical considerations that you need to be aware of and potentially need to take actions for as a traveler. Both sections are written by **Leanne Olson** who is a highly qualified field nurse and has worked in many of the world's conflict zones with such NGOs as Medecins Sans Frontieres and Merlin. This is relevant because any proffered medical advice is most effective if it has the real conditions in mind. In addition, the contribution **"First Aid Knowledge Saves Lives: What to Do at the Scene of a Car Accident and Other Medical Emergencies"** by **Catherine Plumridge** in **Chapter 3 (see Section 3.8)** gives advice for dealing with a medical emergency and there is a first aid kit list. It has to be underlined that you are recommended to take a first aid course before you travel because it is a skill that is best learned through practicing and interacting with the instructor.

PRE-DEPARTURE PREPARATIONS MAKE FOR HEALTHIER TRIPS

LEANNE OLSON

CHARGE NURSE IN THE PEDIATRIC EMERGENCY DEPARTMENT AT THE CHILDREN'S HOSPITAL OF EASTERN ONTARIO AND A FORMER NURSE WITH INTERNATIONAL AID ORGANIZATIONS

Prior planning, preparation, and careful selection of materials can make the difference between getting the most out of a holiday, business trip, or field mission and its ending in illness (sometimes long-term) and wasted opportunity. This section will focus on what can be done before your trip to prevent illness and stay healthy while traveling.

VACCINATION

If your trip is lengthy, it's advisable to get a full pre-departure medical check-up in advance so that any vaccinations that are out of date can be administered. The requirements depend on the country or area that you will visit. However, tetanus and hepatitis A and B are essential wherever you are going. Many countries will refuse immigration to those who do not have a valid yellow fever vaccination certificate with them. This may be required even if you have only transited through a yellow fever–infected area prior to arrival.

MALARIA

Some malaria prophylaxis needs to be commenced in advance of departure. The latest preventative and treatment regimens can be explained to you by your physician/health care provider; however, if you are concerned, attend a specialist travel clinic.

MEDICATION

Any medications taken for chronic illness should be taken with you, as certain countries do not control the quality of medications. If it is necessary to purchase medications, go to a government-controlled pharmacy. Make sure that you take enough contact lens material, spare glasses, sanitary items, and if necessary, condoms.

INSURANCE

It is vital that you are fully insured, including coverage for medical evacuation and repatriation. Be aware that it may be necessary to pay the hospital bill yourself and be reimbursed later. It is also recommended that you register with your country's embassy. Your embassy may have a list of health care facilities, as well as travel safety and health information that you should take with you in case of emergency.

For advice about traveling with your medical supplies, refer to the sections on **Personal Belongings and Documents (see Section 1.10)** and **Airports and Airlines (see Section 1.13)**.

If you want to read more about medical considerations before you go abroad and during your trip, then three recommended resources are the U.S. Centers for Disease Control and Prevention website,[102] the article "Well On Your Way: A Canadian's Guide to Healthy Travel Abroad" available on the Public Health Agency of Canada website,[103] and the "Health and Travel" article on the New Zealand government's Safe Travel website.[104] The "First Aid in the A-Z Situations" article provided by the Indian government is a good resource for medical issues such animal bites and injuries that you might encounter while abroad.[105]

1.9 INSURANCE

"Peace of mind, protection against the unexpected, and protecting their trip investment" are the top three reasons travelers cited for getting travel insurance, according the *Travel Insurance Review* article "How to Select a Plan Based on Your Needs."[106] **Adam Bates** uses similar themes in his contribution to demonstrate the main reasons for getting travel insurance and what to look for.

$80 TRAVEL INSURANCE INSTEAD OF $30,000 IN MEDICAL AND EVACUATION BILLS

ADAM BATES

VICE PRESIDENT, INSURANCE SERVICES OF AMERICA (HTTP://WWW.INSURANCEFORTRIPS.COM FOR U.S. CITIZENS AND HTTP://WWW.OVERSEASHEALTH.COM FOR ALL OTHER NATIONALITIES)

If the U.S. State Department, Indian government, German embassy, Australian and Irish Departments of Foreign Affairs, and the United Kingdom's Foreign and Commonwealth Office, amongst others, each warn their citizens about the need for health insurance coverage overseas, it's probably worth considering before booking your next international trip, right?

Right. And here's why. . . .

The risks of traveling overseas are real, and they vary from simple medical mishaps (twisted ankles, bug bites, a bursting appendix) to natural disasters (think voluminous clouds of volcano ash disrupting hundreds of flight schedules) to world-altering political unrest (the Arab Spring, for example) to acts of terrorism. What follows are a few stand-out cases as well as everyday risks from my 15-year career in international insurance. I also included some helpful advice for traveling with peace of mind.

EXTRAORDINARY RISKS: THE WAR ON TERROR

Many would agree that the world is a different place since the events of September 11, 2001. This past decade's headlining "War on Terror" events have forever changed the perception of how safe we are. On the morning of September 11, 2001, a client of ours was traveling to the Middle East when his flight was diverted to London's Heathrow Airport. The remaining leg of his trip was cancelled and it was four days before he could schedule a return flight back to the United States. Before the terrorist attacks, we were primarily providing international health and life insurance for our clients, but the events of 9/11 broadened the need to insure against "new" risks. Travel medical and health policies now include provisions for acts of terrorism as well as accidental death and dismemberment (AD&D) benefits. Some policies provide additional coverage to protect against kidnapping and ransom scenarios—all features unheard of a little over a decade ago.

EXTRAORDINARY RISKS: NATURAL DISASTERS

In 2004, a devastating tsunami wiped out a major portion of the coast of Thailand and large coastal areas of Indonesia, Thailand, and other countries in Southeast Asia. In 2010, a 7.0 magnitude earthquake demolished Port-au-Prince, the capital and most populous city of Haiti. Yet again, in 2011 a tsunami hit the coast of Japan, causing massive structural and environmental devastation, displacing millions of people, costing billions in damages, and resulting in thousands of deaths. In each of these scenarios, we have had clients who had to be medically evacuated as a result of the natural disasters. Thankfully, medical evacuation coverage included in their travel medical insurance plans not only covered the costs of the evacuation, but managed the complex logistics involved.

EVERYDAY RISKS: TRAFFIC ACCIDENTS

While headlining events like these have made all of us more aware of unforeseen dangers while traveling abroad, the biggest health risks are not tied to terrorist activity or natural disasters. The number one health risk to all overseas travelers is simply the common traffic accident. Using data from 182 countries, which cover 99% of the world's population, the World Health Organization estimates 1.24 million traffic fatalities and approximately 20 to 50 million nonfatal injuries every year. For people ages 15–29, road accidents are the leading cause of death worldwide. According to the *Global Status Report on Road Safety, 2013* by WHO, "Only 28 countries, representing 7% of the world's population, have adequate laws that address all five risk factors (speed, drunk-driving, helmets, seat-belts and child restraints)."[*]

EVERYDAY RISKS: ILLNESS

The Centers for Disease Control (CDC) reports that nearly one out of every two U.S. citizens who travels overseas will become ill. Dr. Edward T. Ryan, director of the Travelers' Advice and Immunization Center at Boston's Massachusetts General Hospital offers this observation about travelers: "American travelers tend to think of the world as a giant amusement park—that they can have a wonderful experience with little risk. The reality is that the world is a risky place."[†] We are reminded of this with the headlines announcing outbreaks of H1N1, avian flu, norovirus, yellow fever, and cholera. But the leader in this all-star cast of illnesses, but much less reported on, is the not-so-glamorous "traveler's diarrhea." The most common health problem faced by travelers is usually the simple result of contaminated food and water. I have had my share of this gut-rumbling killjoy during my trips to Africa and Europe.

MY BROTHER'S $30,000 STORY

Not all foreign hospitals are required to admit patients in a life-threatening emergency. In some countries, medical personnel could demand a guarantee of payment or full-payment prior to hospital admission. Do you travel with an extra $30,000 on hand? Me neither.

While most won't face a life-threatening health emergency while traveling, odds are you might need to see a doctor for a non–life threatening illness or injury. Take my brother, for example: In 2007, my younger brother traveled to Vietnam. He's a seasoned traveler and a former member of the elite Special Operations for the U.S. Army. Despite his general toughness, he wisely purchased a travel medical insurance policy—just in case. Less than a week into his trip he became severely ill, and without being able to speak Vietnamese, was not able to communicate how much pain he was in. His initial visit to a local doctor was in less-than-desirable or sanitary conditions, and he was later evacuated to Saigon's best hospital since the local doctors were unable to

---

[*] World Health Organization, *Global Status Report on Road Safety, 2013*, 2013. http://www. who.int/violence_injury_prevention/road_safety_status/2013/en/index.html.

[†] Christopher R. Cox, "Staying Healthy Abroad," *Travel and Leisure*. July 2006. http://www. travelandleisure.com/articles/staying-healthy-abroad.

diagnose him. In Saigon, he was finally diagnosed with spinal meningitis, a potentially fatal viral infection affecting the fluid surrounding his spinal cord. After five days in the hospital, he was healthy enough to return home to the United States. Since he was initially treated overseas, his travel medical insurance covered follow-up medical care back in the States.

Even though my brother had a domestic (U.S.) health insurance plan, he knew they wouldn't be much help in his international medical emergency. Most policies include limited coverage for international medical emergencies but virtually none can process claims in a foreign language, pay claims in a foreign currency, offer multilingual customer assistance, or have the capabilities to coordinate emergency medical evacuation. Where his domestic policy failed, his international travel medical insurance was able to handle the evacuation, pay claims, and even assist in translating documents and bills. Without his travel medical plan, my brother's U.S. healthcare would only cover part of his expense at out-of-network rates. In short, his $80 international insurance plan saved him close to $30,000 in medical and air evacuation costs.

TRAVELING WITH PEACE OF MIND

True, there are risks involved with traveling, but you can manage them. Get vaccinated, learn how to avoid con artists, familiarize yourself with travel warnings. All of these things help guard you against the risks of traveling. Purchasing international travel medical insurance also helps reduce your risks. My advice to you on selecting the right insurance is this:

- As you would with any regular health insurance policy, verify that the company you choose is experienced in assisting its customers traveling overseas.
- Purchasing a dedicated international health insurance policy from a reliable insurance company will not only limit the financial risk of an unforeseen illness or accident, but you should also receive the necessary international assistance to help locate medical facilities, arrange payment of medical expenses, and, if needed, orchestrate emergency medical evacuation to a hospital that can treat you properly.
- In most cases, international health insurance offers a 24-hour worldwide assistance phone number, which connects you to a live person for help. You don't have to worry about a language barrier because multilingual staff is readily available to translate your symptoms to a local doctor. I was able to use such a phone number to help rebook cancelled flights out of Nampula, Mozambique, a few years ago. It wasn't a medical emergency, but the international insurance policy I had included translation assistance; without it, I would have had a much harder time making sure I didn't miss all my connecting flights to get me back home!

Whether you acquire a dedicated international health and travel medical insurance policy or use your current individual or group health insurance policy, study the terms of the policy to make sure it meets your needs, and be familiar with the procedures for obtaining international assistance before you go. I know reading policy brochures isn't most people's idea of a good time, but understanding how to use your insurance before you have to is something I can't stress enough.

For further help, I recommend contacting an experienced international insurance agent to help you navigate the different policies available and help you choose the best plan to meet your overseas travel needs.

When determining whether you will be adequately insured for your upcoming trip, you can refer to your analysis of the risks **(see Section 1.1)** and your vulnerabilities **(see Section 1.2)** to help you select the right criteria for the appropriate coverage. The circumstances of your destination, your personal situation, and the dynamic interaction between you and your environment should be parts of your insurance calculations. The article entitled "How to Select a Plan Based on Your Needs" claims popular criteria include:

- Medical emergency and evacuation
- Preexisting medical condition
- Cancel for any reason
- Weather
- Hazardous sports
- Rental car coverage[107]

It is important to make sure you are aware of the exclusions and limitations. For example, you may need to pay an additional premium for valuables such as jewelry or electronic equipment. Your pre-trip analyses will assist you with identifying potential issues that you should raise when acquiring insurance. As the following contribution emphasizes, it is better to pay a higher premium than to be without insurance when you need it most.

OMISSIONS CAN COST YOU YOUR INSURANCE COVERAGE—THAT'S RISKY BUSINESS

FRITZ LORENZEN
*GLOBAL PHYSICAL SECURITY MANAGER, CLIMATE
AND ENERGY MANUFACTURING SECTOR*

For various reasons, some employees don't tell the whole truth about their physical conditions such as cardiovascular disease, cancer, recovered injuries, and so forth. This can become a very costly affair. Insufficient health statements can and will result in reduced coverage or no insurance coverage at all. This can be avoided by being honest. It will probably result in a higher premium but compared to the medical and transportation costs when an employee gets sick on the other side of the globe, it's almost free.

For an overview of practical considerations you need to keep in mind when arranging your travel insurance, see the "Top Ten Tips" on the Travel Insurance Guide website[108] and the resources available on the Travel Insurance Review website including the articles "Top 10 Questions Every Traveler Asks,"[109] "Five 'Loopholes' and How to Avoid Them,"[110] and "Four Steps after You Purchase Travel Insurance."[111]

You should obtain your insurance soon after you make your travel arrangements so that the entire trip is covered. However, if you are about to embark on private travels, be aware that often you can get a better deal elsewhere if you do not buy it as part of a trip package.

If you will be traveling for your organization, it can be worth your effort to make sure the department who deals with insurance understands your travel realities so that you can get proper coverage. Results from the 2011 "Duty of Care and Travel Risk Management Global Benchmark Study" show that prior to an expatriate assignment only 32% of the 628 companies surveyed carry out person–location risk assessments.[112] The study does not include figures for short-term assignments, but it can be surmised that it is not a common practice. Especially if you are destined for risky locations or activities, check the coverage because not all organizations invest in proper insurance, as **Neil Mackinnon's** contribution spotlights.

IT'S COSTLY TO OVERLOOK INSURANCE

NEIL MACKINNON

*SECURITY CONSULTANT AND DUTY OF CARE SPECIALIST,
G2X CONSULTING LTD., TRAVEL SAFETY & SECURITY
CONSULTING (HTTP://WWW.G2XCONSULTING.COM)*

The number one area overlooked by organizations is insurance—security/political/natural disaster evacuation, kidnap and ransom (K&R), health and medical, repatriation of remains, and so forth. In a lot of cases, if an organization has solid insurance, then a majority of their internal crisis management and response needs are taken care of, and it can also reduce the possibility of or assist with reputation risk, families, and the media.

I have worked with a number of organizations that do not have suitable (or any, in some cases) insurance, and it quickly became a very costly mistake.

NGOs without K&R insurance when their expats are kidnapped in Pakistan (and still missing), organizations without repatriation insurance when an expat country manager dies of natural causes, expats without evacuation insurance or evacuation plans—these involve all sorts of extra resources, such as crisis management teams, crisis management and response planning, GPS tracking, 24-7 hotlines, intelligence and information provisions, internal communications, and so forth. With or without insurance, there's a lot to deal with in one of these extreme cases such as a kidnapping case—it's better to have the professional experience and support insurance brings.

Of course, your organization should pay and arrange for emergency support. But, dealing with these after the fact can cause delays and inconveniences for you.

1.10   PERSONAL BELONGINGS AND DOCUMENTS

As part of this book's research, several professional networks and LinkedIn groups were asked which topics would they like addressed in a travel security book: A frequent response was the issue of personal belongings and documents. Some sought advice about security equipment in order to assess what was *really* necessary and what was hype. Others wanted tips on keeping their luggage safe and used terms like "peace of mind." Quite a few wanted a checklist.

For protecting your belongings and documents, this section covers the essentials. In addition, throughout this book, you will find supplementary advice. Specifically, two closely related topics are in the upcoming sections on **Information Security (see Sections 1.11 and 2.11)**, which deal with taking safeguards against identity theft and industrial espionage, and **Communication Equipment and Procedures (see Sections 1.12 and 2.12)** because that covers smartphones, laptops, and other mobile devices. As for a travel checklist, a link to a template and tips on how to customize your own list can be found in the **Planning and Preparing** section **(see Section 1.4)**.

1.10.1   PACK WITH SECURITY IN MIND

In which social contexts will your potential activities take place? In some countries, people make about $100 per month: For that type of context, should you pack a watch that is less tempting? Scenario-thinking when you pack can improve your security while traveling because you decrease the chances that you will find yourself in situations like "clash of culture" or being targeted for petty crime. And it will increase your chances of dealing successfully with travel inconveniences or security situations should they arise. Plus, good packing can contribute to your having a more enjoyable trip.

What you wear to the airport should also be considered from a security point of view. Wearing slip-on shoes will speed up your passage through airport security. For your upcoming destination, your clothing should also be appropriate in order to avoid delays and hassles at the security check.

You should consider carrying with you these small and simple items that can enhance your safety and security on every trip:

- A flashlight
- A whistle
- Duct tape
- Safety pins
- A doorstop

These easy-to-carry and lightweight solutions can go a long way. For instance, your context assessment has identified that Nepal is in an earthquake zone, plus you heard from friends that building construction is usually substandard. Part of your preparation for traveling in an area prone to natural disasters should be to always carry a flashlight and whistle, which are quickly accessible. Plus, in many other developing countries, there are holes in the roads and walkways, which are a safety risk, and ill-lit areas, which can be a security risk—again a flashlight and whistle are good to have handy.

Duct tape is disproportionately useful for rare events such as the need to repair your luggage or make windows less vulnerable in a potential bomb blast situation. Similarly, but on a different scale, safety pins are good for small jobs such as pinning the hotel's card into your child's clothes (**see Section 2.2.7**) or firmly closing a hotel's window curtains (Blu-Tack is also good for this; **see Section 3.4**).

You should definitely consider traveling with at least one doorstop/wedge, as you never know when your accommodation could require extra security (**see Section 2.15**). Smaller versions are useful for securing windows.

Regarding other items that you may consider carrying to boost your security, many travelers opt to wear a wedding ring. For both men and women, wearing a wedding ring can deter many would-be-approachers—and if it does not, you can point it out to them.

If you are concerned about your personal safety because you plan to travel solo in some dodgy places, to go trekking, or to enjoy the nightlife until morning's light comes, then you might consider carrying mace or pepper spray. As noted in **Sarah Martin's** contribution (**see Section 3.4**), it can be illegal to carry these across national borders. Instead, there are a few practical alternatives. You can purchase a small spray bottle, and after you arrive at your destination, you can put chili pepper seeds in water: You now have a legal form of pepper spray. Another option is to carry a vegetable peeler: It is handy because it enables you to peel fruits and veggies in places where food- and water-borne health problems are an issue, and it can be a simple self-defense weapon if the situation warrants it. But, then again, a plastic pen, keys, or similar items can be employed instead.

However, before you decide on carrying a self-defense item, you should be aware of some of the important issues related to them. First, something like homemade pepper spray can give a false sense of protection when it is lying at the bottom of a purse. It has to be readily accessible in the appropriate situations. Second, a false sense of protection can also be because of the fact that you are not actually prepared to use the spray, veggie peeler, or keys. In such circumstances, a perpetrator could easily disarm you and will then be in a position to use it against you. Beforehand, you should run through likely scenarios and ideally practice a few drills. Be honest with yourself and reflect on whether you are really willing to use your self-defense weapon and under which circumstances and how you can ensure that it actually benefits your security. Of course, the most important consideration is: What else can you do to *not* find yourself in such a situation?

1.10.2 "Secret Stash"

Upon your arrival and throughout your stay, it is highly recommended that you carry a "secret stash": This is an extra set of money, a credit card, and documents (e.g., a contact list and a copy of your passport) that you hold near to your body. This resource can be invaluable in an emergency; for example, if you are robbed then you can rely on the local currency tucked in your "secret stash" to enable you to catch a taxi to a police station and then to your hotel. Many thieves know about money belts around your neck or waist, so try ones that go around your arm or leg, or use a money belt that looks like an ordinary leather belt. Alternatively, simply safety pin a zip-locked plastic bag to the inside of your pants leg or dress. The important thing is that you have it on you from the beginning of your trip, since you can encounter a security problem at any point during your journey. For instance, in many countries criminals specifically target the road from the airport into the city, especially at night. Or, during the day, there is enough hustle and bustle at the airport that some of your belongings can easily be robbed.

Regarding carrying an extra credit card in your "secret stash," one option is to carry a completely different card as a backup. Another option is to arrange for a second card that is identical to your first card. According to the highly recommended website I Hate Taxis, well before your next trip, order a new card by claiming some excuse. Once it arrives, make sure you clearly mark it as a card you should not use and put it in your "secret stash": If the original card is lost or stolen, immediately use the identical new card—this action voids the original card.[113]

1.10.3 Safer Luggage and Belongings

The measures listed below can make your luggage and belongings safer:

- Critically consider what you *really* need to take with you. Remove unnecessary documents, mail, credit cards, identification papers, and so forth. Your aim is to minimize vulnerabilities by limiting the amount of accessible personal data you carry with you. Also, you want to see your belongings as a whole picture from the perspective of a prying criminal—is there a combination of items that give away more information than you intended? What can you remove, lock up, or black out to prevent intrusion if your belongings are lost or stolen?
- Photocopy your identification papers and credit cards and keep them in a secure, accessible location (e.g., emailing to yourself). In your documentation, include the contact details for your bank, credit card companies, and issuing authority of your identification papers: If your belongings do go missing, then it will be easier to manage the situation (**see Section 2.16**).
- Carry your valuable electronic equipment in ordinary-looking cases because computer, camera, and gaming cases alert thieves to their valuable contents.

- Limit the number and weight of your luggage to an amount that you can carry or manage.
- Check the handles, straps, and wheels of your luggage.
- Opt for bags with hard sides because soft-sided bags with zippers are more vulnerable, even locked.
- Use locks and other protective devices. Coded locks with at least three dials are the safest. Ideally, you should use different codes for your various locks.
- Use a covered nametag on the outside of your luggage. Inside your luggage, you should have a paper with just the necessary contact details in case the outside tags get detached.
- Consider taking a photo of your luggage and its contents, as this will aid you in making a claim if your luggage is lost.

For a downloadable checklist of measures to protect your wallet, refer to the CreditCards.com website PDF called "Wallet Safety Tips."[114]

Regarding your nametag, it is recommended to only write the initial of your first name and your whole last name. And you should not use your home address: Instead, use your organization's address (without the agency's name) or some other neutral address. In some cases, you may decide to stick on an additional nametag that has the local contact details for your next destination.

An extra tip to help make sure that someone else does not accidentally walk away with your bags is to attach something that makes them easy to identify, such as a brightly colored ribbon. You can also place a sticker on the bottom of your luggage because it is this end that usually comes out of the conveyor belt first.

Below is a list of specific advice for those of you who will be:

- Flying: In your carry-on bag, pack extra clothes for 1–2 days and enough of any required medicines to last for several days. According to the "Duty of Care and Travel Risk Management Global Benchmark Study" of 628 companies, lost luggage was experienced by 52% of small companies (less than 1,000 staff), 65% of medium (up to 10,000 staff) and large companies (10,000+ staff), and 68% of Global 500 enterprises[115]: Clearly, this is a normal travel inconvenience. Hence, pack accordingly.
- Carrying medicines or other liquids in your carry-on luggage: You might need to find out about the regulations for your medicine for all the airport security checkpoints you will be traveling through. The general rule for carrying on any liquids, as they say in the United States, is "3:1:1"—3.4 liquid ounces (100 mL) in 1 resealable plastic bag per person. According to the U.S. Transportation Security Administration (TSA)'s website: "Medications, baby formula and food, and breast milk are allowed in reasonable quantities exceeding three ounces and are not required to be in the zip-top bag. Declare these items for inspection at the checkpoint. Officers may need to open these items to conduct additional screening."[116] You should make sure that your medicine (and in some cases, your medical condition) is permissible in your destination: Sometimes you will need a letter from your doctor. It is also advisable to pack enough medicine in case of any delays, say,

due to a tropical storm in the vicinity of your outbound airport. This may mean quantities over the allowable amounts for carry-on bags have go in your main luggage. And this, in turn, may affect your ability to keep the medicine in its original packaging—check if this needs to be resolved before the last minute.

- Bringing electronic equipment: Remember to pack the most valuable equipment with its corresponding cables and adapters in your carry-on luggage so that you will always have it closest to you. If you are carrying a USB drive, then this too should be in your carry-on bags but housed separately from your laptop **(see Sections 1.11, 1.12, 1.13, 2.11, 2.12, and 2.13)**.
- Traveling as a family: Consider packing supplies (food, entertainment, and so forth) and documents in such a way that allows for temporary separation on the aircraft or at security checks **(see Sections 4.1 and 4.2)**.
- Backpacking: A security net that encases your backpack is definitely a good choice for some countries. But the lighter option of a waterproof cover is usually enough of a deterrent in most locations.
- Using a purse: Preferably pick one with a flap and an inner zipper or closure. Drawstring purses are the easiest to rob. In some cases, you might want to consider using purses with security features like slash-proof straps. And do not over-pack your purse because it is important that you can keep it closed **(see Section 2.10)**.

Additional advice on packing considerations, such as taking care that your reading material does not cause problems with custom officials, can be found in the **Airports and Airlines** section **(see Section 1.13)**. To help you organize your belongings and documents prior to departure, you can use the "Travel Wise Checklist" available at http://www.trainingsolutions.dk. For more advice on pre-trip checklists, refer to the **Planning and Preparing** section **(see Section 1.4)**.

1.10.4 Travel Documents

When you book your ticket, write down the booking reference number and contact details for the airline/travel agent. Make extra copies of important documents (passport, vaccinations, blood type, and other medical information) and keep these separate from your originals as a simple security precaution. This information can also be emailed to yourself, as to be readily accessible around the world, assuming there are power and Internet access. Your pre-trip efforts could come in handy if, say, you lose your passport. Simply put, losing your passport and having to deal with the consequences is a common travel risk: 48% of the large companies (over 10,000 employees) surveyed in the "Duty of Care and Travel Risk Management Global Benchmark Study" noted this was something their travelers had experienced.[117]

All countries require valid travel documents, but many countries have additional requirements. A common one is that your passport be valid for several months beyond your date of departure from the country that you are traveling to. Check visa requirements, especially if you will be working or traveling with children **(see Section 1.2.7)**. Carry extra passport-sized photos because many countries require them for documents.

1.11 INFORMATION SECURITY: IDENTITY THEFT AND INDUSTRIAL ESPIONAGE

Information security is a broad category of security risks to information and information systems. Both individuals and companies can be targeted. This section focuses on identity theft, as it affects individual travelers, and industrial espionage, because travelers are a significant source of security breaches. While external threats definitely exist, too often sensitive or confidential information is compromised because travelers do not follow basic safeguards. For example, a 2010 study by the Ponemon Institute found that for European businesses, 32% of lost laptops were lost while staff were traveling or in transit and 42% were lost from a home office or a hotel room.[118] Confidential or sensitive data were not encrypted on 31% of the lost laptops. Health and pharmaceutical, and education and research were the two worst-affected sectors in both the European and the corresponding U.S. studies, probably due to their mobility. Even if your mobile device is lost or stolen, you can take immediate actions to reduce the repercussions **(see Section 2.16)**. Hopefully you can rely on your contingency plan for missing devices **(see Section 1.12)**, which should dramatically speed up damage-limitation maneuvers. However, all said, prevention is always best.

1.11.1 IDENTITY THEFT

The article entitled "Three New Ways to Protect Your Identity in 2012" on the Forbes website indicates the scale of the problem of identity theft affecting individuals: 1 in 25 Americans is victimized by this crime at a total cost of $37 billion a year.[119] However, other sources cite numbers as high as $50 billion, affecting 15 million Americans each year.[120] The Forbes article claims that each person typically loses $631 in direct expenses and 33 hours in time and effort. To make matters worse, in the United States at least, beginning in 2012 holders of new financial accounts may have to pay up to half the total costs of identity fraud.

Referring to a report by Javelin Strategy & Research, the Forbes article proffers three key pieces of advice that help safeguard against identity theft:

1. Monitor your credit.
2. Use a smart card that is embedded with EMV microchip technology because these are more secure that magnetic strip credit cards.
3. Protect your smartphone by, for example, using passwords, limiting Wi-Fi access, and checking that apps come from legitimate producers.

The article "How Identity Theft Works" available on the How Stuff Works website lists several recommendations on how to protect yourself while traveling abroad:[121]

- Don't disclose your identity number unless absolutely required and there are assurances that your information is safeguarded.
- Destroy unwanted credit card offers.
- Shred sensitive information—at the very least, cut across it in several places.

- Only carry essential identification documents and credit cards. Consider storing copies of these in a safe place.
- Review your bank statements monthly (more regularly after you return from a trip) and your credit rating at least once a year.
- Refuse to give personal information to callers who claim to be updating your bank or credit card details.
- Directly post mail containing personal data in official postboxes or offices.
- React quickly to unexplainable charge denials and bank withdrawals.
- Consider getting insurance coverage for identity theft, as this can help with cutting the costs and getting support if you experience this crime.

In addition, you must be vigilant if expected mail (especially bills) does not arrive or if unexplained bills do arrive.

Since credit card skimming is one important means of committing identity theft on a traveler, you can seek further advice in the **Crime and Corruption** section **(see Section 2.16)**. Of course, online banking and shopping are other opportunities for perpetrators to steal and abuse your identity; however, as these areas are outside the scope of this book, you are advised to seek additional resources to stopgap such vulnerabilities.

On the Internet, your personal and organization data can be exposed to criminals who "mine" data and/or use "social engineering." Data mining, in this context, means trolling through social media sites to gather information for criminal purposes: for instance, collecting your date of birth and pet's name that then can be used in attempts to decode your bank account password. Social engineering occurs when someone tries to manipulate another person into divulging confidential information: This could be through a face-to-face encounter like a "honey trap" **(see Section 2.11)** or "friending" in the virtual world. The growing phenomenon of social media facilitates these risks.

The next contribution outlines the social media risks that travelers should be aware of. An interesting point from **Mark Johnson's** contribution is that identity theft is one risk, but additional threats such as burglaries and market distortions can stem from disclosures of information to social media outlets.

SOCIAL MEDIA RISKS: DON'T MAKE IT TOO EASY FOR CRIMINALS

MARK JOHNSON
SECURITY AND FRAUD CONTROL SPECIALIST IN TELECOM AND ONLINE CRIME INVESTIGATIONS AND MANAGEMENT, SOCIAL MEDIA, AND ONLINE GAMES RISKS, TRMG (HTTP://WWW.TRMG.BIZ)

In late 2010, concerned about an increase in the number of burglaries being facilitated by social engineering of victims via Facebook, insurers Legal & General

(L&G) conducted a survey* to assess the willingness of people in the United Kingdom to share personal data with strangers online. The results were startling: 59% of men and 42% of women surveyed admitted to having accepted friend requests from strangers on Facebook based solely on liking the other person's photo. Thirteen percent of men and 9% of women had shared their phone numbers via Facebook and 9% (men) and 4% (women) had posted their home address.

Perhaps more importantly, the L&G survey also found that 64% of 16–24-year-olds admitted sharing their holiday plans on Facebook. This is significant for two reasons. First, because many people in this age group are likely to still be traveling with their parents, by exposing their own plans, they also expose their parents. Second, this behavior indicates that habits are forming amongst younger users that will be difficult to eradicate when they become senior company officers themselves in years to come.

Compounding this problem, a number of services exist online that automatically add travelers' plans to their Facebook and LinkedIn pages, as well as to other social media feeds. Perhaps the most prominent example is Tripit (http://www.tripit.com). We suspect that many people who allow these services to automatically update their public online profiles are simply unaware of just how much information they are revealing. Others might be engaged in what has become known as "face bragging," the practice of showing off via social media channels.

As concerns about vulnerabilities in Facebook and similar social media services grew during 2011, the University of British Columbia conducted its own experiment,† launching 100 fake profiles, which generated 5,000 friend requests to test users' willingness to "friend" strangers. According to the UBC report, 19% (596 users) accepted this first round of requests. The fake accounts then targeted the friends of the 19%, and on this occasion 59% (2,079) of those invited to "friend" accepted.

While the L&G survey focused on the importance of "attractiveness," the UBC study addresses the principle of triadic closure—a theory postulating that you are more likely to accept a request of friendship from me if I am already a "friend of a friend." At TRMG we decided to conduct our own tests, fabricating five Facebook accounts, four with female profiles and one with a Neanderthal man's image and name. Within a week, the female profiles each had up to 140 Facebook friends, and they currently average 175 friends. By friending and recommending the Neanderthal account, the fake female accounts were then able to find 36 friends willing to link with it, despite it clearly being a completely fake profile. One further factor was that the Neanderthal account would often "like" photos and comments posted by others, leading some to offer friendship voluntarily.

From this research, we concluded that the combination of triadic closure, attractiveness, and "liking" represents a valuable tool for those with malicious

* Legal & General, "Digital Criminal Report 2010," 2010. http://www.legalandgeneral.com/_resources/pdfs/insurance/digital-criminal-2.pdf.
† Yazan Boshmaf, Ildar Muslukhov, Konstantin Beznosov, Matei Ripeanu. "The Socialbot Network: When Bots Socialize for Fame and Money." University of British Columbia. 2011. http://lersse-dl.ece.ubc.ca/record/264/files/ACSAC_2011.pdf.

or criminal intent. We also noted that all five profiles were consistently logged on from the same IP address and that after eight months neither Facebook, nor any of the "friends" has challenged any of the five profiles, including the Neanderthal. We have developed several scenarios in which criminals might profit from these vulnerabilities. The main ones are listed below.

KEY SOCIAL MEDIA RISKS

- *Targeting*: LinkedIn, Facebook, and others offer excellent sources for criminals to gather targeted information. Many users post their locations, sometimes updating these automatically. Travel plans are included via services such as Tripit and Trip Advisor. This is compounded when further face bragging occurs and people boast about their wealth via social media sites or post images of their disposable assets. The concerns of L&G arose from this risk and observations about a number of insurance claims related to burglaries.
- *Identity theft and impersonation*: Not only are real names and photos displayed, but email addresses, phone numbers, children's names, and even dates of birth are regularly included in public profiles. All of these data can provide a basis for identity theft attacks and fraud exploits, and there is much anecdotal evidence to suggest that this is a widespread problem (Figure 1.8).
- *Data disclosure*: Social media provides a mechanism for broadcasting confidential data to the whole planet, leading to breaches of data protection law or other issues such as the Wikileaks disclosures.

FIGURE 1.8   Courtesy of Peter Steudtner/www.panphotos.org.

- *Market distortion via fake profiles*: Setting up a fake Facebook, Twitter, or LinkedIn profile is child's play, and the creation of fake company web pages is equally straightforward for even the most novice criminal. Advanced criminal ploys can include putting out inaccurate market information. A person could potentially distort the market with minimal risk of being detected. In fact, a series of false Tweets in December 2011 sent many thousands of Latvians running to their ATMs on a weekend to get their cash in fear that two banks, SEB and Swedbank, were pulling out of the country on the following Monday.
- *Reputational harm and blackmail*: By exploiting the attractiveness principle, a would-be blackmailer could execute a "honey trap attack" on a target, enticing him or her to say or do things that would be harmful if exposed. After this type of social engineering, blackmail can then follow.
- *"Nigerian 419"–type frauds*: These attacks still occur, and social media offers a potential gold mine to those wishing to more effectively adapt their 419 messages to their targets, so as to more effectively engineer them.
- *Exposure to malware*: Social media sites can serve as malware vectors. There have been numerous instances of video and other links promoted via social media leading to malware infections. One piece of malware, "Koobface," has actually been specifically designed to install Botnet malware on Facebook users' systems. In this case, Facebook is fighting back by naming and shaming those behind the attack.

SUMMARY

Even though there is a wide range of security incidents that criminals can perpetrate once they have information about you or your company, following a few simple measures can greatly reduce your vulnerabilities. While preparing for your travels, when abroad, and simply at home, be aware of the risks and limit your vulnerabilities/exposures by:

- Making sure that you as well as others in your circle of family, friends, and colleagues do not give out private information about you (or them) or information related to company activities.
- Disabling GPS and tracking options on public social media platforms.
- Verifying the identity of new contacts via social media.
- Breaking the dialogue if you suspect a new contact (real or via social media) is trying to "phish" information out of you. Or, ask them where and how they know things about you and then take the time to verify that information.
- Following company policies.

Protecting yourself in the social media landscape can be greatly improved by cautiously limiting personal data that are publicly available and ensuring that others (at home, office, school, gyms, and so forth) do not give out private information about you. Simple measures can reduce the chances of potential perpetrators of such crimes as kidnapping, industrial espionage, and burglary gaining the critical information needed to victimize you.

To get an idea of how a criminal could potentially exploit data mining and social engineering to unlock your personal data, try reading the article "What It's Like to Steal Someone's Identity" on the CSO website.[122] A very determined and technologically savvy criminal will access your information if there are specific reasons for doing so, but unless your vulnerability analysis indicates that you are a direct target (in which case you should seek specialist advice), then most travelers should be concerned with not making it too easy for less-determined and skilled criminals.

As for further reading about identity theft, the Scamwatch website is generally recommended because it has several useful articles such as "Identity Theft."[123] The "How Identity Theft Works" article has a good overview of the subject.[124] At http://www.idtheftcenter.org, various risks are explained and advised against. Similarly, http://www.identitytheft.info has various articles and videos. In case you want to see how expensive lost data can be for you or your company, the "Tech//404 Data Loss Cost Calculator" by Allied World is easy to use but sobering.[125]

The "A to Z of Safe Social Media" and "A to Z of Safe Children Online," both authored by **Mark Johnson**, are two in a series available on the TRMG website.[126] Though from 2009, the article "9 Dirty Tricks: Social Engineers' Favorite Pick-Up Lines" available on the CSO website is still an interesting read.[127] The slideshow entitled "15 Social Media Scams" by CSO gives a good overview of various online tricks and cons: The first slide about the 419 scam expands upon the point raised in **Mark Johnson's** contribution and explains how a criminal misuses a person's social media platform like Facebook to plead for immediate cash transfers because the person was robbed or a similar situation.[128] Even though it is a "victimless" crime, the person's family and friends are left worried and a little poorer for the experience. As a side note, "419" denotes the Nigerian Criminal Code for fraud, but nowadays it generally refers to defrauding scams and cons.

1.11.2 INDUSTRIAL ESPIONAGE

The threats to information security for companies are worrying. A study of 600 German companies found that expected losses from industrial espionage could reach $5.5 billion in 2012, and the attacks were expected to come from China, post-Soviet countries, and the United States.[129] In India, the consumer products sector experienced losses of 13% due to industrial espionage in 2010.[130] Figures show that annual cyber crime costs for United Kingdom companies was £21 billion, £2.2 billion to government, and £3.1 billion to citizens: The amount inflicted on United Kingdom businesses is more than twice the Home Office's budget according to a 2011 article.[131]

The U.S. National Intelligence Directors report "Foreign Spies Stealing U.S. Economic Secrets in Cyberspace" from 2011 estimates that the costs to U.S businesses could be $398 billion, though it is not possible to accurately calculate since areas such as lost research and development are difficult to measure.[132] For the first time, the report to Congress cited China and Russia as the biggest perpetrators of economic espionage through the Internet. Of course, cybercrime has many manifestations, but the report points to the rise of mobile devices as a key vulnerability. The report notes a worrying trend of companies that are smaller than Fortune 500 enterprises being increasingly attacked. As an indication of the breadth of the problem, the "2012 Global State of Information Security Survey" of over 9,600 respondents in 138 countries by PriceWaterhouse Cooper, *CIO* magazine, and *CSO* magazine found that there were increases compared to the previous year in the number of respondents indicating 50 or more negative incidents in several sectors including financial, automotive, telecommunication, and utilities.[133]

Whenever heading for China, American companies such as Google, research institutes such as Brookings, and governmental offices such as the State Department follow a strict protocol to protect information and prevent penetration into their systems. A February 2012 *New York Times* article "Travel Light in the Age of Digital Thievery" describes the spy-like steps Kenneth G. Lieberthal, a China expert at the Brookings Institution, takes.[134] Before his departure, he:

- Securely leaves his mobile phone and laptop behind and chooses to bring "loaner" devices. These are erased before traveling and upon return.

In China, he:

- Disables Bluetooth and Wi-Fi.
- Always keeps his mobile phone in close proximity. In meetings, he removes the phone's battery to prevent his microphone from being remotely activated.
- Only connects to the Internet via an encrypted, password-protected channel.
- Never types in a password directly. All are copied and pasted from his USB drive. He said, "The Chinese are very good at installing key-logging software on your laptop."

Ken Nygaard Jensen's advice for avoiding espionage applies to any traveler working for an organization who needs to avoid this crime.

AVOIDING ESPIONAGE: THE EXTREME EXAMPLES OF RUSSIA AND CHINA BUT APPLICABLE FOR ALL BUSINESS TRAVELS

KEN NYGAARD JENSEN

SECURITY ADVISER, MINISTRY OF FOREIGN AFFAIRS OF DENMARK

Common for both Russia and China is that the resources spent on espionage are almost limitless. Foreign business travelers will make very easy targets if they are not aware of this situation before entering one of these countries in particular, but also other countries where other types of espionage are found.

It is confirmed that Moscow has the highest level of general all-round espionage (IP theft, politically motivated surveillance, intimidation, and so forth) in the world! Especially toward people from NATO-member countries! This is why I am posted here in Moscow and not somewhere else in my geographical region of responsibility. In Moscow, you are most vulnerable, but in the major cities throughout the rest of the country, espionage is still a significant threat.

The main reasons for this situation are cultural and historical. Since the beginning of the Soviet Union, Russians have been raised to be paranoid, and this mentality has not died out with the collapse of the Soviet Union. This mentality thrives better than ever, and any foreigner will, by definition, raise suspicion with most Russians.

Comparatively, the profile of the espionage threat in China is simple. It's all about business, competition, and money (industrial espionage). However, under special circumstances, the Chinese authorities will focus on other issues and may even intimidate singled-out individuals. If the government of your nation of origin tampers with matters regarding the Dalai Lama, Tibet, Taiwan, or other matters of a sensitive nature for China, there might be a negative focus on you as a traveler in China.

Specific information about state-sponsored or -backed espionage is very hard to come by. Security analysis companies that provide country assessments and daily briefings will not mention it with one word! If they did write about espionage in Russia and China, they would never be able to operate in those countries again. This is something you need to consider when you are gathering context-specific information for Russia and China and other places you travel to.

The extensive practice of espionage in China and Russia makes them special cases to be aware of, but even if you travel to other destinations, you can apply these general information security tips when on business travels:

BEFORE LEAVING ON A BUSINESS TRIP: PREPARATIONS WITH YOUR COMPANY

- Read your company's policies on travel and information security.
- Conduct a security meeting with a member of your management with security responsibilities and the IT-manager from your company.
- Specifically find out about what kind of information should not be discussed on open lines (telephone and open Internet connection) and which information (hard copy, digital, and the depth of your knowledge about the company) is sensitive.
- Decide whether to upgrade your electronic devices to more secure devices with a level of encryption and other security features. Seek advice on what is legally permissible for both host and transit countries.

BEFORE LEAVING ON A BUSINESS TRIP: YOUR PREPARATIONS

- Be aware of the diplomatic relations between your home nation and the nation to be visited.
- Be aware of social engineering. It is much more commonly used than, for example, electronic surveillance—mainly because social engineering is easier and cheaper.
- Be prepared to keep sensitive information on you at all times! Do not leave it behind at your hotel room when you go out for dinner or when you go to the hotel gym. You can keep cash and other valuables in the hotel safe, but not sensitive information!
- Buy a new and cheap USB memory stick. Keep your digital information on it. It is commonly known that your USB memory stick can be compromised. A virus/Trojan Horse can be installed on this device in an attempt to compromise your laptop and other IT systems. When you have used the information on your new USB memory stick, delete the data and destroy the device.

Organizations are responsible for providing user-friendly and relevant policies, procedures, and support for their staff. Certainly, more can be done when the "2012 Global State of Information Security Survey" found that more than half of the oil and gas respondents, for example, noted that their organization "does not have critical policies in place addressing areas such as data protection, use of technology, security awareness training, and incident response, among many other important domains."[135] Of the aerospace and defense respondents, only 41% have a strategy for the security of mobile devices and 39% have a strategy for social media. The retail and consumer sector has similarly low numbers of 34% and 33%, respectively. As for fulfilling your responsibilities, there are numerous suggestions in this book on how you can protect your personal and organizational information **(see Sections 1.10, 1.12, 2.10, and 2.12)**.

For further reading about industrial espionage, a chronicle of cases can be found in the article "10 Most Notorious Acts of Corporate Espionage" on the Business Pundit blog.[136] Though written for specialists, the article "How to Detect and Stop Corporate Espionage" provides advice that individual travelers can also apply.[137] For example, it makes the critical point that information exists in the four dimensions of paper, visual, oral, and electronic—all of which are vulnerable, and thus protection measures must be employed to fully protect valuable information. The "Cyber Safe" website by the Malaysian government has several relevant downloadable brochures.[138] The "Information Security Awareness" website by the Indian government has similarly useful resources, including a special section for NGOs.[139]

1.12 COMMUNICATION EQUIPMENT AND PROCEDURES

As part of your preparations, you should ensure that you have appropriate communication equipment and procedures for your time abroad. Many of us rely solely on our mobile phones and assume the only the procedure we need is the ability to touch the keypad.

However, before you go, you should understand the communication possibilities and limitations of your destination: These should be decisive factors for the equipment and procedures you use. There are many technical and financial reasons as to why the forms of communication that you may take for granted are not available in other countries. And, in some places, politics plays an important role in restricting or denying access to various communication means. Have, at least, a "plan A" and a "plan B," which accommodate the realities of your destinations. Your back-up plan could simply be to know how to make a call on a local phone and have means to pay, assuming your main plan included carrying an extra set of contact details in your "secret stash" **(see Section 1.10)**. Of course, going to more dangerous places means that you should also have "plans C and D."

As a security-aware traveler, your aim is to prevent security incidents from occurring, but at the same time, you should have contingency plans in place in case an incident does happen. Having these plans will enable you to more efficiently and effectively manage the situation. This approach is particularly important when it comes to your communication.

This section outlines key considerations and "best practice" measures needed for good travel communication. The corresponding section in **Chapter 2 (see Section 2.12)** will build on these, plus list facts and figures that highlight vulnerabilities of mobile devices. The **Personal Belongings and Documents (see Sections 1.10 and 2.10)** and **Information Security (see Sections 1.11 and 2.11)** are closely related sections that you can also refer to. To ensure that you have the most appropriate methods for protecting your equipment, you could also read sections such as **Airports and Airlines (see Sections 1.13 and 2.13)**, **Transportation (see Sections 1.14 and 2.14)**, and **Crime and Corruption (see Section 2.16)**.

1.12.1　Communication Equipment

Abigail Lucas Maia's contribution suggests practical steps you can take to prepare your mobile devices for traveling.

**WHAT IS IT-SECURITY AND WHY IS IT IMPORTANT?
PROTECTING PERSONAL COMPUTERS,
MOBILE PHONES, AND TABLETS**

ABIGAIL LUCAS MAIA

*IT COMPUTER FORENSIC AND SECURITY SPECIALIST.
OWNER AND CHIEF EXECUTIVE OFFICER, SECLUDED
IT AID (HTTP://WWW.SECLUDEDITAID.COM)*

Information technology (IT)-security means in short to protect information and information systems from unauthorized access, use, disclosure, inspecting, recording, or destruction. IT-security has as its goal to protect the confidentiality, integrity, and availability of information. For most travelers, this would also include your personal computers, mobile phones, and tablets. Safeguarding information is key to increasing your own personal safety, as well as the security and safety of family, friends, colleagues, beneficiaries, and business partners.

While an organization usually will have a system in place to safeguard sensitive information about its activities and employees, this does not mean that your private computers, mobile phones, and tablets are secure. Both organizations and individuals have a responsibility to secure technological equipment used at home and in the field.

My experience with humanitarian workers shows that, more often than not, they do not take sufficient action to prevent access to information on their personal devices. In contexts where humanitarian assistance is increasingly politicized, there are often groups who are extremely technologically advanced and will know how to use their knowledge to pose IT-security risks to humanitarians and their agencies. In countries where humanitarians are directly targeted, IT-security can become a matter of life or death. Individual workers are seldom aware of the potential severity of the risks.

The following section provides advice for some of the most volatile and hostile humanitarian contexts such as Afghanistan, Pakistan, Sri Lanka, the Democratic Republic of Congo, Somalia, Sudan, Central Asia, Caucasus, and Occupied Palestinian Territories. But, the same tips are generally applicable to all travelers and expatriates who carry personal computers, mobile phones, and tablets.

PRIOR TO DEPLOYMENT

- Seek advice and consider having your personal computer, mobile phone, and tablets checked prior to deployment.
- Remove personal and sensitive data from your private computers and back them up with an external online hard disk—often referred to as a cloud. One can access data from this external (online) hard disk when needed, assuming your destination has regular power and Internet access. Traveling with personal information on your physical devices increases the chances of information concerning yourself, your family, friends, and organization being easily accessed by external parties.
- Invest in equipment that is relevant to the context. This is essential.
- Consider having your computer installed with a free operating Linux system because this is more resistant to viruses that are caused and developed by the piracy of Microsoft software. Windows-based smartphones are more exposed to bugs and security risks than a Linux-based device (e.g., Samsung Android, HTC, BlackBerry).

- Make sure your computer does not contain any counterfeit software. Apart from being a criminal offense, downloading and applying counterfeited software leaves your computer/tablet open to spyware, hackers, and others that could cause a threat.
- Undertake all available software updates. Many IT users are exposed to hackers and spammers due to their computer running old versions of Microsoft software, Adobe, Skype, or other software or from not running regular security scans. It sounds simple, but is more important than you think.
- Make sure your computer is installed with antivirus programs appropriate for the context you will be working in. A large number of viruses/malware are universal but several are context specific, and particular types of viruses/malware are more common in some contexts than in others. Researching the top ten security risks is not the most efficient way of securing your computer, as types of viruses/malware quickly change and develop. Seek expert advice and install the correct antivirus programs relevant to the country you will be deployed to.
- Be aware that some countries have restrictions on certain types of equipment (e.g., devices such as iPads, iPhones, and Apple computers) due to sanctions on these countries or their perception that the device poses a threat to them (e.g., satellite phones).

Supplementary advice includes:

- Consider the practical side of any potential piece of equipment: Is it robust enough for your demands? Does it attract unwanted attention? Does the battery quickly run low? At all your locations, is the power steady and reliable?
- For every piece of equipment you carry with you, make sure you have the corresponding cables and transformers. The cables should accompany its equipment in whichever bag you put it in; for laptops and mobiles, this usually means in your carry-on luggage.
- Find out if you will have coverage for your mobile phone. It may be worth buying a SIM card once you arrive.
- Check if, where, and when you might have Internet access.
- Make a contingency plan for both your equipment and data.
- Weigh your laptop before and after a trip to help identify potential modifications to the hardware.
- To secure your laptop when it is unattended in an office or conference room (some of the most common places to have it stolen **[see Section 2.12]**) consider buying a cable lock. Check where the cable should be attached to the computer; a nonremovable metal plate is best, a metal casing inside the attachment is good, and plastic attachments are the worst option.

- Consider buying/using a privacy screen to avoid "shoulder surfing."
- If you want to prevent someone from accidentally picking up your computer at airport security, distinguish it in some way, such as an engraving or a sticker. Some opt for invisible markings, but the ink can wear off so you have to maintain it.
- If you plan to carry your equipment while on the streets, consider using a plain bag so it is not obvious that you are carrying valuable items.
- In addition to applying essential security measures like changing your password regularly **(see Section 2.12)**, you may consider steps like engraving your devices and using remote means to lock down the device or delete information. Be particularly aware of the limitations of any measure so that you can mitigate these or, at least, be cognizant of the risks.

The more security layers you add, the better your chances of not having to deal with all the consequences of losing any of your mobile devices and their valuable contents. And if you do, then having a contingency plan will facilitate your recovery.

1.12.2 Communication Procedures

Regarding your communication procedures, it is a good habit to carry a contact list, preferably in two different places. While you should have these numbers accessible on your mobile, you still need to carry two paper versions. You could, for example, have one in your luggage and one in your "secret stash" **(see Section 1.10)**. Mobiles are easily left behind, misplaced, or stolen—you should not carry all your communication resources only in one place, especially one as vulnerable as your mobile is. In locations where kidnapping or fake kidnappings are a threat, do not list your private numbers with telling descriptions in your mobile (e.g., home, son, parents), in case your mobile falls into the wrong hands.

Your contact list should include important numbers at work (and/or family) and the ones at your destination. You may not be able to get all the numbers in a foreign destination, but at least you will identify which numbers you want to obtain in the early stages of your trip. Important numbers to consider adding to your contact list include:

- Bank and credit card companies
- Insurance company
- Accommodations
- Police, embassy, and other authorities
- Airline and local transportation (ideally including the number for a backup means)
- People, companies, and so forth, that you might be dealing with

Your individualized factors **(see Section 1.2)**, such as who you are, what activities you will be engaging in, and where you will go, should affect which numbers you carry with you. As a parent living abroad with your family, you certainly will have your children's school, good friends, and local medical care numbers. If you travel through or work in landmine-affected areas, you definitely should have the numbers for the local de-mining agencies (both governmental and NGO/UN) and hospitals. And as a charter tourist, you will have your travel agent's details.

For all travelers, it is best to inform two responsible people of your travel plans—one might be a family member while the other might represent your company, sometimes known as a life-line (for low risk destinations, one person will suffice). They should generally know your plans, what to do in an emergency, and how to help ease minor crises such as closing down your credit cards and sending you money. They should also know how to reach each other. A "travel plan" template **(see Section 1.4)** that you can share with them is available at http://www.trainingsolutions.dk.

If you are traveling alone or are going to dangerous areas, you should have prearranged check-in times. Organizations who take their duty of care seriously will base their check-in procedures on threat levels. Similarly, as a private traveler you can adjust your procedures accordingly—for low risks you could simply send a quick email a couple of times during a two-week vacation, or if you are traveling through particularly dodgy areas, hourly text messages/SMS and call-ins at set points could be established. Travelers who are not concerned with their security and fail to check in can cause a lot of problems for their organization, as **Syed Ali's** contribution relates.

DON'T BE THE WEAK LINK IN THE COMMUNICATION SYSTEM

SYED ALI

MAJOR (RETIRED) PAKISTAN ARMY AND INGO SECURITY OFFICER

This incident happened in July 2010, when the security situation of Pakistan was really at its worst. I was working with an International Nongovernmental Organization (INGO) and based in South Punjab in an area where agencies had confirmed reports about the presence of Taliban. We had a tracking system in which all traveling employees would send me their location after every hour through text/SMS. This procedure was rigidly followed, so when one of our staff did not report in, I was concerned. I tried on his and his driver's cell number, but that one was switched off. After I reported this matter to my senior management, I contacted the vendor who told me that he had appointed a new driver but did not have his number. I urged him that we needed to know the driver's number now and was is his duty to provide it. After 30 minutes, the vendor got the number from the driver's house and passed it to us.

I immediately contacted the driver and asked his location and situation. After getting reassurances I then instructed him that I wanted to talk to my colleague, who was busy with beneficiaries. After receiving the phone, he immediately said he was sorry and he knew where things went wrong. It turned out he changed his cell number and had not updated me. Worst yet, after he changed his SIM he misplaced my number.

The lesson learned is that employees must keep their colleagues updated about their location and latest contact number.

For high-risk destinations or risky activities, you should have prearranged code words that secretly pass on information to your contact person. These should be normal words integrated into a normal sentence, but the use of the code words triggers a predetermined response. These can function as preventive measures, for example, to avoid eavesdroppers from gathering information, or reactive measures such as using a particular word that identifies one of the perpetrators you had in your threat analysis, for instance.

Especially for longer-term stays or particularly natural disaster–prone destinations (e.g., earthquake zones), find out if a local emergency notification system exists, is reliable, and what it consists of. Having an alternative way to be notified is usually recommended.

You can ask yourself, given the threats in the environment **(see Section 1.1.1)** and your vulnerabilities due to what activities you do and how you do them **(see Section 1.2)**, what communication equipment and which procedures are appropriate?

The next contribution lays out various supplementary considerations for you to review when mapping your communication procedures.

DO TRAVELERS REALLY NEED TO COMMUNICATE? TRAVEL COMMUNICATIONS AND TRACKING FAQS

TONY RIDLEY
CONSULTANT, SPEAKER, AUTHOR, AND ADVISOR, TRAVEL RISK MANAGEMENT SOLUTIONS (HTTP://WWW. TRAVELRISKMANAGEMENTSOLUTIONS.COM)

A lot can happen in an hour, even more in a single day. Almost all of those who travel have someone in their life that cares for them, either family and friends or even their employers. Therefore, these people are interested in knowing that you are healthy, safe, and secure. With the ever-increasing speed of information circulation from sources such as TV and online news and social media, all sorts of information about your destination will reach concerned friends and employers in real time. To help reduce unnecessary concerns and worry, it is up to the traveler to ensure that those who need to know are informed.

While the joy or the focus-on-the-business reasons for traveling may consume the thoughts of many travelers, it really doesn't take much to keep one or more people informed. These communications can be automated or manual, brief or long, simple or complicated, live or old school; there are no rules that must be followed. What is more important is that travelers consider the effectiveness and appropriateness of communication procedures and equipment.

WHAT IS TRAVEL MONITORING, TRACKING, OR SURVEILLANCE?

Travel monitoring is not new. Travel agents, family, friends, governments, airlines, hotels, and many other entities have been following travelers in one form or another for decades. The more modern version is a whole-of-journey process, sometimes achieved by software, for knowing where a traveler is at any given time. This may encompass single or multiple journeys and travelers but the results are the same, knowing where someone is at any given time. It may also extend to being able to communicate with or receive messages and updates from both parties.

Leveraging information, support, and resources while traveling will almost certainly result in more productive, efficient, and safer travel. Travel monitoring, tracking, and surveillance are beneficial for both those traveling and those responsible with the oversight. Free tools, such as social media, and paid-for corporate conscriptions can all be used for this purpose, but scale, context, and cost may result in one or more choices being utilized.

COMMUNICATIONS OPTIONS FOR TRAVELERS

Any traveler can share a message or communicate. The message may just be about his or her location, experience, or observations while traveling or perhaps more targeted to specifically include current health and safety status if aimed at a business objective.

The key is to not limit options to only those considered business applicable. Updates on social media profiles are a means of communication and can convey a lot to a select audience. Business communications can aim to achieve the same. Postcards, text messages, emails, status updates, forum comments, location-based services, near-field communications, phone messages, calls, and predetermined meeting points can all be used independently or collectively to keep travelers in touch.

ACTIVE OR PASSIVE: WHICH IS BEST?

Information can either be pushed (active) to groups and individual travelers or pulled (passive) from data updates and information. Determining which is best really depends on the:

- Traveler, those who want/need to be updated
- Location and environment where someone may be traveling
- Degree to which the overall situation could affect any business objectives

If a business wants to ensure that they are regularly updated on the status and safety of a traveler, in any location, they may opt for an active process that ensures multi-systems checks and reports on the traveler. Businesses often employ an outside service provider and/or software. Conversely, leisure or routine travelers may opt for a more passive process that permits occasional information updates either from or to the traveler via email, for instance.

If in doubt, an active system should ideally be adopted to begin with, and upon review may remain in place or decrease to a more appropriate or context-relevant passive process. Technology can simplify this choice.

TECHNOLOGY

Generally, computers are for creation, notebooks are for consumption, and mobile phones are for networked communications. The latter are ideally suited for routine and emergency travel communications.

Technology also now allows for simplified and diverse options for travel communications. Gone are the days of exclusively relying on travel guides. Travel can now be done virtually, in real time, interactive, in living color, and constantly changing to suit the circumstances. Technology enhances this opportunity.

Caution is appropriate for those that think good, relevant content and management can be substituted by technology. Technology represents the medium and access to the information and messages during travel communications but is not independently responsible for better travel communications.

INTEGRATION

Increasingly, travelers of all kinds (business, leisure, NGOs, etc.) are seeking integrated solutions to travel communications or travel monitoring. Conversely, many travel providers are seeking more independent and bespoke channels for communicating with their guests, customers, or prospects. This is making the choice and selection more challenging for business managers and providers as trends and options come and go over time. Greater integration and universal platforms are likely to prevail, providing scalability and customization to suit the travel and circumstances.

CONTEXTUAL DECISION-MAKING

The net gain for travelers and those that manage travel is that enhanced travel communications and monitoring significantly improve the decision-making process.

Decisions around cost, safety, time, destination, alternatives, threats, entertainment, and schedules are all inputs that provide context for more informed decision-making. This decision-making is relevant to both travelers and managers. Over time, the divisions between consumers (those that passively receive travel content), producers (those that create the content), and prosumers (those that both receive and create) will decrease, and this will result in greater choice and value for all travelers, while perhaps adding to the challenges of managers to select a single solution for all-purpose requirements.

1.12.3   COMMUNICATION CONTINGENCIES

When it comes to communication contingency plans, there are many aspects that these can apply to. Examples of this include having an alternative "plan B" that enables you to communicate despite failure of your main option, and informing two people of your general travel itinerary is a basic contingency plan to assist you, if needed. Copying essential documents (i.e., identification, credit cards) and storing them in a secure, accessible place is another easy-to-implement contingency plan **(see Section 1.10)**.

Similarly, you should outline a contingency plan for both your equipment and data. Start by writing down key information about your equipment such as your laptop's make, model, and serial number. Keep this separate but accessible, perhaps emailing it to yourself. Next, go through the information and access points on the device—is it necessary? If yes, is it protected **(see Section 2.12)**? Then think of realistic scenarios for your destination, such as potential forgetfulness at a San Francisco cafe or a targeted laptop theft in Shanghai, which could threaten your equipment and/or data and review who might potentially be affected and how. Obviously, you will be affected if you lose your smartphone and nothing is password protected **(see Section 2.16)**. Equally important are third parties whose information could be compromised—who are they and how can you inform them if the scenario is realized? The more information contained within your devices, the bigger the task will be to limit the damage. Reviewing the issues that you might have to deal with in the event of loss or theft may help you develop a contingency plan **(see Section 2.16)**.

As for further reading, the "Laptop Security for Aid Workers" PDF by SaferAccess is recommended (despite the fact that it was written for NGOs and some of the advice has "aged" because it was published in January 2008), because it has still relevant discussions about such issues as durability and power usage.[140] You can update and supplement the PDF's advice by browsing other Internet resources such as the OnGuard Online website by the U.S. government, which has links to resources to help you protect your data and equipment.[141] The *New York Times* article "Safe Travels for You and Your Data" gives a good overview.[142]

1.13   AIRPORTS AND AIRLINES

Unless you only transport yourself by sea, rail, or car, you will depend on air travel to reach your destinations. Air travel is relatively safe but it is not without its risks and inconveniences. This section looks at pre-trip actions you can take to manage these.

To mitigate the risks, aim for direct flights and landing in the daytime, as these are your safest options. To find out the safety record of your airline, ask your travel agent or use Internet resources like http://www.airlinequality.com or http://www.planecrash info.com. The About.com Air Travel website has several useful resources such as the articles "Check-In to Arrival," which compiles links to relevant articles, and "The Safest Airplanes in the World: World's Safest Airplanes."[144] It is good to note that wide-bodied aircraft are safest.

To minimize inconveniences, you can use the Internet to research the rules and regulations of the airport security checks that you will be going through. You can brace yourself for normal travel inconveniences such as flight delays by following the advice in the **Personal Belongings and Documents** section **(see Section 1.10)**. A review of the statistics from the "Duty of Care and Travel Risk Management Global Benchmark Study" shows how common these are: The 2011 survey of 628 companies with headquarters in 50 countries revealed that of the small (less than 1,000 employees) and medium sized companies (up to 10,000 employees), 76% and 78%, respectively, experienced travel delays, while large corporations (10,000+ employees) and Global 500 enterprises had levels at 85% and 86%, respectively.[145]

For a more pleasant journey, a useful resource is http://www.seatguru.com. There, you can get practical information about the various airlines and aircraft. For each aircraft, the website also lists specific information for each seat. Another option is to refer to the About.com Business Travel articles "How to Choose Your Airplane Seat: 5 Tips for Getting the Seat You Want" and "Airline Safety: Tips for Business Travelers."[146]

A highly recommended article, for both risks and inconveniences, is "Documents, Info, Policies and Advice" on the About.com Air Travel website simply because it does a lot of Internet research for you: For each pre-trip consideration, ranging from family travel to jet lag, there are links to articles.[147]

If you have any questions about your rights concerning delays or cancellations, then you should check your airline's website for their compensation policies, as these vary from carrier to carrier. Regarding your rights for when you go through airport security or complaints about your treatment by U.S. customs officials, a good resource is "Know Your Rights When Traveling" on the American Civil Liberties Union website. That said, it is focused on the United States but it can give you insights for other destinations, if the airports you will be traveling through do not have Internet resources.[148]

In addition, **Patrick Kane's** contribution offers a range of suggestions that can make your trip safer and more pleasant.

REDUCE AIR TRAVEL RISKS BEFORE YOU GO

PATRICK KANE
*SENIOR DIRECTOR OF SECURITY WITH A GLOBAL
AVIATION SERVICES PROVIDER*

While in many respects air travel can be safer than other forms of travel such as road or rail due to its controlled and regulated environment, it is not without its risks. This is especially true when it is undertaken in some parts of the developing world. Air safety records in parts of Africa and Central Asia in particular can be very poor. This can be attributed to an ineffective regulatory enforcement environment, weak infrastructure, poorly trained personnel, corruption, and a host of other issues. This not only means a greater likelihood of an aviation accident of some sort due to poor maintenance, pilot error, or other factors but also a greater vulnerability to hijacking, terrorism, and other acts of unlawful interference.

Whether traveling in the developing world or not, there are still many steps that travelers can take to reduce the risk of being exposed to a dangerous incident, a loss of their possessions, or other problems, and to mitigate the degree of damage should one of these events occur.

BEFORE YOU GO

- When possible, select an air carrier that has a good safety record. That may seem to be stating the obvious, but in some parts of the world this may be difficult to do. One place to look to get an idea of airline safety records and suitability is the European Union's list of banned airlines (http://ec.europa.eu/transport/air-ban/doc/list_en.pdf). There are also some subscription providers that rate airline safety and security and can provide a report for a price. In some cases, it may be preferable to take a more circuitous or more expensive route to use a safer carrier: Whether or not you do so comes down to the circumstances, your threshold for risk, and other factors.
- Look at routings and avoid changing planes or making intermediate stops in mid- to high-threat cities where you may be delayed or forced to overnight unexpectedly. My colleague and I were traveling in West Africa and had a connection in Abidjan, Cote D'Ivoire. Due to a delay of our inbound flight, we missed the connection and arrived in Abidjan late at night. The airline was prepared to provide us accommodation at a hotel of their choosing. We declined and were able to pay cash to get a flight on a different airline to another West African city and continue on our journey. The moral of the story being, you don't want to find yourself arriving at night (or sometimes in the day) in a city with security issues and be at the mercy of the airline to accommodate you in a hotel that may or may not have good security measures, may or may not be located in a safe area of the city, and so forth.
- If your destination is a location that is known to have security concerns, try to arrive during daylight hours whenever possible to reduce the risks both at the airport and subsequently in transit to your accommodation.
- When packing, put all items of value in your carry-on luggage and only check in items like clothing that can be easily replaced if your bag is lost or stolen. Lock your bags, though if traveling within the United States these have to be TSA locks. There have been a number of instances where security screeners were arrested for stealing valuables from checked bags after detecting them as part of the security screening process.
- Consider packing as lightly or practically as possible. Being encumbered with multiple bags is more likely to make you a target for

criminals who prey on travelers at your destination. It is much harder to pay attention to your surroundings when you are managing multiple pieces of luggage. If you pack lightly, you will be able to move much more rapidly and fluidly through formalities like passport control and customs and get to your chosen mode of ground transportation.

- Be cautious about what you pack in your bags when going to a foreign country. This means everything from medicine to reading material, depending on the location. Regarding medicines, one consideration is that airport security procedures limit the amount of liquids you can bring in your carry-on baggage, so just carry essential medicines to last you a few days and the rest will have to go in your checked-in luggage. Before you go, find out if there are any restrictions on bringing your medicines into the country you will visit. Some countries have very strict rules. What might be over-the-counter in your home country may require a prescription in the country you are going to. Some countries even have very strict rules about bringing in medicines in a prescription bottle and require a letter of approval from the country's health ministry or other advanced approval.

Reading material that may be innocuous to you may be viewed as offensive or prohibited in certain countries with very conservative social or religious customs. Additionally, politically oriented material—especially concerning the politics of the country you are visiting—may be considered seditious or at least may provoke local officials if they find it in your luggage. It is also important to be cautious about bringing military- or police-related clothing, equipment, or paraphernalia because in some countries this material may be illegal and in others it will draw unwelcome attention from the local authorities. It goes without saying that it is important to closely check the law at your destination before bringing any weapons or ammunition into a foreign country, and even where permissible, it is crucial to ensure all the proper paperwork and approvals have been completed. In some places, even empty shell casings, inert devices, and other things that might be considered souvenirs are illegal.

1.14 TRANSPORTATION

This section focuses on the key considerations during the planning and preparation phase, whereas the corresponding section in **Chapter 2 (see Section 2.14)** gives practical advice for different forms of transportation.

During your planning stage, consider your potential activities and means of transporting yourself between them. Will you be walking, taking taxis, using public transportation, or driving? How safe are these? Will you need to take any extra precautions at certain times of day or night? To save yourself the hassle of being stuck somewhere, you can ask what are the acceptable alternatives?

Much of your preparation will depend on which forms of transportation you will be utilizing. Typical actions include:

- Finding out the rules and regulations for your destination if you will be driving. Your embassy in the country is a potential resource for finding answers to such questions as: Can you use your driver's license or do you need an International Driving Permit? Which side of the road do they drive on? Can you turn at a red light? Are you allowed to use your mobile while driving? Similarly, research before departing and notice common practices while driving around in your destination. For example, in some countries they flash their lights before passing.
- Checking your auto insurance coverage including the liability clauses in your rental car agreement, if you are hiring a vehicle.
- Researching local conditions, quantity and quality of the infrastructure, driving hazards like stray chickens and risks like bandits, and availability of police and medical services.
- Arranging your transportation for the first 24 hours of your trip, or at least from where you disembark to your initial accommodation. Many travelers also opt for arranging their transportation for the duration of their trip. Check if your hotel offers a service or can recommend one. If you have arranged for a driver to pick you up at the airport, then consider taking a few precautions: Make sure that the driver's placard does not include your first name—limit your private information in public spaces. And, if your company's or NGO's name is locally contentious, then require that the placard does not include this information.
- Adding to your contact list **(see Section 1.12)** any relevant phone numbers and possible addresses that you might need such as the local police and your insurance company.
- Downloading a map and perhaps a plan of the public transportation, if you will be using that (Figure 1.9).
- Packing the right child seat if you will be driving with your children. A good article about the four stages of seating for children can be found on Transport Canada's "Keep Kids Safe" webpage.[149]
- Bringing a helmet if you will be using any form of cycling.

To aid you with mitigating transportation risks, expert advice and traveler stories are peppered throughout this book. Take, for example, **Jack Chu's** advice in **"Planning Travels to China" (see Section 1.4)** and **Andreas Poppius's** contribution **"24 Hours of Don't Do's in New Delhi" (see Section 2.14.3)**.

As for Internet resources, the website I Hate Taxis is recommended because it is quite clear that the proffered practical advice is by and for international travelers: The website's name is somewhat misleading because it actually covers all types of transportation options and other relevant advice like dealing with money, Wi-Fi hotspots, and so forth—giving both generic and country-specific advice.[150] Moreover, they set the page up so that it can be easily translated into various languages. The About.com website is also a good starting point for country-specific information.

FIGURE 1.9 Courtesy of Carrie Clinton.

For instance, the articles "Getting Around in China—Taking a Taxi"[151] and "San Francisco Taxi Tips"[152] are two such examples.

1.15 ACCOMMODATION

Except for the most adventurous, young-at-heart types, travelers prefer to stay at safe and secure accommodations. But which criteria should you use to select a hotel? Even if you do not personally book your own accommodation because you use your organization's services or external ones, you should have a clear idea of what is acceptable and pass those ideas on to the booking agent.

To provide you with "best-practice" advice and tips, this book asked experts in hotel security, each with a different specialty, these questions:

- How can travelers prepare themselves for a safe hotel stay?
- When comparing various accommodations, what security features should travelers look for?

- What should travelers do at the hotel to have a safe and secure stay?
- What should they do in case of an emergency (i.e., fire, terrorist attack, earthquake)?

The following contribution and the corresponding one in **Chapter 2 (see Section 2.15)** are a joint collaboration to give you practical advice that you can incorporate as needed. This contribution lists guidelines that address the first two questions above while **Chapter 2's** section covers, in detail, the last two questions.

SURFING THE INTERNET FOR A SAFER HOTEL STAY

DARRELL CLIFTON
AUTHOR OF HOSPITALITY SECURITY *AND DIRECTOR OF SECURITY, CIRCUS CIRCUS HOTEL AND CASINO (HTTP://WWW.CIRCUSRENO.COM)*

GABOR BUNTH
DIRECTOR OF LOSS PREVENTION, ST. PANCRAS RENAISSANCE HOTEL LONDON, MARRIOTT INTERNATIONAL (HTTP://WWW.MARRIOTT.CO.UK/HOTELS/TRAVEL/LONPR-ST-PANCRAS)

JOHN J. STRAUCHS
SECURITY DESIGN CONSULTANT AT STRAUCHS, LLC WHO HAS WORKED IN SAUDI ARABIA, KUWAIT, JORDAN, SINGAPORE, HONG KONG, VIETNAM, GREECE, VENEZUELA, AND COLOMBIA, AMONGST OTHERS (HTTP://WWW.STRAUCHS-LLC.COM)

TANYA SPENCER
GLOBAL TRAVEL SECURITY AND CRISIS MANAGEMENT SPECIALIST AND COAUTHOR OF TRAVEL WISELY: A PERSONAL SECURITY GUIDE FOR WOMEN TRAVELERS *(IN DANISH ONLY), TRAININGSOLUTIONS (HTTP://WWW.TRAININGSOLUTIONS.DK)*

Through some Internet research, you can make an informed decision about your accommodations' security by:

- Checking http://www.tripadvisor.com or similar websites written by travelers. While many past guests will not directly refer to the presence of security officers, cameras, or prevention programs specifically, they will allude to security and safety issues in other ways. Look for comments about noisy neighbors, disruptive bar patrons, guest accident response, or access control. These incidents are found in any hotel, but the way the incidents were handled tells you the difference. For example, if a blogger mentions their neighbors keeping them up all night and the hotel finally moving them to a different room the next day, it is unlikely the hotel has security officers.

- Using selection criteria based on the size of the hotel, its age, and name. Larger hotels will generally supplement their security. Hotels that are older are less likely to meet current standards and may have been built before the adoption of certain codes or standards. Earthquake safety, for example, was not factored into most hotel buildings until the 1970s in some Western countries. If a hotel has made upgrades to meet these standards, they will proudly advertise it. Finally, the name is a great indicator of the asset protection in which a hotel invests. A well-known brand is not only more likely to protect the integrity of its brand, but having many locations provides them with the experience needed to protect against all hazards.
- Seeing if physical security features are mentioned (adequate door security, electronic lock systems, safety deposit box).
- Using Google Maps or a similar service to make sure the location of your accommodation, transportation options, and activities work well together. Thinking about convenience when choosing the location of your accommodations can benefit your security in positive ways. Also, try to avoid staying within 500 meters (1,600 feet) of potentially contentious locations like government buildings, military installations, gas depots, political offices, and in some cases certain businesses, NGOs, or UN premises.

For their female guests, some hotel chains make it a priority to provide extra security measures. To find out if a hotel has such measures, visit the hotel's website as they tend to advertise this, or try http://www.journeywoman. com. Some women prefer to stay in bed and breakfast (B&B) accommodations because the owners will notice if anything is wrong.

Particularly for when you will be traveling to politicized contexts, there are a few things you can consider on the geopolitical level before selecting your accommodation. The well-known larger hotel chains tend to have higher security standards. However, in some places, it is worth considering if the hotel brand has been or could be a target. It could be locally targeted because there is opposition to American ownership, for example. You still may choose to stay there but when you arrive you will understand why your hotel has a slight fortress feeling to it. Or you may opt for a local B&B; though these tend to have fewer security measures, they also attract less attention. Being aware of the external factors will help you make informed decisions before your trip and continuously while you are traveling. The choice is yours.

The Internet has plenty of resources about safe accommodation choices and options. One such example is the article "Hotel Security Tips for Small Business Travelers," which seemingly is for a narrow target audience but most of the tips apply to any traveler staying in a hotel.[153] The CNN article "Business Travelers, Avoid These Rooms" provides similar advice.[154] The Lonely Planet Travel Forum has a lot of threads about hotels.[155] If you would rather watch an instructive video, then check out the resources on the Gutsy Traveler[156] and About.com Hotels & Resorts[157] websites.

1.16 HOME PROTECTION

It would be a shame to have a safe and wonderful trip, just to return to a burglarized house. Hence, this section spotlights home protection tips and advice you can implement before you depart for your journeys. If you will be moving to a different country, you can also use these guidelines for your new accommodation. Additional advice about protecting your belongings if you use housekeepers while living abroad can be found in the **Accommodation** section (**see Section 2.15**). However, details about physical security measures like the thickness of doors and types of fencing are beyond the scope of this book, so you should seek information on the Internet or from service providers.

**HOME SECURITY WHILE TRAVELING
STARTS BEFORE YOU GO**

CHRIS E. MCGOEY
*SECURITY CONSULTANT, MCGOEY SECURITY CONSULTING
(HTTP://WWW.CRIMEDOCTOR.COM/HOME.HTM)*

Home burglars are always on the lookout for an easy opportunity. Most of them prefer to break into an unoccupied home that presents itself, without complications, as a chance to steal cash, credit cards, jewelry, electronics, and even weapons that can be easily sold on the street.

Travelers who leave homes unoccupied for weeks are ideal targets for burglars because the crime will not be immediately reported. Here are proactive steps you can do well in advance of your travels:

- Burglarize yourself. As a family exercise, pretend you are burglars and take a critical look at how easy it would be to break in and what property would most likely be stolen. How can you make it harder for burglars to break in and, if they get in, to steal your valuables?
- Talk with adjacent neighbors about a "Neighborhood Watch" by formulating plans to protect each other's homes while away. Invite the police to provide input.
- Fortify your home by installing solid core doors, heavy duty locks, longer screws in the door lock strike-plates and door hinges, and extra blocking devices on all accessible sliding windows.
- Make an inventory of valuables. Record models and serial numbers, and take photographs. This makes filing a burglary loss claim easier. But prevention is better, so make sure you secure irreplaceable items.

- Place high-value items in a home safe that is securely attached or a bank safety deposit box.
- Copy important documents and computer files and keep one copy off-site.
- Review your home insurance policy for adequate coverage and review loss exclusions.
- Use a burglar alarm system. The alarm sign and window decals are a 75% deterrent.

Just before you go, you can do a few more steps that will give you more peace of mind while traveling:

- If practical, provide a trusted neighbor or relative with your house key. A neighborhood burglar will notice the activity such as shades being raised and lowered daily and avoid this house. Consider trading house-sitting duties like watering plants or feeding animals when neighbors go away.
- Create occupancy clues. Don't have outdoor lights burning 24-hours a day. Set interior and exterior lights and radio to operate on a normal schedule with inexpensive light timers to simulate occupancy.
- Consider whether or not to stop newspapers, mail delivery, or garbage pickup. Preferably you shouldn't stop them because these activities are occupancy cues. But, of course, it will depend on your circumstances—if you have a mail slot in your door and you don't want to give your house keys to someone, then you probably should cancel. Whereas, if you have mailbox that a neighbor can empty, then continue the services. A neighbor can be asked to place and remove garbage cans.
- Ask neighbors to park cars in your driveway.
- Arrange for snow removal if that is the normal routine.
- Don't hide spare house keys under rocks, in flowerpots, above door ledges, or other obvious places (remember to think like a burglar).
- Don't post your family name on your mailbox or on your house. A burglar can call directory assistance to get your telephone number and call your home while standing in front of your house to confirm that you are away.
- Don't leave descriptive telephone answering machine messages like, "You've reached the Wilson's. . . . We're away skiing for the holidays. . . . Please leave a message." Burglars love to hear that they have plenty of time to break in and completely ransack your home.
- Authorize neighbors or relatives to makes temporary repairs if forced entry occurs.

For further reading, **Chris McGoey's** Crime Doctor website covers a wide range of security topics and advice.[158] Other recommended Internet resources include: "15 Steps You Can Take to Prevent Home Burglary" available on the Scambusters website,[159] "Home Security Tips" on the generally useful How Stuff Works website,[160] and "Protecting Your Home" by ADT India.[161]

1.17   WELL-BEING: DEALING WITH FEAR, ANXIETY, AND INSECURITY

During the book's research phase, various LinkedIn groups and professional networks were asked what the book should cover for their traveling staff or for themselves. As the article below by **Dr. Donald Bosch** notes, this section is a direct response to a question from a LinkedIn group about travelers' real and perceived fears. For the commenter, who has regional security responsibilities, his concern was for travelers who had misplaced fears or trust, which made them overtly reckless or overly cautious.

While there are all types of fears and anxieties that relate to traveling, such as the anxiety felt by some before a flight or cruise, the contributions below deal with such feelings that impinge upon your ability to accurately assess risks. Since your psychological well-being is an essential part of being a traveler who is ready for every opportunity and challenge, this section offers expert advice and case studies. The aim is to provide insights into such questions as: Why are some people's thresholds for fear lower or higher than others? How do you rate your own levels of anxiety, fear, and feelings of insecurity? What can trigger an anxious response? Which concerns fill your thoughts? What can you do to be psychologically and emotionally ready for your next travels?

In **"Understanding Feelings of Insecurity,"** **Dr. Donald Bosch** explains the psychological and physiological brain functions that allow fear to hijack our brains. He offers advice on how to strengthen your response to fear and lists questions that can help you gain insights into the things that might be triggers for you. In **Mark Snelling's** contribution **"Your 'Secure Base' Aids in Your Ability to Assess Threats,"** he makes the case that when our emotional stability is lacking or worn down, we are less able to differentiate between external threats and internal emotions. He ends by noting that there are steps you and your employer can take to maintain optimal stability. **"Raquel's"** contribution **"Is That the Kenyan Police or My Past Traumas Knocking On the Door?"** about how her fears kept her up at night demonstrates how past traumas, not dealt with, can affect the present. In her description of her personal journey to heal, she names several methods that worked for her. Additional advice and tips can be found in **Sian Kelly's** contribution, **"Stress: Positive, Negative, and What to Do" (see Section 2.17).** The two **Medical Considerations** sections **(see Sections 1.8 and 2.8)** in this book also provide health tips that can support you psychologically.

UNDERSTANDING FEELINGS OF INSECURITY

DR. DONALD BOSCH

DIRECTOR OF CLINICAL SERVICES, HEADINGTON INSTITUTE (HTTP://WWW.HEADINGTON-INSTITUTE.ORG). REPRINTING AND MODIFICATIONS MADE BY PERMISSION. COPYRIGHT © 2012 HEADINGTON INSTITUTE. FOR THE ORIGINAL ARTICLE, SEE "UNDERSTANDING FEELINGS OF INSECURITY," DR. DONALD BOSCH/HEADINGTON INSTITUTE, MAY 2012. HTTP://HEADINGTON-INSTITUTE.NET/WP/?P = 750.

"What is the difference between the feeling of being secure and being secure, and the feeling of being in danger and actually being in danger? A lot of travelers are scared of things not worth being scared of and are comfortable about the things they actually should be paying attention to." I was posed this question in response to a LinkedIn comment during this book's research phase.

The answer to the question lies in how different parts of the brain function. In the simplest of terms, we have a downstairs brain and an upstairs brain. The upstairs is our thinking, reflecting, conscious sense of our self. While we have the feeling that we are in control from this "computer desktop" of our brain, the reality is that it only comprises a small percentage of our brain function. The vast majority of brain activity occurs in the downstairs brain that is busy keeping our whole bodily organism functioning and in balance. Our heart keeps beating without our having to consciously tell it to do so—good thing, or we would be dropping like flies.

HOW FEAR HIJACKS OUR BRAIN

Deep in the center of our downstairs brain is the amygdala, a structure composed of two little nodes that are strategically positioned to evaluate whether we are in any danger. It operates without our conscious awareness but can have a powerful effect on our entire physical and mental well-being. Throughout our lifetime, it collects and stores the sights, sounds, and smells that have been connected to dangerous or threatening situations. These can be both physical and psychological or emotional dangers. The amygdala also comes preloaded with some danger situations passed on over the millennia from our ancestors, such as an infant's awareness of heights and not being willing to crawl over a visual cliff. When the amygdala senses danger, it reacts in a big way. It sends out the message for a massive change in our bodily functioning. Our heart beats faster and our lungs suck in more air to feed oxygen to our muscles to prepare to fight or to run. We feel apprehension and fear. The digestive tract shuts down, sometimes resulting in what normally would be embarrassing results. *And* our upstairs brain struggles to keep some control as the downstairs brain tries to shut it down so as not to interfere with this emergency response. The downstairs brain in essence hijacks the thinking brain in the belief that it can best preserve our lives with its storehouse of automatic defensive maneuvers.

While immensely complicated both psychologically and physiologically, this conflict between the upstairs and downstairs brain is the core of the issue when trying to understand fear and feelings of insecurity. It is hard to make a rational threat/risk appraisal when the brain is locked in this tug of war. The amygdala's neighbor, the hippocampus, tries to aid the upstairs brain by bringing context appraisal to the situation, but it too can be overrun. We are now discovering that over time if we are exposed to too much trauma and too many dangerous situations, the hippocampus actually begins to falter and become less effective in its role. People who have been exposed to a lot of danger, especially during childhood, are more likely to struggle to keep the upstairs brain engaged and therefore may appear to be overreacting without cause. Some people, depending on their history or predisposition, can go into what is called a dissociative state, a kind of being "checked out" from current reality state, which can explain why they may underreact.

A poignant example of the workings of the amygdala and hippocampus happened a couple of years ago when I was in Haiti with a security training team working with humanitarian workers. I was in front of the class actually teaching in more detail about how the brain functions, when a large truck rumbled past the building. The building vibrated slightly, and I could instantly tell who had been in the earthquake or one of the aftershocks. Their amygdala reaction was obvious in their facial expressions. But then the hippocampus kicked in with a contextual appraisal as the participants could see that I and the other trainers were calm, as we were in a position to see the truck go by. Their facial expressions relaxed and they could again attend to the lesson with their upstairs brain.

STRENGTHENING OUR RESPONSE TO FEAR

So is there anything we can do to give our upstairs brain a better chance in this struggle? Indeed, in the immediate moment there is a simple technique, but it needs to be practiced. By consciously slowing down your breathing, you can physiologically interrupt the amygdala emergency response. Essentially we are trying to override this response. Suggestions on breathing techniques vary, but one method often recommended is to inhale down deep from your stomach for four seconds, hold for one second, then exhale for five seconds. By continuing with this pattern we can help tip the balance in favor of keeping our thinking brain in the game. While operating from the upstairs brain doesn't guarantee we will make the correct threat/risk assessment, it certainly can help us make decisions on a more rational and empirical basis.

To understand your fear triggers, some questions you can start off with include:

- Have you been in a life-threatening situation?
- What was your "disaster personality"? Did it surprise you? What would you like to do differently?

- What are your fear triggers—sights, sounds, and smells that have been connected to dangerous or threatening situations?
- What do you need to do to feel and be safer?
- How can you increase awareness for your context? What information do you still need in order to accurately assess risk?

As the answer to the initial question posed is complex, hopefully this article gave you a good starting point. It's important because most people have to struggle to assess a situation on the presented facts alone. These facts get colored by our own history, often unconsciously, and can have a profound effect on how these facts are interpreted. Developing an awareness of your own likely fear triggers can go a long way toward making good upstairs decisions. It is also very helpful for people to develop situational awareness for their travel locations. Are there known risks? Especially if someone is going to a higher-risk environment, consider getting a briefing of current security conditions. Talking with locals is often helpful to get a sense of what is actually worth being cautious of and fearful about. This will allow your upstairs brain to prepare to recognize situations as they develop and hopefully rehearse more appropriate responses.

YOUR "SECURE BASE" AIDS IN YOUR ABILITY TO ASSESS THREATS

MARK SNELLING

PSYCHODYNAMIC COUNSELOR AND TRAINING CONSULTANT, INTERHEALTH (HTTP://WWW.INTERHEALTH.ORG.UK)

A really interesting link between feelings of fear, anxiety, and insecurity can be made with the concept of the "secure base" in attachment theory.

When we grow up in an environment that is adequately protective in terms of food, shelter, and parental understanding and reliability, we slowly internalize that external security to the point where it becomes an inner sense of stability (known as the secure base). This provides us with the inner resources to identify and process difficult feelings, but it also equips us to seek appropriate support when we can see that those resources are running low.

If we have a solid, secure base, then we have an emotional stability that allows us to recognize feelings of fear as an important indication that we are faced with some kind of danger or threat. We can then use that rational fear as a prompt that some action needs to be taken in response to the threat.

If we don't have a secure base, then that very useful fear response will increasingly turn into much more generalized and irrational feelings of anxiety. And if we're feeling insecure and anxious, we're much less able to discriminate between real external threats and inner emotional turmoil. Put simply, it becomes very difficult to accurately assess risks.

People may lack a secure base because of early deprivation or neglect, but in the humanitarian sector in particular, people can also lose their secure base because of lengthy exposure to stress, pressure, and the suffering of others, combined with frequent travel and a lack of sustained relationships. Often, people who have moved countries too many times will finally end up losing their sense of "home," either in terms of an actual place or in terms of an inner sense of belonging.

The more disconnected a person becomes from that inner sense of stability, the more vulnerable he or she becomes to anxiety and depression. They are also more likely to seek out behaviors that mimic feelings of security, such as drinking and sex, but serve only to erode overall resilience, rather than promote it. In the field, we also know that compulsive pursuit of these behaviors poses genuine risks to personal security. Significantly, clinical experience also tells us that this inner disconnection can compromise capacity to recover, should one experience some kind of actual trauma.

A secure base is made up of many different elements: a sound sense of self, the capacity to make good relationships, belief in some transcendent purpose, physical health, and an employer who takes their duty of care seriously with robust policies and procedures. In some ways, those who travel a lot need to put extra energy into preserving and building on these foundations; otherwise they will become increasingly vulnerable to both fear and anxiety.

The next contribution humanizes these psychological insights by demonstrating the effects that past traumas and a weakened "secure base" had on **"Raquel."**

IS THAT THE KENYAN POLICE OR MY PAST TRAUMAS KNOCKING ON THE DOOR?

"RAQUEL"
SAFETY AND SECURITY MANAGER FOR RAPID RESPONSE TEAMS, HUMANITARIAN SECTOR

During a period when I was staying in a hotel/rental apartment compound in Nairobi, there were rumors that the police were targeting people at such "affordable' accommodations late at night. They would wake up the occupants and force them to choose between "giving something to ease the paper work" or going to jail. It's never called what it is, a bribe. So my Kenyan friends warned me that some kind of code would be used and then I should pay a small amount (and not show that I had more money) but I shouldn't pay before hearing the code, otherwise I could go to jail because I offered a bribe.

Even though I had local advice on how to react if my door was knocked upon and I used extra locks (the compound was also relatively secure but the police can just use the main entrance), I couldn't sleep at night. I would stay up "watching" TV, but actually I was monitoring any changes of light outside of my door. It was terrible. My feelings of insecurity were so profound and the lack of sleep didn't help either.

The thing is, because of my work with emergency and relief NGOs, I've had a few experiences that really shook me, but I brushed them all off at the time because that was the organizational culture of some of the agencies I worked for. I now know that I can't just brush off seeing the bodies of ten slaughtered villagers in the Democratic Republic of the Congo, having a bad police experience in Guatemala, or coping with the constant stress levels of being a security manager in Pakistan during a period of floods and terrorist threats.

The organization that I worked for didn't have the resources in Kenya to offer me psychological support. Talking with a good friend was good for me but it wasn't enough to help me to get over my fears, so I started some self-help. I revisited those past episodes in my mind and gave myself credit for the things I handled well and forgave myself for my mistakes, and I used a Native American trick of empowering myself in my dreams.

After a while, I managed to sleep better, which helped me "gain my wits" and be more my usual self. Once I was back in Europe, I got professional counseling. Also, I'm now in the habit of coaching myself before and during a risky mission. I meditate and exercise regularly. The things that I've witnessed, good and bad, are a part of me. I'm at peace with that and I have tools to continuously support myself. I still work in and have responsibilities for teams in dangerous locations, so the potential for something triggering another strong response is there. But since I started to actively work on my insecurities, I feel at ease and self-assured—exactly what is needed for my job!

As for Internet resources, the website The Travel Psychologist has a series of articles that could be interesting for some readers.[162] The Headington Institute has several relevant articles, apps, and video resources: The "How to Manage Yourself during a Critical Incident" video featuring **Dr. Donald Bosch** is one example.[163] The No Nonsense Self Defense website is packed with relevant resources: The "Pyramid for Personal Safety" article is highly recommended because it links security awareness to psychological preparedness[164] and their "Fear Management vs Danger Management" article makes some interesting points using scorpion and vampire analogies.[165]

1.18   WORTH KNOWING, BEFORE YOU GO: CHAPTER 1 SUMMARY

Hopefully, as a reader, you highlighted, took note, or acted upon suggestions that are relevant to you and modified other tips to suit your circumstances. Accordingly, the chapter's key points will differ from reader to reader, so the summary offered here of the three points for each section can be used to "jog your memory." How do these points compare with the ones you identified?

1.1 Proactively Assessing the Risks

- If you get the opportunity to understand the motivation, capacity, and history of the potential perpetrator(s), then you will have a better chance of weighing the likelihood of a threat occurring.
- A country's context entails its history, politics, culture, demographics, climate, infrastructure, economy, etc.
- Your situation analysis should monitor typical trigger points such as contentious elections, price hikes, anniversaries, court cases, or religiously oriented antagonisms.

1.2 Personal Considerations and Vulnerability Analysis

- Your vulnerability analysis should assess your exposure to a given threat by considering who you are, what you do, and how you do it.
- When you travel, you need to see yourself through the local "glasses" of those with potentially good, neutral, or ill intentions.
- Customize your security measures based on your personal characteristics, requirements, and realities.

1.3 Building Situational Awareness

- Taking personal responsibility for your own security is essential to being an aware traveler.
- Build up your security awareness by considering the knowledge, skills, attitudes, and behavior (KSAB) that are necessary to be a safer traveler.
- You can practice situational awareness exercises before traveling.

1.4 Planning and Preparing

- Create a customized travel checklist to make sure you are thoroughly prepared.
- Make a travel plan and ideally share it with a trusted, responsible, and accessible adult.
- Specifically regarding money matters, you should consider how money is best handled (local or international currency, credit or travel cards), exchange rates, how much to bring, etc.

1.5 Organizational Considerations

- Duty of care is the legal, economic, and moral obligations borne by companies to take reasonable steps to protect their employees (and their dependents) from risks associated with their work activities, and it encompasses various aspects such as safety, security, health, and well-being.
- Duty of loyalty refers to your obligations and responsibilities as a traveler to be security-aware and to follow guidelines that safeguard the company's assets, which of course includes you.
- You have the right to require that your organization meet its duty of care obligations. At the same time, you have a responsibility to comply with its

efforts to manage travel risks while always using your best judgment to avoid security incidents and react in appropriate ways.

1.6 Political Considerations

- Let the realities of your destinations determine the time, efforts, and resources you invest in pre-trip research and continuous monitoring of politics while abroad.
- You can utilize models such as PEST (politics, economics, sociocultural, and technological) to help you analyze and navigate situations.
- Adding to your toolbox that helps you to make informed decisions are the World Bank's governance indicators: voice and accountability, political stability, government effectiveness, regulatory quality, rule of law, and control of corruption.

1.7 Cultural Considerations

- Create the conditions for smooth intercultural exchanges by being informed about such key issues as beliefs and religions, dress codes, greetings, and permissible forms of physical contact.
- Your pre-departure preparations can start with considering the differences between your culture and the cultures of the countries you will travel to in terms of values/attitudes/beliefs, motivation, and communication.
- Insights into the structural patterns that define the values of a culture can be used as guidelines for understanding a society's do's and don'ts.

1.8 Medical Considerations

- Vaccination requirements depend on the country or area that you will visit. However, tetanus and hepatitis A and B are essential wherever you are going: In general, it is advisable to get a pre-departure medical check-up so that any vaccinations can be administered, but also to attend to any special circumstances such as getting enough medicine or considerations such as pregnancy.
- Some malaria prophylaxis medicine needs to be commenced in advance of departure.
- Make sure that you bring enough medicines, contact lens material, spare glasses, sanitary items, and if necessary, condoms.

1.9 Insurance

- The main reasons for getting proper insurance coverage are peace of mind, protection against the unexpected, and safeguarding your trip investment.
- It is important to make sure you are aware of the exclusions and limitations and that you take care to avoid omissions that could negate your coverage: There is a limit on how much you can delegate responsibility for making sure you are properly covered, so check that your organization's plan is sufficient.
- You should obtain your insurance soon after you made your travel arrangements so that your entire trip is covered: However, if you are about to

embark on private travels, be aware that often you can get a better deal elsewhere if you do not buy insurance as part of a trip package.

1.10 Personal Belongings and Documents

- You should consider carrying with you on every trip these small and simple items that can enhance your safety and security: a flashlight, a whistle, duct tape, safety pins, and a doorstop.
- When packing, critically assess what you really need to take with you and remove unnecessary items, especially valuable personal and organizational data: For the remaining items, the more valuable it is to you, the closer you should be prepared to keep it.
- Make extra copies of important documents (passport, vaccinations, blood type, and other medical information). Keep these separate from your origi- nals as a simple security precaution but note that you should not rely solely on being able to access electronic versions.

1.11 Information Security: Identity Theft and Industrial Espionage

- Consider getting insurance coverage for identity theft, as this can help with cutting the costs and getting support if you experience this crime.
- Social media risks are a growing trend that can expose you to identity theft or other threats.
- Specifically find out about what kind of information should not be dis- cussed on open lines (telephone and Internet) and which information (hard copy, digital, and the depth of your knowledge about company) is sensitive.

1.12 Communication Equipment and Procedures

- Understand the communication possibilities and limitations of your desti- nation: These should be decisive factors in any decision about the equip- ment and procedures you use, and specifically find out if you will have coverage for your mobile phone.
- Take preventative measures such as removing personal and sensitive data from your mobile devices and proactively take steps to reduce the impact of a potential IT breach by backing up your information before your trip and having a contingency plan for the duration of your travels.
- It is a good habit to carry a contact list, in your mobile and on a separately held paper, of bank and credit card companies, insurance company, accom- modation, airline and local transportation (ideally including the number for a backup means), and people, companies, and so forth that you might be dealing with.

1.13 Airports and Airlines

- Find out the safety record of your airline, and it is good to note that wide- bodied aircraft are safest.
- When booking your tickets, aim for direct flights and landing in the day- time, as these are your safest options.
- To minimize inconveniences, you can research the rules and regulations of the airport security checks that you will be going through.

1.14 Transportation

- During your planning stage, consider your potential activities and means of transporting yourself between them.
- Get a map.
- Research local conditions, as they might apply to you. For instance, check out the infrastructure if you will be driving or find how local taxis are paid and where they operate if you will be using that form of transportation.

1.15 Accommodation

- Check Trip Advisor or similar websites, blogs, and advisories by travelers: While many past guests will not directly refer to the presence of security officers, cameras, or prevention programs, they will allude to noisy neighbors, disruptive bar patrons, guest accident response, or access control, all of which indicate an accommodation's security and safety provisions.
- Use selection criteria based on the size of the hotel, its age, and name. And look for extra security and convenience measures many establishments provide for their female, handicapped, elderly, and family guests.
- Try to avoid staying at accommodations that are within 500 meters (1,600 feet) of potentially contentious locations such as government buildings, military installations, political offices, and in some cases certain businesses, NGOs, or UN premises. In general, use Google Maps or a similar service to ensure you select the safest options for accommodation, transportation, and activities.

1.16 Home Protection

- Burglarize yourself: This is a good way to test your home's vulnerabilities, which in turn helps protect all of its valuable and nostalgic assets while you are abroad.
- Consider fortifying your home by installing solid core doors, heavy duty locks, longer screws in the door lock strike-plates and door hinges, and extra blocking devices on all accessible sliding windows.
- Create occupancy clues by, for example, setting timers for lights and a radio to operate on normal schedule and making sure there is not an obvious stack of mail and newspapers piling up.

1.17 Well-Being: Dealing with Fear, Anxiety, and Insecurity

- Be aware that in an emergency, your thinking brain struggles to keep some control as the part of the brain that deals with vital functions tries to shut it down as to not interfere with bodily responses.
- Developing an awareness of your own likely fear triggers can better enable you to make good decisions during critical situations.
- You can psychologically fortify yourself by having a sound sense of self, good relationships, and good physical health—and by having an employer who takes its duty of care seriously with robust policies and procedures.

All this is to say there is a lot you can do before you travel to ensure that you have a safe, secure, healthy, and enjoyable trip. It is just a question of which measures best suit you and your upcoming travel realities.

REFERENCES

1. "Threat Forecast 2013," Red 24. 2013. http://www.red24.com/threat_forecast/threat_forecast_2013.php.
2. "Interactive Charts," Lloyd's. ND. http://www.lloyds.com/news-and-insight/risk-insight/lloyds-risk-index/infographics.
3. "Heat Map," The Aid Worker Security Database. ND. https://aidworkersecurity.org/incidents/report/map.
4. "What Should I Wear, Where?," Journeywoman. ND. http://www.journeywoman.com/ccc/default.html.
5. http://www.realmenrealstyle.com.
6. "How to Choose Travel Clothing," REI. ND. http://www.rei.com/learn/expert-advice/travel-clothing.html#top.
7. http://edition.cnn.com/CNNI/Programs/business.traveller/archive/index.html and http://www.economist.com/blogs/gulliver.
8. http://www.executivetravelmagazine.com and http://www.businesstraveller.com.
9. "James Bond as Business Traveler: Hotels Worthy of 007," Mark Chestnut, Orbitz. October 2, 2012. http://www.orbitz.com/blog/2012/10/james-bond-as-business-traveler-hotels-worthy-of-007.
10. "5 Business Travel Threats for 2013" Tony Ridley. ND. http://tony-ridley.com/risk-management/5-top-business-travel-threats-2013-travel-risk-management.
11. "Safety and Security for the Business Professional Traveling Abroad," Federal Bureau of Investigation. ND. http://www.fbi.gov/about-us/investigate/counterintelligence/business-brochure.
12. "Attacks and Interference Heighten Humanitarian Risks," Tim Witcher, AFP. April 12, 2011. http://www.google.com/hostednews/afp/article/ALeqM5iP2NK5Bq6s9HrVrLVQ8smi_bndeQ?docId=CNG.339fc2df9b43da9680cd9933ecbd37aa.191.
13. *Good Practice Review 8: Operational Security Management in Violent Environments*, Humanitarian Practice Network, Overseas Development Institute. Updated version, December 2010. http://www.alnap.org/pool/files/gpr-8-new.pdf.
14. *Safety First: A Safety and Security Handbook for Aid Workers*, Shaun Bickley, International Save the Children Alliance. 2010. http://www.eisf.eu/resources/library/SafetyFirst2010.pdf.
15. *Generic Security Guide for Humanitarian Organizations*, ECHO. 2004. http://www.aidworkers.net/?q=node/809.
16. *Staying Alive: Safety and Security Guidelines for Humanitarian Volunteers in Conflict Areas*, David Lloyd Roberts, International Committee of the Red Cross. 2006. http://www.icrc.org/eng/resources/documents/publication/p0717.htm.
17. *To Stay and Deliver: Good Practice for Humanitarians in Complex Security Environments*, United Nations. 2011. http://www.unhcr.org/refworld/type,RESEARCH,,,4d9039e32,0.html.
18. *New Protection Manual for Human Rights Defenders*, Enrique Eguren and Marie Caraj, Protection International. 2009. http://www.protectionline.org.
19. "Women Travel Statistics Explained by Travel Expert," Marybeth Bond. ND. http://gutsytraveler.com/women-travel-statistics-2.
20. "Female Business Travel—Is Your Employer Keeping You Safe Abroad?," International SOS. July 19, 2012. http://www.internationalsos.com/en/pressreleases_6571.htm.
21. http://www.journeywoman.com.
22. http://gutsytraveler.com.
23. http://www.about.com and http://www.streetdirectory.com/travel_guide/singapore.
24. "Her Own Way: A Woman's Safe-Travel Guide," Foreign Affairs and International Trade Canada. 2011. http://www.voyage.gc.ca/publications/woman-guide_voyager-feminin-eng.

25. "Air Travel with Mobility Devices or Mobility Aids: Airlines and Wheelchairs, Walkers, Canes," Arlene Fleming, About.com Air Travel. ND. http://airtravel.about.com/od/accessableairtravel/tp/advicewheelchair.htm.

26. "Travelling with Disability," Natalie Ippolito, Streetdirectory.com Singapore Guide. ND. http://www.streetdirectory.com/travel_guide/215847/travel_tips/travelling_with_disability.html.

27. "Disabled Travelers," Foreign and Commonwealth Office. Updated version, September 19, 2011. http://www.fco.gov.uk/en/travel-and-living-abroad/your-trip/disabled-travellers#.

28. http://www.lonelyplanet.com/thorntree/forum.jspa?forumID=38.

29. "Older People Looking to Achieve Travel Dreams," Tom Dawson, Streetdirectory.com Singapore Guide. ND. http://www.streetdirectory.com/travel_guide/163431/travel_tips/older_people_looking_to_achieve_travel_dreams.html.

30. "Safe and Healthy Travels for Senior Citizens," Centers for Disease Control and Prevention. Updated version, April 2, 2012. http://www.cdc.gov/Features/SeniorTravel.

31. "Over 65's Travel Insurance," Travel Insurance Guide.org.uk. ND. http://www.travelinsuranceguide.org.uk/over-50.html.

32. "Seniors—Air Travel Tips and Advice," Arlene Fleming, About.com Air Travel. ND. http://airtravel.about.com/od/travelindustrynews/tp/seniorstips.htm.

33. http://seniortravel.about.com.

34. "Smart Traveller," Department of Foreign Affairs and Trade. November 2011. http://www.smartraveller.gov.au/tips/travelling-seniors.pdf.

35. http://www.50plusinfobus.com.

36. http://www.senioryears.com/travel.html.

37. "Security—Information and Tips," Gays On Tour. Updated version, March 30, 2011. http://www.gaysontour.com/index.php?page=254&lang=en.

38. "Travel Tips," Queer Trip. ND. http://www.queertrip.com/travel.php.

39. http://ilga.org.

40. "LGBT Travellers," Foreign and Commonwealth Office. Updated version, October 11, 2010. http://www.fco.gov.uk/en/travel-and-living-abroad/your-trip/LGBT-travellers.

41. "Homosexual, Bisexual, and Transgender Travel—FAQ," Foreign Affairs and International Trade Canada. ND. http://www.voyage.gc.ca/faq/homosexuality_homosexualite-eng.

42. "Child Travel Consent," LawDepot.com. ND. http://www.lawdepot.com/contracts/child-travel-consent.

43. "Travelling with Children," Foreign Affairs and International Trade Canada. ND. http://www.voyage.gc.ca/publications/children_enfants-eng.

44. "Traveling Abroad with Kids," Lori Morris, Parents. ND. http://www.parents.com/fun/vacation/international/checklist-traveling-abroad-with-kids/?page=1.

45. "6 Safety Tips for Traveling Abroad with Kids," Jason Brink, The Flipkey Blog. November 11, 2011. http://www.flipkey.com/blog/2011/11/11/6-safety-tips-for-traveling-abroad-with-kids.

46. "Single Parent Travel," Jamie Jefferson, Streetdirectory Singapore Guide. ND. http://www.streetdirectory.com/travel_guide/215976/travel_tips/single_parent_travel.html.

47. "Documents, Info, Policies and Advice," Arlene Fleming, About.com Air Travel. ND. http://airtravel.about.com/od/beforeyougo/u/Docs.htm.

48. "Flying with Children," Sharon, Flying with Children. Updated version, March 2011. http://flyingwithchildren1.blogspot.dk.

49. "Children and Flying Fears," Children's National Medical Center. ND. http://www.childrensnational.org.

50. "Child Safety Tips," Alvin Eden, MD and Elizabeth Eden, MD, TLC Family. 2006. http://tlc.howstuffworks.com/family/kids-safety-tips2.htm.

51. Ibid.

52. "Choose with Care: A Parent's Guide to Choosing Child Safe Organisations," Child Wise. 2004. http://www.crin.org/resources/infodetail.asp?ID=4790.

53. http://www.crescentrating.com.

54. "Defining Faith-Focused Security," David Dose, Safe Travel Solutions. April 11, 2011. http://safetravelsolutions.org/home/index.php?option=com_content&view=article&id=207:defining-faith-focused-security-&catid=41:training-articles&Itemid=211.

55. http://www.flyertalk.com/forum/religious-travelers-604.

56. http://www.independenttraveler.com.

57. "Situation Awareness," Wikipedia. Updated version, September 23, 2012. http://en.wikipedia.org/wiki/Situation_awareness.

58. Ibid.

59. "Got Situational Awareness?," Joe Lavelle. ND. http://thepeakmind.com/dealing-with-setbacks/got-situational-awareness.

60. "Situational Awareness Exercises," Defensive Carry.com. ND. http://www.defensive-carry.com/forum/defensive-carry-tactical-training/110323-situational-awareness-exercises.html.

61. "Pyramid for Personal Safety," No Nonsense Self Defense. ND. http://www.nononsenseselfdefense.com/pyramid.html.

62. "Travellers Checklist," Foreign Affairs and International Trade Canada. ND. http://www.voyage.gc.ca/preparation_information/checklist_sommaire-eng.asp.

63. "5 Tips for Those Who Are Considering Becoming an Expatriate," Donald Saunders, Streetdirectory.com Singapore Guide. ND. http://www.streetdirectory.com/travel_guide/211705/travel_tips/5_tips_for_those_who_are_considering_becoming_an_expatriate.html.

64. "Moving Tips: 12 Amazing Tips to Facilitate Relocation," Abhishek Aqarwal, Streetdirectory.com Singapore Guide. ND. http://www.streetdirectory.com/travel_guide/215930/travel_tips/moving_tips___12_amazing_tips_to_facilitate_relocation.html.

65. "Documents, Info, Policies and Advice," Arlene Fleming, About.com Air Travel. ND. http://airtravel.about.com/od/beforeyougo/u/Docs.htm.

66. "Travel Wise Checklist," TrainingSolutions. ND. http://www.trainingsolutions.dk.

67. "Travel Plan," TrainingSolutions. ND. http://www.trainingsolutions.dk.

68. http://www.compareprepaid.co.uk.

69. "Landmine Awareness," CAT-UXO. 2012. http://itunes.apple.com/us/app/id515291377?mt=8.

70. "Best Apps and Websites for Travelers," Tom Samilijan, NBC News Travel Kit. September 20, 2012. http://www.nbcnews.com/travel/travelkit/best-apps-websites-travelers-1B6002828.

71. "BRIC Benchmarking: Research Uncovers the Top Threats & Coping Strategies," Myles Druckman MD, Dialogues on Duty of Care. August 9, 2012. http://dialoguesondutyof-care.com/2012/08/bric-benchmarking-research-uncovers-top-threats-strategies.

72. http://www.internationalsos.com/dutyofcare.

73. "Corporate Travel Safety," Jim Glab, Executive Travel Magazine. March/April 2012. http://www.executivetravelmagazine.com/articles/corporate-travel-safety.

74. "Duty of Care and Travel Risk Management Global Benchmark Study," Dr. Lisbeth Claus, International SOS. 2011. http://www.internationalsos.com/dutyofcare.

75. Ibid.

76. Ibid.

77. Ibid.

78. "C'est La Vie? A Step-By-Step Guide to Building a Travel Risk Management Program," Advito. 2009. http://www.advito.com.

79. "2011 'Extremely Turbulent' for Business Travelers," Anne Freedman, Risk and Insurance. January 30, 2012. http://www.riskandinsurance.com/story.jsp?storyId=5333 44807&topic=Main.

80. "Lloyd's Risk Index, 2011," Lloyd's/The Economist Intelligence Unit. 2011. http://www.lloyds.com/~/media/Files/News%20and%20Insight/360%20Risk%20Insight/Lloyds_Risk_Index_2011.pdf.

81. "C'est La Vie? A Step-By-Step Guide to Building a Travel Risk Management Program," Advito. 2009. http://www.advito.com.

82. http://dialoguesondutyofcare.com.

83. http://travelriskmanagementsolutions.com/duty-of-care.

84. "Mapping Political Context: A Toolkit for Civil Society Organizations," Robert Nash, Alan Hudson, Cecilia Lottrell, Overseas Development Institute. July 2006. http://www.odi.org.uk.

85. "World Bank's Worldwide Governance Indicators (WGI) Project," World Bank. ND. http://info.worldbank.org/governance/wgi/index.asp.

86. Ibid.

87. "PEST Analysis," Mindtools. ND. http://www.mindtools.com/pages/article/newTMC_09.htm. and "PEST Analysis," Quick MBA. ND. http://www.quickmba.com/strategy/pest.

88. *Do's and Taboos around the World*. Roger E. Axtell. 1993. White Plains, NY: The Parker Pen Company.

89. *When Cultures Collide: Leading across Cultures*. Richard D. Lewis. 2006. Boston, MA: Nicholas Brealey Publishing.

90. *Do's and Taboos around the World*. Roger E. Axtell.

91. *Do's and Taboos around the World*. Roger E. Axtell.

92. *When Cultures Collide: Leading across Cultures*. Richard D. Lewis.

93. *Do's and Taboos around the World*. Roger E. Axtell.

94. *When Cultures Collide: Leading across Cultures*. Richard D. Lewis.

95. *When Cultures Collide: Leading across Cultures*. Richard D. Lewis.

96. *Do's and Taboos around the World*. Roger E. Axtell.

97. *When Cultures Collide: Leading across Cultures*. Richard D. Lewis.

98. *When Cultures Collide: Leading across Cultures*. Richard D. Lewis.

99. "Hofstede's Cultural Dimensions: Understanding Workplace Values Around the World," Mindtools. ND. http://www.mindtools.com/pages/article/newLDR_66.htm.

100. *Understanding Global Cultures*. Martin J. Gannon and Rajnandini Pillai. 2012. Thousand Oaks, CA: Sage Publications.

101. *Do's and Taboos around the World*. Roger E. Axtell.

102. http://www.cdc.gov.

103. "Well on Your Way: A Canadian's Guide to Healthy Travel Abroad," Public Health Agency of Canada. ND. http://www.phac-aspc.gc.ca/tmp-pmv/well-way_bon-depart-eng.php.

104. "Health and Travel," Safe Travel New Zealand Government. ND. http://www.safetravel.govt.nz/beforeugo/health.shtml.

105. "First Aid in the A-Z Situations," Government of India. ND. http://www.healthy-india.org/first-aid/knowledge-of-first-aid-may-help-in-the-a-z-of-situations.html.

106. "How to Select a Plan Based on Your Needs," Travel Insurance Review. ND. http://www.travelinsurancereview.net/selecting-a-plan.

107. Ibid.

108. "Top Ten Tips," Travel Insurance Guide. ND. http://www.travelinsuranceguide.org.uk/top-10-tips.html.

109. "Top 10 Questions Every Traveler Asks," Travel Insurance Review. ND. http://www.travelinsurancereview.net/questions.

110. "Five 'Loopholes' and How to Avoid Them," Travel Insurance Review. ND. http://www. travelinsurancereview.net/small-print.

111. "Four Steps after You Purchase Travel Insurance," Travel Insurance Review. ND. http:// www.travelinsurancereview.net/after-purchase.

112. "Duty of Care and Travel Risk Management Global Benchmark Study," Dr. Lisbeth Claus, International SOS. 2011. http://www.internationalsos.com/dutyofcare.

113. "ATM Locations and Lost and Stolen Cards," I Hate Taxis. ND. http://www.ihatetaxis. com/advice/atm-locations-and-damaged-cards.

114. "Wallet Safety Tips," CreditCards.com. ND. http://www.creditcards.com/downloads/ wallet_safety_tips.pdf.

115. "Duty of Care and Travel Risk Management Global Benchmark Study," Dr. Lisbeth Claus, International SOS. 2011. http://www.internationalsos.com/dutyofcare.

116. "Make Your Trip Better Using 3-1-1," Transportation Security Authority. September 7, 2012. http://www.tsa.gov/traveler-information/make-your-trip-better-using-3-1-1.

117. "Duty of Care and Travel Risk Management Global Benchmark Study," Dr. Lisbeth Claus, International SOS. 2011. http://www.internationalsos.com/dutyofcare.

118. "Lost Laptops Costs $1.8 Billion Per Year," Matthew J. Schwartz, Information Week. April 21, 2011. http://www.informationweek.com/news/security/mobile/229402043.

119. "Three New Ways to Protect Your Identity in 2012," Justine Rivero, Forbes. January 3, 2012. http://www.forbes.com/sites/moneywisewomen/2012/01/03/three-new-ways-to-protect-your-identity-in-2012.

120. "Identity Theft Victim Statistics," IdentityTheft.info. ND. http://www.identitytheft.info/ victims.aspx.

121. "How Identity Theft Works," Lee Ann Obringer, How Stuff Works. ND. http://www. howstuffworks.com/identity-theft.htm.

122. "What It's Like to Steal Someone's Identity," Joan Goodchild, CSO. November 18, 2010. http://www.csoonline.com/article/637763/what-it-s-like-to-steal-someone-s-identity.

123. "Identity Theft," Scamwatch. ND. http://www.scamwatch.gov.au/content/index.phtml/ tag/identitytheft.

124. "How Identity Theft Works," Lee Ann Obringer, How Stuff Works. ND. http://www. howstuffworks.com/identity-theft.htm.

125. "Tech//404 Data Loss Cost Calculator," Allied World. ND. http://www.tech-404.com/ calculator.html.

126. http://www.trmg.biz/publications/the-a-to-z-guides.

127. "9 Dirty Tricks: Social Engineers' Favorite Pick-Up Lines," Joan Goodchild, CSO. February 16, 2009. http://www.csoonline.com/article/print/480589.

128. "15 Social Media Scams," Joan Goodchild, CSO. June 20, 2012. http://www.csoonline. com/slideshow/detail/52935/15-social-media-scams?source=csointcpt_ss#slide1.

129. "German Companies Cite Cost of Espionage, Sueddeutsche Says," Joseph de Weck, Bloomberg. April 23, 2012. http://mobile.bloomberg.com/news/2012-04-23/ german-companies-cite-cost-of-espionage-sueddeutsche-says?category=.

130. "Corporate Espionage on the Rise In India," Shilpa Phadnis and Mini Joseph Tejaswi, *The Economic Times*. September 24, 2010. http://articles.economictimes.indiatimes. com/2010-09-24/news/27571489_1_detective-agencies-corporate-espionage-requests.

131. "UK Cyber Crime Costs £27bn a Year—Government Report. BBC. February 17, 2011. http://www.bbc.co.uk/news/uk-politics-12492309.

132. "U.S. Calls Out China and Russia for Cyber Espionage Costing Billions," Fox News. November 3, 2011. http://www.foxnews.com/politics/2011/11/03/us-calls-out-china-and-russia-for-cyber-espionage-costing-billions/#ixzz1yJqVa8LG.

133. "2012 Global State of Information Security Survey," PriceWaterhouse Cooper, *CIO* magazine, and *CSO* magazine. October 2012. http://www.pwc.com/gx/en/information-security-survey/index.jhtml.

134. "Travel Light in the Age of Digital Thievery," Nicole Perlroth, *New York Times*. February 10, 2012. http://www.nytimes.com/2012/02/11/technology/electronic-security-a-worry-in-an-age-of-digital-espionage.html?_r=1.

135. "2012 Global State of Information Security Survey," PriceWaterhouse Cooper, *CIO* magazine, and *CSO* magazine. October 2012. http://www.pwc.com/gx/en/information-security-survey/index.jhtml.

136. "10 Most Notorious Acts of Corporate Espionage," Business Pundit. April 25, 2011. http://www.businesspundit.com/10-most-notorious-acts-of-corporate-espionage.

137. "How to Detect and Stop Corporate Espionage," Michael Podszywalow, Continuity Central. December 2, 2011. http://www.continuitycentral.com/feature0938.html.

138. http://www.cybersafe.my/guidelines.html.

139. http://infosecawareness.in/downloads.

140. "Laptop Security for Aid Workers," SaferAccess. January 2008. http://www.eisf.eu/resources/item/?d=1656.

141. http://www.onguardonline.gov/topics/secure-your-computer.

142. "Safe Travels for You and Your Data," Riva Richmond, *New York Times*. February 17, 2010. http://www.nytimes.com/2010/02/18/technology/personaltech/18basics.html?_r=1&scp=7&sq=laptop%20and%20theft&st=cse.

143. "Check-In to Arrival," Arlene Fleming, About.com Air Travel. ND. http://airtravel.about.com/od/airlines/u/checkintoarrival.htm#s6.

144. "The Safest Airplanes in the World: World's Safest Airplanes," Arlene Fleming, About.com Air Travel. ND. http://airtravel.about.com/od/safetysecurity/qt/safestairplane.htm.

145. "Duty of Care and Travel Risk Management Global Benchmark Study," Dr. Lisbeth Claus, International SOS. 2011. http://www.internationalsos.com/dutyofcare.

146. "How to Choose Your Airplane Seat: 5 Tips for Getting the Seat You Want," Greig Waddell, About.com Business Travel. ND. http://businesstravel.about.com/od/airlines/tp/choose_your_airplane_seat.htm; and "Airline Safety: Tips for Business Travelers," Greig Waddell, About.com Business Travel. ND. http://businesstravel.about.com/od/healthsafety/tp/airline_safety_businesstravel.htm.

147. "Documents, Info, Policies and Advice," Arlene Fleming, About.com Air Travel. ND. http://airtravel.about.com/od/beforeyougo/u/Docs.htm.

148. "Know Your Rights When Traveling," American Civil Liberties Union. ND. http://www.aclu.org/technology-and-liberty/know-your-rights-when-traveling.

149. "KeepKidsSafe," TransportCanada.ND.http://www.tc.gc.ca/eng/roadsafety/safedrivers-childsafety-car-time-stages-1083.htm.

150. http://www.ihatetaxis.com.

151. "Getting Around in China—Taking a Taxi," Sara Naumann, About.com China Travel. ND. http://gochina.about.com/od/tripplanning/p/Taxi_China.htm.

152. "San Francisco Taxi Tips," Ingrid Taylar, About.com San Francisco. ND. http://sanfrancisco.about.com/od/gettingaroun1/qt/sftaxitips.htm.

153. "Hotel Security Tips for Small Business Travelers," Paul Davis, Business Know How. ND. http://www.businessknowhow.com/security/hotelsafety.htm.

154. "Business Travelers, Avoid These Rooms," Jill Becker, CNN. July 9, 2012. http://edition.cnn.com/2012/07/09/travel/hotel-rooms-avoid/index.html.

155. http://www.lonelyplanet.com/thorntree.

156. "Marybeth Speaks about Travel Safety on CNN News," Gutsy Traveler. ND. http://www.gutsytraveler.com/hotel-security-2.

157. "Hotel Room Safety," Jonathon E. Stewart, About.com Hotels & Resorts. ND. http://video.about.com/hotels/Hotel-Room-Safety.htm.

158. "Home Security," Crime Doctor. ND. http://www.crimedoctor.com/home.htm.

159. "15 Steps You Can Take to Prevent Home Burglary," Scambusters. ND. http://www. scambusters.org/homeburglary.html.

160. "Home Security Tips," How Stuff Works. ND. http://home.howstuffworks.com/home-improvement/household-safety/security/home-security-tips.htm.

161. "Protecting Your Home," ADT India. ND. http://www.adt.in/en/index.aspx?page=Protect.

162. "Travel Psychology 101," Michael Brein. ND. http://www.michaelbrein.com/travel-psychology-101.html.

163. "How to Manage Yourself during a Critical Incident," Dr. Donald Bosch, Headington Institute. ND. http://www.youtube.com/watch?v=9QI7CSUO-Rg&feature=youtu.be.

164. "Pyramid for Personal Safety," No Nonsense Self Defense. ND. http://www. nononsenseselfdefense.com/pyramid.html.

165. "Fear Management vs Danger Management," No Nonsense Self Defense. ND. http:// www.nononsenseselfdefense.com/FEARvsDANGER.html.

2 While Traveling

To aid you with being a safer traveler throughout all your journeys, this chapter relies on "best practice" advice and real stories from experienced travelers to give you insights into such questions as:

- Which travel risks should you be concerned with **(see Section 2.1)**?
- What specific measures address your personal considerations **(see Section 2.2)**?
- How do you identify a changing security situation and feel prepared to deal with it **(see Section 2.3)**?
- What preparations are needed at this stage **(see Section 2.4)**?
- In a globalized world, what are some of the organizational considerations that need to be managed in order to safeguard local and international staff **(see Section 2.5)**?
- Should you SWOT your PEST analysis **(see Section 2.6)**?
- How can you apply cultural frameworks to travel situations **(see Section 2.7)**?
- How can you avoid travel aches and pains **(see Section 2.8)**?
- Can you get insurance after a trip has started **(see Section 2.9)**?
- What else can you do to safeguard your personal belongings and documents **(see Section 2.10)**?
- Which opportunistic and determined threats pose a risk to your personal and organizational data **(see Section 2.11)**?
- How can you protect your mobile devices, data, and apps while on the move **(see Section 2.12)**?
- From gate to gate, what security considerations you should be aware of for safer air travel **(see Section 2.13)**?
- Since many security incidents happen while travelers are in transit, how can you make your transit safer **(see Section 2.14)**?
- If hotel security is like an onion, what should you expect at each layer **(see Section 2.15)**?
- What can you do to avoid being a victim of crime and corruption **(see Section 2.16)**?
- How can you avoid stress affecting your travels **(see Section 2.17)**?
- What are the key points you should keep in mind while traveling **(see Section 2.18)**?

In many regards, the security measures you put in place while traveling in San Francisco may be similar to those you employ in Singapore, but these will be radically different than for San Pablo: To mitigate travel threats, your security measures need to realistically address the risks you might face. Accordingly, the chapter demonstrates frameworks, models, and tools that you can flexibly apply to the dynamic situations that traveling brings.

"Prior proper planning prevents problems and poor performance": In other words, planning and preparation are essential for preventing security incidents and reacting well in worst-case scenarios.

2.1   UNDERSTANDING THE POTENTIAL RISKS WHILE TRAVELING

Just as food and culture vary from location to location, so do the risks you might face abroad. Part of understanding the potential risks while traveling is deciding which indirect threats (those that are in the environment, such as a demonstration against the regime or grenades thrown in a marketplace) could affect you and which direct threats (those in which you are the target because of who you are, what you do, and how you do it) could be aimed at you. Such an analysis will let you know which threats, if any, you need to spend time and energy on.

This section outlines a global overview of statistics and facts about the risks you might encounter. While traveler-specific facts are cited, most of the figures in the listed examples apply to the nation's citizens who are, in any case, the main victims. If any of the listings below apply to your next destination, then you could, for example, update your **Risk Management Framework (RMF)** by asking:

RMF 1: Threat analysis—where and how likely are you to encounter that threat **(see Section 1.1.1)**?

RMF 1: Context assessment—what power base (weapons, tribal loyalties, voters) do the perpetrators rely on **(see Section 1.1.2)**?

RMF 1: Situational analysis—which indicators point to increased likelihood of a threat occurring **(see Section 1.1.3)**?

RMF 2: Vulnerability analysis—when are you potentially exposed **(see Section 1.2)**?

RMF 3: Analysis of options—what is needed to implement various plans?

RMF 4: Continuously monitoring and adjusting—which additional measures should you implement if the local situation becomes insecure?

RMF 5: Confidence in your security precautions and reactions—what does it take to have "peace of mind" while traveling?

Additional facts and, more importantly, advice on mitigating measures are covered in the relevant sections of the book.

2.1.1   SAFEST AND MOST DANGEROUS LOCATIONS: WORLDWIDE COMPARISON

Mercer Consulting's "2011 Quality of Living Worldwide City Rankings" survey weighed "internal stability, crime levels, law enforcement effectiveness and the host country's international relations" to rank the cities in terms of personal safety.[1] On the safer side of life, the report notes that Luxembourg ranked number one for personal safety. Actually, European cities dominated the top ten with seven placements.

Tbilisi at 215 and Moscow at 199 were Europe's lowest ranking cities. For the Asian-Pacific region, Singapore in 8th place was the highest for the region followed by Auckland and Wellington, both ranked 9, while Karachi at 216 was the lowest. Five Japanese cities ranked 31st. Abu Dhabi (23), Muscat (29), and Dubai (39) placed highest in the Middle East and Africa while Baghdad and several African cities in the listing below clustered at the low end. All tying for 17th place, the safest places in The Americas were five Canadian cities. The United States had three cities ranked 53rd. Caracas (205) and Port-au-Prince (202) occupied the worst places for personal safety in the region.

Based on the "Duty of Care and Travel Risk Management Global Benchmark Study" by International SOS of 628 companies with headquarters in 50 countries, the article "2011 'Extremely Turbulent' for Business Travelers" on the Risk and Insurance website cites the perceived riskiest countries as:

1. Mexico—due to drug-war homicides
2. Nigeria—kidnappings for ransom
3. Afghanistan—terrorism
4. India—medical and safety issues, especially traffic accidents
5. Pakistan—terrorism
6. Iraq—sectarian violence
7. Papua New Guinea—medical care
8. China—industrial espionage
9. Democratic Republic of the Congo—medical care and unstable environment in eastern part of country
10. Indonesia—terrorism[2]

The list of the ten most dangerous cities and their main threats from the article "The World's Most Dangerous Cities" in *Economic Policy Journal* and based on Mercer's personal safety report are:

1. Baghdad, Iraq—car bombings and sectarian violence
2. N'Djamena, Chad—destabilization due to upheaval in Libya and threats of terrorism and kidnappings
3. Abidjan, Ivory Coast—muggings, robberies, burglaries, and carjackings pose security risks. Yellow fever, cholera, and measles have been health risks since 2011
4. Bangui, Central African Republic—outbreaks of violence, government-imposed curfews, and direct attacks on some Europeans
5. Kinshasa, Democratic Republic of the Congo—armed robbery by groups posing as law enforcement officials in both urban and rural areas, especially after nightfall, and robberies by gangs of street children
6. Karachi, Pakistan—violent crime, sectarian violence, and political instability, internally and with other nations
7. Tbilisi, Georgia—potentially explosive regional situation, given the breakaway regions of South Ossetia and Abkhazia
8. Sana'a, Yemen—kidnap by armed tribes, criminals, and terrorists

FIGURE 2.1   Courtesy of Peter Steudtner/www.panphotos.org.

9. Nairobi, Kenya—local unrest and random grenade attacks
10. Conakry, Guinea Republic—criminals operating at the airport, traditional
    markets, near hotels, and restaurants frequented by foreigners[3]

(Figure 2.1).

2.1.2 MURDER

Specifically regarding murder, if you live in the United States, you are 13 times more likely to face it than in Japan and 16 times more likely than in Germany.[4] The United Nations Office on Drugs and Crime (UNODC) conducted the first global study on homicide and revealed that there were 468,000 homicides in 2010. Of these "36% were committed in Africa, 31% in The Americas, 27% in Asia, 5% in Europe, and 1% in Oceania."[5] The article "Murder Most Foul: A Global Picture of Homicide Rates" on The Economist website summarizes the UNODC's study findings as two broad trends and one worrying thought: First, there is a correlation between low scores on the UN's human-development index and high murder rates and vice versa.[6] A cluster of exceptions in relatively developed countries point to the second trend in which the perpetrators are organized crime and violent gangs who engage in drug trafficking and have a firearms culture. Honduras and El Salvador, ranked first and second highest, exemplify this. The article's final worrying thought is "sudden dips in economic performance have also been known to increase the homicide rate, usually with a lag." Given the recent series of economic wobbles, crashes, and faltering recoveries, how has your destination's economy fared? Who are the economic winners and losers?

An article on the Seguridad, Justicia y Paz website used the "City Council Public Safety and Criminal Justice AC, 2012" as a source to list the world's 50 most dangerous cities in terms of the number of homicides compared to the population. Caracas had the most homicides at 3,164 in 2011. But, because there are over 3 million people living in the city, it was ranked number six. The top city was San Pedro Sula with 1,143 homicides affecting a population of 719,447. The top 30 cities were all in Latin American countries, with the exceptions of New Orleans (21) and Detroit (30). Five of the top 10 cities were in Mexico. Actually, there were 41 Latin American and Caribbean cities in the top 50. The United States and South Africa each had four and Iraq rounded out the list.[7]

Indicating how the hazards in the environment can affect you, five Canadians were murdered in Mexico in 2011 and four in 2010. However, there were 1,626,200 Canadian visits to Mexico in 2010.[8] For U.S. citizens, the number murdered in Mexico climbed to 120 in 2011 from 35 in 2007.[9] But, to put these numbers into perspective, there are about 60 million Americans who live and work abroad: Of these, about 6,000 die per year but "only" 600–900 die from unnatural causes.[10]

While the majority of the homicides affect local people, innocent and complicit alike, a context in which there are high murder rates generally increases the likelihood that you might be affected as an indirect target because murders are a part of the environment, and/or you could be a direct target due to a certain vulnerability. For example, an ongoing database of NGO workers' fatalities shows that 90% are a consequence of intentional violence, and of these, half are caused by ambushes (direct and indirect targeting) and killings (direct).[11] In places such as Honduras or the Democratic Republic of the Congo, the environment is dangerous, while in countries such as Afghanistan or Sudan, NGO workers have to be aware of both direct and indirect threats. When considering any threat, understanding the context **(see Section 1.1.2)** is essential for assessing how risky (or not) the destination is for you.

2.1.3 TERRORISM

To look at the risk of terrorism, a search on the Global Terrorism Database for the period of 2000–2010 of all types of terrorist acts and attempted attacks shows that there were 29,820 incidents worldwide.[12] In the vast majority of the incidents, zero or 1–10 people were either killed or injured. For the same period, there were 3,292 incidents directed toward businesses, 343 against NGOs, and 132 targeting tourists.

To put these numbers into context, using Americans as an example, from 2005–2010 a total of 158 private citizens died in terrorist attacks, averaging 16 per year, which puts the likelihood at 1 in 20 million according to the article "How Scared of Terrorism Should You Be?," reporting on figures from the U.S. National Counterterrorism Center.[13] The article goes on to compare the risk of death resulting from terrorism with much higher daily risks such as "dying in a car accident of 1 in 19,000; drowning in a bathtub at 1 in 800,000; dying in a building fire at 1 in 99,000; or being struck by lightning at 1 in 5,500,000." To understand the risk of terrorism, it is essential to assess the likelihood **(see Section 3.9)**.

2.1.4 SEXUAL VIOLENCE

Particularly for female travelers, but not exclusively, there is the gender-specific threat of rape and sexual violence **(see Sections 2.2.3 and 3.4)**. Worldwide, an estimated 13% of females and 3% of males have been sexually assaulted, according to the Australasian Medical Journal (Online) article "Sexual Assault: An Overview and Implications for Counselling Support" from 2011.[14]

The Delhi police filed 489 rape cases in 2010, meaning that a woman was raped every 18 hours in the capital: That said, women's groups claim that there are many cases in which the police would not file a report and would harass the woman.[15] In the United States, about 1 million women are raped each year.[16] The 2010–2011 report of crime statistics for South Africa shows that a sexual offense occurs about every 8 minutes. However, in 2009, several police stations were shown to have substantially reduced crime statistics in order to win a large government bonus.[17] In general, most crimes are underreported for various reasons and sexual violence, in particular, is prone to this.

2.1.5   KIDNAPPING

Kidnapping, in its various forms, is a threat that many travelers are concerned with, so it may be comforting to know that over 90% of victims survive the ordeal (see Section 3.3). According to the "Annual Kidnap Review 2011" by Special Contingency Risks Ltd., Mexico City averages 60 express kidnappings and 49 longer-term kidnappings per day, but it's suspected that only 10% are reported to the police.[18] In the same report, three kidnappings occur on average each day in Guatemala.

These nationalities had the highest risk of being kidnapped according to "Annual Kidnap Review 2011":

1. Pakistani
2. Iranian
3. American
4. Chinese
5. South Korean
6. Indian
7. Turkish
8. Spanish
9. Malaysian
10. French, Canadian, and Singaporean[19]

Different nationalities are vulnerable for different reasons, as exemplified by comparing the cases of Pakistani and Chinese nationals. On land, Pakistanis face the problem of Taliban militants using kidnapping as a way to make a political statement, while at the same time, making money.[20] At sea, they contend with the risk from pirates.[21] In comparison, many of the over 800,000 Chinese who worked abroad in 2012 live in isolated compounds, making them an easy target for militant groups.[22]

2.1.6   CARJACKINGS/HIJACKINGS

Carjackings (also known as hijackings) are a serious threat in some countries. South Africa, known for high rates of this crime, had 10,600 reported cases in 2010–2011, which is a dramatic decrease of 23.6% from the previous year.[23] In other countries, the crime is not widespread but exists in certain locations and targets particular types of vehicles. According to the article "Sydney the Carjacking Capital of Australia," of the 16,600 vehicles stolen in the New South Wales state, of which Sydney is the capital, only 50 incidents involved a carjacking in 2010: Prestigious, luxury models were targeted in the majority of the incidents.[24] Police surmise that some of the vehicles were stolen to make money, but often the perpetrators committed this violent crime simply to get a cool car to do other crimes **(see Section 3.5)**.

2.1.7   CIVIC UNREST

While demonstrations, protests, riots, strikes, and other forms of unrest are not new, the past few years have witnessed quite significant ones. The demonstrations across the Muslim world against the Mohammed cartoons first published by the Danish newspaper *Jyllands Posten* in 2005 and subsequently republished by newspapers in many countries are another example of a global protest.[25] In this book, there are two traveler stories about the demonstrations: **"The Mohammad Caricatures in Yemen: Protected By Relationships"** written by a security consultant and adventure traveler **(see Section 1.1.3)** and **"It's No One, It's the Mob: Meeting an Angry Demonstration during a Family Diving Vacation in Sri Lanka"** by a frequent business traveler and avid diver **(see Section 3.6)**.

According to "Arab Spring: An Interactive Timeline of Middle East Protests" on the Guardian website, the "Arab Spring" ignited when the Tunisian jobless graduate Mohammed Bouazizi died from setting himself on fire after police had confiscated his vegetable stand on December 17, 2010, and young Tunisians protested.[26] Establishing a pattern, on January 7, 2011, Algerians took to the streets over unemployment and food prices—and an Algerian man was the second to set himself on fire. On January 14, 2011, the Tunisian president Ben Ali fled the country. After this first example of regime change by people power, there was a chain reaction in the region that was coined the "Arab Spring." On January 16, 2011, an Egyptian man was the third in the region to set himself on fire. By February 11, 2011, president Hosni Mubarak had stepped down. Unbeknownst to Colonel Gaddafi, his downfall started with the eruption of protests in Benghazi on February 16, 2011. From Algeria to Yemen, the region continues to feel the affects of the uprisings.

Referring to the Spanish "Indignados" in May 2011, Wikipedia notes: "For some journalists and commentators the camping marked the start of the global 'Occupy' movement, though it is much more commonly said to have begun in New York during September."[27] The website's "Occupy Movement" article explains that a Canadian activist group, inspired by the "Arab Spring" and the Spanish "Indignados," initiated "Occupy Wall Street," which received widespread media coverage from September 17, 2011. By October 9, 2011, there were 95 protests in 85 countries, representing a global movement with the slogan "We are the 99%."[28] Even though the speakers for the protests gave various goals, essentially the movement was against social and economic inequalities within their own countries and globally.

Despite these examples of headline-making global protests, most demonstrations, riots, strikes, and other forms of unrest revolve around local matters—corrupt local officials, mass job cuts, environmental degradation, and so forth. It normally takes a lot before people will get out of their comfort zones and take to the streets, so it usually involves cases that include a serious grievance that affects them personally. With slogans like "Water is more precious than gold," the weeks of unrest in the poor communities of Argentina's mining areas represent a typical local issue, as written about by *Le Monde* in March 2011.[29] Even for the countries involved in the "Arab Spring," they were inspired by each other, but the issues were mainly national.

By some estimates, there are approximately 500 daily protests in China, as reported by *The Economist* magazine in June 2012.[30] According to the blog Facts and Details by an amateur researcher that cites the China Academy of Social Sciences, land disputes "account for 65 percent of rural 'mass conflicts' and [are] also a serious problem in cities."[31] The blog's article "Protests and Demonstrations in China: The Tensions and Methods Behind" goes on to list other causes as: "protests over unpaid wages, taxes, lay offs, land seizures, factory closings, poor working conditions, environmental damages, corruption, misuse of funds, ethnic tensions, use of natural resources, forced immigration and police abuse." These issues that fundamentally affect people's lives can ignite not only into mass protests but increasingly into individual actions of civil disobedience, which is significant in the Chinese context.

2.1.8 INFORMATION SECURITY

As mentioned in the **Information Security** section **(see Section 1.11)**, the 2011 report "Foreign Spies Stealing U.S. Economic Secrets in Cyberspace" estimates that the costs to U.S businesses could be $398 billion. Mobile devices are a key vulnerability, asserts the report. A study of 600 German companies found that expected losses to industrial espionage could reach $5.5 billion in 2012.[32]

As a traveler, your personal information can be threatened too. Some sources state that 15 million Americans are victims of identity theft with a total cost of $50 billion.[33] However, most sources claim between 9 and 12 million. To put this in perspective, if there are 10 million American victims annually, then that means the crime happens every four seconds.[34] "You are 15 times more likely to have your identity stolen than to have your car broken into," says Todd Davis, chairman and CEO of LifeLock, as quoted in the article "Travelers at High Risk of Identity Theft, Experts Say" on the USA Today Travel website.[35] The average amount taken from a victim is $4,841,[36] but the recovery process can cost about $8,000 and take about 600 hours for a person to clear his or her name, with 70% still having difficulties or never managing to completely rid their records of the negative consequences of the crime.[37]

Too often, it is the busyness and forgetfulness of travelers that are the biggest risks to their personal and organizational data. In July 2012, Credant Technologies revealed findings from their "2nd Annual Airport Survey," based on seven major airports in the United States, in which travelers lost 8,016 devices: 44.6% laptops, 43% smartphones and tablets, and 12.4% USB drives.[38] According to five of the seven airports, the security checkpoints were the common place for travelers to forget their devices: Overall, 71% of the lost devices were forgotten at checkpoints. For the other two airports, it was in the restrooms.

One global enterprise that many might be surprised to hear has experienced numerous losses of mobile devices is the United Kingdom's Ministry of Defense (MoD). In 2011, it revealed that, for an 18-month period, employees lost 188 laptops, 73 USB memory sticks, 72 hard disks, 18 mobile phones, 10 Blackberrys, and 194 CDs or DVDs.[39] The MoD stated that encryption and other security measures protected the information. In terms of a quick risk assessment for the threat of lost devices **(RMF 1)**, with 250,000 staff working globally, the MoD has a high exposure, which increases its vulnerability **(RMF 2)**, but it has guidelines in place to reduce the likelihood of losses and contingency measures to reduce the impact of protocol breaches **(RMF 3)**.

Lost or stolen mobile phones are a significant and growing vulnerability to information security. According to the *USA Today* article "Lost Cellphones Added Up Fast in 2011," an estimated $30 billion worth of mobile phones were lost in 2011 in the United States.[40] The article refers to an app by Lookout Labs, a mobile security company with 15 million users, which recovered a phone every 3.5 seconds. The top five cities for phone loss were Philadelphia, Seattle, Oakland, Long Beach, and Newark.

"The Symantec Smartphone Honey Stick Project" study, conducted in late 2011, in which 50 smartphones were deliberately lost in five U.S. and Canadian cities, worryingly revealed that 89% of the finders tried to access apps and information that were clearly personal and 83% looked at corporate-related ones.[41] Writing about the same study, the MSNBC Digital Life article "The 'Lost' Cell Phone Project, and the Dark Things It Says about Us" notes that on average only 50% of the mobiles were returned even though the contact list of just two persons made it deliberately easy to identify and locate the owner of the phone. However, there was a gap between return rates: the highest was Ottawa (70%) while the lowest was New York City (30%).[42]

2.1.9 CRIME

The 2011 "Duty of Care and Travel Risk Management Global Benchmark Study" reveals that all but 1 of the 20 industries that the respondents were categorized into perceived "opportunistic crime" as a high threat: Interestingly, it was respondents from the transportation, travel, and tourism industry that ranked it as a medium risk, but their inputs were generally lower than for the other industries.[43] In the same survey, respondents were asked if their staff had experienced opportunistic and violent crime—the figures are telling (see Table 2.1).

TABLE 2.1
Occurrence of Crime

	Global 500 Enterprises	Large Corporations (10,000+ staff)	Medium Companies (1,000–10,000 staff)	Small Companies (less than 1,000 staff)
Opportunistic crime	69%	60%	50%	45%
Violent crime	47%	43%	29%	20%

Source: L. Claus, "Duty of Care and Travel Risk Management Global Benchmark Study," International SOS. 2011. http://www.internationalsos.com/dutyofcare.

The Maps of the World website has a page called "Top Ten Countries with Highest Reported Crime Rates" that gives a visual overview, but suffers from reporting issues.[44] Different types of criminal pursuits, including corruption, are covered in the Crime and Corruption section **(see Section 2.16)**.

2.1.10 CORRUPTION

The United Nations Office on Drugs and Crime (UNODC) states "Corruption is a crime committed by officials (public or private) abusing of their role to procure gain for themselves or somebody else. Several forms of corruption exist: bribery, embezzlement, abuse of power, just to name a few."[45] The amounts taken by bribes and corruption are outstanding. According to the 2011 article "Corruption in Business: Power to Destroy Firms" on a blog called Bizshifts:

- $2.5 trillion are lost to corruption and $1 trillion is paid out in bribes per year. That is more than 5% global gross domestic product (GDP).
- Corruption adds approximately 10% to the cost of global business. In some developing countries, procurement contracts can have an extra burden of 25%.
- Moving operations from a country with low corruption levels to one with medium or high levels is the equivalent of an additional 20% tax.[46]

To take one example of how corruption is a perverse influence on an economy, the 2011 KPMG India survey of top companies found 68% believed "India can achieve more than 9% GDP growth if corruption is reduced" and 31% agreed that "Corruption is a deterrent and a key risk to the projected 9% GDP growth rate."[47] Perhaps there is hope that companies will get better at tackling corruption: Responding to the question "In your opinion, how can your industry fight bribery and corruption?," from a survey by Ernst & Young in 2012, respondents selected the following statements:

- 73%—Zero tolerance to bribery and corruption such as taking legal actions against the perpetrator
- 62%—Stringent disciplinary procedures
- 54%—By improving the tone at the top
- 42%—Training
- 40%—Transparent disclosures about company policies on bribery and corruption[48]

2.1.11 NATURAL DISASTERS AND COMPLEX EMERGENCIES

Though this book is focused on human-made threats, natural disasters are included here because these large-scale cases of human suffering are often followed by periods of insecurity and/or instability, which in some cases can intensify an already critical situation (e.g., Pakistan, Haiti, Sri Lanka). Such situations can result in "complex emergencies" where destabilizing factors compile and compound upon each other, opening the gateway for multiple threats. Accordingly, these risks, and possible subsequent ones, should be included in your context and threat analyses **(see Section 1.1)**.

The infographic entitled "Danger Zones! Worldwide Deaths from Natural Disasters" illustrates that Africa was inflicted with the most deaths resulting from droughts and epidemics. Droughts are the top killer in the natural disasters category of risks, causing nearly as many deaths as the next two (earthquakes and tsunamis), claiming 558,540 lives in the period 1979–2008. Asia bore the brunt of the most deaths caused by earthquakes, floods, tsunamis, and storms. High temperatures affect Europeans the most.[49]

Food insecurity is another issue that unravels the social fabric of a people and instills desperation, thus creating the ideal conditions for increased opportunistic threats (it is important to underline that poverty in itself does not necessarily result in high crime rates, but it is an unstable foundation to add extra pressures onto). According to figures available on the World Bank's website, the hike on food prices in 2011 resulted in an additional 44 million people crossing the poverty line: This, in turn, compounded the already shockingly high number of 1.2 billion human beings living below the extreme poverty line of $1.25 per day.[50] The food crisis has been ongoing since 2008, the depth of which has not been experienced in 40–50 years.

The outlook for the global food crisis is bleak according to the *Guardian* newspaper article "The World Is Closer to a Food Crisis Than Most People Realize" from July 2012, which urges politicians to hastily recognize the problems that crop failures in the United States will have on the world.[51] It cites that in the summer of 2012, 26% of the corn crop was rated good/excellent compared to a 77% rating in May: These are some of the lowest recorded figures. Furthermore, 74% of the crop was rated fair/very poor in the summer. The *Forbes* article "The Coming Food Crisis: Blame Ethanol?" posted in July 2012 states:

> If you believe the folks at the New England Complex Systems Institute in Cambridge, Mass., the global food supply system is stumbling into a drought-induced supply shortage that could galvanize a global food crisis far more severe than those implicated in the widespread uprisings known as the Arab Spring.[52]

In other words, as a traveler you should pay attention to a destination's dynamic situation if it is one of those affected by the burden of the food crisis and particularly if there are indications that potential destabilizing factors are lurking in the near future.

2.1.12 LIFE IS FULL OF RISKS, BUT OPPORTUNITIES COME TO THOSE WHO MANAGE THEM

While these risks do exist, billions of people live in and millions of people travel safely to the countries listed in this book and the hundreds of thousands of locations not referred to. How can you manage risks so that you can concentrate on the task at hand, whether that is vacationing with your family or overseeing your company's international operations?

The best advice is to proactively manage risks by having the appropriate knowledge, skills, attitudes, and behavior for your destination (**see Section 1.3**). Adjusted accordingly, you should have the right levels of knowledge about the threats, context, and current situation; possess security and cultural awareness and first aid skills;

maintain an attitude that respects others while requiring respect for you; and behave in ways that optimize the opportunities by mitigating risks. Throughout this book there are lessons learned and expert advice that you can apply to better understand the potential risks that you might face while traveling, which in turn, better enables you to take the appropriate actions. The world is full of risks, but opportunities come to those who manage them.

2.2   PERSONAL CONSIDERATIONS

The corresponding section in **Chapter 1 (see Section 1.2)** highlighted that who you are, what you do, and how you do it are all key factors when assessing your vulnerability to any particular threat. While abroad, actively and continuously use these insights to aid you with taking appropriate mitigating measures. This section mixes expert advice and real-life cases to illustrate how, generally speaking, a few simple measures and a dose of common sense can keep you safer while traveling, as in the next contribution.

INCONSPICUOUS IN SÃO PAULO

FERNANDO LANZER PEREIRA DE SOUZA
MANAGEMENT CONSULTANT, EXECUTIVE COACH, AND
INTERNATIONAL TRAINER IN CROSS-CULTURAL MANAGEMENT
(HTTP://WWW.LCOPARTNERS.COM)

An American lady friend of mine was spending a week in São Paulo, accompanying her husband on a business trip. While the husband spent long days in business meetings, she wanted to see the city, as it was her first visit to Brazil. The staff at her hotel, which was a few kilometers (about 1 mile) from downtown, told her flatly: "Don't go out of the hotel on your own. It's not safe!"

That did not deter her. She donned a pair of jeans, plain sneakers, and a shirt and sneaked out of the hotel through a side door. She hailed a bus on the street and rode it downtown. She spent the afternoon strolling the streets and then took another bus back. She took great pride in her "adventure."

Her behavior did entail some risk, of course, but my point here is that she took some measures to mitigate the risk: by dressing as simply as possible and not carrying a camera, she was barely noticed in a densely populated area.

If you are about to go off exploring in a similar situation, it is advisable to also take some easy contingency measures like leaving note in a sealed envelope with your departure and expected arrival times and general plans on the bed at your hotel **(see Section 2.15)** and carrying a "secret stash" **(see Section 1.10)** and a map, though not openly carrying it **(see Section 1.14)**. That said, **"Inconspicuous in São Paulo"** is a good example of being aware of how your appearance will potentially be interpreted by your environment. And it is also a classic case of pushing oneself to meet new challenges while traveling. Being adventurous is certainly one reason why many people enjoy working and vacationing abroad. But, as **Ali Hayat's** contribution ends, "There is no problem in enjoying the nightlife in a foreign country; just learn about the local "nightlife etiquette" before you go out." The same practical advice applies to all your activities.

NIGHTLIFE SAFETY TIPS FOR TRAVELERS: KNOWING HOW TO ENJOY

ALI HAYAT

SECURITY CONSULTANT (HTTP://WWW.DFACTOWORLD.COM)

I have worked with nightlife security for more than a decade and spent many nights working the doors as a bouncer, security manager, and doorman in the nightlife and hospitality industry. Today, I work as a nightlife security consultant, and one of my greatest concerns is making clubbing safer and preventing nightlife-related violence.

One thing I have learned throughout the years is that all to often ordinary people become victims of crime. I have seen how businessmen and women, tourists, and average Joes from all over the world make poor decisions and end up as either victims of crime or causing themselves unnecessary embarrassment. What should be a fun way to relax on a business trip or vacation all too often ends up as a nightmare and leaves the person asking, why did this happen? Or, why did I end up here?—in worst cases, hospitalized or in jail.

The most common reason for people ending up in these risky situations is not the actual consumption of alcohol as many would people would think. Drinking alcohol is a natural part of a night out. The problems begin to appear when people do things they normally would never do, but they do them because they feel that they can and because they are not in their own community or environment. The mindset is often "I am on vacation and I am free to do what I want" or "I have been closing these deals with my business partners and we deserve to let loose." This is when the problems begin.

Some travelers run into problems because they don't know the local "nightlife etiquette"—this is different from country to country, and in larger countries, even from city to city. In some parts of the world, spending money in the bar will make bar staff, from managers to doormen, take good care of you. They will call a cab when you leave, they will make certain that no one "hustles" you, they will keep thieves away, and even when you become obnoxious and drunk they will take care of you and make sure that you get back to your hotel safely. In other countries, however, the same staff will gang up on you, con you, get you drunk, let prostitutes engage you, rob you, and perhaps even drug you. Travelers, including businessmen, from all over the world become victims of crime because they simply don't know the rules. Before you go out to enjoy yourself with business associates, ask your hosts what you can expect and what you can and, just as importantly, can't do.

Common advice such as never leave your drink unattended, never accept drinks from pretty girls that you don't know, never flash bundles of cash, don't wear your $1,000 watch, and so on, may seem simple, but believe it or not, people all over the world commit these simple mistakes because they forget that they are not "back home." Businessmen do get conned, they do get tricked by prostitutes, and they do get beaten up in back alleys because they took unnecessary risks.

There is no problem in enjoying the nightlife in a foreign country; just learn about the local "nightlife etiquette" before you go out.

The rest of this section supplements the advice mapped out in the **Chapter 1** corresponding section **(see Section 1.2)** by proffering specific personal considerations for various categories of travelers. The categories allow you to concentrate on your individual factors. However, glancing over the other sections might also provide you with insights that augment your travel risk management.

2.2.1 BUSINESS TRAVELERS

In many places, business people are particularly targeted because, as a group, business travelers tend not to report a crime against them for various reasons, including the inconvenience of taking time out from work or fear of harming their reputation at work and career chances. Business people also generally carry valuables, enticing to a variety of criminals—from watches and cash for street kids to snatch to laptops with sensitive information that your competitor might want to buy from sophisticated information technology (IT) crooks. Combined, these represent increased rewards, optimally joined with a decreased risk of getting caught. In other words, it makes good business sense to rob business travelers. You need to make it hard for a would-be thief by increasing the costs and decreasing the benefits.

As with other travelers, when you lock up your valuables, apply layers of IT security, or call a contact to say that you are in the taxi and casually mention some detail about the taxi (e.g., its number, name of the driver, etc.). You are increasing the costs for a criminal. Similarly, you are increasing the potential risks for anyone planning to detain you, as in the next contribution about sour business dealings in China, if you arrange for the meeting to be conducted in a neutral, public place you can safely enter and exit.

CHINA'S SPECIAL RISKS FOR BUSINESS TRAVELERS

JACK CHU

PRESIDENT, RA CONSULTANTS LTD. (HTTP://WWW.RA.COM.HK)

Even though China is a safe destination, you can find yourself with special risks. Ideally, it is best to avoid such situations by knowing your risks. For example, if you had a business dispute with your local partners, wrongful detentions may happen.

- Contact a security consultant or in-house security manager for advice. Find a local security professional if needed.
- Try to set up meetings with your local partner at a public venue, such as a hotel. Avoid meeting in their facilities. In most of the cases, once you have entered their facility, you will be controlled by others. When this kind of situation happens, even after it is reported to the local government, the local government or police might not be able to help, as they may believe this is a business dispute between two parties, into which the government cannot step. Then you might have to stay in that facility against your own will. In other situations, you might be retained in a hotel room but guarded and escorted by their employees. They won't allow you to communicate with outside parties until you agree to pay their demanded money.

Keep in regular communication with your company and friends to ensure your safety. If there is no communication, that means you are being held and they can start trying to get you out of the situation.

By decreasing the benefits to criminals, you also take away the incentive. Let's take an example from Poland, where you opt for driving a luxury rental car like a Mercedes or BMW. Unfortunately, these are the preferred targets of carjackers/hijackers. As someone who manages his or her travel security, your context assessment should have informed you that Polish thieves are making good money selling stolen cars in Germany. Seeing yourself from the local perspective will show you that you are more vulnerable to carjackings that target expensive rental cars. Your preventative measures could be to keep a low profile by choosing car models that blend in and, if possible, removing any rental car markings on your car **(see Section 2.14)**.

Travel risk management is a calculation of costs and benefits. For the costs of the time, effort, and money you invest in preventative measures, the benefits you could potentially gain include having peace of mind so that you can concentrate on maximizing your opportunities abroad. For criminals, on the other hand, these same measures increase their risks and decrease their benefits. This is a "win-win" situation for you.

2.2.2 Nongovernmental Organization (NGO) Travelers

"The Aid Worker Security Database" is a good resource for statistical graphs and charts covering countries, locations, trends, and more—all searchable by date range.[53] For the period 1997–2011, the "Location of Attacks" graph shows where incidents occurred:

- 54% road (in transit)
- 15% office, compound
- 12% private home
- 9% project site
- 2% official forces/police[54]

However, as the corresponding section in **Chapter 1 (see Section 1.2.2)** highlighted, even though aid work can be a dangerous job, that is not the case in all places, situations, or times. Therefore, it is important to be informed of the real situation and to test any assumptions, especially the extremes of "it's absolutely safe" or "it's always terribly dangerous."

Using figures from the Security in Numbers Database (SiND), the PDF entitled "Comparing Urban and Rural Security Incidents" found that 578 incidents occurred in rural areas while 306 were recorded for urban centers.[55] They charted the results into a six W's model: "Who and what affected? Where? What type of incident? Who did it? What weapon? When?" For the period of June 2008 to July 2010, the main findings were:

- Who and what affected? In rural areas, incidents tended to target both people and agency infrastructure, whereas in urban settings, mainly people were affected.
- Where? Service buildings were targeted more in rural areas than in urban centers, but urban compounds and private residences were riskier than rural ones.
- What type of incident? Carjackings were typically experienced while conducting rural fieldwork, and burglaries/robberies were more common in urban settings.
- Who did it? Groups or gangs were the typical perpetrators of rural security incidents; in comparison, somewhat more organized criminals tended to focus on urban victims.
- What weapon? In both rural and urban settings, small arms were involved.
- When? Daytime was riskier in rural places, whereas evening/nighttime posed extra risks in urban settings.

The six W's model is quite similar to the threat analysis provided in this book **(see Section 1.1.1)**. To help you safely do your job, use whichever model, or combination, that makes the most sense to you and best suits the realities of the environment. Before you go, you can enlist these models to help you prepare yourself and while abroad you can continuously apply them to stay updated.

2.2.3 Women Travelers

As evidenced by the abundance of websites and articles about female travelers avoiding, facing, or coping with the aftermath of sexual assault and/or violence, these are a serious concern and reality for many women traveling or living abroad. In the corresponding section in **Chapter 1 (see Section 1.2.3)**, there is a list of Internet resources: Many of these have several relevant articles about avoiding sexual aggression on public transportation, facing harassing men, or coping with being raped while abroad. Some of the recommendations are preventative, like taking your cues from local women in regard to dress codes, customs, and social interactions, while others focus on contingency measures like maintaining regular contact with someone at home or in the office when you travel solo.

The purpose of this section is to help you prevent sexually oriented threats. The next contribution adds to your toolkit by explaining the buildup to violence and your preventative options. For further advice about avoiding and reacting to sexual harassment/assaults, refer to the **Sexual Violence** section **(see Section 3.4)**.

PSYCHOLOGICAL TECHNIQUES THAT PREVENT VIOLENCE

CHRIS POOLE

AUTHOR, TRAINER, AND CONSULTANT IN VIOLENCE PREVENTION, ESPECIALLY FOR WOMEN AND GIRLS. DIRECTOR, VIOLENCE PREVENTION IN PRACTICE (VOLDSFOREBYGGELSE I PRAKSIS) (HTTP://WWW.VOLDSFOREBYGGELSE.NU)

What can we do to prevent becoming the victim of sexual harassment and other forms of violence? This question is not only relevant when we are going to travel. All women know that sexual harassment, rape, and domestic violence exist. But often, what we don't know enough about are the forms of behavior and attitudes that really are effective in preventing these forms of violence. Part of what can be done to stop these crimes, which predominantly affect girls and women, is for us to know how to prevent them.

The tools and techniques we will go through in the following section are based on research results, have been developed for the prevention of gender-specific violence, and are taken from the Danish book *Psykisk selvforsvar for kvinder: nedsæt din risiko for krænkelser og vold (Psychological Self Defense for Women: Reduce Your Chances of Experiencing Harassment and Violence)*.[*] They can, however, also be used to improve our general personal safety and security.

THE PSYCHOLOGICAL BUILDUP

The kinds of violence women are typically subjected to, both at home and while traveling, all have a psychological buildup. This refers to the process and the period of time that comes before and leads up to the assault. It begins the moment you feel that the situation you are in is going in the wrong direction, and you feel uneasy, unsafe, or you register an aggressive atmosphere. For example, you are out on the town and a man starts getting intimate and you don't like it. Or while walking down the street you feel someone is following after you and they are getting closer and closer. These are psychological buildups—90–95% of the violent episodes women experience are preceded by a psychological buildup.

---

[*] Chris Poole, *Psykisk selvforsvar for kvinder: nedsæt din risiko for krænkelser og vold (Psychological Self Defense for Women: Reduce Your Chances of Experiencing Harassment and Violence)*, self published, 2012.

A psychological buildup almost always progresses through several stages, each with increasing seriousness and intensity. It can vary in time from a couple of minutes to a half hour, to a whole evening or even longer. Initially, the attacker "checks us out" and "tests" us in ways that overrule our needs and ultimately jeopardize our safety. This could culminate in a physical or sexual assault, if the circumstances are right and depending on how you respond.

Most swindlers and sex criminals begin by trying to take control from you in a psychological buildup. By being aware of and listening to your intuition and common sense, you have a chance of recognizing a psychological buildup in time to get out of the situation before violence occurs. Knowing that a psychological buildup exists makes it easier to find a multitude of options to react in ways that avoid an assault.

SEVEN ELEMENTS THAT PREVENT VIOLENCE IN A PSYCHOLOGICAL BUILDUP

Figure 2.2 is an illustration of how the seven elements work together to prevent violence. Although each element is important individually, they all become very effective when used in combination.

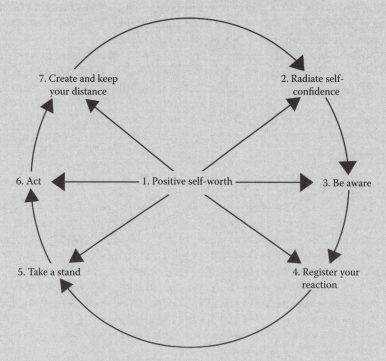

FIGURE 2.2   The seven elements that prevent violence in a psychological buildup. Copyright © Chris Poole 2003.

1. **Positive self-worth:** A feeling of self-worth and confidence in your own actions is a primary foundation for preventing violence. Personally, I think this is a prerequisite for a satisfying life.

   All our actions should be based on an overall feeling that we care about ourselves, in knowing that we have the right to express our feelings and wishes, and in the recognition of the fact that we are worth defending. A positive self-feeling is not something you simply have or don't have—it can be built up and must be maintained.

2. **Radiate self-confidence:** Studies show that women who express in their body language self-confidence and courage are less likely to become the victims of crime. We can learn to feel and show that we can and will take appropriate action in all situations. Walk with purpose and show self-confidence.

3. **Be aware:** This is about paying attention to what is happening around you—being aware of people, circumstances, and atmospheres. Awareness should include both the positive as well as the negative aspects of a situation, and it should take into account the whole spectrum of things ranging from objects and people we like, to ugly things and people we do not like or feel safe with. We are already unconsciously aware of many things when we travel. This kind of awareness should be expanded to become a natural part of our way of being no matter where we are.

4. **Register your reaction:** Intuition is an excellent tool. It's when you have a "gut feeling" or "protective voice." The more you listen to your intuition, the easier it is to follow. There are many advantages to learning to listen to your intuition, both in your daily life and in psychological build-ups to dangerous situations. Intuition is an important source of information that can contribute to a higher quality of life and travel safety.

5. **Take a stand:** Ask yourself: "Do I or don't I like what is happening right now?" Dare to make your own evaluation of the situation you are in. And trust your right to follow your assessment, no matter what others might think.

6. **Act:** It is important that you clearly and in direct terms express what it is you want and what you do not want. We need to know and express our boundaries. We can make our opinion clear through many different means using facial expressions, body language, and words. In all cultures, there are facial expressions that definitively mean "stop" or "don't"—use them at home and find out how to use them while abroad. Via body language, we can take a step away. In words, a refusal can range from a mild and friendly "I do not want to do this" to the more assertive "This is completely unacceptable!" How you react is completely dependent on your individual feelings and wishes. It is not possible to make a set of rules that work for everyone in the same situation. The point is you need to act and the sooner you do so, the more options you will have.

American studies that compared women who were raped with women who got away from an attempted rape showed that if the woman's reaction in the psychological buildup was primarily angry, assertive, and included a clear refusal, the rape was usually not carried out. If her reaction was fear, passivity, or paralysis, there was a greater risk that the rape would be completed.* Even if you are not an assertive person by nature or culture, you can find ways to express your boundaries so that they will be respected.

7. **Create and keep your distance:** Perhaps the most important technique is to create distance, psychologically as well as physically. Keeping your distance is essential because if you have distance between you and an attacker, he cannot sexually or physically assault you.

There are strong and weak ways of creating distance. These can again be done using your facial expressions, body language, and words. For example, you are having dinner with someone you met at the hotel who is attending the same conference as you. Because you are aware of what is going on, you notice at some point that sex is "in the air"—perhaps he has made more than one sexual comment. You are not interested. While looking down at the table you can say "Hmm, I think I have to get back to my room and read my travel book and wash some clothes and...." Or you can look him in the eye and say firmly but friendly, "You know what? If it's sex you are interested in, you can count me out. I am not interested." The difference and effect will be quite apparent. If the situation continues to develop in an unpleasant or dangerous direction, then it is time to put space between you and him so the situation does not escalate.

Remember, it is your intuition and "gut feeling" that you should respect and base your actions on. If someone, no matter who, starts to bother you, you don't need to be 100% sure that the situation will end in an assault (by then, it's an assault!). All you need to know is that if you do not like what is happening, then it is your right to react based on your evaluation of the situation. Potential attackers unfortunately have no special physical signs, like bad teeth. Therefore, we cannot know if a man we know or a complete stranger is a potential perpetrator just by his appearance. We can only listen to and act on our intuition.

In your daily life, you should practice listening to your intuition, thinking and expressing positive self-feelings, projecting confident body language, being aware of your surroundings, and registering your reactions. Then if you are faced with a situation with a psychological buildup, you can quickly take a stand and act by maintaining the distance you feel safe with.

---

* Pauline B. Bart and Patricia H. O'Brian, *Stopping Rape: Successful Survival Strategies.* Pergamon Press, 1985; Lindsey M. Orchowski, *Risk Reduction Interventions to Prevent Sexual Victimization in College Women.* Ohio University, 2006.

2.2.4 TRAVELERS WITH DISABILITIES

The subsequent contribution deals with general preventative and contingency measures that you can put in place as a disabled traveler or his or her travel companion. In addition, a few specific tips for various disabilities are also prescribed. The concluding scenario demonstrates the key points.

**FOR TRAVELERS WITH DISABILITIES
AND THOSE ASSISTING THEM**

CBM INTERNATIONAL

*MODIFIED EXCERPTS FROM 2011 "SAFETY AND SECURITY FACTSHEETS"
(HTTP://WWW.CBM.ORG). REPRINTING AND MODIFICATIONS MADE
BY PERMISSION. COPYRIGHT © 2011 CBM INTERNATIONAL*

Whether you are a seasoned traveler or not, always remember that each new journey should start with thorough preparation and a (renewed) familiarization with the country you will be traveling to. Without proper preparation, it's more likely that events might catch you off-guard. Travel considerations for persons with disabilities and those assisting them include:

- Beforehand and on arrival get/provide a thorough orientation on security and safety protocols. A cursory "show around" for a person with disabilities is not enough to prepare them for the eventual chaos that follows immediately after a crisis.
- Note that in emergency cases, some of the regular routes cannot be used (e.g., elevators should not be used, doors might be blocked after an earthquake) so consider alternatives (e.g., carrying a person who is usually using a wheelchair, escape through the window, etc.).
- Make sure regular safety information channels (e.g., emergency numbers) are known and accessible to the person with a disability. If these are not accessible, consider pragmatic alternatives, for example, arranging to send text messages to the companion of the person with disabilities.
- Be and make people aware of local perceptions of disability and how best to respond to this. These will vary widely and if interpreted wrongly it can increase your exposure and thus make you more vulnerable. This attitude can also vary between urban and rural settings and is not necessarily positive.
- Be willing to sacrifice some of your independence. In many places around the world, it might not be wise to travel or stay alone.
- Ensure you travel with somebody you trust. You will be spending intensive days of travel together, including the hours you would normally want some privacy. Plan and communicate what you will do if and when you might need assistance.

FIGURE 2.3   Courtesy of CBM International and photographer Ingrid Vekemans.

Here are some additional points for specific disabilities:

- A visually impaired person cannot see what the local clothing customs are nor how people greet each other. Ask about and discuss this.
- Ensure that a person who cannot see is kept informed on what is
  going on. For a visually impaired person it is vital that you immediately tell factually what is happening outside and what can be
  expected. Communicate also when a relatively calm situation escalates to a tense situation.
- Persons who cannot hear and/or speak should always carry a notebook and writing utensil. It may be helpful to already have text in the
  local language(s) and the traveler's language in the notebook. In an
  emergency situation, sometimes a drawing can help to make a situation understood quicker. Also for critical situations, you could have
  a prewritten message about your emergency treatment in your native
  language and the local language.
- Somebody who is hard of hearing will struggle to understand information provided in a sudden chaotic situation. Make sure that in such
  a situation you face the person you talk to and try to find a quiet place
  to convene basic information one on one.

For persons with disabilities, being well prepared and briefed enhances
your confidence, and this will help you to handle each situation much better
thus reducing your vulnerability (Figure 2.3). For companions, try to be well
attuned to the requirements of the person with a disability that you travel or
work with. Consider the following scenario.

Jonathan and Eileen are participating in a workshop in a hotel in Wellington, New Zealand. Eileen is visually impaired and Jonathan travels with her to participate in the workshop. Eileen has prepared herself well before this trip. She knows Wellington is in an earthquake-prone area. She also realizes that their workshop is on the fifth floor of the hotel. In case an earthquake should strike, it would not be straightforward for her to find shelter and later leave the building safely.

On arrival she has therefore asked Jonathan to show her around the floor where their workshop is as well as the hotel where she is staying. They sought the assistance of the managers and got a thorough briefing on the emergency notification and procedures. She is now able to locate the emergency exits and has practiced going down the stairs. She also knows what to expect once she comes outside. She keeps her telephone and a few other items she needs in a small bag by her side at all times. She keeps her white cane and a pair of extra shoes by her bed when she is in her room.

Jonathan also recognizes that in case of an emergency, Eileen would need his help. On arrival in New Zealand he has offered his assistance to Eileen and together they have assessed the situation and have agreed what each will do in the unlikely event that something might happen. Jonathan ensured that Eileen got a hotel room on the ground floor near the emergency exit of their corridor. The staff of the hotel are also aware that in case of an emergency, Eileen will need assistance and have agreed to help.

2.2.5   ELDERLY TRAVELERS

If you have already started your travels, you should simply be enjoying your trip by taking stock of the relevant advice, modified to suit your personal circumstances, that will help you prevent security incidents from occurring and assist you with reacting in the best ways if the worst should happen. As described in the corresponding section in **Chapter 1 (see Section 1.2.5)**, most of your special considerations revolve around medical and mobility issues.

Regarding keeping you medically fit and healthy while traveling or living abroad, you should follow your doctor's advice and any appropriate general advice from the **Medical Considerations** sections **(see Sections 1.8 and 2.8)**. As for mobility issues, good Internet resources include "10 Safety Tips for Seniors Using Public Transportation" on the About.com Senior Living website[56] and "Train Travel Safety" on the About.com Senior Travel website.[57]

2.2.6   HOMOSEXUAL, BISEXUAL, AND TRANSGENDER TRAVELERS

As long as you follow the relevant advice from this book and continuously apply your security knowledge, skills, attitudes, and behaviors that are most befitting for your travel realities, then you should be in a position to get the most out of any journey. While being cautious to not perpetuate stereotypes, it has to be pointed out that several experts and Internet resources mention that "cruising" in public places for the purpose of seeking sexual encounters can be a security risk because this can be illegal in some countries, and in many places the police actively set up traps. Of course, this is only a concern if your intentional or sometimes even unintentional activities can potentially make you vulnerable to such a risk. However, your pre-trip risk **(see Section 1.1)** and vulnerability **(see Section 1.2.6)** assessments should have alerted you to the potential risks. On the Internet, there are various websites and blogs that focus on homosexual, bisexual, and transgender travel issues—many of these are directly or indirectly related to travel risk management. To name a few, try the forum on Lonely Planet's website,[58] Globe Trotter Girls,[59] and My Gay Travel Guide[60]: These are in addition to the resources cited in the corresponding section in **Chapter 1 (see Section 1.2.6)**. An interesting read, which has loads of links, is "Why You Can't Bulletpoint Gay Travel."[61]

2.2.7 Traveling Families

While a traveling family tends to stay close together, it is possible to be separated from each other for various reasons. For instance, you may not be able to sit together on the airplane because of the seating configuration. For families with members holding different passports, you may be required to go through different customs and security checks. Similarly, families may be split up along gender lines. You should prepare for this in terms of your supplies for the trip (food, entertainment, travel documents) and your family's plans to meet up again.

It is becoming more common for airports to provide activities spaces for young travelers. Though mainly focused on the United States, the "Kids Airport Diversion Guide" on the Cheapflights.com website lists some of the available exhibitions, museums, and play areas.[62]

Before leaving your accommodation, you can take a picture of your children, so if they are separated from you, you can get others to assist you. Some people place a picture of themselves on their child so that whoever is assisting a child can find the parents. You should avoid clothing that has your child's name on it because children tend to trust people who know their name.

You can have your young children wear brightly colored clothes, a special hat, or "glow-in-the-dark" jewelry. However, even if the unthinkable happens and someone actually tries to steal your child, be on the lookout not just for your brightly dressed child but any child who has the same height and build. That is because a very determined person will change your child's appearance.

You should tell your children about a prearranged meeting spot or destination, so even if they get separated from you en route they can get assistance to find you. If they are old enough, explain what they should do if they are lost—for example, they should approach an employee of the amusement park. Ideally, you should direct them toward seeking help from official services, say, at a train station: But another option, especially good for young children, is to approach another family. As mentioned in **Chapter 1**, security does not have to be scary: Role-plays and games are easier for your child to remember and fun too.

Place your hotel's card on all your children. Put your last name on the back of the card or, if you are traveling with your mobile phone, then you can also include that. Even if you have done that, it is advisable to have your children memorize your mobile number, hotel name, or some other contact detail, if your children are old enough. For water-bound activities, you may consider writing your mobile number or hotel name on your child's arm—it will wear off in a few days.

While these precautions are necessary for worst-case scenarios, it is highly unlikely that a stranger will grab your child: According to experts, strangers are responsible for "only" about 25% of child abductions, while the majority are taken by an estranged parent.[63]

The "Tip Sheet: Crowd Safety" on the We Just Got Back website is a highly recommended resource fueled by good advice from parents.[64] The article "Preventing Abductions" on the Kids Health website also has some good advice.[65]

2.2.8 RELIGIOUS TRAVELERS

The next contribution raises some of the social, cultural, and political considerations you should keep in mind when discussing religion and/or religious activities in public spaces.

TRAVELING AS A PERSON OF FAITH

SCOTT A. WATSON
SECURITY MANAGEMENT CONSULTANT

In 2006, I was traveling to Southeast Asia as part of a short-term mission team. The purpose of our team was to assist a local congregation in a church building project. Our team had been invited to participate in the project and was working under the authority of the local church. Due to the poverty of the area, staying at the work site would have been a burden on the local church. As a result, arrangements were made to stay in a hotel some 40 minutes away from the work site.

Each morning the team would gather in the hotel lobby prior to departure. One morning, I came down to the lobby a little early and noticed that "Sally," one of my teammates, seemed a bit shaken. Sally told me that she had had a run-in with another hotel guest in the elevator. The guest, an American man, had overheard Sally speaking about the purpose of the trip and took offense. When the elevator doors closed and they were alone, the man became verbally aggressive and accused her trying to "impose her religion on another culture." When the elevator reached the lobby and people were again around, the man stopped speaking and quickly left.

Although Sally had not been physically harmed in the incident, it was an eye-opening experience for her and the team. Since arriving in country, all the nationals we had met, whether Christian or not, had been exceptionally nice to us. A fundamental underpinning of our supportive mission as church builders was that people from the same culture can more easily share the gospel with their countrymen then we could. As a result, we had not attempted to evangelize anyone. Nonetheless, we did not hide the purpose of our trip either.

We never saw the man again nor did we did experience any other incidents of this sort. Nonetheless, this event illustrated some important points about traveling as a person of faith.

LESSONS LEARNED

1. *Under the microscope*: If you are a person of faith traveling on a mission trip, then you are under a microscope. Some people will watch you so they can point out real or perceived incongruence between your words and deeds. While others will observe you because they are curious about you and your culture. How you respond to the situations around you makes a difference in how you and your message are received. By being respectful of the culture and showing that you care for people, you can slowly gain the opportunity to speak into their lives about spiritual matters. This, however, does not happen overnight and may not happen at all on a short-term mission trip. It is also important to keep in mind that sharing the gospel with non-Christians can be exceedingly dangerous in some countries. The decision to do so should be taken at the prompting of the Holy Spirit and with an understanding of the potential consequences. Regardless of your role in the process, being a good ambassador will allow you to set a positive example of faith in action. Some sow seeds and others reap a harvest.
2. *Unexpected sources of resistance*: Sometimes, those who most vocally oppose your missions are not the nationals that you've come to help, but Westerners with an anti-faith bias.
3. *Travel in groups*: The incident above illustrates why it is important to travel in groups. While Sally was not physically harmed, the behavior of the man in the elevator was clearly designed to intimidate her. Thankfully, Sally could rely on her teammates and her faith to feel better after the incident.

Since religion, like other areas such as politics and culture, can be a crucial part of people's identities, then even in private conversations it is generally advisable to steer clear of contentious subjects, unless you are quite certain the other interlocutors are open to such discussions. And still, it probably is prudent to be particularly sensitive with your articulations and extra alert to potentially hostile turns in the conversation. Of course, what is more important is your judgment in the situation, based on your knowledge of the context, interpersonal skills, and attitude of giving and requiring respect, all of which add up to your behavior that helps create the space for open dialogue.

2.3　IMPLEMENTING SITUATIONAL AWARENESS

As an aware traveler, you should constantly be reading your environment and listening to your intuition and "survival instincts." Doing such better enables you to take mitigating measures, preferably early on. Throughout this book, there are tools you can use to improve your skill set. In the **Building Situational Awareness** section **(see Section 1.3)** the situation awareness exercises help you draw out and alert your attention to details that may be significant for your personal well-being while traveling. In the following contribution, "Nena's" awareness actually benefited an elderly woman's safety.

UNDER THE RADAR IN SAN DIEGO: IS AWARENESS IN THE EYES OF THE BEHOLDER?

RUDY FRIEDERICH

CHIEF INSPECTOR (RETIRED) U.S. MARSHALS SERVICE

I like to take pride in being alert and aware of my surroundings. My track record of seeing trouble in advance is a pretty solid one. On the other hand, "Nena" has always come across as totally oblivious to her surroundings in terms of security and safety issues. She never sees anything until I point it out to her. Well, after this, I came to see awareness from another perspective.

One day, we were getting ready to have lunch at one of these outdoors cafes, in one of those cutesy villages north of San Diego, and had, more or less, just sat down at the table. Out of the blue, a police officer walks up to us and essentially asks if we have been sitting there long enough to see a little old lady walk by carrying a shopping bag. I hadn't. But Nena suddenly says that she had seen such an older woman about five blocks up about 10 minutes earlier. Nena then went on to describe what the woman was wearing, to include her type and color of hat, *and* the name of the store on the shopping bag the lady was carrying. Nena also added that she believed the woman was about to turn up a side street near the 7-Eleven shop.

I was simply stunned. We had both walked by this lady at the exact same time and I never even noticed her. Nena, on the other hand, *noticed every single thing about her.*

The officer calls it in and walks off. About 15 minutes later he comes back and essentially says "I thought you would like to know we found her sitting on a low wall up the block you described. She's okay. She had walked off from a local seniors' home some time a little earlier today."

And so it occurred to me that while I might be pretty good about being observant about situations that appear sinister, or perhaps hot babes, or people in good shape, somebody like this old lady was completely underneath my radar. Apparently, in my mind, there was simply no reason to notice her. When I asked Nena how come she noticed this woman, her response was essentially that "She seemed out of place and almost lost." I certainly walked by this woman and saw no such thing.

I came away from this event appreciating that other people are attuned to different things that register with them. I was blind-sided because the old lady didn't present a danger to me. It was a heck of a humbling moment, as well as a learning experience.

What do you normally observe about the people, places, and events around you? What else should you be noticing, especially given your threat and contextual assessments of your location (see Section 1.1)? From a security perspective, under what circumstances should your awareness be at its most heightened? And when can you relax it? You can gain insights into those questions by reading the contribution "Psychological Techniques That Prevent Violence" by Chris Poole, which covers seven elements from self-worth to intuition to taking action. Trusting your intuition is a key resource available to you at all times: Listening to those forewarnings can help you avoid insecure incidents, and on the flip-side, not paying attention to what are essentially your "survival instincts," as in the following contribution, can result in an unpleasant experience.

FOUR HOURS IN A SENEGALESE JAIL FOR NOT TRUSTING MY INSTINCT

SOLÈNE
HUMANITARIAN AID WORKER

I'm used to traveling alone, but one time in Dakar, I went on a work trip with my husband. We went to a colleague's house who invited us for a drink at his local bar. When we arrived, I looked around and realized that we were the only foreigners and this place was obviously not safe! I thought we should leave immediately. But then I thought, don't worry you're not alone this time, don't be paranoid, and I ended up not saying anything.... And we stayed. Fifteen minutes later the police raided the bar, arrested two or three drug users (dealers?) and ended up arresting us after my coworker argued with them. The cops said it is unlawful to be out without your passport when you're a foreigner, so we spent four hours under arrest until someone at my office came to negotiate our release. That night I learned a big lesson: Trust your instinct at all times. If you feel something is wrong with the place, leave (and carry a copy of your passport at all times)!

The next two contributions give tools for reading and reacting to your environment. **Tom Givens** explains how you can use the Cooper Color Codes as a sliding scale of readiness: This is a functional tool that many self-defense instructors use in their courses for individuals and security professionals. The short contribution **"Get**

into Your Peak State to Get Away" is about how to optimize your chances of physically getting away if you need to.

STATES OF AWARENESS: THE COOPER COLOR CODES

TOM GIVENS

*OWNER AND CHIEF INSTRUCTOR, RANGEMASTER.
AUTHOR OF MORE THAN 100 MAGAZINE ARTICLES AND
FIVE TEXTBOOKS INCLUDING* FIGHTING SMARTER. *HE IS
AN EXPERT WITNESS IN CASES INVOLVING FIREARMS AND
FIREARMS TRAINING (HTTP://WWW.RANGEMASTER.COM).*

Most people stumble through life, blissfully unaware of the world around them. They remain preoccupied with thoughts of work, or personal problems, or how to get a date, or other trivialities, with no thought to their immediate environment. By not paying attention to their surroundings, they place themselves in needless jeopardy.

The vast majority of criminals are opportunists, who only strike when presented with a viable opportunity. Remove the opportunity and you remove much of the risk to you!

By learning to observe your environment, constantly evaluate it, and react appropriately to what you see, you can achieve a large degree of control over your fate. This requires you to learn to shift up and down a scale of readiness, just like shifting gears in a car, so that you can match your level of awareness/ readiness with the current requirements of your situation. In a car, you shift gears based on the grade encountered or the speed desired. On the street, you must learn to "shift gears" mentally, to match the threat level encountered. There is a sliding scale of readiness, going from a state of being oblivious and unprepared to a condition of being ready to instantly do lethal violence if forced. One cannot live stuck at either end of this spectrum.

If you try to live at the bottom of the scale, you will fall victim to an accident or to a criminal, eventually. It's just a matter of *when*, not *if*. On the other hand, you can't go through your daily routine with your hand hovering over your holstered pistol, ready to shoot if anything moves! What you must learn to do is escalate and deescalate up and down this scale as the circumstances around you dictate. This is an easily learned system, and one that will help you be in the right frame of mind to deal with any conflict you might encounter.

If you should find yourself faced with a life-threatening attack by a criminal, as a typical normal person, you will be faced with three enormous difficulties. They are:

1. Recognizing the presence of the predator in time
2. Realizing, internalizing, and accepting that *that man, right there* is about to be violent to you for reasons you do not understand, if you don't stop him

3. Overcoming your reluctance to do lethal violence against a fellow
   human being

Let's look at each of these in turn. First, you have to see him and realize that
he is a threat. They typically walk right up to you unnoticed because of the fog
most people operate in daily. Learn to lift that fog and see the warning signs
earlier, so you can be prepared.

Second, it is very difficult for normal, rational, socialized, civilized people
to grasp that there are people who are *not* like you. There are people out there
who do not care about your hopes or plans for the future, they do not care about
your family, they do not care about the pain and suffering they inflict—they
just don't care. They may seriously injure you for the contents of your wallet
so they can buy one more day's supply of drugs. They may rape you because
they feel powerless, degraded, and abused except while they are degrading and
abusing someone else. They may kill you simply to move up one rank in their
street gang. A typical victim reaction is, "But why would anyone want to hurt
me?" Guess what? The "why's?" don't matter. You need to be concerned with
how to prevent an attack from happening.

Third, regarding reluctance to do lethal violence against a fellow human
being: If you have a gun, for example, it will be difficult for you to pull the
trigger. Don't let anyone tell you that will be easy. As a society, we don't
want it to be easy, do we? This is why legally armed citizens don't shoot
people over arguments or traffic accidents and so forth. Private citizens are
reluctant to actually shoot, even when it is necessary. You must overcome
this obstacle if your life is on the line. I feel that there are times when
lethal violence is not just excusable, or justifiable, or acceptable, but actually *required*.

Fortunately, there is a system available to help you overcome all three of
these problems. By learning to use this system, practicing it, and making it
part of your daily routine, you can be assured of seeing an attack in its developing stages, and become both mentally and physically prepared to defend
yourself. Jeff Cooper, who taught it at Gunsite and later gave an excellent vid-
eotaped presentation, first publicized this system called the Color Code. I had
the great fortune of being taught this by Jeff early in my career, and I can say
without reservation that this system saved my life on several occasions. Not
what kind of gun I had, nor the brand of ammunition, but this mental system. I
feel so strongly that this is one of the most important weapons in your arsenal,
that I feel it is my duty to share it with you.

I mentioned earlier learning to move up and down a scale of readiness,
just like shifting gears. The scale consists of four mental states, which Jeff
gave color names. The colors simply let us conceptualize and discuss the basic
mental states. You must learn to go up and down this scale as the situation and
circumstances around you change, as they invariably will as you go through
your daily routine.

CONDITION WHITE

White is the lowest level on the escalator. In Condition White one is unaware, not alert, oblivious. This state can be characterized as "daydreaming" or "pre-occupied." You see examples of this frequently. People in White tend to walk around with their heads down, as if watching their own feet. How often do you see someone in public talking or texting on a cell phone, absolutely unaware of the people around him?

These same guys will be the victims of violent crime, because the criminal targets the inattentive, the complacent, the lazy, the distracted, and the preoccupied. Why? Because the criminal wants to get to him, get what he wants from him, and get away from him, without being hurt or caught. Who would be the easiest person to do that to? Someone in Condition White.

So, when would it be acceptable to be in Condition White? When in your own home, with the doors locked. If you leave your home, you leave Condition White behind. The instant you leave your home, you escalate one level, to Condition Yellow.

CONDITION YELLOW

This is a relaxed state of general alertness, with no specific focal point. You are not looking for anything or anyone in particular; you simply have your head up and your eyes open. You are alert and aware of your surroundings. You are difficult to surprise, and therefore, you are difficult to harm. You do not expect to be attacked today. You simply recognize the possibility.

Anything or anyone in your immediate vicinity that is unusual, out of place, or out of context, should be viewed as potentially dangerous, until you have had a chance to assess it. Someone who looks out of place, or someone engaged in activity that has no obvious legitimate purpose, should be looked over carefully. When your mental radar picks up on a blip, you immediately escalate one level on the scale, to Condition Orange.

CONDITION ORANGE

This is a heightened state of alertness, with a specific focal point. The entire difference between Yellow and Orange is this specific target for your attention. Your focal point is the person who is doing whatever drew your attention to him. It might be the fact that he is wearing a field jacket in August. It might be that he's standing by a column in the parking garage, instead of going into the building or getting into a car. It might be that you have been in five stores at the mall, and saw this same guy in every one of them. His actions have caused you to take note of him, so you must assess him as a potential threat.

How do you assess someone as a threat? You have to take into account the totality of the cues available to you. His clothing, appearance, demeanor, actions, anything he says to you, are all cues. The single most important cue is body language. About 80% of human communication is through body language. Predators display subtle pre-aggression indicators, which are obvious once you learn to look for them.

When you shift upward to Orange, you begin to focus your attention on this individual that caught your eye, but do not drop your general overview. You don't want to be blind-sided by his associates. You begin to watch him and assess his intentions, again looking at all of the cues available to you. Nine times out of ten, after a few seconds of observation you will be able to see an innocuous reason for his behavior and then dismiss him. Once you figure out he's not a threat, dismiss him and deescalate right back down to Yellow. If he is a predator who would have gotten to you if you had been inattentive, now that you are aware of him, you are in far less danger.

As you assess this individual, and you see things that convince you he has evil intent, you start to play the "what if" game in your mind to begin formulating a basic plan. This is how we get ahead of the power curve. If he acts suddenly, we must have at least a rudimentary plan for dealing with him already in place so that we can react swiftly enough. By saying to yourself, "That guy looks like he is about to stick me up. What am I going to do about it?," you begin the mental preparation vital to winning the conflict. With even a simple plan already in place, your physical reaction is both assured and immediate, if the bad guy presses his intentions. If, after assessing him, you believe he is an actual threat, you then escalate to the highest level, Condition Red.

CONDITION RED

In Red, you are ready to fight! You may, or may not, actually be fighting, but you are *mentally prepared* to fight. In many, or perhaps even most, circumstances where you have gone fully to Red, you will not actually physically do anything at all. The entire process of escalating from Yellow, to Orange, to Red, then deescalating right back down the scale as the situation is resolved, occurs without any actual physical activity on your part. The key is that you are mentally prepared for a conflict, and thus could physically act if the situation demanded.

When you believe a threat is real, and you have escalated to Red, you are waiting on the mental trigger, which is a specific, predetermined action on his part that will result in an immediate, positive, aggressive, defensive reaction from you. This is how you achieve the speed necessary to win. By having a "premade decision" already set up in your mind, you can move physically fast enough to deal with the problem.

Your main enemy is reaction time. If you're caught in Condition White, you will need five to six seconds to realize what is happening, get your wits together, and respond. You simply don't have that much time. On the other hand, if you are thinking to yourself, "I may have to hurt that guy if he doesn't wise up," you've probably already won that fight, because you have a better understanding of what is transpiring than he does!

There are a couple of mental tricks you can use to train yourself in quicker response time. Every morning visualize realistic situations in which you practice seeing yourself going through the Cooper Color Codes. When you pick up on a potential threat and escalate to Condition Orange, tell yourself, "I may have to harm him before he harms me!" Believe me, if you have internalized that a specific threat might happen to you, then you have the means to deal with real-life situations.

Let's work through a scenario to illustrate these principles. Let's say you are working in a jewelry store, a small storefront shop in a strip mall. All of the other employees went to lunch. There are not even any customers in the store, so you're alone. What mental state are you in? Yellow. So you keep your head up, and occasionally you scan out through the glass storefront and check out the parking lot. You want to know about a problem while it's out there, not when it's standing across the counter from you.

As you glance through the glass, you see two men in their early twenties back up an old car to your store, get out in identical jogging suits, enter your door, and split up. Immediately, you go to Orange. They have done nothing illegal, and nothing aggressive, but they are out of place, out of the ordinary, so you escalate your mental state, and begin to think: "This looks like a hold-up in the making. I may have to hurt these guys. What should I do now? If things go bad, I'll drop behind this safe and I can shoot into that wall without endangering anyone in the parking lot. I have a plan." At this point, you watch them and continue to monitor their movements. If they leave, you deescalate to Yellow once they are gone.

If they stay, they will then move toward your position at the counter, and after trying to distract you ("Can I see that ring back there?"), pull their guns and announce a stick-up. If you have been using the system, you went from Yellow to Orange when they came in, and went to Red as they approach your counter. You are ready. Because criminals have to be adept at reading body language (their lives depend upon this skill), they will see that you are prepared and simply leave. About nine out of ten pairs will leave at this point, without a confrontation. As they drive away, deescalate from Red, to Orange, to Yellow.

What about the tenth pair? They failed to recognize your level of readiness and they may go ahead foolishly with their hold-up. In this situation, probably 80% of the ones you will actually have to fight will be under the influence of drugs and/or alcohol at the time. What's the good news? They're drunk and/or drugged, which plays hell with their reflexes, reaction time, and motor coordination. They'll be relatively easy to deal with, if you are mentally prepared (Condition Red) and have done your homework.

If they come in, and upon observing them you go to Orange, then as they approach, to Red, but then they leave, and you deescalate, you will have gone all of the way up the scale without even reaching for your weapon, which is very common. The point is, you would have been ready if necessary. This is how you win fights, by being mentally prepared to win.

The subsequent contribution is a tip to help get in your "peak state" to get away. To further understand the dynamics of a potentially violent situation and the options available to you, refer to the discussion about violent crime in the **Crime and Corruption** section **(see Section 2.16)**.

GET INTO YOUR PEAK STATE TO GET AWAY

DAVID BRIENT
EXECUTIVE COACH, DB COACHING LTD.
(HTTP://WWW.DAVIDBRIENTCOACHING.COM)

When I conduct conflict management courses, I advise my participants to get into a "peak state" with the right physiology, focus, and language.

- Physiology—steady, calming breathing. This should be raised to a level that enables the explosive energy release required for fight or flight responses to be effective.
- Focus—determination to get away and an absolute confidence that *I will not become a victim*!
- Language—clearly expressing "no" and making specific commands for someone to change their behavior.

You can visualize it as a triangle, with each component in its own corner. Something that I have found as a business person, executive coach, and conflict management course leader is that avoiding and reducing the threats should be tried 99% of the time and self-defense is the last option: When all else has failed ... then you need to be ferocious!

It is important to mention that in the build-up to a potentially critical situation, people tend to assume that their mobiles benefit their security. They can, but a lot depends on the circumstances. In some situations, displaying your mobile can attract criminals, or worse yet, using it can distract your attention from your surroundings. Some security experts say that up to 75% of your attention can be focused on your conversation. In London, posters remind pedestrians of the risk of being hit in traffic due to being distracted by their mobiles.

If you want to use your mobile as a tool in an insecure situation, such as walking from the train station to your accommodation, then have it call ready in your hand, but usually you will want to keep it out of sight. Times when you might want to visibly display your mobile could include if you use it in a way that makes a taxi driver think that you have informed someone of your ride **(see Section 2.14)**, or when stopped by police, because in many countries police are incredibly corrupt and one way to get them to behave lawfully is to let them know someone else is listening or watching **(see Section 2.16)**.

Throughout your travels, you should aim to apply the ABC's: Awareness, Behavior, and Common Sense. Using your situational awareness to continuously read your environment will help you to prevent security incidents from happening and to react with the best available options in the worst-case scenarios.

For further reading, the article "Situational Awareness: How Everyday Citizens Can Help Make a Nation Safe" available on the Stratfor website is seemingly about American homeland security, but it is actually a good explanation of the Cooper Colors, using a driving analogy to clearly illustrate the main points.[66] The article "Color Codes of Awareness" by Self Defense Resource.com covers the issues in a straightforward and concise way.[67] The corresponding section in **Chapter 1 (see Section 1.3)** lists additional resources about situational awareness.

At the same time, this book also gives you advice on how to mitigate personal considerations such as witnessing a traumatic event **(see Section 1.17)**, working sequential periods on a stressful contract abroad **(see Section 2.17)**, or being blinded by your own cultural glasses **(see Sections 1.7 and 2.7)** that, potentially, can reduce your ability to correctly interpret your surroundings. By adding these insights to your travel toolkit, you gain greater maneuverability and choice in your preventative options because you know how to read your environment and take appropriate actions.

2.4   PREPAREDNESS

This section depicts three checklists that are particularly useful for preparing for the early stages of your trip. They represent different countries but also their scope varies. **"Security Tips for Traveling and Working in China"** exemplifies an overall list from money exchange to police contact details that helps you be prepared for most common eventualities. The contribution **"Words of Advice for Travelers to Papua New Guinea"** illustrates the interplay between contextual factors (i.e., poor infrastructure and high unemployment) and your security. The last contribution, **"Enjoyable Street Life and Safe Dining in Romania,"** contains the type of information you want to gather so that you can fully take advantage of social and cultural opportunities during your trip. Supplementary checklists can be found in the corresponding section in **Chapter 1 (see Section 1.4)**.

SECURITY TIPS FOR TRAVELING AND WORKING IN CHINA

JACK CHU
PRESIDENT, RA CONSULTANTS LTD. (HTTP://WWW.RA.COM.HK)

Overall, China is a very safe country for any travelers around the world, but as with any other country there are criminal activities in China aiming at travelers. I have the following recommendations for people traveling to China.

LOCAL CULTURE

- China is a massive country. It is important to understand the local culture and customs of your destination. Do not do anything against local societies.
- Pay respect to your local guide or staff and ask them in advance about what to do or not to do.

MONEY EXCHANGE

- Exchange your money at the hotel, airport, or banks. Photo ID will be required.
- Be aware that counterfeit bank notes are popular.

AIRPORTS IN CHINA FOR ARRIVAL AND DEPARTURE

- Preferably you should have arranged for the hotel's pickup service at the airport, as they are safe and convenient.
- You can also use a licensed taxi at the airport to take you to the hotel. Ask them to start the meter before driving, and ask for a receipt before you get out. Avoid hiring an unmarked taxi.

TRANSPORTATION FOR DOMESTIC AND CITY TRAVEL

- You can travel by airline or train in China domestically. Chinese airlines and train services do meet international standards. You can book domestic travel tickets in China, as there are a lot of online booking agencies—the hotel business center can be helpful with this.
- Most of the cities are safe and well managed.
- For city travel, you can hire taxis from the hotel. Keep the name card of the driver, just in case you lose something in the car, and do ask for a receipt. Again, avoid unmarked taxis.
- Try not to use public transportation, as they are crowded and not safe for international travelers.

HOTELS

- Four and five star hotels are up to international standards.
- Try to eat inside the hotel if you are on your own. You can dine outside if you with a group of people. At least one person should know the place. If you are not sure where you are going, get details from the hotel service.
- Try to keep your confidential documents, computer, and electronic devices with you all the time. You can keep your passport, money, and valuables in the safe in your hotel room.

LOW PROFILE

- Do not use your company name or brand on your bag or clothing. This can identify your employer.
- Do not tell other people your nationality and company name unless necessary.

TOURIST SPOTS

- Most of the tourist spots have English services.
- Avoid talking with strangers who volunteer to provide a guide service, especially a female.
- Avoid beggars at tourist spots. They travel in groups, so if you pay one of them, others will start bothering you.
- Make transportation arrangements in advance, as it can be hard to get a taxi.
- Use a local guide from the official agency or one arranged by your hotel.
- Beware of a typical tourist scam known as the "tea scam." At almost every tourist spot, you will find teahouses. They will invite you to sit down and have a tea tasting party. Of course, you will be told it's free. If you are thinking that it's not a bad idea to rest your feet and try some free tea, you have already fallen into their tea scam. They will find many different ways of persuading you to lose money. At the end of the day, you will be forced to pay for the tea you thought was free or to buy lots of overpriced tea from them.

RESTAURANTS, BARS, AND SHOPPING MARKETS

- Visit restaurants and bars that are hotel suggested.
- Be aware who is drinking with you or around you. Do not believe the people you meet in the bar and their excited stories nor feel any sympathy toward them.
- More and more often, the police get reports of violence against foreign citizens in bars and nightclubs over small issues such as bumping into each other or picking up girls.
- In most of the shops, you cannot bargain. You have to pay the price marked on the item. Some places, such as small shops, you can bargain with. You can start your bargaining from half price at least.

ROBBERY, BEGGARS, KIDNAPPING, AND HONEY TRAPS

- You need to pay attention while in public areas with a lot of people.
- Be careful if there is a motorbike. They may snatch your bag or cell phone away.
- Do not walk on the quiet street alone at night.

- Do not give money to the beggars near the hotel or on the street. They are professionals at getting money. Many pretend to be beggars.
- The men around the hotel who polish shoes will make trouble for you if you do not pay them well.
- Kidnappings have happened to foreign travelers in China. In most of these cases, they took the foreigner as a hostage to negotiate with the government officials.
- Local business partners who claimed to not have been paid have arranged for a wrong detention or kidnapping of their foreign visitor.
- Honey traps work in China because the traveler hopes to find true love or one night of luck. These stories normally end up in some kind of nightmare for the traveler. The key to these situations is to tell yourself you will never be that lucky. When a girl or a guy you don't know invites you to visit somewhere you don't know to continue the great night together, say "NO."

NATURAL DISASTER AND SOCIAL ORDER

- Earthquakes, floods, or other natural disasters do occur in China. Try to cooperate with the local hotel or local government. They will have good organization for this event.
- There can be some demonstrations in the cities in China, especially in a small city. Keep away from them. Do not watch them if you are nearby. Do not read or take the publications distributed by them.
- Some areas in China are more dangerous than others, such as Yunan where drug trafficking is very popular. Do not keep or carry anyone else's bag, keep your eyes on your bags, and always carry them around you so you will not be a blind contributor to the drug trafficking industry. Bear in mind, carrying 50 grams of heroin could be worth capital punishment in China.

ASSISTANCE AND POLICE

- Get a good local contact. The hotel desk can be very helpful if you have any questions.
- Call 110 (like 911 in the United States) for police support.
- Call 119 for fire.
- Call 112 for medical emergency transportation to the hospital. Your hotel will make that arrangement for you if you are in need.

RESOURCES

- You can book air tickets and hotel accommodations on http://english. ctrip.com—it is one of the best online services in China.

If you conducted an analysis of the context and situation (**see Section 1.1**) as part of your pre-trip preparations, then you will have information similar to that found in **Brittany Damora's** contribution. While traveling, the trick is to continuously monitor the situation and implement mitigating measures, as required by the realities of the location.

WORDS OF ADVICE FOR TRAVELERS TO PAPUA NEW GUINEA

BRITTANY DAMORA
POLITICAL RISK ANALYST

The main concern in Papua New Guinea is a lack of law and order. Crime, particularly in urban areas, is fairly rife and Port Moresby has been described as one of the world's most difficult cities to live in. Security concerns are less pronounced in rural areas, although the provision of law enforcement is even less evident.

Another notable concern is that infrastructure is poorly developed, a factor that is particularly evident in New Britain. Most roads are badly maintained and driving conditions are generally appalling. Medical facilities are also underdeveloped. If something were to go wrong, it may well be extremely difficult to find assistance.

The lack of jobs and the difficulty of policing urban areas in the 1980s encouraged the development of "rascal gangs" in Port Moresby and other urban centers. These gangs continue to pose a serious threat to Port Moresby residents, principally those who do not take adequate precautions. Random or opportunistic crime is also common, however. The situation is not unreservedly bleak. Public disorder in Port Moresby, for example, is rare. It is ordinarily safe to travel on main routes in Port Moresby during the day.

The absence or weakening of traditional village social controls is a major contributor to both urban and rural crime. Tribal fighting may break out without prior warning throughout the highlands. These fights are increasingly fuelled by the drug trade, and those taking part are constantly acquiring increasingly sophisticated weapons.

PRECAUTIONARY ADVICE FOR PORT MORESBY

- Papua New Guinea's principal airport is Jackson airport (POM), 11 kilometers (7 miles) from Port Moresby. Direct flights normally only arrive from Australia or Singapore. The national airline is Air Niugini (PX). There is little security at any of Papua New Guinea's smaller airports.
- Remain inside your vehicle and with your driver at all times during the journey from Jackson airport. Foreigners have been assaulted when traveling on buses, which are known as PMVs (Public Motor Vehicles). These buses are rarely properly maintained.

- Do not travel by rental car outside of Port Moresby at night, even on major highways.
- If you encounter a roadblock that does not appear to be manned by uniformed police, or notice a disturbance on the road ahead, turn around immediately if possible and seek an alternative route. Police vehicles are sky blue with a red insignia.
- Drivers involved in an accident may be threatened with violence. Get away and seek police assistance as soon as possible, particularly if you feel that you are in danger; crowds may form quickly and you and your vehicle may be stoned and burned.

An important component for feeling and being prepared involves having the right information so that you can make the appropriate decisions and actions. Call upon examples such as the next contribution to map out the type of information you need for your destination.

ENJOYABLE STREET LIFE AND SAFE DINING IN ROMANIA

DAN BELAI

SECURITY CONSULTANT, ATC SYSTEMS AND ASIS INTERNATIONAL ROMANIA CHAPTER CHAIR

During your visit, you should enjoy the Romanian tradition of eating out. But, as with other countries, there are a few things you should be aware of:

- Seek advice from your host or hotel receptionist for suitable dining venues and routes. Take normal precautions for hygiene. Poor hygiene is poor hygiene and good restaurants are clean.
- If you are uncomfortable eating alone, use room service or hotel eateries but it's not necessary to make yourself a prisoner of your hotel.
- Check service charges on bills; 10% is the norm although less scrupulous establishments will try to coerce you into paying more.
- Romania is mainly a cash economy, but in good shops/restaurants you can use your credit card. Do not allow transactions to be done outside of your sight.
- Wealth and perceived wealth make you a target. Avoid wearing expensive jewelry or showing accessories like your music player.
- Beware of street criminals, especially bag-snatchers, who specifically target diners leaving expensive restaurants. Your dining choice may indicate potential wealth.
- Street touts operate in Romania like in any other country. If it looks or sounds to good to be true, it probably is.

- Be wary of using ATMs on the street and avoid exchanging money at any location other than Cambios or banks. On trams and trains beware of pickpockets and bag-snatchers.
- Wear the right clothing. High-heeled shoes and shoes with little grip raise the risk of slips, trips, and falls and reduce your ability to move quickly should you need to.
- Avoid walking alone and be careful of short cuts, alleyways, and poorly lit streets, especially after dark.
- Walk with the shoulder strap of your bag across your chest. Carry wallets in your front trouser pocket.
- Look purposeful when you move about.

Street life in Romania is generally less rowdy than in other European countries like the United Kingdom. Dining and drinking outside of restaurants can be an enjoyable part of your experience in Romania. Just keep your wits about you.

In this book, there are several sections that are related to this contribution: You can enjoy such a situation with "peace of mind" because you know you are equipped with well-honed situational awareness skills **(see Sections 1.3 and 2.3)**. As street life and street crime, unfortunately, often go hand in hand, then you can read about mitigating measures for snatching, distracting, and other petty crimes **(see Section 2.16)**. And, in case one of your trips gives you the chance to be a night owl, you might want to consider the advice about enjoying the nightlife **(see Section 2.2)**.

2.5 ORGANIZATIONAL CONSIDERATIONS

Part of your organization's responsibilities to you is to understand the threats you might face **(RMF 1)** and your vulnerabilities **(RMF 2)**, and to take proactive mitigating measures to reduce the likelihood and impact **(RMF 3)**. Using cases from South Korea and Mexico, this section illustrates two duty-of-care scenarios in which proactive risk management plays an important role.

Anthony Hegarty's contribution is a good example of the interface between duty of care, duty of loyalty, and risk management: As such, it represents an argument for a holistic and proactive approach for steering your company toward successful ventures. In his piece, he explains how societal trends could result in certain Korean staff being vulnerable to external pressure to compromise company secrets. Hopefully, if your company is in a similar situation, then the context assessment that your company did or paid for highlighted this vulnerability that exposed the company to an insider threat. His contribution provides advice on how your company can proactively avoid any unnecessary risks to both the staff and the company.

To apply the lesson to your company's situation, you could ask: What about a staff member's position, access to valuable or critical information, access to cash, and so forth, makes them vulnerable to which threats? Your local cleaning staff should not have to face the terrible dilemma of feeling obligated to give a third cousin access to your offices at night while knowing this is at the expense of a valued employer—she knows that she will have a bad conscience if they are not caught or go to jail if they are. To plug security loopholes, an organization must implement a risk management process similar to the one mapped out in this book. Of course, the consideration of risks for an enterprise is broader than those discussed in this book, but the process is the same.

PERSONNEL'S VULNERABILITIES ARE THE COMPANY'S VULNERABILITIES: PROACTIVELY PROTECT YOUR INVESTMENT IN KOREA

ANTHONY HEGARTY
MANAGING DIRECTOR, DISCREET RISK & SECURITY MANAGEMENT SERVICES (HTTP://WWW.DISCREET-SERVICES.COM)

Unlike in many Asian countries, in Korea loyalty to the company has been largely replaced by a stronger emphasis on loyalty to one's family. It's something that has always existed, but with competitive threats from China and elsewhere, Koreans now concern themselves more with the future of their children. The difference between a university and a high school education is life changing because it essentially dictates whether someone will become a white-collar manager or blue-collar worker.

In an attempt to control wages and thus attract investment in Korea, there has been a mass culling of employees once they are around the age of 50. Perhaps another reason for forcing staff to retire early is because of the uncomfortable work environment that would be created when a younger person has authority over an older individual. This would conflict with Confucian teachings of seniority and respect for one's elders.

At retirement they will receive one month's wages for each year they have worked. Many struggle to find further employment, and if they do, it is at a far lower salary. These individuals generally have late middle or high school aged children. Traditionally, the company covers the costs of education right through university, which is not cheap in Korea. Thus, the burden of education fees lands on the now unemployed father.

Professional intelligence gatherers are attracted to these very vulnerable individuals during the period when they are most nervous about losing their jobs. At this time in their careers, they often are in a position to have access to critical corporate data.

Business people creating their own companies in Korea, or those seeking partnerships with Korean organizations, thus need to examine very carefully what data they hand over, what the demographic make-up of the organization they are seeking to work with is, and how they can mitigate this risks.

Training staff for life outside their former company is one such example. To a lesser extent, advice on how to set up one's own small business, or on how to invest retirement funds can be very reassuring to the employees. These are the types of solutions available to offset these threats, but these should be designed around the dynamics of the particular company.

Using an example of managing external threats, **Pablo Weisz's** contribution asserts that it is an organization's duty of care to have robust response measures and mechanisms in place. This, in turn requires a multi-prong approach aimed at proactively managing the safety and security of traveling staff. Policies, procedures, and preparations have to be operable before an incident. For both the affected individuals and the organization, being proactive versus reactive can make the difference between a minor security incident digressing into a major one or a major one spiraling into a nightmare.

ENSURING YOUR ORGANIZATION'S DUTY OF CARE: LESSONS FROM MEXICO ON THREAT ANALYSIS AND ROBUST RESPONSE

PABLO WEISZ

REGIONAL SECURITY MANAGER (THE AMERICAS), TRAVEL SECURITY SERVICES, A JOINT VENTURE BETWEEN CONTROL RISKS AND INTERNATIONAL SOS (HTTP://WWW.INTERNATIONALSOS.COM)

We live in an age of significant economic uncertainty that pushes companies to explore increasingly remote and unfamiliar environments. This is triggered by the drive to develop new markets and financial growth in an unstable global economy. While the financial crisis that began in 2008 reduced the overall volume of corporate travel, it has pushed businesses to operate in places previously deemed as less than safe. That means business travelers are faced with new types of risks for which they may be unprepared.

As travel to unfamiliar environments has grown, so have responsibilities borne by the companies exploring these areas. Moral responsibilities over the protection of travelers have been accompanied by a parallel rise of legal liabilities, holding businesses accountable for the safety and well-being of employees sent abroad. When an employee suffers an incident abroad, a company will likely be held accountable for the adequateness of its preventative measures and its reaction to the event. The organization can suffer significant legal and reputational damages that may lead to financial losses and negative affects on its bottom line.

I will share a story in which a client was faced with a trying security situation that could have turned into a crisis (some details have been modified to protect client confidentiality). The client used our advice, which allowed corporate decision makers to react accordingly; thus the company handled the situation adequately. The story shows that a swift and robust response to an incident affecting corporate travelers is crucial to meet all duty-of-care responsibilities.

The incident happened in Mexico, a country that is both "near" geographically to the United States (and, in many respects, also culturally) and at the same time "far," or unfamiliar due to its significantly challenging and changing security environment.

We'll start by succinctly stating what many, but not all, of those in charge of the well-being of traveling employees know about Mexico. It's no surprise that the country poses significant challenges to the visitor. Mexico has seen a rapid deterioration in its security environment, which is intricately tied to the rise of powerful organized crime syndicates and the ongoing "war on drugs" regionally espoused by the United States and locally implemented by the government of Felipe Calderon (2006–2012). The numbers are astounding: Since the beginning of Mr. Calderon's presidency in December 2006, drug-related homicides have sky-rocketed. The latest count stands at 50,000 deaths since this date. In 2011, 12,903 homicides related to drug violence were reported, an 11% increase from the previous year. And likewise, the year 2010 saw a 73% increase from 2009. This seems to point to a trend where homicides may be reaching a plateau. While these numbers put Mexico below the homicide rates of Honduras, El Salvador, Venezuela, and Brazil, the sheer speed at which the country reached these levels of violence is one of the main reasons for concern. Other crimes such as street robbery, carjacking, and kidnap for ransom have also grown exponentially.

It is kidnapping and its more common "cousin," express kidnapping, that often keep clients up at night. The crime, where the victim is taken for a period of no more than 24 hours and forced to withdraw as much money as possible from ATMs before being released, has affected travelers, albeit a relatively low number.

One late evening, an American client with operations in Mexico contacted my team to report a potential kidnapping. A female traveler, of Colombian descent but an American resident, failed to provide her daily report of well-being that same morning in the city of Chilpancingo, in the western coastal state of Guerrero. The company kept a stringent traveler tracking protocol in which travelers called in daily to state they were safe and sound. The traveler had also missed an important appointment with a local partner that day. Naturally, the client felt immediate action was necessary, but they were unsure as to what the next steps should be. They had valid concerns, including the need to contact local authorities, the prospect of receiving a call from the abductors, and the viability of initiating a search and rescue operation.

Our initial action was to run the client through the different scenarios that the traveler could be facing. With our understanding of the threats and vulnerabilities, we questioned the assertion that we were already dealing with a long-term kidnap for ransom case (in such situations, we would advise our clients about the involvement of "special risk" consultants and local authorities). We pointed out that much more likely alternatives could be disappearance "off the radar" situations. These included everything from a lost telephone scenario to a potential illness, preventing the traveler from making contact. That we could be dealing with an express kidnapping was a possibility, but we considered long-term kidnapping a much less likely scenario because that kind of kidnapping rarely affects foreign visitors. Having a starting point based on threat and vulnerability analysis allowed the client to prioritize their next steps, which ran the gamut from merely waiting for further communication from the traveler to activating their crisis management plan and convening their crisis management team.

As key players within the client's organization convened, my team followed internal standard operating procedures, which included alerting local providers of a potential request for assistance. Local providers included both security specialists, who could initiate a search for the individual, and medical professionals, who could prepare for the triaging of a potentially sick or injured person.

To our client's surprise, the traveler made positive telephone contact less than two hours later. Although the traveler was now safely back at her hotel, three men had taken her against her will as she attempted to retrieve money from an ATM across the street. The company's travel policy prohibits cash withdrawals from ATMs precisely because of this danger and it proved to be crucial for her abduction. The men forced the employee into their car and demanded she withdraw all money available to her through her four debit and credit cards in two different locations. Once she had completed these actions the traveler was released, unharmed and roughly 3 kilometers (2 miles) from her hotel. She had taken a taxi back, asking hotel management to pay the fare. Practicalities aside, she was rightfully extremely shaken and fearful for her safety.

My team's next actions were to first determine the nature and source of the threat and the type of aggressor we could be dealing with and provide immediate assistance to the employee to get her out of danger. Because the incident had all the markings of an express kidnapping, we deemed the likelihood of a subsequent incident affecting the individual as low. This was despite threats made by her captors that any communication with her company or authorities regarding the event would be met with repercussions. However, the potential for these threats to materialize could not be left to chance. Our assessment was that the next step was to assist in her safe and secure repatriation to the United States. Approval for this action was agreed upon with the client, but not before our team spoke to her to calm her nerves and contacted the hotel to have her transferred to another room. Our local providers were sent into action, discretely retrieving the individual, transporting her to Mexico City, and flying her back home, accompanied by a medical professional with crisis counseling expertise. Once the traveler had returned home safely, she was provided with counseling and leave until she considered herself to be well. She was also fully debriefed by her company to ensure her experience would not be repeated with another employee.

This incident of express kidnapping, compared to graver examples, had limited and reversible consequences for those affected. The traveler quickly recovered and felt well taken care of by her employer, as she was supported every step of the way. For the company, the incident represented a valuable learning experience in security management and duty of care. It prevented a crisis and emerged unscathed, as it suffered no additional legal or reputational repercussions. The client applied corrective measures in the following weeks that included mandatory travel security awareness training for employees before deployment to Mexico and countries with similar risk profiles. Nonessential travel to Guerrero was deferred until a threat assessment could be completed to prevent a recurrence.

This serves as a case study in exemplifying the correct handling of a company's duty of care to protect its traveling employees, including the following key lessons that other companies can apply:

- Creating actionable travel security policies that outline what the traveler should and should not do.
- Appropriate planning and training at all levels of the organization to have the structures in place to deal with an incident and prevent it from turning into a crisis.
- Assuming corporate responsibility for the training of employees in travel security.
- Communicating the potential risks faced at unfamiliar locations and higher threat environments.
- Instituting security protocols that allow for the tracking of and accounting for the location of every traveler.
- Deploying necessary medical and security resources in the event of an incident.
- Addressing immediate and long-term medical and security needs for the victim.
- Finally, assuming a central and decisive role in the duty of care to the traveling employee.

2.6 POLITICAL CONSIDERATIONS

According to International SOS's TravelTracker, 651,543 business travelers went to India in 2010, whereas the numbers jumped to 955,195 in 2011.[68] With its being an important work and tourist destination, this section uses India as a case study to go over some of the political considerations that you might also be able to apply to other locations. As mentioned in the corresponding section in **Chapter 1 (see Section 1.6),** if your circumstances warrant it, it could be worth your effort to analyze the political, economic, sociocultural, and technological factors (PEST). In **Abhimanyu Singh's** contribution, he concentrates on the first three factors.

INDIA'S UNIQUE BUSINESS RISKS

ABHIMANYU SINGH

HEAD OF RISK ADVISORY, RECON-RISK EVASION & CONTROL. LEAD ON APAC AND MENA REGIONS FOR THE INTERNATIONAL PROTECT AND PREPARE SECURITY OFFICE (IPPSO) BASED IN DELHI, INDIA. HE IS AN AUTHOR, SPEAKER AND CONSULTANT (HTTP://WWW.RECONADVISORY.COM).

The huge growth opportunities in India's emerging economy also contain unique risks due to the diversity of cultures, government structures, business practices, and legal framework. These risks are further compounded by a combination of a weak and unsupported enforcement arm, lack of infrastructure, and insufficient allocation of resources across the entire geographic expanse, leaving gaping holes that are exploited by vested interests.

Hence for businesses looking toward India, it is important to choose your partner with care: Do thorough due diligence and seek independent advice. Consider what kind of agreement you need—and don't give away too much information in advance of finalizing any agreement.

In India, businesses have little or no control over external events that can adversely affect the commercial viability of current and future business plans. When operating in India, be aware of the top political and social considerations:

- Potential slow-down in government decisions due to political instability both in the national and regional/state/provincial political scene
- Adverse changes or unpredictability on foreign investment, import, ownership, pricing, or tax issues
- Labor unrest and industrial action
- Disruption of normal business due to social and political unrest
- Corruption and bureaucratic inefficiency
- Unexpected delays and cost-overruns due to overlapping governmental jurisdiction
- Cultural problems, delays, or legal disputes due to local partners and suppliers
- Fluctuation in interest, inflation, and currency rates

India is a huge country where risks vary from region to region and city to city, depending upon the situations and local customs. Some of the issues can be broadly categorized as geopolitical, societal, and environmental issues. It is always better to take a good in-country briefing from people who have traveled to India before and also connect with a reputed risk management company to get travel advisories. Travelers are advised to ensure their insurance cover illnesses, accidents abroad, and social/political unrest.

In "Spotlight on India: Navigating the Barriers" available on the Dialogues on Duty of Care website, a survey of 101 webinar attendees asked the question, "Which of the following considerations will most affect your organization's approach to planning international business travel or expatriate assignments to India in the near future?," with the responses:

- Health risks (diseases, level of health care, etc.): 41%
- Political corruption/red tape—rapidly evolving policy/rules and regulations: 34%
- Gaps between business demand and technological availability: 15%
- Infrastructure issues (traffic, pollution, etc.): 10%[69]

This information touches upon the political, sociocultural, and technological factors of the PEST model.

For the Asia-Pacific region, the "Lloyd's Risk Index, 2011" found that on a scale where 10 is the highest, the 500 companies surveyed scored political considerations as a 6.1 on the priority scale and 6.8 on the preparedness scale.[70] Critical questions you can ask include: Has your organization correctly prioritized political considerations for the work you do and how can it improve its preparedness, if that is required?

One option for you is to SWOT the PEST model: You can see your personal strengths and weaknesses, and external opportunities and threats (SWOT) in light of the information that you gathered from the PEST model. Use any insights to update your mitigation measures. Take **"India's Unique Business Risks"** as an example, and let's say you are concerned about the possibility of any eventual cultural disputes turning into a legal challenge: Options available to you include inviting a few Indian staff to the company's European headquarters to assist with developing and implementing cultural awareness training or you could have external consultants do an introductory briefing before expatriate staff head abroad and then stage a series of cultural exchanges at the workplace. Essentially, by analyzing political considerations you can create more options and make better decisions.

2.7 CULTURAL CONSIDERATIONS

"To my friends, anything: To my enemies, the rigors of the law" is a popular saying that holds true for hierarchical societies. As it turns out, 90% of the world's population lives in such societies. Accordingly, after laying out a conceptual framework with comparative examples, **Fernando Lanzer Pereira de Souza's** contribution gives advice to travelers destined for hierarchical societies.

For smoother intercultural relations, you can apply the KSAB model of knowledge, skills, attitudes, and behavior **(see Section 1.3)**. You can be knowledgeable about conceptual frameworks that you find useful, be skilled through training before your trip and observation of key areas of culture while you travel, have a respectful attitude when interacting with people, and behave in a way that is open to different cultural inputs.

At work, you can use your cultural insights to ensure successful operations: Could an oversight result in lunch from the office canteen sometimes including beef, which your Hindu staff cannot eat? Could rules that staff cannot take unscheduled personal time off during working hours mean that Muslim employees do not have the opportunity to pray, especially on Fridays? Once you are aware of the potential missteps **(RMF 1 and 2)**, you can start planning and implementing problem-solving measures **(RMF 3)**.

TAKE OFF YOUR CULTURAL GLASSES TO SEE DOLPHINS FROM SHARKS

FERNANDO LANZER PEREIRA DE SOUZA
MANAGEMENT CONSULTANT, EXECUTIVE COACH, AND INTERNATIONAL TRAINER IN CROSS-CULTURAL MANAGEMENT (HTTP://WWW.LCOPARTNERS.COM)

We all develop starting in early childhood a "culture bias": what we perceive as similar to our own cultural values, we consider to be "good" or "right"; whatever we perceive to be different from our own cultural values, we consider to be "bad" or "wrong."

We look at the world through colored spectacles or sunglasses, which distort our perception. We see everything through these tinted sunglasses, and each culture has its own biased vision, shared by members of that culture. This has been demonstrated repeatedly in research.

TAKE OFF YOUR GLASSES

Understanding a bit about the culture and adjusting your expectations may help you mitigate "culture clashes" when you face security issues, or in daily situations, for that matter. When traveling, in order to understand the world outside of your own culture, you first need to be aware of your own cultural bias. You need to be aware of your glasses and take them off, in order to see other cultures as they really are.

Most of the world's people are living in hierarchical and collectivistic societies, accounting for 90% of the world's population. In collectivistic cultures, people belong to groups who take care of them in exchange for their loyalty. The law is applied differently, depending on which groups you belong to.

Anglo-Saxons, Germanics, Dutch, and Scandinavians are all "egalitarian" cultures. They value low "power distance" and a reasonably flat hierarchical structure in society, where everyone has a similar amount of power, since all persons are basically equal. These "egalitarian" cultures are also "individualistic" (I) rather than "collectivistic"; people value individual responsibility and the universal application of the law. Only Northern Europe and North America are egalitarian and individualistic (E+I). Therefore, if you are not destined for one of these locations, you are arriving in a hierarchical and collectivistic culture (H+C).

The thing to bear in mind is that in E+I cultures, control and discipline tend to come from within each individual (including respect for the law). In H+C cultures, control and discipline are expected to be enforced from outside, by figures of authority who have that responsibility. For instance, in E+I cultures people tend to observe the law whether there is a policeman in the vicinity or not; in H+C cultures the law is observed when the police are around, but not necessarily when there are no police in sight.

With such different cultures, it's understandable that misgivings and aggravations arise. For example, the "power distance" within hierarchical cultures is quite annoying for people who come from egalitarian societies, because it goes against values they have learned since childhood. It seems morally wrong to display such authoritarian behavior on one side, and such submissive behavior on the complementary side of authority.

On the other hand, people from H+C cultures tend to be annoyed when they see others from egalitarian cultures "talking back" at them, expressing opinions in a way that, for them, shows "lack of respect."

Actually, there is no "right" or "wrong" when it come to culture, in spite of our feelings: another culture is just "different." In my own life, I've had to get used to different cultures—I'm a Brazilian, an H+C culture, and I have lived in the United States and in The Netherlands, both E+I countries. Plus, I travel extensively because I have clients in 40 countries. I start with understanding my own cultural glasses and biases. And when I travel, I go with an open mind, ask a lot of short, open questions, listen extensively, and emphasize relationships. I consider these to be key behaviors in seeking to understand different cultures.

TRAVELING TO HIERARCHICAL CULTURES

No matter what your cultural background is, you should be aware of the cultural aspects of the places you will visit. Since most countries are hierarchical/collectivistic, I am going to focus on those.

Normally, when you are strolling down the street, you do not want to attract attention. But if you need to get assistance from security professionals, you need to use the power distance dimension in your favor. If you want to be respected by security officials in hierarchical countries, you need to look like a VIP and behave like one. If you go into a police station dressed like a slob, you will be treated like one. If you come in dressed in a suit and tie, you will be treated like a VIP. In hierarchical countries, appearance counts (a lot). Position yourself as the figure of authority, demanding service in a confident, authoritarian way. State how outraged you are that some disrespectful individual has dared to commit a crime against you. Assert that you expect them to do whatever is necessary to assist you, as the important person you are.

Most hierarchical cultures are also collectivistic. This means that the law is applied differently, depending on who your friends are, to which groups you belong, and how powerful they are. If you need assistance from security officials, try to contact them accompanied by a local friend, preferably someone who is perceived to have power of some sort; and dress up, so you also look important.

This is summarized by a popular saying: "To my friends, anything; to my enemies, the rigors of the law."

"TO MY FRIENDS, ANYTHING"

I was recently in Nairobi and I took a taxi to one of the slums outside the city. I had a large suitcase full of donations for an NGO operating there and I was going to meet my daughter at an intersection, since the NGO operated from a shack in a narrow alley, inaccessible by car.

As the cab drove there for almost an hour, we chatted along the way and I told him why I was going there, plus we swapped the stories of our lives. When we got to the intersection and met my daughter, who was there waiting, he refused to leave us on our own.

"You are not going to carry that heavy suitcase full of stuff all the way through that alley to the middle of the slum! Let me help you. There must be another way to at least get closer to the NGO shack. I won't charge you."

Eventually we made a long way around the slum and found an entrance that the car could take to a clearing some 50 meters (160 feet) from our final destination. He helped us carry the suitcase inside the shack and met the local NGO staff.

My point here is that developing a relationship by chatting with the local people will help you to be regarded as "part of their group," at least temporarily—although not as a "full member" (never assume that) but as a "guest member." They will protect you, without your asking, as they protect each other in the groups they belong to.

"TO MY ENEMIES, THE RIGORS OF THE LAW"

A couple of years ago, a Brazilian woman in her forties was refused her fourth whisky on a flight from the United States to Brazil on an American carrier. She made a quarrel of it and was swiftly handcuffed to her seat by a couple of U.S. Marshals who were on the flight.

Arriving in Brazil, the Marshals proceeded to turn her over to local authorities. She revealed in outrage that she was the wife of a prominent judge and had never been so badly treated in her entire life. In the ensuing discussion, the Brazilian Federal Police agents arrested the American Marshals for abusing their authority and freed the lady.

The point here is that she was used to getting special treatment in a hierarchical, collectivistic society. In her mind, she was not abusing her privileges. To the American flight attendants and Marshals, her behavior was unacceptable, and they were doing their duty.

The American Marshals were probably thinking, "Who do you think you are, to behave in this way, disrespecting rules and disturbing other passengers?!" The Brazilian lady was probably thinking, "Do you know who you are talking to?! You can't treat me this way, disrespecting my status as the wife of a judge!"

Yet once they were on the ground, local cultural values prevailed. That was no way to treat a privileged member of the elite (in the minds of the Brazilian Federal Police agents). Security officers will behave differently in different places, consistent with their culture. Do not expect otherwise.

SHARKS AND DOLPHINS

The challenge for a foreigner, of course, is being able to "read" people and situations so that you can differentiate "sharks" from "dolphins." "Dolphins" will help you and protect you, while "sharks" will take advantage and harm you. They look alike, are roughly the same size with large fins on their tails, and swim close to the surface, yet they are very different.

People who have been brought up in collectivistic societies have learned to read situations, contexts, and the nonverbal signs sent by other people. It comes naturally to them by the time they are adults. Contrarily, people brought up in individualistic societies (the ones previously mentioned) are more focused on content rather than context. They often miss the subtle signs that differentiate "sharks" from "dolphins." Be aware of your limitations and engage the assistance of a trusted local before accepting the invitation to go out for a swim with a large marine animal.

Robert's contribution about killing a pig, which is highly important in Papua New Guinea's society, illustrates how proper handling of a potentially volatile situation enabled him to continue using that stretch of highway throughout his stay. Having cultural awareness in his toolkit insured his personal safety and allowed his organization to continue working in the area.

DON'T HIT A PIG IN PAPUA NEW GUINEA

ROBERT
EDUCATIONAL PROJECT FACILITATOR

For my work as a project facilitator in Papua New Guinea, I frequently drove the Highlands Highway to and from the airport in the next province—a drive that is equally stunning as it is exciting. Poor road conditions combined with anything from heavy traffic to drying coffee beans kept you alert during the full two and a half hours. During one of these trips, a couple of year-old pigs suddenly crossed the road. I didn't drive fast, but couldn't avoid running over the last one. When you've lived in Papua New Guinea (PNG) for long enough, this situation rings two alarm bells.

First, there is the generic warning about traffic accidents. Groups of bystanders tend to get excited fairly quickly in these kinds of situations and often turn violent some way or the other. Second, there is the involvement of a pig: not so much a sacred animal in the sense we would see it, but certainly a pivotal element in any of the numerous ceremonies that mark Papua New Guineans' lives, groups, or organizations. They are also the clearest indicator of someone's wealth. Its importance for PNG society cannot be overestimated, and I just killed one!

My colleague and I quickly agreed that we should not stop, so we drove on, apparently unseen. But we knew the bush has eyes and news travels quickly. Even without the immediate danger of the inflamed crowd, compensation would be demanded somehow if the owners found out our or our organization's identity. This in itself could have created intimidating situations at a later point.

Upon arriving at the airport, we picked up our passenger; an expat with years of experience working in PNG. We made contact with a local NGO who had recently implemented preventative health projects in that particular area. One of their local staff agreed to come along in order to find the owners and to mediate in the negotiations for compensation. When we were nearly there, we were joined by a local magistrate who came in handy as a local agent of the national judiciary system. Approaching the location where the pig was hit, we drove slowly enough to make sure that we would have been recognized. After driving up and down a couple of times, we had to conclude that we were not recognized and assumed we hadn't been seen in the first place when the collision happened. For me, this was enough as it ensured me safe passage for my travels along this stretch of highway.

A claim, directed to my organization's main office, was made after a few months and subsequently paid. I have not been stopped in that area by anyone since.

If you sense a situation is deteriorating due to a cultural misunderstanding, you can try employing the advice from the following contribution.

DEESCALATE CULTURAL MISUNDERSTANDINGS: LISTEN ACTIVELY, HIGHLIGHT AGREEMENTS, AND RESPECTFULLY STATE YOUR MEANING

TANYA SPENCER

GLOBAL TRAVEL SECURITY AND CRISIS MANAGEMENT SPECIALIST, TRAININGSOLUTIONS (HTTP://WWW.TRAININGSOLUTIONS.DK)

In my experience as a conflict resolution trainer working volatile intercultural, interethnic, and interreligious conflicts, I found that while there are loads of models and frameworks, the best tactic for deescalating interpersonal conflicts simply involves:

- Actively listening to the person—hear his or her underlying needs, values, assumptions, and motivations. Listen without commenting too much and make sure your interruptions are mainly engaging questions.
- Highlighting agreements—what about what they specifically said, the general circumstances, or your own situation can be positively discussed?
- Making clear points—while having a respectful attitude and an attitude that demands respect, you can discuss your side of the issues. That said, in some heated circumstances, you might opt to not confer inflammatory opinions.

I've used this myself on several occasions. Once in Kosovo, before the NATO war but with war raging in other parts of former Yugoslavia, I was taking pictures of a public library, and a suited man in his fifties aggressively approached me. I responded in broken Serbian but he quickly switched to English and was angry with me about American bombs hitting Serbian targets in Bosnia: Then, he suddenly began hitting my camera! Working for peace organizations meant I had a negligible income and the camera was the most expensive thing I owned. So, firmly I told him he better stop hitting my camera or I would have to fight him back. I meant it. And more calmly, I said that he could hit me but not my camera: In any case, it was better that we talked.

I explained that I agreed with him about the regrettable waste of life caused by the war—for me, all the war-related loss of life was unnecessary. I had held various jobs in the region, so at that point I had a fairly good understanding of the people and politics. I told him that I had met with all sides: Then, I named several national and local Serbian politicians and church leaders. In my job, I had even met with representatives of the holy Patriarch of Serbia so it helped the situation when I told him about the icon of the Virgin Mary that was given to me as a gift.

When he threatened to take me to the police, I said that would be fine. (The irony was that I knew I was under police surveillance because the day before I had been interrogated by the secret police, technically due to a visa issue but actually because of my human rights work. The only reason I wasn't deported was because I was scheduled to leave in two days.) When he said that I couldn't take pictures, I asserted the library was a public building that was architecturally interesting. When he bemoaned the war, I agreed with him. We ended up shaking hands and he went his own way. But, unfortunately, I never took the picture—my hands weren't steady enough after *that* experience even though by standing my ground, listening, and agreeing the overall confrontation ended positively.

Regarding the skill of active listening, the website Rethinking Learning has a practical and recommended article entitled "10 Tips for Active Listening."[71] The Power to Change Student website also has a list of 10 pieces of good advice: Its "10 Tips for Effective & Active Listening Skills"[72] article focuses on body language and physical aspects, whereas the previous one actually concentrates more on the techniques needed to develop and implement active listening skills.

2.8 MEDICAL CONSIDERATIONS

The advice in **Leanne Olson's** contribution covers a plethora of medical considerations that you may need to be aware of while abroad. As with security, knowing how to prevent and react appropriately to medical situations will potentially save you a lot of headaches, belly aches, or other aches and pains. **Andreas Poppius's** contribution **"Sunstroke in Syria"** is integrated into the text as an example of how not taking basic measures can negatively affect your trip. Most of the proffered information is to help you identify and treat the common health issues travelers face. That said, in serious or prolonged cases, you are always recommended to seek professional assistance, preferably while you are still in your destination, because some local illnesses can be quickly treated there yet misdiagnosed in places unfamiliar to it. Follow-up care and second opinions can always be administered in your home country.

HEALTH CARE CAN MAKE OR BREAK A TRIP

LEANNE OLSON

CHARGE NURSE IN THE PEDIATRIC EMERGENCY DEPARTMENT AT THE CHILDREN'S HOSPITAL OF EASTERN ONTARIO AND A FORMER NURSE WITH INTERNATIONAL AID ORGANIZATIONS

There are many simple steps that you can take to ensure your well-being. Hydration and sanitation are two of the most essential areas where you should make an effort to prevent difficulties. Most of the diseases that visitors and workers catch when overseas are waterborne or water-related.

That said, maintaining your health while abroad can be a challenge for a number of reasons. Adapting to a completely different climate can be difficult, be it intense heat, cold, rain, or desert. The type and availability of food mean your usual diet may be completely altered. Limited water may be difficult to adjust to. Hygiene practices may be less than ideal, and sanitation measures far from what you're used to. Not to mention, you may be subject to any number of tropical diseases and water-related illnesses that you have not encountered before. Plus living in very different and sometimes difficult circumstances can lead to added stress.

There is no single correct way to deal with all these changes. You are responsible for maintaining as high a standard as possible for your own health and well-being. The important thing is to allow yourself time to adjust to the changes working overseas brings and don't hopelessly use energy on the things you have no power to change. And there will be many things you can't change. If you can't get rid of the mosquitoes, use a net and bug spray. If you can't do much about the local diet, supplement it with tinned goods, lots of spices, and try some recipe exchanges with colleagues. If you can only get poor quality beer, you may at least be able to refrigerate it.

Prevention is the best way to deal with your health issues overseas. On a basic level, this means getting all your vaccines, taking your malaria prophylaxis regularly, and following measures to prevent common diarrheal diseases. This can be done by staying away from raw foods and salads, ensuring people who are preparing your meals are trained in hand-washing techniques, and washing your hands before you touch food. Those are the basics. There's more advice below.

HYDRATION

It is essential that during your journey, you are adequately hydrated. Men and women should void straw colored urine around eight times per day. If your urine is dark, cloudy and smells strong, you may be dehydrated and/or have an infection. Thirst is a poor indicator of hydration because you are already dehydrated if you feel thirsty. Usual signs apart from thirst are dry lips and a white coated tongue. There must be an adequate supply of clean drinking water for the duration of your visit. It is essential to take an adequate supply of oral rehydration solution (ORS) sachets with you. This will allow you to replace electrolytes lost through diarrhea, sickness, and general dehydration through being in hot or high altitude environments. To make ORS, take one liter of clean water, add eight teaspoons of sugar, one teaspoon/a good pinch of salt, and mix until it is dissolved. Sips of room temperature ORS of approximately 200 mL per hour or up to 1–2 liters per day can resolve dehydration.

SUNSTROKE IN SYRIA

ANDREAS POPPIUS

SECURITY CONSULTANT, ADVENTURE TRAVELER, AND
FORMER SENIOR SECURITY OFFICER/SWEDISH EMBASSY
KABUL, AFGHANISTAN (HTTP://WWW.U3KOMPETENS.SE)

Some years back I spent a summer studying and traveling in Syria. During a one-day travel to Palmyra from Damascus, I got sunstroke. In the summertime, temperature in the desert can reach at least 45°C (113°F), and this time was no exception.

Due to poor planning, I did not bring enough water and fluid replacement (and I was not fully acclimated to the climate, since I arrived in Syria from Sweden a week and a half before this trip) but managed to complete the trip. When back in Damascus, I got really ill—fever, ague, and diarrhea. By mixing what fluid replacement I had left with water (drinking about 12 liters a day), combined with diarrhea medicine and staying in bed between moist towels, I managed to get well after four to five days. But it was still a complete waste of time.

Make sure when you are traveling in hot climate environments to always:

- Acclimatize to the climate step by step—don't rush and don't push yourself into physical challenges that you are not up to. Acclimatization to climate can take up to two or three weeks—it varies for each individual.
- Bring a sufficient amount of clean water and fluid replacement (at least salt and sugar) and don't be afraid to drink—a lot. Up to six or eight liters a day in the beginning is not unusual.
- Study your destination's most common health problems and make sure to cover them with vaccine, medicine, and other medical supplies. Don't forget to check if the medicines you intend to bring with you are legal in your destination and/or any other place you travel to or through.
- Use sun block; wear a hat with a brim, sunglasses, and loosely fitted cotton clothing.
- If you have any health conditions, ask your physician before traveling and make sure that your travel insurance covers any medical emergency—both local treatment as well as medical evacuation if necessary.

If bottled water is available, it is advisable to drink that, ensuring that the seal has not been broken and it has not expired. In hot countries, people tend to drastically underestimate the amount of fluid required per day. It is not unusual to require 5–6 liters of fluid when the temperature is above 35°C (95°F). Feelings of weakness, dizziness, fatigue, and headache can all be symptoms of early dehydration. Canned juice and soda are safe sources for extra fluids. It is essential to emphasize how important it is to have adequate hydration while overseas.

If water is sufficiently available but it is not clean, then take steps to make it so. During a humanitarian mission to South Sudan by the author, all of the water for the clinics, feeding center, and compound was taken from a muddy river. The water was boiled for ten minutes. After cooling, it was filtered through a guinea-worm net and chlorinated. Not one single episode of diarrhea was recorded.

Water boils at lower temperatures at altitude, so allow it to boil for longer. Use a purification tablet. If you are in an area where the *Giardia* protozoa is present, it is necessary to take these steps and to use iodine. Iodine is light sensitive, so keep it in a dark bottle or in dark conditions. Pregnant women, women over fifty years old, anyone on lithium, or anyone with an allergy to iodine should not use it, but instead use a special filter. Iodine tastes disgusting, so you may wish to add some juice or flavor.

SANITATION

Most diseases that people catch while working overseas are waterborne or water-related (for example, contaminated food or water), so ensuring adequate water and good sanitation is very important. Do not assume that essential items such as soap and toilet paper can be found locally, and often local facilities do not keep restrooms stocked. Wash and dry your hands thoroughly after using the toilet or latrine.

Sanitation systems can also vary tremendously depending on where you are. You may have a citywide flush toilet system that makes one's life very easy. If not, you may end up with a septic system to deal with, or a pit latrine. If you are staying in a hotel and the sanitation is not of a reasonable standard, insist that the toilet is cleaned with bleach.

HYGIENE

Make sure if you are staying in a hotel that you choose the cleanest possible (which is not always the one with the most stars to its name). Be assertive if you feel that more can be done to ensure cleanliness.

Most people working overseas for extended periods end up living in a compound with their colleagues. This means that often cooks and cleaners are hired locally to care for the team and the living quarters. These employees require training in hand hygiene, food hygiene, and preparation. All countries have their own cultural and belief systems when it comes to hygiene standards, but you have to ensure that your own hygiene standards are met. The most important thing you can do is train your staff in good hand-washing techniques and appropriate food hygiene. This includes providing them with sufficient quantity and quality of water, cleaning supplies, soap, buckets, brooms, washbasins, cooking utensils, and other essential items that enable them to do their jobs.

Particularly if you will live in the Tropics, sheets should be changed regularly and the mattress left in the midday sun for a few hours every month to prevent bed bugs and other insects from making it their home. In some places, particularly in Western and sub-Saharan Africa, washed clothes should be ironed after they have dried in the sun. This is because tumbu flies tend to lay eggs that can hatch in one's skin unless the clothes have been ironed, killing the eggs. You might feel strange ironing your undergarments (or asking someone else to do it) but you will feel worse as an incubator for tumbu flies! Ask your local contacts about pests and other health issues. This also applies for short-term visits.

SIMPLE WOUNDS

If you have a cut or scratch that starts to appear red and infected, address it immediately and do not wait for things to get worse. Access to medical care in some places can be difficult, if not impossible. If there is a medical organization in the area with qualified staff, it would do you well to pay a visit if you develop a medical condition that you think requires care.

FOOD AND NUTRITION

It may sound simple, but basic nutrition and adequate food is often overlooked in the field. For example, it is seriously not advisable to live for prolonged periods on a diet high in carbohydrates and very low in nutrients, vitamins, and protein. It is important to include a wide variety of food from a number of sources to provide you with adequate nutrition. Fruits and vegetables may be hard to come by, depending on where you are, so a variety of canned items should be considered. Proteins such as meat, beans, and legumes are necessary in one's diet. Avoid salads and raw foods unless you are certain they've been washed in a weak chlorine solution and are well cleaned. It is strongly advised to cook your vegetables and to peel your fruit. Ensure that any meat or seafood products are thoroughly cooked. The risk of parasites from undercooked meats is quite high.

It is also advised that during illness, especially bouts of diarrhea, it is important to continue with as regular eating habits as possible. You may need to substitute soup and bread for your normal intake for a time, but as soon as you have an appetite, it is important to try to resume regular eating habits.

At least with the many NGO, UN, or ICRC staff that we know, quite a lot of them lose weight in the field for negative reasons such as pressures of work, not taking time to make food when fast food is not available, stress, and so forth. However, a weight loss of 7–10 kg (15–22 lb) over a six-month period of time is probably too much. This depends, of course, on your starting weight.

Security, weather, and transport problems can all lead to a rupture of supplies, and planning ahead should be a crucial part for being able to continue your work. Depending on your situation, it would also be wise to stock up on basic supplies of food and water, enough to last the team several days/weeks if necessary. Even if you are not responsible for the supplies, you could ask about them as part of your own emergency planning and preparations.

If you are responsible for the supplies by one degree or another, then consider the climate when ensuring you have adequate storage for food and water. This means having a good refrigerator with a reliable power supply. If the power supply is not continuous, then get a generator. Be aware that a refrigerator is no longer safe storage for temperature-sensitive foods if the temperature is not maintained at 2–8°C (35–45°F). For other food, make sure you have lockable storage to keep out pests, bugs, and mice. For many reasons, canned foods are a good option, though remember to monitor the expiration dates.

PRESCRIPTION MEDICINES

In most cases, you should carry enough prescription medicines to last for the duration of your trip plus an extra amount in case of any unexpected delays. If you do need to refill your prescription or buy over-the-counter medicines, be aware that drugs with similar names can actually be different medicines. The "International Drug Names Database," with information from 185 countries, can assist you with avoiding a mistake.*

SHELTER

Whether you are living in a luxury house or a mud hut, the need for a clean and managed household remains the same. Regular cleaning of the house and regular washing of linens and clothing can really keep infestations at bay. Take proactive steps for the actual health risks such as using mosquito nets and fumigating with insecticides, laying out rattraps or poison for pests, and keeping the grass cut and allowing good drainage of pooling of water that breeds mosquitoes.

Always check with your national staff in regards to what are safe or unsafe practices, as they tend to know a great deal. If you find yourself in Chad in a house with a new thatch roof, for example, and you get severe itching caused by small mites, then by gaining local knowledge you would know to prevent this by covering the inside of the house with a local material, or you could live with it for a couple of weeks until the thatch settles. (This is a possibility if you packed an anti-itching product or got a hold of a good local option.)

STRESS

As for stress management, individuals need to find their own successful techniques for handling stress. A good diet, regular exercise, and time out to read or see a movie can all help. These moments away from a hectic schedule are really important for one's mental and physical health and should not be ignored regardless of how "busy" you find yourself to be.

---

* "International Drug Names Database," Drugs.com. ND. http://www.drugs.com/international.

DRUGS AND ALCOHOL

It is strongly advised to stay away from illicit drug use, as consequences in some countries can be legally severe. Use of alcohol or any drugs should be moderate. Overuse tends to cause more stress than it relieves.

SEXUAL HEALTH

Maintaining good sexual health practices while traveling or working abroad is also part of being responsible for your health and well-being. Approach any new relationship with caution, especially in areas where HIV/AIDS is prevalent. Keep in mind that many people do not know their HIV/AIDS status, and treatment probably remains out of reach for large numbers of the population (Figure 2.4).

Your organization may well have a code of conduct in regards to fraternizing with national staff, but whether they do or not, consider carefully the consequences of what is likely to be a short-term relationship and what both parties stand to gain or lose. Local customs and laws need to be considered. Talk about these issues with your new partner. This is different than the serious ethical and legal consequences caused by a sexual relationship with a stakeholder in your project. Those cases often have wide-reaching ramifications, such as female staff being raped as a revenge for the inappropriate conduct of male staff. It's important to know that prostitution is illegal in most countries. Even though that leaves few options for a sex life when traveling or working overseas, the best advice is if in doubt, do not do it.

FIGURE 2.4   Courtesy of Peter Steudtner/www.panphotos.org.

If you are or become sexually active, it would be strongly advised to use preventative measures, especially a condom, which is the only safe method to prevent HIV/AIDS transmission as well as a number of sexually transmitted infections. Unless you are sexually active with a known partner, it cannot be stressed enough that the risks of unprotected sex, particularly in certain countries, can be lethal. Only practice safe sex.

SEXUAL VIOLENCE

From a physical health perspective, the most important thing you can do after sexual violence is to get medically checked out by a reputable medical officer, and start on the HIV prophylaxis as soon as possible. Again, since most people do not know their status and the risk may be high, you have a 72-hour window in which to begin taking HIV PEP (post-exposure prophylaxis). If this cannot be accomplished in the country where you are, evacuation should be considered.

RETURNING HOME

When you get back from a prolonged trip, a medical check-up may be required by your organization, but even if not, it is advisable to check out any health concerns that you may have.

CONCLUSION

Taking care of oneself while working overseas can be difficult and challenging, and it requires some time and attention. Putting standards and systems in place that keep your living quarters and nutritional needs in good standing can cut down on illnesses and help maintain a decent quality of life. This is not a luxury. Your employer will benefit a lot more from you if you are healthy than if you spend much of your time sick in bed. Most importantly, you need to enjoy your new experience and not let yourself be overwhelmed with the details of your work. Take time for yourself as you need it and find activities that give you pleasure. Try to eat, sleep, and exercise regularly. It is up to you to take care of yourself, and if you are feeling that you can't, seek help and support. Working overseas should be a good adventure, and to meet the challenges instead of being overwhelmed by them, you need to be healthy.

To expand upon some of the topics listed above, you can refer to **"First Aid Knowledge Saves Lives: What to Do at the Scene of a Car Accident and Other Medical Emergencies"** in the **Medical Emergencies** section **(see Section 3.8)**. Stress and the related topic of fear are orientated in the **Well-Being** sections **(see Sections 1.17 and 2.17)**. The subject of sexual violence is covered in **Chapter 3 (see Section 3.4)**.

2.9   INSURANCE

The corresponding **Insurance** section in **Chapter 1 (see Section 1.9)** emphasized the importance of obtaining insurance before the start of your trip. But it
is possible to buy a new policy or extend your existing one while you are abroad.
That said, not all insurance companies offer policies after a trip has started.
World Nomad is one company that has such an option.[73] Most insurance companies do allow for extensions but they may set limits on how many times this can
be done.

On the Travel Insurance Review website, you can read the article "Can You Buy
Travel Insurance after Your Vacation Has Begun?"[74]

2.10   PERSONAL BELONGINGS AND DOCUMENTS

Many of the measures for protecting your belongings and documents actually should
be put in place before you depart on your journey **(see Section 1.10)**. While traveling, the key is to remember to use the right advice at the right times. For example,
it is recommended that you wear a "secret stash" of reserve money and essentials:
This should be done from the time you leave home **(see Section 1.10)**. And perhaps
you should install an encryption program on your laptop **(see Section 1.11)**. And you
should be particularly diligent with your belongings as you pass through the various
airport security checks **(see Section 2.13)**.

To supplement the advice from other relevant sections of the book, this section
offers additional measures to safeguard your personal belongings and documents
that you can easily integrate into your travel habits.

2.10.1   WALLETS AND PURSES

The best way to carry a wallet in your pants is in the front pocket; furthermore,
a rubber band around it is an annoyance for would be thieves and it slows them
down. The front pocket of your coat, however, is an easy target. For readers who
use "mobile wallets," or are planning to, according to the article "Mobile Wallet
Pickpocket Risks Low" on the ZD Net Asia website, you should maintain similar
safeguards as for a traditional wallet: In addition, consider using a shielded holder for
your near-field communication (NFC) enabled device and checking that the service
provider does not store sensitive data on the device.[75] That said, as the technology
spreads, criminals will be motivated to find ways to profit from it fraudulently, so
it is advisable that you continuously keep abreast of what is on the threat horizon.

Preferably pick a purse with a flap and an inner zipper or closure. Especially for
crowded places, avoid drawstring purses, as these are the easiest to rob. Whichever
type of purse or bag you carry, it should be closed. Keep a hand or arm in contact with your purse or laptop bag, preferably on the front part of your body. Some
experts say not to wear the strap across your chest because you could get hurt if
someone did mug you. However, others recommend wearing it across the chest with
your hand draped across it.

POTS OF GOLD: WHAT A PICKPOCKET
THINKS OF WOMEN'S PURSES

TANYA SPENCER
GLOBAL TRAVEL SECURITY AND CRISIS MANAGEMENT
SPECIALIST AND COAUTHOR OF TRAVEL WISELY: A PERSONAL
SECURITY GUIDE FOR WOMEN TRAVELERS *(IN DANISH ONLY),*
TRAININGSOLUTIONS (HTTP://WWW.TRAININGSOLUTIONS.DK)

During my research for a travel security book for Danish women, *Rejs Sikkert,*
I interviewed a former pickpocket. He said he preferred small designer purses
because they were guaranteed to have valuables. Many women assume these
cute little purses are safe because they carry it under their armpit. But, in
reality, many women wear them to the back of arm, leaving these little "pots
of gold" exposed. Large purses were less desirable because they were often
full of junk. His method for large purses was to wait until they were on the
ground.

Even before looking at the potential "pot of gold," he first assessed the
targets—did they radiate arrogance or fear? People in those extremes were
easy prey because they were self-absorbed. His next question was: Did they
look like someone carrying valuables, preferably cash? When asked which
gender was easier to pickpocket, he said women. "They are more distracted,"
he stated. But he admitted that he would pickpocket a man if his wallet was
an easy target.

2.10.2 PRIORITIZE SAFEGUARDING VALUABLE DOCUMENTS

You should protect both your physical and electronic documents including your passport, identity cards, and sensitive organizational documents. Remember, however,
that money is just money, whereas your passport can be used for all sorts of crimes
(see Sections 1.11, 2.1, and 2.16). And, just as important, your passport enables you
to transport yourself away from trouble, as in the next contribution.

"PLAN B" IN KARACHI WITH PASSPORT IN HAND

JEROME
FREQUENT BUSINESS TRAVELER AND DIVER. RETAIL,
MANUFACTURING, AND CUSTOMER GOODS INDUSTRY

As divers, we're use to having normal operating plans and emergency plans.
At a depth of 30 meters (100 feet) under water or at the surface, what may get
you out of trouble, if anything, is to train yourself to execute the following in

FIGURE 2.5   Courtesy of Peter Steudtner/www.panphotos.org.

sequence: Stop. Breathe. Think. Act. A key part of that is being observant and always asking: "What am I going to do now and for the next step?"

That approach served me well in November 2010 when there was a powerful car explosion near my hotel, the Sheraton in Karachi, Pakistan. Luckily, I was in a taxi when it happened—I had worked late so the traffic was heavier resulting in the driver taking the route to the back entrance. Even though my hotel was not the target, the blast was powerful enough to blow out windows at the Sheraton and it was a chaotic scene there.

With little reliable information about the situation, the obvious immediate action was to get away from the place and avoid the even more dangerous chaos the aftermath can become. Sitting in the back seat of the taxi, I knew I had my passport and key documents with me so I made an instant decision to head for the airport and abandon my belongings at the hotel. I already had a Plan C, to pay the taxi to drive the long distance to the nearest alternative airport in Lahore, if getting out of Karachi proved to be problematic. It helped to have my passport in hand so that I could be nimble when planning my emergency exit from Pakistan (Figure 2.5).

2.10.3 As You Move About

Upon your arrival and throughout your stay, you should carry your money, credit cards, and identification in at least two separate places—in an obvious place like a wallet, purse, or money belt and an extra stash. This "secret stash" will help you cope if you are robbed because you will not be left empty-handed **(see Sections 1.10 and 2.16)**. At the same time, the amount in the most obvious place should be realistic so that the thieves do not suspect anything. Many thieves know about money belts around your neck or waist, so try ones that go around your arm or leg, or use a money belt that looks like an ordinary leather belt. Even a zip-locked plastic bag safety pinned to the inside of your clothes will suffice.

Know how many bags you are carrying and recount them regularly whenever you are away from your accommodations. The more valuable it is to you, the closer you should keep it to your person.

Whenever you remove something, say at airport security, take care to return it to your bags. Figures for 2010 showed, on a daily basis, an airport in Las Vegas, Nevada, found about 82 items, a hotel in Chicago gathered 20 items, and an airline collected about 333 lost things.[76] Books, mobile phones, jewelry, passports, and credit cards were amongst the most common items that were left behind.

While in transit, keep your luggage and belongings in front of you. Or, even better, stand over your luggage in such a way that the lock side is not accessible from behind you. In crowded places, always keep in physical contact with your belongings. Leaving your possessions beside or behind you and in the case of sitting, underneath you, leaves them too exposed to criminals. Your body language at all times should indicate that you are aware of your belongings and surroundings. Your aim is to exercise that fine balance between being casual enough to blend in yet alert enough to signal that you are not an easy target, as the your circumstances warrant.

After you have exited the airport's security area, it is advisable to remove any baggage claim tickets and information about your flight. Once in your accommodation, keep your valuables out of sight by locking them up. One cheap trick is to place your money and valuables in a self-addressed envelope (not your private address), and if possible, add local stamps: Perhaps someone may post it to you if you lose it.

Be aware not to leave a public trail of where you leave your valuables: Let's say, after enjoying a cappuccino at a street cafe, you walk a short distance to your car to drop off your laptop in the trunk before you stroll around the city center. You have not been observing anyone in particular, so it never occurs to you that someone has been watching you and waiting for the opportunity to take ownership of your laptop (**see Section 2.16**). If you are going to leave valuables in your car, then try to place them there at your departure point, not at your arrival point, especially if they will be unattended (**see Section 2.14**).

These basic precautions can be applied even in relatively safe places: There is no need to let criminals, abroad and at home, get a chance to ruin your work or relaxation times. For all your destinations, you need to have security measures that reduce the likelihood that you are robbed and increase the resources available to help you cope if it happens.

But, too often, travelers are so absorbed in what they are doing or are about to do that they forget to keep track of their possessions (**see Sections 2.1, 2.12, and 2.16**)—like the case **Paul Devassy** recounts in his contribution. However, if you pay heed to the proffered advice, perhaps you can avoid such predicaments and their consequences.

GROWLING STOMACHS RESULTED IN
LAPTOPS LOST IN NEW DELHI

MAJOR (RETIRED) PAUL DEVASSY, CPP
ASIS INTERNATIONAL INDIA CHAPTER MEMBER.
REGIONAL SECURITY MANAGER IN AN MNC IN INDIA

"Ajit," "Varun," and "Jitender" work for a multinational manufacturing company in India. Their normal routine involves sales meetings across the city of New Delhi. Lunch used to be had at any restaurant falling en route to their next meeting. In March, the three of them used Ajit's car to visit a customer located in the heart of New Delhi.

Growling stomachs dictated that they stop over for lunch at a road side eatery. They carried their laptop bags into the restaurant and placed the bags under their chairs. After enjoying their scrumptious lunch they were in a hurry to reach the next meeting venue. Ajit quickly settled the bill while Jitender and Varun went to the washroom. After settling the bill, Ajit picked up his laptop bag and proceeded to the parking lot. Jitender and Varun emerged from the washroom engrossed in a discussion and seeing Ajit in the car, boarded and drove off. About 15 minutes later, Varun reached for his laptop bag to take out a file to only discover that he and Jitender had left behind their laptop bags in the restaurant.

They drove back to the restaurant and discovered to their dismay that the laptops were missing. They checked with the waiters and inquired with the other diners but unfortunately no one had noticed the theft. The trio also noticed that the eatery did not have any CCTV system, which may have given them a chance to see the thief.

The trio subsequently lodged a complaint with the nearest police station. The police are still inquiring into the incident and have not made any significant headway on the case. The laptops, with company information on them, have not yet been found.

Quick pointers on how to avoid such situations:

- If traveling alone, carry the laptop with you at all times. Do not leave your bags unattended.
- Inform your colleagues that you are moving away from the table or place where you are leaving the laptop bag.
- Laptops and other such expensive IT equipment are at maximum risk when you are in transit. Thieves often are on the lookout for owners who fail to be careful.
- Carry your laptop in a less attention-grabbing bag. Potential thieves target expensive laptop carrying cases.

In the trio's case, the incident ultimately led to a waste of about 120 hours of productivity. After hearing of such a foolish mishap, the other employees have been more vigilant and proactive in their measures to safeguard their belongings.

2.11 INFORMATION SECURITY: IDENTITY THEFT AND INDUSTRIAL ESPIONAGE

The ability to move data while traveling is a great convenience for modern travelers: Actually, on average, a businessperson carries 3.5 mobile devices, a number that has doubled from 2009 to 2012.[77] At the same time, mobile devices expose our private and corporate information and systems to a range of threats. This section illustrates a few opportunistic and determined threats and offers practical tips. But, as with other threats, there are multifold variations, each metamorphosing with time, so you should continuously seek specific and updated advice. For example, during the Olympics of 2012, an estimated 80% of websites with the word "Olympics" were set up for scamming or spamming purposes with many targeting travelers who wanted to watch missed events.[78] Or in another case, written about on the USA Today Travel website in an article entitled "Travelers at High Risk of Identity Theft, Experts Say," the identity theft and fraud expert John Sileo suspects that someone used their smartphone to photograph his card number when he paid his family's admission to Disney World.[79] Ironically, he was in Orlando to give a speech to the U.S. Treasury Department about avoiding identity theft. These technological crimes indicate the dynamic innovation of data-mining thieves.

2.11.1 OPPORTUNISTIC THREATS

Curiosity and opportunistic criminality are amongst the threats to sensitive or confidential data, as a study by the Symantec Corporation illustrates: In different cities in the United States and Canada during late 2011, they intentionally placed 50 mobile phones in obvious public locations with the aim of finding out how curious the average person was about another person's information.[80] As the Digital Life article "The 'Lost' Cell Phone Project, and the Dark Things It Says About Us" reveals, the finders opened folders and apps clearly indicated as:

- Private photos: 72%
- Personal social media tools and email: 60%
- Saved passwords: 57%
- HR salaries: 53%
- Online banking: 43%[81]

In total, 89% of the finders tried to access information that was in clearly personal apps and information and 83% looked at corporate-related ones.[82] Symantec highlights that most of the finders were probably average people, and not professional criminals, who took advantage of someone else's mishap. Perhaps some of this prying was innocent to some degree, but in this "day and age" when bank account information can be sold for around $900 and email account details for $20 on special black market sites on the Internet, then it is important to also see the financial benefits of luckily finding such information.[83]

Furthermore, even though the contact list of two entries made it easy to contact the owner, only 50% of the mobiles were returned. Even for the returned phones, it was common that those too were searched. Therefore, the preventive measures, such as using passwords wherever possible and limiting the types of information on your device, can stop less skilled perpetrators. Remember, if you are lucky and your lost mobile is returned, assume that someone has at least attempted pry into it. For facts and advice about steps to prevent your mobile phone from being lost or stolen, refer to the **Communication Equipment and Procedures** sections **(see Sections 1.12 and 2.12)**.

2.11.2 DETERMINED THREATS

Of course, determined threats by skilled perpetrators pose a greater risk to your personal and organizational data. The examples and cases below indicate the range of skills employed to commit identity theft or industrial espionage.

Social engineering involves psychological manipulation for criminal gains such as collecting information from you or setting you up in an exploitative scenario, ready to use in blackmail. It is an increasing trend to be aware of as a traveler. As noted in **"Avoiding Espionage: The Extreme Examples of Russia and China but Applicable for All Business Travels" (see Section 1.11.2)**, social engineering is cheaper to operate than electronic surveillance, and thus it is widely used.

"Honey traps" are one form of social engineering that is getting more media attention. Two interesting articles for their historical perspective are "Hush … It's a Honey Trap" on *The Times of India* website[84] and "The History of the Honey Trap" available on the Foreign Policy website.[85] The next contribution by a former intelligence officer and current chief security officer outlines the buildup of one such trap and offers a good starting point for avoiding victimization.

SHANGHAI HONEY TRAP

"JOHN"

CHIEF SECURITY OFFICER, ENERGY SECTOR

In November 2010, I was in Shanghai on business and I went to a Halloween party at a very fine international hotel. The party was loaded with happy people, many business people from the United States, Europe, Russia, and a few Chinese. The evening started with local entertainment and dinner, followed by live music.

At the end of the evening, when the band had stopped, only a few remaining groups lingered and folks sat at the bar. When my companions left, I went to the bar. After I drank a beer, I was approached by two Chinese ladies, one on each side of me. I had spotted them earlier—to me they looked out of place with all those international business people. They had been sitting with a Chinese man who was probably in his fifties. They were in their mid twenties. They looked like escort girls but with more knowing eyes.

I have a background as a former intelligence officer—I know how these traps are set up. But it was the first time that I was the target and saw it live.

This "honey trap" was really about social engineering. They started with polite chatting and asking basic "getting to know you" questions. They quickly moved on, telling something personal about themselves. It was an informal chat, a kind of ping-pong. As time went by, they tried to pump me for work-related information. I just told them lies, big lies. When the bar closed and the ladies offered me drinks from the bar in their room, I declined and ended the conversation. I reported the incident to my office that evening.

Social engineering scams and cons do exist and they are trying to get information about your company. My advice is to know what and how much you are willing to tell—about your personal life, work life, and so forth.

You're always on the job when you travel as a company representative so you need to always be alert. Even on vacation you need to think about how much information and what information you are willing to tell inquiring strangers. A good starting point for preventing this type of crime is to set limits about what you can and cannot tell.

Be forewarned that perpetrators of "honey traps" often use drugs to ensure that they are able compromise your reputation with your company and/or family and make you feel obligated to pay the price of blackmail: But will you ever be really free from that skeleton? Or what if they accessed valuable data or systems through your mobile device? How would it feel to tell your boss that? To be aware of the various types of drugs that are typically used and their indicators, as well as preventative measures you can take, refer to the **Sexual Violence** section (see **Section 3.4**). Of course, if you are in a situation like **"John's"** in the Shanghai story, then simply do not expose yourself to the risk by refusing the enticing offers for a private nightcap: It could cost you more than the free drink.

Electronic surveillance demands motivation, skilled labor, and resources, but a determined perpetrator will muster these. **Ken Nygaard Jensen's** contribution about avoiding espionage when holding meetings supplements his advice in **Chapter 1** (see **Section 1.11.2**). If industrial or political espionage is a realistic threat to you or your organization, then in addition to the measures provided in this book, you should acquire specialized advice.

AVOIDING ESPIONAGE: CONDUCTING SAFER MEETINGS

KEN NYGAARD JENSEN

SECURITY ADVISER, MINISTRY OF FOREIGN AFFAIRS OF DENMARK

To avoid becoming easy targets for industrial or political espionage while working abroad, travelers can take a few steps to conduct safer business meetings. These are general tips. The extent you use these or other measures will, of course, depend on the risk analysis your company provided you and your discussions with a member of your management with security responsibilities and the IT manager from your company.

CONDUCTING MEETINGS

- If possible, do not talk about the location of the meeting place/conference room on open and unsecure lines. This would allow electronic surveillance to be set up there beforehand.
- If possible, have people meet (e.g., at a hotel lobby) and leave together for the meeting.
- If there are only a few people to take part in the meeting, simply choose the meeting place spontaneously (e.g., a random cafe, restaurant, or hotel lobby).

Be aware what kind of electronic devices you bring to the meeting. Laptop computers and smartphones can very easily be compromised. If your laptop computer or smartphone is compromised, the built-in microphone and camera can be remotely activated and used to spy on you. If possible, take out the battery during meetings that deal with sensitive information (this is not possible on some products such as iPhones).

In this "day and age" when manipulation of hardware and software is an ever-present threat, as a security aware traveler you should be ready to implement mitigating measures for those times when you are "on the move." Most travelers tend to travel with their laptops, though for destinations with high risks of espionage such as China and Russia, you probably should opt to bring "loaner" devices instead (**see Section 1.11**). It is common for travelers to use their laptop to log onto a Wi-Fi hotspot—what risks should you proactively counter? You might find yourself needing to quickly use another computer, say, at an Internet cafe. What can you do to protect against prying? The follow advice aims to assist you with answering these questions.

The article "Preventing Digital Identity Theft," available on the About.com Asia Travel website, notes that Internet cafes in Asia are prone to invasion risks.[86] Either an employee has installed key-logging capabilities or the cafe has poor browser security, which exposes you to other external risks. The article laments that there is not much you can do about key-logging except use trusted computers, but you can be safer on public computers by using portable web browsers installed on a USB memory stick, although you need to be wary of viruses infecting your USB. Conveniently and securely, you take your bookmarks, cookies, and personal data with you when you leave.

If you must use a public computer then try:

- Using Firefox or Google Chrome rather than Internet Explorer
- Turning off the "remember password" option in the various programs

- Logging completely out of every program
- Clearing cafe computers of cache, cookies, and user names at the end of your session[87]

The New York Times article "Safe Travels for You and Your Data" gives additional tips:

- Ask if the public computers are reset after each user. Better hotels and cybercafes do this.
- Check if there is a security icon at the bottom of the screen and if it is updated.
- Soon afterwards, change your passwords to any sites you visited once you safely can.[88]

Regarding Wi-Fi hotspots, the "Preventing Digital Identity Theft" article warns of a sophisticated scam called "channeling attacks": This is when a fake Wi-Fi hotspot is created with the purpose of gathering your personal information.[89] Often, these offer "free" Internet access, but, of course, there is a real cost to you if they are successful. This type of attack is not common yet, but it does occur in traveler-frequented places like airports and public areas. Past examples show them using alluring and trusted names like "Free Airport Wi-Fi" or "Starbucks." These are illegitimate but difficult to detect. Avoid using these and turn off your Bluetooth and Wi-Fi. If you must use a hotspot of unknown origin, then do not carry out any particularly sensitive tasks such as online banking.

Another IT threat is "sniffing" the airwaves for data that you send, according to the "Safe Travels for You and Your Data" article.[90] The means to do this is free on the Internet and easy to set up. The article recommends you set up firewalls, encrypt information, and check if the Wi-Fi uses encryption.

Remember, when you are implementing your IT security measures, you need to have a holistic approach. You could take steps like not using public Wi-Fi hotspots and turning off the Bluetooth but then risk exposure when you leave your laptop unattended in your hotel room, for example. A 2010 study by Trustwave's SpiderLabs discovered that 38% of data breaches happen at hotels or resorts.[91]

2.12 COMMUNICATION EQUIPMENT AND PROCEDURES

"Protect the device, protect the data, and protect the apps on the device," said John Dasher, senior director of mobile security at McAfee in an *Information Week* article, adding, "If you don't do all three, inherently, the device is not secure."[92] He was referring to smartphones, but this also holds true for other mobile devices. Mobile phones and laptop computers have become standard fare for most travelers, and the use of smartphones and tablets is on the rise: As such, these devices are the main communication equipment and involve the most common procedures. This section first examines security for mobile devices in general, and then focuses on mobile phones and laptops.

According to the *Information Week* article entitled "5 Essential Mobile Security Tips," good advice includes:

- Lock your devices—This is the first line of protection for cases of lost or stolen items. Preferably, you should combine a password lock with an autodestruction of data mechanism. However, data should not be whimsically deleted, so the system should require numerous attempts (around eight); therefore, your password should be complicated and long. Remote wiping software has the benefit of being more lenient on the autodestruct policy.
- Avoid questionable apps—"DroidDream" posed as a real app and managed to infect a quarter million Android devices in March 2011, making it, at the time, the most successful malicious app. Best advice is to *only* use trusted, vetted, and popular app stores. "Some are better vetted, such as Google's Android Marketplace and Amazon's and Verizon's app stores," said Michael Sutton, vice president of research for the cloud security firm Zscaler. And look for comments and reviews to indicate any problems.
- Accept the patches—Simply put, do this regularly because patches and updates safeguard against vulnerabilities found by professionals.
- Backup your data—While you will still have to deal with the consequences of the lost item, one less worry can be resolved if you have recently backed up your data. Not to mention you can sleep easier if you know that any situation calling on the autodestruct mechanism will keep your data safe from prying eyes and you can get back to work.
- Stay safely behind bars—"Jailbreaking" a device means breaking free of any limitations that your carrier might have imposed but this can weaken the security of the device.[93]

The *Information Week* article ends by quoting one expert who claims that installing antivirus software is not necessarily recommended, though he was open to changing his mind.

Your tablet's mobile security and productivity is essentially the same as the other mobile devices. In addition, the article "iPad Data Protection: 5 Insights to Secure Your Data" on the Kensington blog suggests:

1. Apply passcodes to your apps to restrict access.
2. Keep your touch screen clean because fingerprints may indicate your entry code.
3. Use text passwords, preferably complex ones, as these are more robust than numerical passwords.
4. Physically lock up your device in an appropriate carrying case.
5. Enable the device to erase data if there are 10 failed attempts at entry.[94]

The ingenuity of IT criminals usually means they try to find some means of bypassing a security system. For example, there are ways to use a paper clip to circumvent an iPhone's passcode, thus gaining access to the data and programs, and an iPad 2 can be opened using a magnet—YouTube clips make it easy to replicate these intrusions anywhere.[95] Therefore, you should have layers of security to protect your devices and data, as advised in **Abigail Lucas Maia's** contribution, plus continuously seek updated advice.

PROTECTING YOUR PERSONAL COMPUTERS, MOBILE PHONES, AND TABLETS THROUGHOUT YOUR TRIP AND WHEN YOU RETURN

ABIGAIL LUCAS MAIA

IT COMPUTER FORENSIC AND SECURITY SPECIALIST.
OWNER AND CHIEF EXECUTIVE OFFICER, SECLUDED
IT AID (HTTP://WWW.SECLUDEDITAID.COM)

Although seldom highlighted as a cause for incidents of kidnapping, hijacking, and killing of humanitarians, unsecured IT systems, personal computers, tablets, and mobile phones often provide governments, non-state armed groups, and criminals with critical information: This poses a severe security risk to workers who do not protect their information. In my work providing information technology (IT) security to humanitarian organizations, I know of several examples where relief workers were on the target lists of a technically capable group. Most of them were not even aware of it.

The following IT security advice is for in country and, more importantly, before you connect to your home or office network. Although based on my advice for some of the most volatile and hostile humanitarian contexts, a lot of the points also apply to any of you who use personal computers, tablets, and mobile phones while traveling or working abroad and therefore need to protect your equipment and information.

IN COUNTRY

Once you are in country, a range of simple measures will contribute to increasing the general level of your personal safety and security as well as those whom you communicate with.

- In order to enhance the security of your computer/tablet, change passwords to your email, Skype, bank, and social media accounts (LinkedIn, Facebook, Twitter, etc.), as well as the login to your computer every 14 days.
- As an extra security measure, add a system boot password. This reduces the risk of someone accessing your computer with passwords that could have been retrieved from unsecured networks.

- Undertake software updates.
- Scan your computer on a weekly basis for log files. Log files would be displaying key-log information that you typed in the past week. Alternatively, have your computer scanned by a remote IT security team.
- Showing care with information exchanged through the Internet and by phones is general advice most should be aware of. However, in many cases, expatriates in the field reveal far more information about their personal whereabouts and personal life/affairs using their private computers than what is recommended security-wise. Information is power, and the more information that is available about you and your personal life, the greater the risk of being targeted or blackmailed.
- The dangers connected with downloading and installing counterfeit software cannot be emphasized enough. In doing so, your computer will be open for what we would call "a can of worms" and by this made accessible to outsiders. Instead, authentic products, both for free and for sale, are available at various Internet sites.

Particularly for expatriates and long-term visitors, the next advice warns against the risks associated with using local services.

- Many expatriates approach local IT shops to have their computers repaired—however, that is gambling with your security. While you may want to support the local economy, the IT security concern is that these retailers seldom have access to genuine software and updated equipment. And, too often, they lack the knowledge necessary to secure your computer. Many of my clients have experienced their staff's computers being installed with nonlicensed software and even viruses: A security risk to both the individual and the agency.
- As a general rule, avoid buying computers, mobile phones, or software in country. The risk of these products being fakes is high. The same goes for external hard drives, USB sticks, and the like. The product might look genuine and is usually far cheaper than what the case would be in, for instance, Western Europe. However, more often than not, these products are not genuine and by using them you open up the possibility of others accessing your technical devices.
- Many expatriates use their computers or tablets at local cafes and restaurants in countries where they are deployed. They might perceive these places "neutral" ground. They are not. In so doing, IT security risks that might have been mitigated by systems put in place by your organization could easily be jeopardized. These networks are seldom

or never secure. Because various groups are aware of this behavioral pattern by international relief workers in particular, this poses a security risk. Accessing such public networks grants anyone that wants it access to your personal data, banking, Skype conversations, and so on. Those at risk are not only you, but anyone you communicate with through these networks.

UPON RETURN

Few seem to realize that returning home represents the most important point for securing their IT system and computer, tablets, and mobile phones. Most start using their computer and other devices on their home and office networks without mitigating the risk of infection. The returnee's lack of awareness results in these IT systems also being compromised. A couple of precautions could help you avoid the most common risks:

- Ideally you should clean your computer before connecting to your home or office network. Your computer, tablets, and mobile devices should all be scanned, formatted, reset, and backed up to remove any failed unauthorized certificates as well as open access points.
- Pirated software that may have been installed by local service providers should be immediately removed, as they make your system volatile. Because updates are not genuine, this creates access for hackers, phreakers, and crackers through an open backdoor (to your TCP/IP ports) causing spoof/spam attempts on your personal email and social network accounts.
- Avoid loading personal data back onto your personal computer before you have had it checked properly.

If you are in need of assistance, or are uncertain on "how to," and/or need advice on any of the points mentioned in this section about IT security, we recommend you contact qualified computer forensic teams within your organization or externally. These teams, like at my company Secluded IT Aid, can secure your computer and other devices prior to deployment, and after deployment can view your event files as well as log files and security audits of your system to make sure that your computer poses no security risk to you and those you communicate with.

But external threats are not the only risk on the horizon. Lack of knowledge, missing skills, lax attitudes, and/or risky behaviors can all contribute to your potentially exposing your data. Even though the information contained in our mobile devices is often incredibly important to us, and many know that our personal and organizational information could be at risk if lost or stolen, too many mobile device owners still choose not to protect their valuables. According to the Kensington Infographic article "The Cost of Stolen Laptops," 50% of owners of mobile devices carry personal data such as credit card information and passwords on their devices.[96] The NBC News Technology article "Report: Most People Don't Rush to Lock Devices with Passwords" notes:

- Of the people who use their own tablets for work, less than 10% utilize autolocking. Of these, one in ten use autolocking with password protection.
- About 25% of smartphone owners have enabled autolocking. Less than a third of these owners used autolocking with password protection.
- Approximately a third of laptop owners switched on autolocking, and of these, less than half did so with password protection.[97]

Or, take the 50% of business managers who intentionally disengaged the encryption on their laptops, of whom 40% admitted that this violated company policies according to the Kensington ClickSafe slideshare "Laptop Theft Statistics" from 2011.[98]

Needless to say, the threats are real, more so in some contexts than others: But, then again, IT crimes are boundaryless. So, the only issue is which advice is applicable to you and which do you want to implement now, before your next trip, or at some point "when there's time"?

In the case that you do lose your mobile device or if it is stolen, you can still take a few steps to limit the repercussions: The discussion about what you can do after a crime in the **Crime and Corruption** section **(see Section 2.16)** gives you practical advice to reduce the consequences.

2.12.1 MOBILE PHONES

The handiness of mobile phones makes them too easy to lose or have stolen, as statistics from various places around the world illustrate. The Asian Correspondent article "Smartphone Boom Raises Identity Theft Fear" cites that over 4,600 phones were reported lost in Hong Kong in 2011.[99] The article advises phone owners to set up screen-lock passwords and to establish the ability to remotely lock and delete data.

In the United States, an estimated $30 billion worth of mobile phones were lost in 2011.[100] The mobile security company Lookout Labs has 15 million users of its app and reports that "each day, $7 million worth of phones are lost by Lookout users alone, and if unrecovered, it would take a significant toll not only on our wallets, but on our psyche, too," said Kevin Mahaffey, cofounder of Lookout, in the *USA Today* article "Lost Cellphones Added Up Fast in 2011."[101] According to the *USA Today* article, 67% of mobile phones are lost at night, between 9 p.m. and 2 a.m. The most likely places to lose a phone were in workplaces, restaurants, bars, and coffee shops. You are recommended to utilize features and apps to allow you to remotely lock or reset the password and wipe data. At a minimum, you should use passwords to enter your mobile and your various accounts, in order to limit access to your social media accounts, for example.

In the Moscone Center of San Francisco, California, a survey of area hotels found 2,316 lost mobile devices in their vicinities, of which 81% were smartphones or tablets, 12% laptops, and, 7% USBs.[102] One hotel chain stated that 92% of the lost items were unclaimed. However, a series of surveys around the city uncovered that, on average, 45% of the devices were not claimed, "putting personal and enterprise data at serious risk indefinitely," noted a February 2012 press release by Credant Technologies, the purveyors of the surveys.

Airports, especially at the security checkpoint, are a common location for people to forget their mobiles. In another survey by Credant Technologies, this time their "2nd Annual Airport Survey" of seven airports in the United States, found that 45% of the 8,016 lost devices were smartphones and tablets.[103] **Paul Devassy's** contribution about his colleague "Naveen" is a typical example of a traveler being so distracted that an essential device is forgotten.

COSTLY ERROR COMMITTED BY MY PRODUCT DEVELOPMENT HEAD FOR ASIA: "NAVEEN'S" STORY ABOUT BEING SO PREOCCUPIED THAT HE FORGOT HIS BLACKBERRY AT SHANGHAI AIRPORT

MAJOR (RETIRED) PAUL DEVASSY, CPP
ASIS INTERNATIONAL INDIA CHAPTER MEMBER. REGIONAL SECURITY MANAGER IN AN MNC IN INDIA

"Naveen's" position as the Product Development Head for Asia for a multinational company (MNC) based out of India entailed frequent travels across Asia. All too often, his busy schedule forced him to extensively depend on his Blackberry especially while in transit. On one occasion, there were some hectic parleys with a client he just had visited in Shanghai and he was waiting for a connecting flight to Hong Kong.

At the same time, he was eagerly awaiting information via email on the result of a test, which would swing the implementation of a critical process for the company. His anxiousness to get that important email before boarding made him constantly check his Blackberry, while intermittently scribbling some notes and doing calculations using his notepad. He got so preoccupied that he did not see that the check-in process had commenced and so was considerably delayed and had to pack in a hurry and run pell-mell to catch the connection. On completion of the security check, he discovered that he had forgotten his Blackberry in the passenger's lounge.

He remembered precisely where he had inadvertently left it on the seat. Naveen coaxed an airport official and returned to the lounge, but the device was missing. Frantic inquiries to other passengers were made but nobody could give any useful answers to trace the missing device. Naveen approached the airport police who, though sympathetic, could not retrieve the lost Blackberry.

Due to paucity of time, the search was forsaken and he boarded the connecting flight. The device still remains untraceable.

His colleagues subjected him to some never-ending ribbing—it was hilarious because Naveen used to vociferously profess the importance of information security amongst our colleagues. He invariably used to lecture everybody on the need of securing handheld devices and related precautions. Worst of all, he very much understood the importance of data integrity and the need for securing company information but ended up losing the device anyway. The lost device potentially put our company's proprietary information open to abuse, even though there are IT locks and bolts in place.

Naveen could have easily prevented this from occurring if he had adhered to the basic principles of securing assets while on the move. That is, make a schedule for emplaning and stick to it because this will avoid last minute packing up and rushing. Avoid using handheld devices while waiting in high loss-potential areas (e.g., airport lounges, waiting rooms, charging points, public toilets, hotel lounges). If a situation necessitates this, then immediately after use put the device into its holder, which you keep in close contact.

In London, in any two-week period about 50,000 mobiles are lost or stolen, and approximately 40% of these are smartphones.[104] According to the article "Mobile Devices at Risk of Theft during London Olympics: Report" available on the eWeek website, the influx of people during the Games could mean an additional 17,000 phones were at risk of being lost or stolen: In total, it is estimated 200 million books' (214.4 terabytes) worth of information could have been lost or stolen during the two-week period.[105] Given that these figures do not calculate other vulnerable mobile devices such as laptops and tablets, the exposure of data appears to be potentially even greater. The article recommends that organizations can leverage encryption and manage digital certificates as two measures that can reduce access via mobile devices.

2.12.2 Laptop Computers

According to the article "Lost Laptops Costs $1.8 Billion per Year" by *Information Week*, the 275 European businesses that were surveyed by the Ponemon Institute lost 72,000 laptops at a total cost of $1.8 billion in 2010.[106] On the average, each company lost 265 laptops per year, yet typically only recovered 12. The *Information Week* article goes on to look at the Ponemon study for the United States: The total cost to the 329 surveyed American companies was $2.1 billion, or $6.4 million per business. These companies, combined, lost more than 86,000 laptops a year. Of the costs to companies, the data breach accounts for about 80% while the costs of replacing the laptops is a mere 2%. The real expense for companies is the costs due to forensics, lost productivity, legal bills, regulatory expenses, and the "joker card" of lost intellectual property. If you are interested in learning how much a data breach could cost your company, then the "Tech//404 Data Loss Cost Calculator" by Allied World can assist you.[107]

The 2010 report "The Billion Dollar Lost Laptop Problem: Benchmark Study of U.S. Organizations" by Ponemon Institute/Intel states:

> What do you think your organization would do if it realized that each year it is losing millions of dollars because of the carelessness of employees and contractors entrusted with laptops? While organizations may be aware of the lost laptop problem, we do not believe they understand fully the adverse affect it may be having on their bottom line. If they did, we believe they would be more diligent in protecting these devices.[108]

According to the 2012 infographic "Security Breaches Are on the Rise, but Preventable," available on the Druva website:

- In the United States, data breaches cost $48 billion in 2011.
- On average, businesses lose $53,000 per lost or stolen laptop.
- 92% of security breaches are avoidable.

The Kensington Infographic article "The Cost of Stolen Laptops" presents an interesting overview of statistics and facts.[110] For example, the typical places Americans lost laptops in 2010 were:

- Office/work: 52%
- Conference: 24%
- Meeting room: 13%
- Car: 6%[111]

The next contribution from India tells the story of "Padmaj" leaving his laptop in his car, just momentarily, but long enough for someone to steal it.

RECOUNTING A FRIEND'S STORY: "INTERNATIONAL FINANCIAL ANALYSIS FIRM EMPLOYEE LOSES LAPTOP FROM A SHOPPING MALL PARKING LOT—EEEEK!"

MAJOR (RETIRED) PAUL DEVASSY, CPP

ASIS INTERNATIONAL INDIA CHAPTER MEMBER.
REGIONAL SECURITY MANAGER IN AN MNC IN INDIA

A lawyer friend of mine, "Padmaj," works for an international financial analysis firm in Kolkata, India. Recently, he told me this story:

> I was packing up in my office to go home early to attend a social gathering in my neighborhood. I was to fly out early the next morning for a business meeting so I had a lot of important documents in my laptop bag. I dropped it on the front seat of my car and drove off in a hurry.
>
> I was about 15 minutes from home when I received a frantic call from my wife asking me to pick up some wine from the shopping mall. I turned my car

into the underground parking lot and ran in to get the wine. I rushed back to my car to see that the side window was broken and my laptop bag had been taken. On confronting the security staff, I found that this happened during their changeover period and this particular spot was in the "blind zone" of the CCTV system. A complaint was lodged with the police and they are still working on the case.

The incident nearly wrecked my business trip—I managed to access documents from the company's server, but I lost my handwritten documents (these weren't easy to remember after the frustrations of the failed coverage by CCTV system). The episode and its aftermath proved to be a drain on my energy and increased my already busy workload along with my immense embarrassment when my colleagues discovered the incident. It was my fault that the laptop and the files were stolen. We have layers of security on our devices, but still it didn't look good to my bosses.

MY ADVICE TO ALL WHO CARRY ELECTRONIC DEVICES WHILE ABROAD (AND AT HOME)

All of us should keep in mind that the more we travel, the more we are prone to encounter risks of theft to our electronic devices and their information. My advice to "Padmaj" and all those who carry electronic devices is:

- "Out of sight is out of mind" holds true for all electronic devices. When carrying laptops/expensive handheld devices in public areas, ensure that these devices are not prominently displayed as it may attract the eyes of a criminal.
- These devices should always be within your possession.
- As a good practice, do not expose your laptop in public places, as it could draw unnecessary attention to the device. Remember that persons nearby also have the chance to indulge in shoulder surfing, perhaps leading to them gaining your company information.
- While in a car, keep your bags away from the public eye as unscrupulous elements always attack an easily visible targets rather than a concealed one.

Maximum occurrences of laptop/expensive handheld device thefts occur in restaurants, airports, railway stations, trains and bus stations/terminals, and buses. Common opportunities for theft are:

- Placing your laptop/Blackberry on an airport x-ray belt and becoming delayed in the line for the bag scanner so that your laptop is unattended at the belt's exit.
- Setting your laptop on the ground or in a seat while waiting for transportation/picking up coffee/sandwich.
- Forgetting your expensive handheld devices where you sit/wait, or even at charging stations. Some are even forgotten in restrooms.

If a gang of street kids stole a laptop or another mobile device out of your car, for example, there would be costs, but the risk to your private and company information is minimal, of course, depending on who the new owner is. But if the thieves are professionals who either work for your competitors or are willing to sell to them, then the risks to the information are significantly greater.

2.13   AIRPORTS AND AIRLINES

While most airports have improved their security since 9/11 in terms of terrorism, threats from thieves and terrorists still apply for the entry and exit halls. Terrorism is covered in **Patrick Kane's** contribution. As for thieves, in some places, they take advantage of the accessibility of the entry or exit halls to people without tickets or the availability of cheap tickets. As the "Airport/Airline Safety" article on the Safe Traveler website laments, "Airports can give travelers a false sense of security"; because of their security cameras, guards, and public notices people let their guard down and instead focus on the hustle and bustle of their trip.[112] Even with all their cameras, guards, and public notices, airports are often prime locations for thieving criminals.

A popular scam used at airports is for a team to "guide" you when you are about to go through the metal detectors. A thief or two manage to get ahead of you and cause a delay. Meanwhile, you have already placed your valuables on the conveyor belt and these make it into the hands of a third thief who is waiting at the end. They will usually exit the area whereas you might look for them on the plane side. Instead, avoid the hassle and wait until all is clear before you let go of your valuables. And do not be your own distraction because you have not removed all your metal. Wearing slip-on shoes can speed things up.

Also, be aware that there are plenty of cases of airport personnel stealing cash and valuables: To help you avoid those threats, the article "4 Ways to Protect Your Stuff at Airport Security" on the ABC News Travel website offers the practical suggestions of limiting the amount of cash you carry with you (but that still does not mean to pack it in your checked-in luggage), removing any cash from your wallet before you place it in the tray, and knowing what you placed on the conveyor belt so you can retrieve all of your possessions.[113]

If you experience flight delays or other en route problems and require overnight arrangements, it is worthy to note that airlines are not bound to provide accommodation unless the problem occurs between midnight and 5 a.m., according to the "Airport/Airline Safety" article by Safe Traveler.[114] But the article suggests that you can ask for a distressed-passenger rate. Plus, many airlines are inclined to give future discounts or other advantages to passengers who write a complaint letter that clearly and objectively explains the bad experience. Meanwhile, if you are standing in a long line and getting frustrated over trying to reschedule a cancelled flight, then sometimes calling your travel agent can provide quicker results. Every traveler knows it, but it is worth stating that you should not take your frustrations out on airline or airport personnel—they literally hold your ticket to travel.

The following contribution covers the essentials for safer and more convenient travel through airports and on aircraft.

TRAVEL SECURITY AT AIRPORTS AND ON THE AIRCRAFT

PATRICK KANE
*SENIOR DIRECTOR OF SECURITY WITH A GLOBAL
AVIATION SERVICES PROVIDER*

While traveling by air is relatively safe because of its regulated environment, there are risks. The greatest risk, of course, is the possibility of a crash. As mentioned in Chapter 1, you can avoid airlines with poor safety records by doing some research before you travel. Once you have booked a safe airline and are ready to travel, you can generally avoid risks at the airport and onboard an aircraft by following a few measures.

AT THE DEPARTURE AIRPORT

- After checking in, move directly to the secure area. Even though airport security measures have increased throughout the world, the public areas of airports are still an easily accessible and attractive location for staging an attack. One of the most dramatic attacks on an airport public area occurred on December 27, 1985, when terrorists from the Abu Nidal Organization attacked passengers lining up to check in at the Rome and Vienna airports. A smaller scale but still deadly attack occurred at Los Angeles International Airport on July 4, 2002, when a lone wolf attacker, Hesham Mohamed Hayadet, opened fire at a ticket counter, killing two and wounding four. While these extreme examples are rare, on a daily basis the public areas of airports are accessible to all manner of criminals and scam artists.
- Be polite and cooperative with passport control officials and security checkpoint personnel. Arguing with checkpoint personnel or making jokes about security are almost certain to make the situation worse and may even lead to detention.
- Watch your bags continuously while in the departure area and keep them with you all the time. If your bags are unattended, they are not only subject to theft but also to the possibility of someone concealing contraband or an explosive device. Therefore, in many airports, security teams may treat unattended luggage as a suspicious item.

ON THE AIRCRAFT

- There is some legitimate dispute about which seat is safer to have on an aircraft—the window or aisle. In the event of a hijacking, the window seat may offer some protection from being harassed or selected for special attention by the hijackers in comparison to the aisle. Conversely, in the event of an emergency situation that requires the aircraft be evacuated quickly, the aisle seat offers some clear advantages. Statistically, the chances of being in a situation where an emergency evacuation is necessary are greater than the chances of being in a hijacking, so it would seem the aisle seat might be preferable.

- When boarding the aircraft and taking your seat, count the number of seats between you and the nearest two exits. In the event of an emergency where there is reduced visibility, you may need to find an exit in the dark. Knowing where two exits are is for the event that one is blocked.
- Place your carry-on luggage with any valuables under the seat in front of you when possible. If you have a seat at the emergency exit this will not be possible and you will need to use the overhead bin.
- When placing items in an overhead bin, try to use a bin across the aisle and in front of your seat rather than the bin directly above your seat. This way you will be able to observe it and ensure nobody tampers with it.
- After taking your seat, take some time to assess your fellow passengers as they board. Considering the fact that you will be sealed in a metal tube with these people for the duration of the trip, it is beneficial to identify people who may pose a potential threat during the flight. Most in-flight security incidents involve intoxicated passengers or mentally or emotionally disturbed persons, so watching boarding passengers and observing aberrant behavior can help you identify people who may be a concern and better prepare you should an incident occur.

IF THAT RARE INCIDENT OCCURS

- In the event there is an incident with a violent passenger, the cabin crew may resist the assistance of other able-bodied passengers to subdue and restrain the passenger. There may also be legal ramifications for getting involved, especially if the crew declines your assistance, so only enter such a situation if necessary. You can, though, prepare yourself by going through scenarios so that you have considered your actions and the reactions of others.
- In the event of a hijacking situation, be cautious about intervening, as there may be other hijackers among the passengers that have not disclosed themselves yet. Also, there may be air marshals on board who might mistake you for a hijacker.
- In the event the aircraft is on the ground and held by hijackers, there may be an armed assault by law enforcement or military forces ready to retake the aircraft. It is important to keep as low as possible: Do not stand up or attempt to assist, as there is a significant risk of being killed either inadvertently in the crossfire or because you are mistaken as a hijacker. If counterterrorism forces assault the aircraft,

understand that you will be treated as a suspect until all identities have been verified and the situation has stabilized. During this period, keep your hands in full view, follow security forces instructions, and don't argue with them.

AT THE ARRIVAL AIRPORT

- As with recommendations for the departure airport, it is important to be polite and cooperative with officials at passport control. This is even more true at the arrival airport where travelers are typically under much greater scrutiny than they are during departure. If you are selected for customs inspection, then it is essential that you are polite with the customs officials, as they can make things very difficult for any traveler (how you are dressed can be a factor in how they treat you).
- After clearing formalities and picking up your luggage, you should locate your appropriate ground transportation. At many airports this will mean dodging unofficial porters and offers for transportation services. Particularly in higher risk locations, it is important to determine your method of ground transportation in advance. Do not accept offers of rides from touts that may solicit you in the terminal building. There is a high risk of being overcharged at the very least, and in some cases accepting these offers may lead to a robbery or express kidnapping.
- If you will be met by a prearranged transportation provider, a good choice in many high-threat locations, then be sure to have a positive way of meeting and identifying the driver or coordinator.

Upon your arrival, taxi-hustlers and con-artists are there to welcome you in many destinations: If these are an issue, then hopefully you have arranged for a driver to pick you up at the airport **(see Section 1.14)** so at this point all you need to do is ask the driver for identification before leaving public spaces. Confirming that your driver is actually from your hotel or another arranged service is necessary in countries such as Kazakhstan where it is a common trick to gain access to airline passenger lists and greet visitors with placards using their names. In some cases, they simply copy passengers' names from the placards that drivers are holding and then catch you before the legitimate driver does. There are many variations of these types of scams: And too often, the scam ends with excess charges and threats to ensure that the passengers pay up. To help you avoid falling victim to such scams, a good resource is the I Hate Taxis website, which also has information for all forms of transportation.[115]

2.14 TRANSPORTATION

Whether you are going on an extended family vacation in North America, closing an important deal for Southern Asia, testing your photo taking skills on a safari in East

Africa, or studying for your higher education degree in Western Europe, you will probably use some form of transportation to get you from A to B. A general estimate is that 50% of all security incidents occur while people are in transit. Accordingly, this section starts with a general overview and then covers a wide range of transportation options: walking, using public transport, taking taxis, renting cars, driving, parking, and getting through checkpoints. Related sections include **Personal Belongings and Documents (see Sections 1.10 and 2.10)**, **Communication Equipment and Procedures (see Sections 1.12 and 2.12)**, **Crime and Corruption (see Section 2.16)**, and **Surveillance (see Section 3.2)**. And, of course, the corresponding section in **Chapter 1 (see Section 1.14)** can be consulted for pre-trip advice.

To be safe and secure throughout your travels, conduct a local threat assessment **(see Section 1.1.1)** and a personalized vulnerability analysis **(see Section 1.2)**. What's the likelihood of a threat occurring? As with other aspects of travel security, your knowledge of the local conditions could make a crucial difference. Take the example of having a punctured tire but the next gas station being a part of the trap set by carjackers **(see Section 3.5)**. **Abhimanyu Singh's** contribution, as an overview of risks and advice for India's various means of transportation, is particularly useful if you are traveling in India, but even if you are not planning a trip there in the near future, you can review it for the type of information you need to mitigate risks wherever and however you travel. Several of the points he raises are expanded upon in this book, in particular, flying safely **(see Sections 1.13 and 2.13)**, avoiding criminal cons and tricks **(see Section 2.16)**, and protecting your belongings throughout your trip **(see Sections 1.10 and 2.10)**.

KNOWING THE RISKS FOR INDIA'S VARIOUS MODES OF TRANSPORTATION

ABHIMANYU SINGH

HEAD OF RISK ADVISORY, RECON-RISK EVASION & CONTROL. LEAD ON APAC AND MENA REGIONS FOR THE INTERNATIONAL PROTECT AND PREPARE SECURITY OFFICE (IPPSO) BASED IN DELHI, INDIA. HE IS AN AUTHOR, SPEAKER, AND CONSULTANT (HTTP://WWW.RECONADVISORY.COM)

Because India is a vast country, you may need to use various modes of transportation (air, rail, road, and water). To be an informed traveler, know the risks:

- Air: Air travel is considered one of the safest forms of transportation. Some of the risks associated with it include hijacking, accidents, and health issues. Indian airports and commercial aircraft are well guarded with Industrial Security Forces and Special Forces and there have been very few such events/incidents (the last hijacking took place in December 1999) in Indian aviation history that have posed a security concern.

- Rail: Risks on rail include bombing, theft, robberies, and sexual harassment. Though the authorities are taking necessary precautions, travelers should still avoid overfriendliness with strangers and distraction, and ensure proper guarding of luggage.
- Local metro network: In the national capital of Delhi, the local metro network is amongst the safest in the world. However, the metro network infrastructure in other major cities including the commercial capital of Mumbai may take months or years to come up.
- Road: Risks on roads include, but are not limited to, accidents, getting delayed, robberies, road jam, extortion, and rape. Travelers are suggested to verse themselves with the route and driving and pedestrian rules if self-driving.
- Water: India has limited ferry connectivity in the coastal areas. Travelers should opt for such services offered by reputable companies with a track record of safe and secure operating practices.

TRANSPORTATION SECURITY ADVICE

If using public transport, the do's and don'ts remain the same as with rail transport. A few of the travel scams and cons include the "metal detector" scam, a sympathy story, a compensation plan, the "snooze and lose" scam, unlicensed taxis (overcharging), confidence tricks (drugging and poisoning), and pickpocketing. You can avoid becoming a sad statistic by the following:

- Be vigilant while traveling and take care of your belongings.
- Never put your belongings on the conveyor belt unless the metal detector is clear.
- In no circumstances should a traveler lend money to a stranger.
- If in any trouble, ask to resolve the situation at a police station or hotel lobby; the crook is more likely to give up the ruse.
- If alone, be on the cautious side and never lose sight of your baggage.
- Never, however tempting, get in an unlicensed taxi in a foreign city.
- Avoid accepting eatables from strangers during travel, especially during train travel.

2.14.1 WALKING

Being safe while walking involves doing many of things you already know: not reading a map on the street or flashing your money and paying attention to traffic. Often, you want to keep a low profile and blend in as much as possible. A good trick is to visibly carry a local newspaper. You definitely need to remove any airline tags or the like, which indicate that you have just arrived. Do that before you leave the airport or station.

Particularly when you are walking, you need to look and be a secure traveler. Avoid, or pay extra attention when you walk (or run) in, areas that offer criminals an easy hiding place such as a tree-lined path. In general, the best advice is the simplest: Ask trusted local people advice on where the troublesome places are (decreases likelihood) and carry your "secret stash" **(see Section 1.10)** of emergency money (reduces impact).

Resources on the Internet include several articles on the About.com Walking website such as "Stranger Danger Safety Tips for Walkers"[116] and "How to Walk Safely."[117] The article "Basic Safety for All Travelers" has advice for drivers, walkers, and bicyclists.[118]

2.14.2   USING PUBLIC TRANSPORTATION

When using public transportation, apply the advice that is appropriate for you and your travel realities:

- As you approach a station, think what kinds of problems could be lurking there. What types of perpetrators could you expect to find and where would they likely be positioned? Typically, escalators, stairwells, and near elevators are favorite spots for criminals to victimize people, for instance.
- While at the station, preferably stand near personnel but being visible to a CCTV camera is the second best option. It is important to realize that often such cameras are not monitored "in real time" by someone so they can give a false sense of safety since help may not be on its way when you need it. However, being near a camera can signal that you are aware of your surroundings and indicate that you are a harder target. All said, waiting near other people, preferably personnel, is the best option.
- Especially at night, avoid empty carriages and try to sit near the personnel.
- When observing your surroundings at the station and on your transportation, notice if there is some kind of emergency communication system that allows you to speak with personnel.
- Choose a seat in which you can see who enters and exits the transportation. Some security experts advise you to take the aisle seat because when you take the window seat you might get trapped when a stranger takes the aisle seat. However, different experts note that an aisle seat exposes you more to traffic in the aisle. There are pluses and minuses to every choice.
- If your belongings are in the luggage compartment, then sit where you can see the compartment.
- If you are feeling insecure because of other passengers, then take action by moving or seeking assistance.
- If you are traveling by train over long distances, book the top bed and use the upper luggage space so that you can sleep close to your luggage.

If you are a female, especially if traveling alone, you may also consider sitting next to other women on public transportation. Be aware that in many countries, there are "women only" services. When you are using the metro in Mexico City, for instance, you are advised to use these sections during crowded times. Let's say you come from a country without gender-segregated transportation, then you may not think it is important to ride in the "women only" sections or that it is your right to ride wherever you want. It is. But you should be aware that in Japan, when women use the mixed carriages during crowded times, they are often groped and fondled because the owners of all those anonymous hands believe the women are knowingly "asking for it." Similar examples are found around the world.

For further reading, the articles "How to Stay Safe on Public Transportation"[119] and "Tips for Your Safety while Riding Public Transportation"[120] both give advice for various forms of public transportation. If you are a senior traveler, then a good resource is the article "10 Safety Tips for Seniors Using Public Transportation" on the About.com Senior Living website.[121] And because this article deals with mobility issues, it is also useful for travelers with disabilities.

2.14.3   TAKING TAXIS

Knowing the latest local trends will help you avoid being overcharged, robbed, or harmed while using taxis. In Shanghai, tourists arriving from Pudong Airport can be charged outrageous fares by the unofficial taxi service. In one case, a passenger paid $1,000 for a ride that should have cost a few dollars.[122] At same time, it is important to be aware of the 35% surcharge when using taxis at night—knowing this could help you avoid making a fuss over the rates when the price hike is legitimate.

In Kazakhstan, drivers sometimes demand double fees and will not take your luggage out of the trunk before you have paid. There are also known cases where the taxi drove off with passengers' belongings after payment. One way to proactively show the driver that you are an alert traveler is to call someone and within the conversation comment on something that identifies the driver and/or vehicle—you could tell your concerned spouse the taxi's license plate number or inform your office colleague that you expect to make the meeting because that taxi company has a good record and your driver, (name), seemed like a competent driver. Surely, you do not want to offend your driver, hence creating an insecure situation: But you do want to clearly state, with subtlety, that you are not easy prey. If a driver tries to bribe you, threaten to call the police.

When in Mexico City, it is worth knowing that street taxis, in particular the common green and white Volkswagen Beetles, have frequently been involved in robberies and "express kidnappings" **(see Section 3.3)**. A safer choice is a taxi that is operated out of a base called a "sitio" and radio-dispatched.[123] To make sure that you have a trustworthy means to return, then be sure to get the sitio's card with their contact details.

Before you go, learn about the local taxi scams and dangers (Figure 2.6). While you travel, keep informed and be alert. General advice that you might draw upon includes:

- Find out how the taxi services generally function in terms of payment (cash, credit card), use of a meter, or the need to negotiate prices for each ride, and where the reputable ones are normally found in the areas you will be frequenting. Similarly, if you will be riding public transportation, check how payment is done, especially because many services are using cashless systems.

- Get local advice and support by asking your hotel to order a taxi for you. It can be useful to find out the normal price for such a journey and the directions or key landmarks.
- When you call a taxi, try to get the driver's name and/or vehicle number and check this when the taxi arrives.
- As soon as possible, get the contact details of a trustworthy service. Generally, authorized taxis are safer.
- Avoid overly aggressive or assertive taxi drivers.
- Look for a taxi-meter and radio. Check that the driver starts the meter.
- Ensure that there is a door handle for the door next to you.
- Keep your valuables nearby.
- Try to keep your luggage near you instead of using the trunk, and if the trunk is required, make sure all your bags are loaded, while you also maintain a general alertness to your surroundings, and demand that the trunk is locked.
- Once you are in the taxi, ask the driver to lock the doors or manually lock yours.
- Call someone while in the taxi and explain your transportation means and expected arrival time but don't discuss your detailed plans in the driver's presence.
- Feel free to talk with the driver—it could be an opportunity to learn about your destination—but do not give out private or sensitive information and be careful when discussing political, cultural, religious, or other "hot topics."
- Unless it is clearly a shared taxi, demand that the driver does not stop for additional passengers. Leave the taxi if this occurs.
- Unless your luggage is in the trunk, pay while in the taxi so you will have time to count your change and put your money away. If your luggage is in the trunk, then pay after you have possession of it.
- Instruct the driver to wait until you go in to your destination before he departs.

FIGURE 2.6   Courtesy of Peter Steudtner/www.panphotos.org.

If you feel at all threatened by the driver, you have two basic options: Demand that the driver stop the taxi and get out. However, beforehand, be alert about the situation outside of the vehicle. You do not want to go from the "frying pan into the fire." In such a "worst-case scenario" your second option is to give clear verbal and physical messages of what you want, create physical distance between you and the driver, and demand to be let out in a safe place, as in the next contribution.

24 HOURS OF DON'T DO'S IN NEW DELHI

ANDREAS POPPIUS
SECURITY CONSULTANT, ADVENTURE TRAVELER, AND FORMER SENIOR SECURITY OFFICER/SWEDISH EMBASSY, KABUL, AFGHANISTAN (HTTP://WWW.U3KOMPETENS.SE)

During 2010, I traveled from Kabul, Afghanistan, to Bangkok, Thailand, via a short sleepover in New Delhi, India. Since my budget was quite low, I tried to keep expenses for accommodations down. Unfortunately, I ended up doing this in not the brightest of ways. And it all started to go wrong at the airport, as it usually does.

Instead of using a prepaid taxi, somewhat controlled by the government, I chose a standard cab (a lot cheaper) just outside the terminal and explained to the driver (who spoke poor English) that I wanted an inexpensive hotel just for the night. This resulted in his driving me to the less fashionable suburbs of New Delhi, following me from hotel to hotel as I was trying to lower the price, and also offering me narcotics and prostitutes. Eventually, I found a place for the night and told him that he could pick me up and drive me back to the airport the day after, at a price that we agreed on. The hotel room was on the fourth floor, had no emergency exits whatsoever, no windows, and the lock was on the outside of the door. And there were electric wires in the shower. But it was cheap.

The taxi driver arrived the day after to pick me up for the trip to the airport as arranged, but just outside the checkpoint for the airport, he turned off the main road onto a small gravel road and stopped his vehicle. He told me he would like half the money now, and half when we arrived. I, politely but firmly, told him no and after a few minutes of discussion, he continued to the airport. Once there, he made a U-turn into the parking lot, let a presumed colleague of his into the back seat of vehicle, and started to drive off, away from the terminal building!

The man in the back started to argue about the price with me, so eventually I told them both that I won't pay a dime until the car is parked outside of the terminal building and the engine is turned off. Finally, after yet another U-turn, the driver stopped the taxi in the parking lot and the man in the back explained to me what I had to pay. The price just went up, from 800 rupees to 3,300 rupees. I got mad, of course, resulting in my paying the 800 rupees but having two mad Indian taxi drivers who threatened to call the police. Which, in the end, they did not.

To avoid this hassle—and the related risks it brings, I recommend the following transportation advice:

- Plan your travel and don't try to cut costs on safety and security arrangements.
- If possible, use prepaid or at least government-controlled transportation. Agree on the total cost before using the service.
- If possible, make sure that your driver knows that others know where you are going and whom you are in the car with.
- Make sure to be aware of—and don't accept—any diversion made by others to your arranged travel plans.
- Use only hand luggage and make sure to wear on you your most important documents (e.g., passport, tickets, and travel insurance), and spare money should be hidden in your clothing.

My cheap accommodation also raised avoidable risks, so my advice is to stay at a hotel with acceptable safety and security arrangements and building standards—preferably also in a safe and secure neighborhood.

For further reading, the articles "Airport Taxi Scams and How to Avoid Them" on the Price of Travel website[124] and "7 Common Taxi Scams—And 7 Steps to Beat Them" by Scambusters[125] are both good overviews of common tricks and cons employed by crooked taxi drivers.

2.14.4 Renting Vehicles

Good advice you should keep in mind when renting a vehicle includes:

- Before leaving the agent, make sure of:
  - Rental rate and terms.
  - Emergency procedures and contact details.
  - Full gas tank and gas agreement.
  - No damage to the car.
  - The car is good working order and has emergency equipment.
  - You know how to operate the car and have tested the brakes.
  - Remove any interior and exterior signs of it being a rental car.
  - Choose a model that blends in and is known for not attracting criminals.
  - You can also try requesting power locks and windows and make sure it has airbags and seat belts.
- Do not leave the contract in view—preferably take it with you when you leave the car.
- Know your route.
- Make your car look as if it is a normal, private car—leave a jacket or local newspaper in the car.

The video entitled "Travel Security—Rental Cars, What to Check For" on the TrainingSolutions website adds supplementary advice such as checking the braking system and tire pressure.[126] The "Car Rental Tips" article on the Travel Sense website contains a lot of advice about insurance and other documentation issues.[127]

2.14.5   APPROACHING YOUR VEHICLE

As with other forms of transportation, there are pluses and minuses to driving your own vehicle, whether it is privately owned or a rental. Besides the chance to take a great road trip, a car is convenient for daily use. And convenience often supports your security. Let's say you own a restaurant on a Greek island. Then getting home late at night can be an issue. Driving could be the best option for your security and convenience.

When you approach your car, maintain a "relaxed alertness." Is there a parked van next to your car, for example? As vans are often used to commit a kidnapping (see Section 3.3) or sexual violence (see Section 3.4), a parked van could indicate the presence of a heightened risk. Do you have any reason to suspect the behavior of someone nearby? These types of questions should be quickly assessed as you approach the car. While doing so, follow these five steps:

- Be aware of your surroundings.
- Do not dally or loiter.
- Have your keys ready.
- Inspect the inside of the car as you move toward the driver's side.
- Quickly get in, lock up, and fasten your seatbelt.

These steps should be a natural process or habit. If you have children and they are old enough to understand, you should explain their part in this routine.

Beyond these steps, your knowledge of the local context should affect how you approach your car: If the threat is troublesome street kids, pickpockets, or even kidnapping, you want to get in quickly. You still need to scan the inside of the car beforehand. In places where car bombings or tracking by professional criminal gangs are the threat, you should use a different approach. Here, you should visibly inspect the car. Look underneath it—of course it is helpful to know what to look for, but often the act of looking signals that you are not an easy target. The old trick of using a mirror to look under the car will only be necessary in some contexts. You want to balance looking secure by inspecting your car and being secure by quickly getting into your car and locking the doors.

2.14.6   DRIVING AROUND

Once you are ready to drive, with the doors locked and seatbelt fastened, other good advice includes:

- Have a good idea of where you are and a general sense of where safe places are en route.
- Only partially open the windows—not enough for a small hand to get in but enough to let some air in and to allow the window to be flexible if someone tries to smash it.

- Keep valuables out of sight. If you have anything (i.e., purse, briefcase, camera) in the front part of the car, keep it on the floor of the vehicle and preferably covered up. If you are going to leave valuables in your car, then try to place them there before your departure, not when you arrive at your destination and will be leaving them unattended.
- Any time that you have to stop, keep the vehicle in gear. Use your rear and side view mirrors to help you monitor your surroundings.
- Maintain space to maneuver by keeping distance between you and the vehicle in front of you—you should be able to see its rear tires.
- In traffic, be aware of potential avenues of attack and escape (both in your car and without it).
- Within a distance of about 2 kilometers (1 mile) from your residence and regular arrival points, be extra vigilant about your surroundings.

In most places, it is sufficient to use your common sense and "relaxed alertness" while driving around: The equivalent of being in a "yellow" condition according to the contribution **"States of Awareness: The Cooper Color Codes" (see Section 2.3)**. However, in some contexts, you have to be quite focused on your safety and security: Or, the "orange" and "red" conditions. The next contribution provides a practical tip for driving in hostile environments.

SINGLE PROFILE IN HOSTILE ENVIRONMENTS

STEVE PHELPS

OWNER, SECURITY & INTELLIGENCE SOLUTIONS LTD. (HTTP://WWW.SISOLUTIONS.CO.UK)

Here is a tip that I used to follow in the Niger Delta that you can use when traveling in a car in an environment with an elevated threat of robbery or kidnapping—particularly if expatriates are being targeted. Most people who have a chauffeur or driver tend to sit in the rear seat on the opposite side to the driver. (This is the side that most passengers enter the vehicle from.) However, if you sit behind the driver, the profile of the passenger in the rear seat merges with that of the driver and presents a front/rear profile of a vehicle with only one silhouette in it. This can reduce the likelihood of your vehicle being targeted—especially if expatriates are being targeted. Obviously, in bright daylight, people following the vehicle will be able to see the passenger in the rear seat so it is not a perfect solution. But every little bit of advantage you can give yourself is worth having.

To learn what actions you can take if you suspect that you are being followed, review the tips and advice found in the **Surveillance** section **(see Section 3.2)**.

Since road accidents are a serious hazard in most countries, you can review the medical advice for dealing with casualties and the list of contents for a first aid kit that should be in your vehicle at all times **(see Section 3.8)**. It is important to note that in some contexts, it is not advisable to stop at the scene of an accident, even if you were involved, because crowds will inflict their own justice, without facts or reason and sometimes apportion blame on you simply because you are a foreigner at the scene, as in the contribution **"Don't Hit a Pig in Papua New Guinea" (see Section 2.7)**. In such circumstances, you are advised to go to the police: If you can safely inform others at the accident scene of your intentions, then do so with caution.

It is important to note that accidents are a serious risk while on the road. Globally, about 3,287 people die in road traffic accidents each day, nearly 1.2 million in total each year, according to the article "Road Crash Statistics" on the website of the Association for Safe International Road Travel.[128] Plus, another 20–50 million are injured annually. Even though low- to middle-income countries have less than half the world's vehicles, over 90% of fatalities occur in those countries. Another telling fact is that these countries spend about $65 billion on road traffic accidents, which is more than the amount received in developmental aid.

Because international business travelers are also on the roads in the countries they work in, figures from the 2011 "Duty of Care and Travel Risk Management Global Benchmark Study" show fairly high percentages of companies whose staff were involved in an accident: Large companies with over 10,000 employees had the highest levels of occurrences at 63%, while small companies of less than 1,000 staff had the lowest at 39%.[129]

The article "Coping with a Car Crash Abroad" on the highly recommended Travel Insurance Review website articulates six things you can do at the accident scene:

- Contact the authorities.
- Get medical assistance if there are any injuries.
- Note down and exchange with the other involved persons relevant information such as license plate numbers, driver details, and place and time of the accident.
- Take a picture of the scene and vehicles.
- Notify your insurance company as soon as possible.
- Get a copy of any documentation you signed.[130]

These are things you should do if the security and medical situations allow it: If either of these are in jeopardy, then the contribution **"First Aid Knowledge Saves Lives: What to Do at the Scene of a Car Accident and Other Medical Emergencies" (see Section 3.8)** gives you practical advice to cope with the emergency.

2.14.7 Parking Safely

When considering safe parking options, your common sense will serve you well, such as parking in busy areas, near your destination, or in a well-lit place if it is going to get dark. Additional precautionary steps available to you are:

- As you approach the general vicinity where you will park, be alert—take mental note of potential hiding places that criminals might utilize near your vehicle as well as to and from it.

- Park in well-lit and public areas. Also consider using valet parking or an attended garage, especially at night.
- Avoid parking near walls, heavy greenery, or other places where an attacker can hide. Clear these, as much as possible, from the driveway of your private residence. Good lighting is another measure you should take if it is within your control or influence.
- Park so that you can get away quickly, for example, leaving the car in gear for your next maneuver and pointing the car in the direction you will want to drive.
- Have a prearranged signal if the gate at your residence is manually opened. During the brief interlude while you wait, have the car in reverse gear so you can quickly back out if you suspect anything. Of course, you should be ready to change gears and drive in.
- Casually, but purposefully, scan your surroundings before you load items in the back of the vehicle.

For added security at a parking lot, measures you can take include:

- Selecting one that has guards, cameras, good lighting, and other security measures.
- Preferably using lots with clearly visible and see-through stairwells.
- Backing into your spot so you exit more quickly, if necessary.
- Being alert when using the stairwells.
- Not using the elevator if someone in it or nearby you makes you feel insecure.
- Being the last person to press for a floor, if other people enter the elevator.
- Opting not to go to your car alone if any of the following occur: You feel uncomfortable, there is a parked van next to your car, or if you spot other "red flags" such as two men sitting in an idling car.

Your analyses of the contextual risks **(see Section 1.1)** and your vulnerabilities **(see Section 1.2)** can help guide you with developing appropriate options.

2.14.8 GETTING THROUGH CHECKPOINTS

Checkpoints exist for various reasons: The main purpose of both legal and illegal checkpoints is to monitor/regulate the movement of people and goods. Many checkpoints are benign but some can be malignant. If you will have to pass through a checkpoint, here is some general advice:

- Quickly assess the situation.
- Remember that soldiers/guards may be scared or frustrated.
- Slow down as you approach.
- Have your identification documents (and vehicle papers) ready in a clearly visible place. In some countries, it is appropriate to put a copy of a friendly flag in the window.

- Have a designated spokesperson. The rest of the passengers should avoid talking as a group, especially not in a foreign language. Passengers should not make demands of the spokesperson so that person can concentrate.
- Be visible—take off sunglasses during the day and turn on the vehicle's interior light at night.
- Turn off the radio/music.
- Stay calm and be nonthreatening.
- Wait for instructions. Do not do anything until you are told what to do.
- Keep the engine running unless told otherwise.
- Keep your hands on the steering wheel and the passengers should keep their hands visible and relaxed on their laps.
- Use slow movements and inform the soldiers/guards of your actions (remember from their perspective, an innocent action such as unfastening your seatbelt can look like you are reaching for a weapon).
- They may ask where you have been and where you are going.
- They may want to inspect the car—have the driver open the hood and trunk. In some contexts, you can ask to have the spokesperson/driver get out of the vehicle and follow the progress of an inspection, if they have not offered.
- At night, dim your headlights because soldiers/guards will be blinded and may react aggressively.

Even though this is "best practice" advice that generally applies, it is critical that you follow measures that are contextually appropriate. Take as an example how in most cases, passengers can keep their hands visible and relaxed on their laps: Yet in high-risk, postconflict, and/or "fragile peace" situations, the standard advice for all the passengers is for them to raise their hands to just about chest level and stare straight ahead, within reason. For these types of destinations, a pre- and posttrip briefing is highly recommended to make sure everyone is "on board" about security. Another example from the other end of the spectrum could be guards who rarely ask for documents, and when they do, they will patiently wait. And they do not mind if people wear sunglasses. Then, of course, you can be more relaxed about having your documents ready, but these should still be handy.

For additional reading about checkpoints, try the Wikipedia articles "Random Checkpoint"[131] and "Security Checkpoint"[132] for explanations of the different types of checkpoints. For additional advice, many of the recommended books in the **Nongovernmental Organization (NGO) Travelers** section **(see Section 1.2.2)** such as *Safety First: A Safety and Security Handbook for Aid Workers* by the International Save the Children Alliance[133] contain good tips.

2.15 ACCOMMODATION

You have arrived and are ready to settle into your accommodation. As a security-aware traveler, you know that at your accommodation you can be exposed to numerous threats from theft to terrorism, depending on the context. Since most travelers will stay in some type of a hotel, this book shares the insights of experts in hotel security and international travelers regarding safer hotel visits. The result is a collection of "best practice" advice and tips, covering the full spectrum of hotel security while traveling—from the moment you arrive until you leave and what to do in an emergency.

HOTEL SECURITY FROM CHECK-IN TO DEPARTURE

DARRELL CLIFTON

AUTHOR OF HOSPITALITY SECURITY *AND DIRECTOR OF SECURITY, CIRCUS CIRCUS HOTEL AND CASINO*

GABOR BUNTH

DIRECTOR OF LOSS PREVENTION, ST. PANCRAS RENAISSANCE HOTEL LONDON, MARRIOTT INTERNATIONAL (HTTP://WWW. MARRIOTT.CO.UK/HOTELS/TRAVEL/LONPR-ST-PANCRAS)

JOHN J. STRAUCHS

SECURITY DESIGN CONSULTANT AT STRAUCHS, LLC WHO HAS WORKED IN SAUDI ARABIA, KUWAIT, JORDAN, SINGAPORE, HONG KONG, VIETNAM, GREECE, VENEZUELA, AND COLOMBIA, AMONGST OTHERS (HTTP://WWW.STRAUCHS-LLC.COM)

TANYA SPENCER

GLOBAL TRAVEL SECURITY AND CRISIS MANAGEMENT SPECIALIST AND COAUTHOR OF TRAVEL WISELY: A PERSONAL SECURITY GUIDE FOR WOMEN TRAVELERS *(IN DANISH ONLY), TRAININGSOLUTIONS (HTTP://WWW.TRAININGSOLUTIONS.DK)*

The following is general advice, with some specific pointers for female travelers and travelers to more volatile destinations, that you should modify as the circumstances call for it.

PUBLIC SPACES DO'S AND DON'TS

An aware traveler always exercises a degree of caution when giving out private information in public spaces. When registering, you may want to use your business address instead of your home address. If your room number is spoken too loudly by a clerk or if someone is nearby and you feel uncomfortable with their overhearing, quietly explain to the clerk that your privacy is important and have him or her reassign you a room number and write it down if necessary. In some countries, you may want to discretely hand over your passport, if you don't want others to see it in the reception area.

Inform the clerk that no one should be given your room number nor should anyone be allowed to your room. Instead, you should be called to the front desk. If this is not a standard procedure for them, then have them note this in their records so that all the shifts know. For females traveling alone, one option is to make it seem as if you are with other people by getting a double room or mentioning that you expect to be contacted by your colleagues. An extreme precaution a traveler can take would be to tell the manager that you are a "nonregistered guest." This is usually reserved for celebrities and trial witnesses. Anyone calling the hotel inquiring about you will be told that you are not registered.

A good basic precaution is to only use your first initial and last name whenever your name is in public spaces. For example, when preordering breakfast, you may leave the order form on the outside of your door and any curious person walking by could have a look. If you do have to sign the bill at the hotel's restaurant and include your room number, hand it directly to your server; don't just leave it on the table.

CHECK THE HOTEL'S SECURITY

Casually look for visible security features as you check in at the registration desk and as you go around the hotel. If your gut feeling tells you that security practices have a poor standard, leave and go to another hotel, as **Jytte Hollender** did in the next contribution. We all have survival instincts wired into our DNA.

- Inquire from the desk clerk if they have any security information for guests. They often do. Once in your room, look for security information in your room's welcome folder and door.
- As you go to your room, check if there is a video monitoring system. Avoid hotels where video cameras are rarely watched, especially if you notice that monitors are sitting on a table or under the counter at the front desk.
- Avoid staying at a hotel that doesn't have an automatic fire detection system and/or sprinklers.
- Be particularly security conscious or change hotels if the hotel:
  - Doesn't have security guards.
  - Relies on other staff members to also perform security functions. This shows that the hotel does not feel the necessity to invest in the safety of its guests.
- Ask hotel staff about the hotel's neighborhood, other areas that you will be in, and areas to avoid—have them point out things on a map if possible.
- If you have any questions or issues, don't be shy to discuss security with the concierge.

CHANGE FOR THE BETTER: FEELING SAFE AND SECURE IN A HOTEL ROOM IN THE UNITED STATES

JYTTE HOLLENDER
DIRECTOR AND OWNER, HOLLENDER.DK APS
(HTTP://WWW.HOLLENDER.DK)

On one of my trips to Los Angeles, California, it was not possible to get space in the conference hotel for my first night, so the hotel had kindly referred me to one of the other hotels that was within walking distance. I checked into that hotel and got a room in which the door and only window faced a passageway that was accessible to anyone off the street. I had a creepy feeling and at first, tried to ignore it. But after a few considerations, I decided to return to the conference hotel and use my best persuasion skills to get a room. I consciously contacted a female receptionist and told her how I felt uncomfortable to stay at the other hotel. We managed to get a room and at the special conference rate. I was much more comfortable staying on the fourth floor of a 4-star hotel, where there were many other conference guests.

PARTICULARLY FOR DESTINATIONS WITH HIGH THREAT LEVELS

- Make emergency exit plans for yourself and meeting point plans if you have travel companions.
- Avoid hotels where private vehicles arrive at the hotel entrance without being checked and vehicle barriers are easy to bypass or are poor obstacles to a ramming attack.
- Avoid hotels where vehicle inspections are conducted 30 meters (100 feet), or less, from the hotel entrance.
- Prefer hotels where valet parking is mandatory for all guests. It is not a common practice, however.
- Avoid any hotel that does not control access through *all* entries at *all* hours.
- Prefer a hotel that has a long "retreat distance"—the distance an attacker has to travel from the hotel to an area of safety, such as to a public road in heavy traffic (Figure 2.7).
- Don't discuss sensitive business, political, social, or economic issues in your room because in some countries governments and competitors will bug your room to gather such information.
- Ask the concierge about the hotel's counterterrorism program.

SELECT A SECURE ROOM

A secure way to enter your room is to leave the door propped open with your bags while you quickly search the room, including the bathroom. Or you could

FIGURE 2.7   Courtesy of Peter Steudtner/www.panphotos.org.

ask one of the hotel's security guards to escort you to your room and to stand there while you check your room. Clearly, these procedures are not needed in all locations, but in every case you still want to check if someone is in your room and also to see if anything was left by the previous occupant as the first thing you do when you enter your room.

When you initially view the room, security criteria you can use include:

- Between the third and sixth floors.
- Facing the hotel's inner courtyard.
- Close to the elevator/stairs.
- Operable and lockable windows and other physical security features.
- A working phone.

While we recommend the third floor and some experts say the second floor, the point is try to avoid ground floor rooms, which are more accessible to intruders. However, if you are traveling as a family, for example, you may prefer to be on the ground floor for easy access to the pool, but then you have to be extra careful about locking up and keeping valuables out of sight. Closing the curtains is an additional measure.

Of course the decision to stay above the sixth floor is yours and there are many good reasons for doing so. But, in general, the sixth floor should be the upper limit because in most countries fire ladders don't extend higher than this. One only has to think of the Karachi Marriot bombing and fire where people hopelessly jumped to their death because they could not be rescued.

The inner courtyards of hotels tend to be more closely monitored than the exterior of the building. Especially if you stay on one of the lower floors, a room facing the inner courtyard is a good option. Particularly for locations with threats such as terrorism or violent political demonstrations, avoid rooms on the front facade, as these will probably bear the brunt of any potential attack. The front is not only accessible, it makes for good TV coverage, which, for political attacks, is part of the motivation.

Although it may be noisier, a room close to the elevator/stairs allows you to exit quickly. However, don't accept a room immediately next to the emergency exits since these can be an easy way for criminals to access the building undetected. Wherever you are, you should know how many doors there are between your room and the exits.

Check that the room has adequate physical security features: door quality, peep hole, safety deposit box, window security measures, working phone, and lock systems including extra latches that can only be locked from the inside (i.e., deadbolt, chain lock). Make sure the windows are operable but limit the degree they can open (especially on the ground floor) and have good locks. If there is a ledge, terrace, fire escape, or other way to access your room from the outside or through another room, then ensure the locking system is robust.

The next contribution illustrates the perils of not having a working phone and good locks.

HELP! A DRUNKEN RUSSIAN IS TRYING TO BREAK INTO OUR ROOM IN TURKEY. WHAT? THE PHONE DOESN'T WORK!

"GEANIE"
EDUCATIONALIST

As a young backpacker, I traveled throughout Turkey with my fiancé. With a wide range of places to explore, one of the stops we made at was in Trabzon to see the Sumela Monastery. We had noticed the large number of Russians in the area but hadn't given it much thought. On our first night in town, after an exhausting day of hiking and sightseeing, the door suddenly banged and roared in the middle of the night.

As I rushed to get some jeans on over my long johns (it was very cold in the mountains), my fiancé checked the peephole of the flimsy door. He described the thunderous source as a drunken Russian or more like a mountain of man. I had picked up the phone to call for help: My eyes widened in disbelief when I realized the phone line was dead. He insisted that I lock myself in the bathroom while he guarded the bedroom door. Before we got a chance, the lock had given up and the man was pushing his way in! The two of us were barely strong enough to keep him from pushing the door open, but in any case, he had an arm, the size of thigh, inside the room. All the while, he was as noisy as a bear but that didn't seem to stir any of our neighbors.

My fiancé was able to effectively use a few moves to push the guy out of our room and into the hallway. Luckily, years of martial arts training had made him skilled in avoidance techniques and stronger than he looked. He yelled, "stop" in four languages and gestured with his hands but the guy attacked again. On the third repulsion, my fiancé hit him hard: Watching the Russian go down was like watching a heavyweight fighter fall in slow motion but made real with the sound of his head banging the metal edging of the elevator doorway. Scared that he was injured, my fiancé watched him until the man tried in a befuddled way to make a fist and dazedly attempted to move his legs.

My fiancé ran back to the room and said something about "someone could get hurt if the Hulk gets up again." We barricaded the door and were ready to jump into the bathroom, as our next line of defense. I had a pocketknife and my fiancé was "armed" with our camping frying pan. To our relief, the Russian had had enough and eventually left but we kept an adrenaline-fueled watch for the rest of the night. The early morning receptionist explained that Russian prostitutes and their drunken pimps often made problems. He looked sheepish about the phone but didn't bother to make promises. We had already seen the sights, so with no reason to stay, we headed for our next excursion.

If a room is unacceptable to you for any reason, including listening to your intuition, demand a change.

CREATE A SAFE ENVIRONMENT

Most hotels provide all of the tools you need to keep you and your property safe. Just make sure you use them and follow these reliable measures:

- Familiarize yourself with safety procedures, especially evacuation routes and procedures (these are displayed on the back of the door to your room).
- Always use the main and extra locks whenever you are in your room. Because the main lock system can be opened with a master key, it's important to also use the extra lock (and/or your doorstop) particularly when you are vulnerable (e.g., sleeping, bathing, or watching TV). If you are concerned and there is no extra lock, a simple motion detector you can arrange almost anywhere is to put a hanger on the doorknob so it rattles if disturbed.
- Never open the door if someone knocks and claims that he or she is a hotel employee or hotel inspector.
- If you aren't expecting room service, call the front desk to confirm the identity of the person.
- Before allowing someone you know into your bedroom, even if you are certain it's completely innocent, take two seconds to think how others may view this and instead consider meeting in a public space. This applies to men and women—men in some cultural contexts and women in most countries.

- Take advantage of in-room safes and deposit boxes at the front desk. Most hotels will not cover missing valuables.

Taking these basic precautions once you are in your room can help you stay safer. Conversely, forgetting to, say, use an extra lock can result in a potentially insecure situation as in following contribution.

HOTEL ALLOWED SOMEONE TO BRIBE THEIR WAY INTO MY ROOM IN KENYA: LUCKILY, IT WAS MY BOYFRIEND

"ANITA"

INTERNATIONAL BUSINESS TRAVELER

I was in Nairobi for business and my boyfriend was going to fly in to meet me at the hotel. His flight was really late so I fell asleep waiting for him. I woke up terrified to the presence of someone in the room. My boyfriend had arrived, and wanting to "surprise" me, he was able to bribe the clerk to let him into my room. Thankfully it was only my boyfriend. Always keep the chain on the door.

On your night table, under your pillow, or some other easily accessible place, keep your flashlight and whistle. Your money, ID, and other resources should be nearby and in the same place every night, as well as your keys. No matter if you stay at the Hilton or the youth hostel, you should be able to react quickly in an emergency such as an earthquake. The accessibility of a few essential resources will expand the options available to you, which increases your chances of coping with critical situations, if the worst case should happen.

That said, most accidents in hotel rooms occur in the bathtub! For some reason, a few of us cannot remain upright in a foreign shower. Whether it is the soap, the surface of the tub, or the poor drain, be careful how you step. Almost every hotel provides safety handles and non-slip mats. And, most importantly, the shower curtain goes inside the tub.

It is probably because most travelers like to retreat to their hotel room after a long day of working or being a tourist that they let their guard down. But, as **Darrell Clifton's** examples show in his contribution, there are plenty of scams to be aware of.

LESSONS FROM CREATIVE HOTEL SCAMS AND TRICKS

DARRELL CLIFTON

AUTHOR OF HOSPITALITY SECURITY *AND DIRECTOR OF SECURITY, CIRCUS CIRCUS HOTEL AND CASINO (HTTP://WWW.CIRCUSRENO.COM)*

Scams in hotels have reached some pretty outrageous heights in recent years. One common identity theft scam is a person who calls your room, "Hello, this is Mr. Johnson from the front desk. Unfortunately, the credit card that you gave us declined and I will need a new credit card number." Most of us would provide the number, the man would tell us it worked that time, and everyone would be happy. Meanwhile "Mr. Johnson" could be anywhere in the world using your credit card number to buy a new big-screen TV. A reputable hotel will never call your room asking for information. If they do, go to the front desk and take care of the matter, including reporting it if it was not legitimate.

The old tricks, such as posing as a housekeeper or room service, still keep some criminals amused. But they are not as popular as some of the scams that are just downright silly yet successful. In 2010, many hotels experienced pranks where scammers called the guestroom posing as the manager and convinced guests to activate fire alarms, flood the bathroom, or throw the chairs out the windows. Amazingly, many gullible people did just as they were told and caused millions of dollars in damage. People who are that naïve are likely to provide any information over the phone. Just like you do at home, be wary of phone pranksters and those fishing for information.

One of the most common methods of hotel theft is committed by "door-pushers." These opportunists walk through hotels—sometimes posing as guests and often as delivery persons or coupon distributors. When they find a door that is open or not quite latched, they enter the room. If the room is occupied but no one is in the room, they take whatever they want. Sophisticated door lock systems only detect entries with a key so the housekeeper generally is accused of the theft. If the room is unoccupied, the person enters the room and becomes a "squatter." Depending on the time of day, they can remain in the room undetected for up to 24 hours. If the prior guest has vacated without a proper checkout, it is very simple for the squatter to call the front desk and say he has decided to stay two more nights. "Just put it on my credit card." Then the real guest gets charged and does not realize this until receiving the next bill, long after the squatter has gone. One "door-pusher" in Nevada spent months finding shelter in various hotels. Even if the occupants were in the room sleeping, he would enter the room, sometimes hiding in the room until the guest left in the morning.

The obvious preventative action for these types of problems is to make sure the door closes and latches every single time—just like you do at home. Also, guard room keys with great care. Use the locked express checkout box or personally check out at the desk.

LEAVE YOUR ROOM WITH SECURITY IN MIND

When leaving your room, do so with security mind.

- Ensure you store your valuable items, including private and sensitive documents that you don't carry with you, in the safety deposit box.
- Never leave valuable items unattended in the bedroom, particularly your personal or organization information on paper or in your mobile

devices—research in 2010 by Trustwave's SpiderLabs found that 38% of data breaches transpire at hotels or resorts.[*]
- Consider leaving the TV or radio on to give the illusion that someone is occupying the room.
- Lock windows and doors.
- Leave a note of your plans (you can do this clearly but discretely by using a sealed envelope) if you work in risky places, are traveling alone, or going out at night.
- Don't use the "service please" sign. Consider using the "do not disturb" sign.
- If your hotel requires you to surrender your key to the front desk when you leave for the day, try to keep the key—ignore the requirement unless you are challenged.

You can go as far as staging your room if you want to check if someone is going through your things. It's well known that hotel employees are sometimes used to collect information about guests. Place a coin on top of something inside a closed bureau drawer. Have the face of it pointing directly toward something you will remember. It only takes a second to do this and costs nothing. If the coin disappears or moves, then someone has gone through your belongings. The extent that you use this or any of the guidelines will depend a lot on the context and general situation.

I CAME BACK TO MY ROOM TO FIND MY TRASH HAD BEEN GONE THROUGH IN YEMEN

TANYA SPENCER
GLOBAL TRAVEL SECURITY AND CRISIS MANAGEMENT SPECIALIST AND COAUTHOR OF TRAVEL WISELY: A PERSONAL SECURITY GUIDE FOR WOMEN TRAVELERS *(IN DANISH ONLY), TRAININGSOLUTIONS (HTTP://WWW.TRAININGSOLUTIONS.DK)*

During a recent trip to Yemen, I had a pleasant stay in a hotel in Sana'a. Even though an American had been murdered that week in the south of the country and there were several tribal clashes in Sana'a, I felt safe (the head of security was a former trainee of mine) and I took good safety measures.

At the end of facilitating a Training of Trainers course, I was ready to head home. My departing flight was at some awkward time of night but after I arrived at the airport it was cancelled due to a dust storm. I returned to my hotel and room to find some documents that I had thrown away at the bottom of the trash now on top of my desk. I felt that my space had been violated (even though I had

---

[*] Nancy Trejos, "Travelers at High Risk of Identity Theft, Experts Say," USA Today Travel. December 12, 2011. http://travel.usatoday.com/news/story/2011-12-12/Travelers-at-high-risk-of-identify-theft-experts-say/51841144/1.

checked out) by one of the nice night receptionists. It was just some extra copies about adult learning, but the course was for humanitarian workers, so perhaps he thought it could be of interest. I never throw away sensitive documents while I'm in a foreign country because this sort of thing does happen. Actually, I am extra careful when it comes to sensitive documents and try to avoid carrying them.

I reported the incident to my employer but requested that it should be taken up after I left because I could be there some days, and the night staff had a master key (in any case, I always use my doorstop and extra door locks). As it turned out, the dust storm caused me to extend my trip by three extra days.

ADD THE NEXT LAYER OF THE ONION:
THE HOTEL'S ENVIRONMENT

When you think of accommodation security as the layers of an onion, then your room is the core, the hotel building is next, followed by the hotel's perimeter and surroundings. As part of your ongoing situational assessment, notice, for example, if there is glass or other sharp objects cemented into the perimeter walls that are high enough and encompass the entire property, if hotel security actually checks underneath cars, and if the hotel guards are armed. Knowing what you do about the context, are these reasonable measures given the threats? If you are shocked by the measures or find them extreme, then proactively ask questions to better understand the dynamics of your location. Also ask staff about the hotel's surroundings and neighborhood.

In general, the concierge and other hotel staff are good sources of information to help you have a more enjoyable trip.

DON'T GET BLINDED BY THE BLING: LOOKING
AT THE HOTEL'S SECURITY FROM ALL ANGLES
IN KENYA'S NORTH-EAST PROVINCE

PHIL
SECURITY MANAGEMENT TRAINER, HUMANITARIAN SECTOR

In January 2012, I went to Kenya's North-East Province to deliver some safety trainings for an INGO. The town I visited is only 100 kilometers (62 miles) from the Dadaab refugee camps and has seen plenty of fallout from the Kenya incursion into southern Somalia with grenade and IED attacks blamed on Al Shabab occurring within the town. Given the recent kidnapping of INGO workers in Dadaab and attacks on local bars and hotels, I was booked into the best (and reputedly safest) hotel in the town.

This was a large, fairly new hotel with rooms in separate three-story blocks. The front of the hotel was very impressive with thick and high brick walls topped with razor and electrified wire. Uniformed guards, who manned the front gate, checked the car for explosives as we drove in. Before entering the lobby, our bags were searched and we were put through a (working) metal detector. These procedures were repeated pretty much every day when we returned to the hotel in the late afternoon.

The rooms had decent wooden doors with good locks although each room had a patio or balcony with full length sliding glass doors fastened with a fairly flimsy metal clip. Given this, and given our usual advice to avoid the ground floor, we requested that the hotel move us to second floor rooms, which they agreed to.

And I'm glad they did. On our second day, the other trainer and I went for a walk around the hotel grounds and quickly discovered that the nice high elec-trified walls only went as far as the last of the guest rooms. The entire back half of the hotel compound was enclosed by a simple brick wall about 5 feet (1.5 meters) high and overlooking vacant bush. No razor wire, no electrified fence, no metal detectors, no physical security!

It proves that the "security bling," at big hotels can give a false sense of safety, as it may just be for show. It never hurts to have a look yourself.

GO TO A DIFFERENT HOTEL IF YOU ENCOUNTER THE FOLLOWING

Seriously consider changing hotels if you encounter:

- Weddings and other private parties open to many guests if no security screening is being conducted. Be vigilant even if there is security screening.
- Beachfront parties, even those hosted by the hotel, if the beach is public or accessible to the public.
- The hotel has scheduled seminars or conventions involving groups or causes that are unpopular in the host country.
- Senior government or military officials are known to frequent the hotel.

RESPONSES DURING AN EMERGENCY

There are really two possible responses to every emergency. You will either evacuate or stay where you are.

Whether you are on a cruise ship, in a hotel, or traveling on a bus, take a moment to make a mental plan of what you will do if an emergency strikes. Locate the exits as soon as you arrive. Use that route at least once to exit so you are familiar with it. Have your essentials, such as wallet and shoes, ready to go if you have to leave in a hurry. Imagine other emergencies such as earthquakes, active shooters, a flood, or riot. Some of these will require an evacuation and you will use your preplanned exit. Depending on the situation, you may decide that you should stay in place, maybe even hide.

It takes only a couple of minutes to run through a few scenarios and decide on your action plan. That way, you and others can avoid panicking because the solu-tion will already be in your mind. If traveling with family or co-workers, arrange a meeting place and contact methods to reach each other if you have to evacuate.

2.15.1 SAFE RESIDENTIAL LIVING

What if you have a longer contract and will be living abroad? Which security measures should you consider for your housing? Security considerations for this type of accommodation are very location-specific but some general guidelines are:

- Find out about the area's safety. Ask advice from your local contacts.
- Preferably choose a place where there are multiple ways to get to and from your residence (e.g., living at the end of a dead end street severely limits your escape options).
- Seek advice on physical security (e.g., secure gates, lighting, not having accessible roof areas, emergency exits).

As for daily security measures, it is usually enough to follow basic home safety and security procedures like locking doors, closing the curtains before turning on the lights, and keeping a flashlight in your room, with the inclusion of any measures that address specific local issues. For example, in many locations it is advisable to place a bar and lock over windows, especially basement ones. But, if there is a fire, then you will not have time to search for keys. Instead, you can leave the keys on a hook near the window but far enough away so a potential intruder cannot access it from outside.

In many parts of the world, house help is normal for both locals and expatriates to employ. In addition to the local advice you gather, you can review the next contribution.

**MAKE SURE HOUSEHOLD HELP AREN'T TEMPTED
TO HELP THEMSELVES TO HOUSEHOLD ITEMS**

MAJOR ELIUD MUITA IKUA

HEAD OF SECURITY, COMMUNICATIONS COMMISSION OF KENYA

- You must have copies of the household staff's identification documents so in case any of them takes off you have ways of catching up with them.
- Install a fixed line in the house so that you can always call back and know when domestic staff is in the house.
- Ensure the security personnel have clear instructions that your house help are not allowed to leave your house with a bag without your written authority.
- Lock the bedrooms that are not in use during your absence.
- You should have a friend or close family member make impromptu visits.

You can also consider "localizing" the advice given in the **Home Protection** section (**see Section 1.16**). As with a hotel's security, think of your housing's security as an onion and ask yourself which measures are needed for each layer.

2.16   CRIME AND CORRUPTION

Criminals will try anything to separate your possessions and money from you. Every place has its own particularities: In Nairobi, some people have been robbed by "poo-point"—a terrible dilemma of either giving up your money or being covered in human excrement. In Mexico, a current trend is to press tourists into signing a timeshare contract. When people refuse to be victimized, then often they are treated poorly.

This section provides you with advice on how to deal with common criminal tricks and corrupt officials. The subjects discussed in this section include snatching, distracting, befriending, ATM-related crime, credit card skimming, violent crime, after a crime, and corruption. Normally, a few modifications to the general advice will help you adapt to local conditions. The old saying "prevention is better than the cure" applies to avoiding crime. Even the pettiest of crimes can feel like a violation of your space and still requires you to face the consequences such as dealing with foreign police and replacing the stolen items.

In addition, other cases, examples, and expert advice on how to avoid being a crime victim can be found throughout this book: For instance, the **Information Security** section **(see Section 2.11)** addresses "honey traps," in **"Lessons from Creative Hotel Scams and Tricks" (see Section 2.15),** there are several examples related to your accommodations, and "tea scams" are described in **"Security Tips for Traveling and Working in China" (see Section 2.4).**

As with the other threats, an aware traveler who is concerned about security needs to be informed about the risks **(RMF 1)**, understand vulnerabilities **(RMF 2)**, create options to feel and be safer **(RMF 3)**, monitor and adjust to the situation **(RMF 4)**, and be confident in their abilities to prevent and react appropriately to security incidents **(RMF 5)** (Figure 2.8).

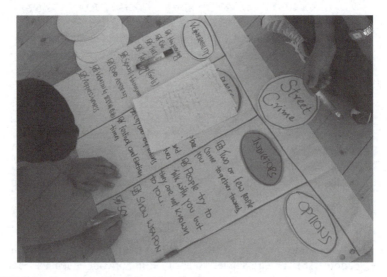

FIGURE 2.8   Courtesy of Peter Steudtner/www.panphotos.org.

To be mentally prepared in the event of pending danger, according to the No Nonsense Self Defense (NNSD) article "Mental Preparation," you should understand five key aspects:

- Recognition—knowing that crime is a process and trying to recognize where you might be in that process if you sense an incident is unfolding.
- Palatability—understanding your own limitations, contradictions, and assumptions.
- Available time—increasing your reaction time by being aware of the potential dangers.
- Appropriate response—remembering that your subsequent reactions have to be within the legal boundaries of self-defense; otherwise there will be serious repercussions.
- Experience with operating in an adrenalized state—moderating the effect of the shock of the situation on you, because high adrenal levels affect your physical and mental functioning and influence your perceptions.[134]

An example from the "Travel Safety: Tips and Information" article on the BugBog website illustrates some of these aspects: The situation happened in Rome on the metro train when one smartly dressed man "accidentally" blocked the entrance while an accomplice attempted to rob unsuspecting passengers.[135] But the author of the story recognized the setup and was ready when a criminal hand tried to steal his wallet from his pocket that was Velcroed shut. He clearly understood his limitations when he wrote: "No further action was taken as an Italian metro car is not a good place to challenge a couple of desperate Albanians." To help you avoid falling prey to crime, you can boost your situational awareness skills (see Sections 1.3 and 2.3).

2.16.1 SNATCHING

Typically, street crime (both snatching and distracting) occurs in crowded places such as stations, shopping centers, and street walkways; tourist attractions such as amusement parks, monuments, and religious sites, and places with valued commodities such as ATMs or jewelry stores. According to the "Travel Safety: Advice and Information 2" article on the BugBog website and citing information from the MoneyGram money transfer service, the world's least safe streets are:

1. Snake Alley, Taipei
2. Khao San Road, Bangkok
3. King's Cross, Sydney
4. Times Square, New York
5. Tverskaya Ulitsa, Moscow
6. Bois de Boulogne, Paris
7. Chandni Chowk, Delhi
8. Frenchtown, Shanghai
9. Las Ramblas, Barcelona
10. Stazione Termini, Rome[136]

While the locations on such top ten lists will change, the common point that tends to remain the same over time is that these are crowded places, drawing many tourists.

At these types of locations, and the local variants at your destination, you need to be particularly alert and advised to take basic precautions such as:

- Only carry what you can afford to lose—minimize the contents of your wallet and bags or take extra precautions when you need to carry valuables (e.g., after going to the bank). And remember to back up photos and store separately.
- Tuck away, in your "secret stash" **(see Section 1.10)**, enough money to cope with an emergency—it could be enough local currency to take a taxi or enough U.S. dollars to fly you to at least a neighboring country.
- Physically radiate that you are a security-aware person by using subtle body language—casually but thoroughly monitor your surroundings, keep in physical contact with your belongings (the more valuable, the closer to you it should be), walk in normal strides, and be ready for your next action by, for example, having your car keys ready.

Additional advice on protecting your belongings can be found in the **Personal Belongings and Documents** sections **(see Sections 1.10 and 2.10)**.

"Lisa's" example of having her handbag snatched while enjoying time with her family at a local cafe shows that you do not have to travel abroad to find street criminals who will simply, but skillfully, take your belongings.

I DIDN'T EXPECT TO BE ROBBED AT MY LOCAL CAFE IN LUZERN

"LISA"
FREQUENT BUSINESS AND FAMILY TRAVELER

On a Saturday, I went to a local cafe in Luzern, Switzerland, with my husband and two children. I had brought along needed items for the children in a nice leather handbag, which I left by the foot of my chair. I had purposely left my wallet at home, thinking I would not need it. Thank goodness I did, because when I reached for the bag, it was gone.

When I reported the crime to the police they told me that this sort of thing has begun in the last years and particularly in the cafes around the train station. My bag had nothing valuable in it, but I still felt violated and nervous for a couple of weeks after it had happened. I was so surprised as I could not expect something like this to happen in such a small, safe place. Now I keep my handbag on my lap at all times and I tell all of my friends to do the same!

A trend that has spread throughout Asia and is found in countries such as Cambodia, Indonesia, and Vietnam (and **Jack Chu** refers to it in China **[see Section 2.4]**) is the "snatch and grab"—here a motorcyclist approaches you from behind and grabs your purse, hanging backpack, mobile, or whatever they can get a hold of. This crime can happen any place and particularly during festivals, at markets, or in other crowded places. Simple measures such as wearing a loose shirt that covers any straps, not carrying a purse, wearing your backpack on your front side, or avoiding walking near the curb will greatly reduce your exposure **(RMF 2)**.

2.16.2 DISTRACTING

A common distraction trick involves asking you if that is your money on the floor. Let's say you are sitting on a tall chair and eating at a food stall, you might turn to automatically look at the money. Meanwhile, a colleague of theirs, who is standing adjacent to you, takes your mobile that is lying on the counter and your laptop because your carrying case was on the floor. There are many variations and locations for this trick, including in the hotel lobby, at the airport, in the shopping center, and so forth.

A trick found around the world is called the "stall-dip-shield-dish," which typically occurs in any crowded place, including even in your home area. The "stall" finds some way to distract you—bumping into you, spilling something on you, using a child to talk with you, asking you the time, or, as in the previously mentioned example from BugBog, blocking the entrance to the metro. The "dip" or "pick" steals from you while the "shield" blocks the view from potential witnesses. The "dip" can then leave the scene with your valuables or pass them on to the "dish" who moves away without being suspected. While the "stall-dip-shield-dish" is the elaborate version, many street criminals successfully apply the simplified version of "stall and dip." To avoid being victimized, use your body language to radiate that you are someone who protects their belongings **(see Section 2.10)**. If you are distracted by a stranger, you should immediately think of your possessions. The "How Pickpockets Work" article on the How Stuff Works website is a recommended resource because the detailed descriptions together with pictures make it very practical.[137]

"Flash mobbing" or "flash robbing" are a less savvy version of the "stall-dip-shield-dish." A child approaches you, begging in a sweet manner, while the rest of the gang gathers around to rob you. This crime is typically found in the tourist areas of southern European cities, such as Milan, Florence, and Rome, but can occur anywhere.[138]

2.16.3 BEFRIENDING/CONFIDENCE SCAMS

When someone is friendly because they have criminal intentions, that can be called a "befriending" or "confidence" scam. These work because con artists know how to make the scam appear real and manipulate people. And the variations are almost endless. In the 1990s, the U.S. government warned American businesses of Nigerian scams involving fraudulent government contracts, business opportunities, or charities.[139] In the 2000s, Asian "honey traps" were and still are regularly featured in the international news.[140] When these types of scams affect businesses, then usually money, information, and reputations are at risk. However, from the perspective of the affected individual, the risks are personally felt. Even though these con artists use their charm and wit to draw their victims in, they can also inflict physical harm to reach their goals. The tea used in the following contribution was a local medicinal herb that could have easily been overdosed.

"FRIENDS" WITH CRIMINAL INTENTIONS MAKE DANGEROUS TEA IN KENYA

TANYA SPENCER

GLOBAL TRAVEL SECURITY AND CRISIS MANAGEMENT SPECIALIST, TRAININGSOLUTIONS (HTTP://WWW.TRAININGSOLUTIONS.DK)

Many years ago, when I was a conflict resolution trainer working with local peace groups, I was the victim of a befriending scam in Kenya. During my first weekend, before starting work on Monday, I met a great group of three Kenyan women and one Dutch guy living in the youth hostel. While my apartment was lonely, theirs was a fun place to hang out. We did all kinds of things that weekend. On Friday night, we went to a grill restaurant that turned into a late-night disco on the outskirts of Nairobi. Since the whole place was crowded, we took turns "guarding" our table with our things while the others danced or whatever.

What I didn't know was that it was all part of a plan to steal my passport and cash, if they could get some. Over the weekend, they managed to make copies of my apartment and locker keys when we went swimming on Saturday. (They said it was safer to leave the keys in the guarded parked car than to store them in the amusement park's lockers.) Later that night, while watching a video together, they drugged my tea so I would fall asleep in their apartment and they could commit the crime downstairs in mine.

My new "friends" were kind enough to assist me with reporting the crime to the police. However, since it was a Sunday, the police wouldn't write a report until Monday and the American Express office was also closed. My embassy did block my old passport even if they couldn't issue me a new one over the weekend. That was possible because I had a copy of my passport.

Since I had done everything I could do and still did not suspect them, I went with them to visit one of their grandparents on a farm outside of Nairobi. Unfortunately, since they hadn't maintained the car properly, one of the tires blew out on the highway on the return trip. By lucky chance (and seatbelts!), we survived what should have been a fatal accident because several cars in the five lanes that we crossed had to swerve and because the wall we finally hit had recently been built since other accidents in that spot resulted in cars going down into the steep ravine. Needless to say, it wasn't easy to report all these incidents to my headquarters in Germany.

The whole thing was planned and schemed, with two very important exceptions: That I blocked my passport and the car accident, plus the ensuing hospital and police station visits. These meant that the Kenyan woman behind the scam was not able to leave for London with her Dutch boyfriend (they had said they were married). Sadly, they burnt my passport, which had sentimental value for me. I learned this after one of the women who had had a small part in it confessed to me a few weeks later. She also told me that the couple had quickly cashed the travelers' checks on the black market before I made it downtown to the (closed) American Express office. I give them credit for being well prepared!

In hindsight, I realize that I hadn't appreciated what others were willing to do to obtain a passport. At that time, a passport for me was a required travel document and a cool "thing" to house my collection of visas and stamps. I had heard of passport theft but I was blinded by the belief that "it can't happen to me." These criminals used this, and my trust, to con and rob me.

What I now know is that "good passports" can have a black market value of about $10,000. That is a strong motivation for the would-be thief. An even stronger motivation, your passport with someone else's photo in it, represents a chance for a better life—perhaps hope for a better future for their children. Needless to say, your passport should be among your most carefully guarded possessions. Keep it close unless the situation better warrants that you carry copies and leave your passport safely locked back at your accommodations.

This book highly recommends resources produced by SCAMwatch, a service of the Australian Competition and Consumer Commission: For example, the article "How Scams Work" maps out psychological tricks criminals use to manipulate their victims:

- Reciprocation—maneuvering the situation (i.e., gave you a gift or special deal) so you feel obligated to do or buy something in return.
- Better offer—presenting with you an outrageous offer, which you reject, but their next offer is comparatively a great deal that is hard to refuse.
- Commitment—getting you to agree to something early on and later referencing back to a much bigger commitment.
- Social proof—convincing you that others are doing it so you should too.
- Liking—charming you so you would never suspect true motivations.
- Authority—relying on your automatic compliance to authority figures.
- Scarcity—tapping into that human desire not to miss out.[141]

The Friday night situation of "guarding" the possessions at the table in the previous contribution is a good example in which the "friends" entangled several tricks (reciprocation, social proof, and liking) into one con.

To safeguard yourself against confidence scams while retaining the ability to be flexible, you can use scenario thinking: Perhaps you are enjoying your holidays in southern Europe, and while sipping refreshments at a sunny cafe, a student-aged person politely asks you if you could take a minute to speak English with him. After a delightful discussion, the student offers to show you the "real" city in exchange for some more time to practice. Who knows if this person is setting you up for a scam: But, in any case, you should be on the alert.

A cautious traveler would probably not let the scenario develop past saying "No" to the person from the beginning. But, if sunshine and coziness means that you are more open than usual to exploring the sights and sounds on offer, then before leaving a populated place with this person, think as a security-aware person. Did this type of scam show up in your risk analysis **(see Section 1.1)**? Can you remember any warnings or indications from other tourists, hotel staff, or vendors? What does your "gut feeling" or instinct tell you about the situation?

Now that you have assessed the situation, go over likely scenarios and proactively consider possible options and measures that could keep you and your belongings safe. One situation could be during your time together, the student passes you his mobile phone to take a picture and somehow in the exchange, it is dropped. The student bemoans his meager allowances, which are particularly tight during the financial crisis—this is an expense that cannot be paid off for ages—and, pleadingly asks, "Couldn't you pay?"[142] The less polite version is to forcibly demand that you pay, perhaps threatening to turn a crowd against you or call on friends who are nearby. Since you proactively considered this scenario, then you would have it clear in your mind *not* to take the phone, if faced with this situation or some version of it.

In another scenario, you show attention to some local trinket, jewelry, carpet, or the like or perhaps the student points something out to you: Let's say at around this point, the student suggests taking you to a shop he knows where you will get the "best price" reserved for "special friends" (often owned by a family member, friend, or employer). Your options could include not going, only browsing without touching items nor accepting anything (especially foods or drinks), or going into the situation knowing that it will cost you, in one form or another, and start listing possible options to handle that situation. Options could be clearly stating your limits early on (and continuously), bringing out your sharpest bargaining skills, or having a bodyguard just outside the door.

The point is, the choice is yours. While it is easier to simply recommend that you do not enter into such a situation, that automatically eliminates a potentially great opportunity to see the sights and maybe make a new friend. Instead, this book advises you to continuously employ your security awareness skills to help you mitigate risks. Together with some basic cautions (e.g., carrying in your main wallet only an amount that you are willing to lose while also carrying a "secret stash," staying near places where you can get assistance quickly and never getting into some form of private transportation with this person), your ability to continuously assess the situation should aid you in making informed decisions and taking appropriate actions.

2.16.4 At Automated Teller Machines (ATMs)

When you use automated teller machines (ATMs) or cash points you are vulnerable to an old-fashioned robbery, as well as the trendy crimes of ATM skimming and "ATM kidnapping." The crime of ATM/credit card skimming, which involves stealing information from the card, is detailed in the next section. The term "ATM kidnapping" refers to the kidnappers forcing the victims to withdraw money from their bank accounts **(see Section 3.3)**. This crime is often initiated at an ATM, as in the case study presented in **"Ensuring Your Organization's Duty of Care: Lessons from Mexico on Threat Analysis and Robust Response"(see Section 2.5)**.

While abroad, conditions differ for using ATMs. In some locations, there are not any ATMs, while in others, they exist but you would be ill advised to go near one. As crimes in or around ATMs are a growing trend worldwide, when you use any cash machine, you can avoid various threats to you and your credit card by:

- Using ATMs during daylight hours.
- Utilizing only secure locations, with 24-hour daily protection; for example, inside banks, shops, or malls.
- Avoiding machines in tourist or other areas that are typically targeted (e.g., an upscale restaurant area).
- Preferring not to use machines where you swipe the card through a raised-reader because these are easiest to manipulate.
- Always stopping the transaction if the keys seem hard to press or use.
- Immediately informing the institution that issued the card and the owner of the machine, if there is a contact number, in cases in which your card is not returned.
- Limiting your withdrawals or currency exchanges to small sums.
- Putting your money away before moving from the bank or machine.
- Consider not carrying an ATM card, or at least only carrying one, when you go about your daily life.
- Avoiding wearing clothes and jewelry that make you look rich.
- Going with someone who can focus on being alert to the surroundings while you proceed with your transaction.

For safer transactions, you should follow the steps of:

- Looking around as you approach the machine and at least once during your transaction. Observe safe places you can potentially escape to or persons you can call the attention of.
- Being aware and alert to anyone watching you.
- Wiggling parts of the machine to make sure a scanning device has not been attached to the card reader or elsewhere. Particularly look for gaps and slightly differing colors of the metal or plastic materials.
- Checking out the actual machine and its immediate surroundings for anything that appears suspicious, particularly anything that can record your transaction in anyway. Cameras can record your exposed PIN up to 100 meters (330 feet) away.
- Using your credit card instead of debit card since these tend to have better protection for you.
- Always covering your PIN with your hand and using your body to block the console from any potential camera.

With minor modifications, you can apply much of the above advice to other high-value places such as banks and jewelry shops.

To protect your credit cards, it is best that you seek advice from your bank before you travel. At a minimum, be weary of assumptions and myths: For instance, it is an urban legend that you can type in your PIN in reverse order to alert the police of an emergency at an ATM. Even though, the technology exists, it is not common for banks to use it.[143] For more advice about traveling with cash and credit cards, see the next section, as well as reviewing the advice in the **Personal Belongings and Documents** section **(see Section 1.10)**.

2.16.5 CREDIT CARD SKIMMING

Credit card skimming is one of the fastest growing criminal threats across the world. The Business Insider article "Hackers Tech: Credit Card Skimming" cites the American ATM Association when defining card skimming as "the unauthorized capture of magnetic stripe information by modifying the hardware or software of a payment device, or through the use of a separate card reader."[144] The SCAMwatch article "Card Skimming" notes that the purpose of skimming is to gain access to your accounts, make online purchases, and/or steal your personal identity details. With both personal details and account information in hand, the criminals are ready to make purchases, borrow money, or take out loans[145]—all in your name and paid for by your hard earned money. Some criminals use the information to forge fake credit cards: In Malaysia alone, about 5,000 fraudulent cards are produced daily.[146] The Business Insider article cites research by *The Indian Times* stating that criminals have successfully withdrawn more than $1 billion in the past decade using cloned cards.[147]

The article "Credit Card Skimming Affects One in Five ATM Users," posted October 2010 on the credit card blog UniBul, calls on facts from several sources that indicate the size of the problem:

- ATM (automated teller machines) skimming theft is approaching $1 billion annually.
- It is estimated that ATM skimmers have hit one in five people.
- A bank robber will traditionally gain about $5,000, compared to average profits of $50,000 from ATM pinching.[148]

In 2010, Australian consumers lost $172 million through 657,000 incidents.[149] The Australian Crime Commission (ACC) warned that, for organized crime, online fraud is becoming the new front line and card skimming is the main form of identity theft. To quote the April 2011 *Daily Telegraph* article "Credit Card Skim Scams Net $170 Million" citing the ACC, "When new chip and PIN technology becomes compulsory in Australia in 2013, so-called 'card not present' fraud, when the card is used online or via the mail, is likely to explode."[150] Criminals from Romania, Southeast Asia, and Sri Lanka were the main perpetrators.

A December 2011 *Sun Sentinel* article "Threat of Credit Card 'Skimming' Rises during the Holidays" warned readers in South Florida about the risk to Americans:

- According to the Secret Service, thieves, using the stolen credit and debit card numbers, annually make purchases for about $8 billion. Since 2008, skimming cases rose consecutively by 10% each year.
- Citing ADT Security Services, more than 3 million Americans have been victimized by ATM skimming, losing an average of $1,000 per person. A device can store information from up to 2,000 cards.[151]

As a tourist spot, South Florida is a magnet for this type of crime. If you are working in or visiting Florida, typical locations where you might encounter this crime are at ATMs, pay-at-the-pump machines at gas stations, or hand-held devices (e.g., carried by a waiter at a restaurant). In a local case from July 2010, one criminal stole $45,000 using the ATM skimming method. In another case, this time affecting the New York City area, a single Bulgarian national stole more than $1.8 million from more than 1,400 customers reported the Federal Bureau of Investigation (FBI) in July 2011.[152] Typically, criminals target a series of banks because the card readers are kept in place for just a few hours, as they are simply taped on, according to the FBI article "Taking a Trip to the ATM? Beware of 'Skimmers.'" As Rob Evans, marketing director at NCR, an ATM manufacturer, said in the Bankrate.com article "Skimming the Cash Out of Your Account," "They're not idiots or drug-addled junkies trying to get $20. They're consummate businessmen. They adjust for the last countermeasure that we put in place. We build the wall higher, but they keep coming back with taller ladders."[153]

In 2009, the top seven cities known for being hotbeds of credit card skimming were:

1. New York City, United States
2. London, United Kingdom
3. Istanbul, Turkey
4. Dubai, United Arab Emirates
5. Dublin, Ireland
6. Washington, DC, United States
7. Sydney, Australia[154]

Even though larger cities are typically affected by this crime, it is important to note that it has spread into smaller towns because people are unaware of the risk.

While modified payment machines are a significant threat, another means of skimming cards is to use a separate device. The SCAMwatch article "Why That mp3 Player Is Stealing Your Identity with Skimming" gives the example: "Someone delivering packages can use their Java enabled phone to operate alongside an official credit card reader installed by the employer. When configured properly, this type of application can transmit the credit card information to servers overseas."[155] The example continues with a twist: the consumer gets an error message and automatically swipes again when asked to. Unbeknownst to the victim, the first swipe was transmitted to an illegal server, which prompted the error message, while the second was needed to carry out a legitimate transaction. As a traveler, the common ruse that you need to be aware of is for someone who served you at a cafe, restaurant, bar, or so forth, to run your card through her or his pocket device as part of the process of billing you. Since the card machine is at the back of the establishment, of course, you gave your card to the server. The problem is you also gave him or her the opportunity to discretely use a skimming device.

Clearly, card skimming is a serious threat both at home and abroad. But what can you do about it? Start by finding out where you are vulnerable. The article "2012: Year of the Skimmer" on the Bank Info Security website, highlights several top skimming trends, of which the ones applicable to travelers are ATM skimming, network hacks (i.e., via Wi-Fi at an airport, hotel, or cafe), and attacks on retailers where you might be a shopper.[156]

Typical situations in which you are vulnerable to card skimming include:

- Potentially modified payment machines—ATMs, cash points in small shops, ticket stands in transportation centers, pay points at gas stations, self-checkout stands in grocery stores, rental movie boxes, and any cash machine that is not secured and, therefore, could have been tampered with.
- Out-of-sight transactions in which a separate device can be used—at restaurants, bars, and so forth.

The best advice to protect you, your identity, and your money from this threat is:

- Avoiding potentially modified payment machines.
- Do not use any cash machine that is not secured around the clock and, therefore, could have been tampered with.
- Follow the advice about ATMs in the **Crime and Corruption** section **(see Section 2.16)**.
- Avoiding out of sight transactions in which a separate device can be used.
- Don't allow your card to be out of your sight.
- Knowing what to look for—you could review the photos and descriptions in the "Credit Card Skimming: How Thieves Can Steal Your Card Info without You Knowing It" article on the NetworkWorld.com website[157] or watch one of the many clips on YouTube.com. From the film clips, you will probably notice how determined criminals are, and from the pictures, you'll see how small their equipment is.
- Detecting abuses early on.
- Check your bank account daily while abroad and the period after your return. That said, you should make sure that you have secure means of using web banking.

According to the PCWorld article "Keep Your Credit Cards Safe from Skimmers," you are advised to use a credit card instead of a debit card because debit cards are not always covered by zero liability programs; conversely, credit card consumers are often protected.[158] Also, look out for programs by retailers who want to fight this crime. For instance, the Association for Convenience and Fuel Retailing in the United States introduced security labels, which if lifted to insert a skimming device, will display a "void" message.[159]

If you want to know more about credit card skimming, the "How Credit Card Skimming Works" article on the About.com Credit/Debt Management website is a good starting point[160] as is "Card Skimming" by SCAMwatch.[161]

2.16.6 Violent Crime

Violent crime denotes the use of weapons or physical strength to threaten or harm a person. It can manifest as a sexual assailant using a knife, a petty criminal threatening you with a gun, or a group of carjackers beating on you.

An article entitled "Five Stages to Violent Crime" available on the No Nonsense Self Defense (NNSD) website underlines that in order to avoid crime and violence, it will be useful for you to see them as dynamic processes that can be influenced.[162] The five stages of violent crime are:

1. Intent—perpetrator intends to attack and is ready to evoke violence.
2. Interview—criminal decides on suitability of target and conditions.
3. Positioning—a person with ill intent will aim to overwhelm you.
4. Attack—perpetrator uses force or threat of force.
5. Reaction—the interactions and aftermath of the violence.

For a crime to occur, there must be the ability, opportunity, and intent (AOI triangle) and the five stages. The NNSD's AOI triangle is similar to the threat analysis presented in this book **(see Section 1.1.1)** and you can interchangeably use the models.

Of the five stages, the first three give you the greatest chances of mitigating the situation before it escalates to violence. For example, at the interview stage, you can head off an unfortunate chain of events by not being a suitable target and creating anti-crime conditions. There are several options available to you: You could reduce the benefits (e.g., not wearing an expensive watch) and increase the costs (e.g., by going out with a group in the evenings), as outlined in the **Business Travelers** section **(see Section 2.2.1)**. You can also draw upon your situational awareness skills **(see Sections 1.3 and 2.3)** to detect and deter danger.

If the situation has reached the point in which an attack is imminent, you generally have five possible responses:

- Fight—attack the perpetrator.
- Flight—run from the scene.
- Posture—bid for time to think.
- Submit—follow instructions.
- Freeze—consider your options.[163]

All of these of have their strengths and weaknesses depending on the circumstances. That said, fighting is usually the worse option. It is better to **"Know When to Be Cool and Not a Hero"** as accounted in the following contribution. Whatever response you opt for, remember to value your life and the people around you over property or assets.

**KNOW WHEN TO BE COOL AND NOT A HERO: A BRAZILIAN
FRIEND'S STORY ENDS WITH A CALL TO HIS HOME**

FERNANDO LANZER PEREIRA DE SOUZA
*MANAGEMENT CONSULTANT, EXECUTIVE COACH,
AND INTERNATIONAL TRAINER IN CROSS-CULTURAL
MANAGEMENT (HTTP://WWW.LCOPARTNERS.COM)*

Do not try to use your authority when looking down the barrel of a gun. In such situations, the golden rule is: do not resist at all. This may be difficult for those who come from cultures where heroic behavior is highly valued, but your behavior might be the difference from surviving the episode and being a dead hero in next morning's news.

A Brazilian friend of mine was approaching his parked car at around 11 p.m. in São Paulo when he noticed someone leaning against the car, apparently waiting for him. The man said, "It's about time! I've been waiting here for almost an hour! Hand over the keys!"

He was not pointing a gun, but my friend (a senior banking manager) knew better than to try to find out whether the guy was armed or not. He reached in his pocket and gave him the keys.

As the guy started the car, he opened the window, called my friend closer, and asked, "I'm not familiar with this neighborhood.... Which is the shortest way to the Marginal Avenue?" My friend replied, "Take the first street on the right three blocks down to the first traffic light; take a left and that will lead you to the Marginal."

The next evening, my friend was at home with his wife. The phone rang and she picked it up. "It's for you," she said. "The guy says he's your friend from the parking lot...."

He froze.... He realized he had documents in the car with his name, address, phone number, all kinds of information. As he took the receiver in his hand he was sure this guy was going to threaten him, ask for money, who knows what....

The guy told him: "You were cool last night, you gave me the right directions. If you want your car back, it's parked in front of number 720 Santana Avenue."

My friend found his car at the assigned place, without a scratch. All his stuff was in the car. He figures the guy must have used the car to stage a couple of robberies during the night and then abandoned it.

The point is simply to avoid reacting. Swallow your heroic pride, be wise, and play it cool. In the end, you might not lose anything and gain a story to tell.

2.16.7 After a Crime

Imagine you have been living abroad for more than a year when one day your backpack is stolen, or perhaps someone took it from you on the crowded commuter train. Your immediate response could be to return to your apartment, for a sense of security after a violation of your space. Stop and think of the consequences of someone having both your address and keys: You will see that your apartment is the last place you should go unattended. To mitigate your vulnerability at your accommodation then consider having extra people stay with you, or you should stay elsewhere until the locks have been changed. Ideally, extra layers of protection should be added and maintained at least for a period of time. If you are staying in a hotel and there is any information about the hotel in your stolen belongings, then you should inform the concierge to discuss if you should take additional precautions such as changing rooms or hotel. The following contribution gives additional advice.

IF YOU ARE LUCKY, YOU MIGHT FIND YOUR DESIGNER BAG IN THE TRASHCAN

TANYA SPENCER
GLOBAL TRAVEL SECURITY AND CRISIS MANAGEMENT SPECIALIST, TRAININGSOLUTIONS (HTTP://WWW.TRAININGSOLUTIONS.DK)

After an intensive week of conducting a security management workshop in Nepal, I went to a disco with a group of internationals. Even though there had been a coup just two weeks before, the disco was packed. At the end of the night, one woman said she had been robbed—she had left her purse in the big pile of coats at their feet. I advised her to look for it and report it to the disco. The next day, the disco called her with the bag. She retrieved her expensive designer bag with some of her personal items, but she lost her valuables and she had to consider the security implications for her housing and work.

If you have the unfortunate experience of being robbed, it is worth looking around the vicinity for your purse, backpack, wallet, and so forth. Often criminals don't want to hold on to it because this easily links them to the crime, increasing their risk of being detected and arrested. If you are robbed on the street, for example, look in trashcans, near the base of trees, places with litter, down a nearby alley (but don't make yourself vulnerable to other threats), and in general scan the area. If indoors, then check the bathrooms and "tucked away" places. Inform people or get guarantees from a key person that they will inform others and make arrangements for follow-up contact.

While it is important to know what to do after a security incident, prevention is still preferable. That night, I had checked in a larger bag with my bulky winter clothing. That bag was locked. I kept a small purse with my essentials strapped across the front of my body. In addition to that, I wore a leg safe with extra cash, one credit card, and a piece of paper with important phone numbers.

In most countries you have to report the attempted or actual crime to the police, though it is not advisable in some destinations. Mentally prepare yourself, as dealing with foreign police may not be a pleasant experience. Any language barrier can stop the process before it starts. Add to that their attitude toward you, the crime, or their job in general—if any of those are negative, then you can end up feeling like you experienced another violation. Try to bring a local contact. You can also try contacting your embassy or consul to see if someone can accompany you. If you are in the 90% of the world that is a hierarchical society, then take **Fernando Lanzer Pereira de Souza's** advice to represent yourself as an important person whose case warrants attention and use your key contacts **(see Section 2.7)**. Regardless of the situation and the resources available to you, you have the right to be treated with respect and you should show respect to the local authorities.

When recounting the incident, it will be helpful to remember details about the place, transportation, and people. For people, try A, B, C, D, E, F, G:

- A = Age
- B = Build/body size and shape
- C = Clothing
- D = Distinguishing marks
- E = Elevation (how tall)
- F = Face
- G = Gait (walk)

Perhaps writing about or drawing the incident will help you remember key details that you can tell to the authorities.

If the crime occurred while you were representing your organization, then most organizations will require that you report the incident to them. This can feel as though your organization is prying into your affairs, especially if the incident happened during your personal time. But, from the organization's perspective, this information helps them track threats and vulnerabilities, identify trends, and continuously improve their security measures. Assuming your organization takes its duty-of-care responsibilities seriously and understands that security management protects its assets, brand, and bottom line, then collecting this information is part of its efforts to safeguard you and your colleagues. To be honest, the treatment of incident reports by organizations can be a weak spot in their security management: Some do not analyze the reports, others have taken care of that issue but failed to communicate this to staff in a way that people feel their report made a difference, and of course in many cases the organizational culture stifles reporting such as when staff fear an incident will affect their career. The next contribution reviews some of the issues around reporting to your organization.

WHAT, WHEN, AND HOW TO REPORT SECURITY INCIDENTS TO YOUR ORGANIZATION

TANYA SPENCER

GLOBAL TRAVEL SECURITY AND CRISIS MANAGEMENT SPECIALIST, TRAININGSOLUTIONS (HTTP://WWW.TRAININGSOLUTIONS.DK)

In my travel security workshops and consultancies, I'm often asked if staff should report incidents that occur during their private time to their organization.

Every organization should, hopefully, have its own procedures that will guide you. I normally advise people to report it if the incident:

- Involved organizational property or assets or has implications for the organization. Then it definitely has to be reported.
- May also affect other staff. Then staff are strongly encouraged to report it so that their colleagues can be informed of the threats, and the organization can provide everyone with updated guidelines.

Depending on the case, the affected staff member may withhold some details or request that only key managers are informed of them and the organization may not process the report in the same manner as the other incident reports.

Equally important to report is a "near miss," which is any security incident that almost happened but didn't because of luck or skill. On an organizational level, that information can be collected to analyze the trends and threats with the aim of revising security guidelines. Similarly, as an individual traveler, you can assess the "near-miss" incident to improve your own measures.

If you do report an incident to your organization, then in addition to the basic points detailing the incident, it can be useful to comment on your lessons learnt and advice. Perhaps your organization can draw on these types of insights when it updates its security guidelines.

If the crime compromised any of your personal data and/or equipment, then you need to take steps to limit the repercussions to you and your organization. For stolen (or lost) confidential data, the "best practice" recommendations are:

- List the items that are missing. Hopefully, you are traveling "light" and not carrying superfluous items and, better yet, you can access copies of essential documents (see Section 1.10). A recommended website, Protect Your Financial Identity, has several practical fact sheets: The "Fact Sheet—If Your Wallet or Handbag Is Stolen" is a list of important documents that you may have been carrying. And on the same page, there is an additional matrix for mobile devices.[164] A similar PDF called "What Was in Your Wallet?" by CreditCards.com is equally as good[165] and their "Your Wallet Recovery Kit" is quite useful.[166] However, this book suggests you use these resources *before* an incident so that you can be better positioned to take the appropriate countermeasures. That said, this list becomes a valuable document that needs to be handled with care.
- Prioritize which relevant third parties should be contacted. If the crime compromised any financial data, then reporting the incident to and seeking advice from your bank and credit card company will be urgent priorities. The article "My Wallet Was Stolen: 4 Lessons Learned" on the Kiplinger

website relays how quickly a thief bought things before the article's author could get home and cancel her credit cards: An interesting point the author learnt from the police was that petty criminals will often use the card in a nearby shop to test it and then move on to bigger-ticket items.[167] The key point is that at this stage, you want to just focus on critical contacts because you will be busy with time-critical actions. For example, even though informing the department of motor vehicles of your missing driver's license is important, blocking key accounts will be more urgent.

- Change passwords to exposed bank accounts, emails, apps, social media access points, etc. If these are not password protected before the incident then take this action urgently. If you previously enabled passwords, then you "gained" a bit more time (assuming they are not highly skilled IT thieves) but it is still something that should be done shortly after the incident. You may even consider closing accounts and opening new ones.
- Report the incident to the police. There are cases in which that is not possible, but generally speaking, every effort should be made to obtain a police report because often it is the key to other processes. For instance, in the United States, you can make an initial fraud alert, which lasts 90 days but with a police report you can get an extension of seven years.[168] Dealing with foreign police can be a challenge for various reasons, and be forewarned, they may require that you go through certain procedures such as fingerprinting in order to confirm that you were not involved in the crime.
- Document every exchange you have with authorities and agencies: The CreditCards.com website has a timesaving PDF, "What to Do If You Lost Your Wallet," containing details that you should record.[169]
- Check your insurance coverage. Unless you specifically purchased identity-theft coverage, your other policies may or may not cover this crime so it is worth checking.
- Contact the credit rating agency, if your home country has one. Carefully review your credit activities, looking out for unauthorized activity. Continue to regularly check this.
- Make sure your mail has not been rerouted. This is one way criminals try to gather more information about you in order to perpetuate additional crimes or to cover the tracks of their criminal activities.
- Change the locks to your home or car, if the keys are missing. Your home and car may be vulnerable to further crimes if the keys are missing. And even if returned, they might have been copied: It is safer to assume so.
- Be prepared to contact a lawyer. Data theft cases often have legal ramifications.

The recommended articles "Fact Sheet: Immediate Steps" by Protect Your Financial Identity,[170] "Stolen Purse, Lost Wallet? What to Do, Step by Step" by Identity Theft Labs,[171] and "How to Protect Data after Laptop Theft" by *The New York Times*[172] were the main sources for this list.

It is important to highlight that this list of steps is reactionary and after the fact. To be in a better position to reduce the impact of losing vital data, you can create a contingency plan for your valuables, especially your IT equipment and data **(see Section 1.12)**, based on this list. Copying relevant information, such as your passport **(see Section 1.10)** and the serial numbers of your mobile devices **(see Section 1.12)**, will be a part of this process.

2.16.8   CORRUPTION

Corruption is not just an irritation, it is "an insidious plague that has a wide range of corrosive effects on societies" according to the United Nations former General Secretary Kofi Annan, as cited in **"How to Avoid Bribes and Facilitation Payments"** below. In South Africa, the *Times Live* wrote in March 2012 that the corruption at the government level cost taxpayers around $3.4 billion per year.[173] Conservative estimates place corruption in Nigeria between $4 and $8 billion.[174] The Indonesia Corruption Watch announced that an estimated $238 million was lost to corruption in 2011.[175] It is claimed that a 2011 report released by the Chinese Central Bank but then quickly removed stated that corrupt officials took $180 billion overseas from the Chinese Treasury.[176]

An article entitled "An Analysis of India's Pathetic 95th Rank in the Corruption Index and Its Far Reaching Social Impact!" on the Business and Economy website reveals:

> India has more black money stashed in Swiss banks than all other countries combined! The number eclipses $1,500 billion: A distant second on this ignominious list is Russia with $470 billion black money, followed by UK with $390 billion and China at $96 billion.[177]

According to the "Corruption Perception Index 2011" on the Transparency International (TI) website, the top five countries with the best perceptions were:

1. New Zealand
2. Denmark, Finland
4. Sweden
5. Singapore[178]

At the bottom of the TI index, the countries with the worst perceived levels of corruption were:

177. Sudan, Turkmenistan, Uzbekistan
180. Afghanistan, Myanmar
182. North Korea, Somalia

On the website of the United Kingdom's Serious Fraud Office, there is an extensive list of corruption indicators. To quote just a few:

- Abnormal cash payments or lavish gifts.
- Pressure exerted for payments to be made urgently or ahead of schedule.
- Payments being made through a third party country.
- Private meetings with public contractors or companies hoping to tender for contracts.

- An individual never takes time off and insists on dealing with specific contractors him/herself.
- Raising barriers around specific roles or departments, which are key in the tendering/contracting process.
- Bypassing normal tendering/contractors procedure.
- Invoices being agreed to in excess of contract without reasonable cause.
- Missing documents or records regarding meetings or decisions.
- The payment of, or making funds available for, high value expenses, school fees, and so forth, on behalf of others.[179]

Birgitte Bang Nielsen's contribution **"How to Avoid Bribes and Facilitation Payments"** maps out the consequences of corruption and suggests ways on how you can avoid it. Supplemental advice includes **Ken Nygaard Jensen's** tip to use any language barrier to frustrate corrupt officials. The last contribution by **Dmitry Budanov** first contextualizes corruption in Russian history and then moves on to forecast future developments for international businesses operating there based on positive current trends.

HOW TO AVOID BRIBES AND FACILITATION PAYMENTS

BIRGITTE BANG NIELSEN
BOARD MEMBER, TRANSPARENCY INTERNATIONAL, DENMARK

I am from Denmark and here we don't think of corruption in everyday life. The explanation is, as several international surveys have shown, that Denmark for several decades has had a severe corruption case neither in the public nor in the private sector. The latest survey from Transparency International points out that bribes or facilitation payment in public services such as education, health care, courts, and policy are not happening to an extent worth mentioning. Denmark has been in the top five of Transparency International's Corruption Perceptions Index for many years as a corruption-free zone.

Unfortunately, this is not the situation in most of the emerging markets and developing countries where more and more companies are doing business and NGOs operate. Subsequently, a lot of us are traveling to countries where corruption is a part of everyday life. It is important to remember that corruption is a big—if not the biggest—threat to development in these countries. This is because corruption stifles all initiatives to growth, which could lead to better distribution of income and wealth and reduce poverty and encourage development.

As former General Secretary Kofi Annan said at the approval of the United Nations Convention against Corruption in 2003:

> Corruption is an insidious plague that has a wide range of corrosive effects on societies. It undermines democracy and the rule of law, leads to violations of human rights, distorts markets, erodes the quality of life, and allows organized crime, terrorism and other threats to human security to flourish.

This evil phenomenon is found in all countries big and small, rich and poor but it is in the developing world that its effects are most destructive. Corruption hurts the poor disproportionately by diverting funds intended for development, undermining a government's ability to provide basic services, feeding inequality and injustice, and discouraging foreign investment and aid. Corruption is a key element in economic underperformance, and a major obstacle to poverty alleviation and development.*

Transparency International clearly defines corruption and bribery as "the misuse of entrusted power for private gains."

When operating in corrupt countries, you will often meet bribery in the form of "facilitation payments." These are small payments or gifts used to secure or expedite the performance of a routine or action to which the project company is entitled. Facilitation payments are typically demanded by low level—and low income—governmental officials. Even though they are small amounts, they are as prohibited as bigger bribes in most countries. They are considered as bribes no matter how small or big. But in many developing countries these laws are weakly enforced.

AVOIDING CORRUPTION WITH YOUR COMPANY

When you are traveling you will often encounter bribes or facilitations payments—one way or the other. There are ways you and your company can mitigate the risks associated with corruption. Your company should:

- Have a clear policy about bribes and specifically on facilitation payments. Often, companies have an unclear and fluffy policy on facilitation payment because it has been seen as a necessary evil, but more and more companies are setting up zero tolerance policies and starting to combat all kinds of bribes including facilitation payments.
- Make suppliers, customers, business partners, agents, and other stakeholders aware of the company's anti-corruption commitment.
- Inform all staff about the policy and train in the dilemmas it will cause.
- Provide during the pre-trip briefing a section about the corruption risks you will face.

AVOIDING CORRUPTION BY KNOWING WHAT TO EXPECT AND WHAT YOU CAN ACCEPT

As a traveler operating in a country with corruption, you should find out before your departure:

- What kind of bribes and facilitation will you meet? In what situations? What are the possibilities to avoid? The best solution is to

---

* Secretary General Kofi Annan, "Statement on the Adoption by the General Assembly of the United Nations Convention Against Corruption," October 31, 2003. http://www.unodc.org/unodc/en/treaties/CAC/background/secretary-general-speech.html.

never get started. Once a public official knows that you are a potential offer and willing to pay, he will keep chasing you and the amounts he requires will increase.

- Will your company accept the consequences of your saying "no"? The consequences could be a delay of the service you are asking for or reduced quality of the service.
- Exactly what are you allowed to do regarding social events such as sightseeing, dinners, theatres, sporting events, concerts, clubs, etc.? Is the event at all acceptable, and if so, what is a reasonably priced event? May spouses participate? How long can it take? Would you feel OK if the event was reported in the newspaper the next day?
- What could an acceptable gift be? Is cash OK? Are gifts like sunglasses, bags, or electronic equipment OK? What if it is a birthday present? Remember that flowers are an appropriate gift in most countries.

AVOIDING CORRUPTION WHILE TRAVELING

An initiative in India that might give you some ideas of what to do when combating facilitation payments is a website called "I Paid a Bribe" (http://www.ipaidabribe.com). It is an initiative to tackle corruption by harnessing the collective energy of citizens. One can report and register any kind of corrupt act on the website. The reports will, perhaps for the first time, provide a snapshot of bribery. It will be used to argue for improving governance systems and procedures, and tightening law enforcement and regulation. In the first five months, 3,000 stories were posted. Today, the number of hits, inputs, and chats are enormous and it is linked to Facebook and Twitter.

The website has set up the top-ten tips for avoiding bribes and facilitation payments:

1. Be confident. Be firm. Be assertive. Address officers by their names without being rude.
2. Do your homework. Read rules, regulations, and citizens' charters. Demand services accordingly.
3. Do it yourself. Avoid touts, agents, and middle men.
4. Get receipts. Insist on receipts for all payments. Demand acknowledgement for documents/forms submitted.
5. Seek reasons. Do not accept verbal rejections. Demand in writing why your document/form is being rejected.
6. Use "right to information" regulations. Apply for information if officers refuse to provide information.
7. Refuse to bribe. Firmly and openly say that you will not give bribes.
8. File complaints. Report demands for bribes, unnecessary delays, and rude behavior.

9. Record evidence. Record conversations on your mobile, take photographs of the corruption, and attach these to your complaints.
10. Try *Gandhigiri*. Gandhigiri, meaning do as Gandhi did—demonstrate your protest nonviolently.[*]

Following the advice might not be easily implemented from day one, but it is certainly worth trying because stopping corruption will take everyone's efforts.

---

[*] "Say No to Corruption! Follow the 10 Commandments!" I Paid A Bribe. ND. http://www.ipaidabribe.com/blog/say-no-corruption-follow-10-commandments.

In addition to the advice that **Birgitte Bang Nielsen** cites from http://www.ipaidabribe.com, specific tips for dealing with corrupt police include:

- Ask for and write down their badges and names. A legitimate cop on legitimate police business will not mind, while a fake cop may not follow through on any ill intentions.
- Do not expose your wallet.
- Do not give them your passport or other documents before you have verified that they are police.
- Never leave busy areas to follow a police officer.
- Insist on calling your embassy.
- Show documents from your embassy, if you have any.

You could also try using language as a barrier, as suggested in the following contribution.

IT'S NOT POLITICALLY CORRECT TO SAY, BUT MAKE LANGUAGE A HOPELESS BARRIER FOR CORRUPT OFFICIALS

KEN NYGAARD JENSEN
SECURITY ADVISER, MINISTRY OF FOREIGN AFFAIRS OF DENMARK

In some cases in Russia, you can actually make a language barrier work to your advantage. If faced with a policeman who demands money of you or you encounter a person who upholds the notoriously extreme levels of Russian bureaucracy, simply act out your role as the stupid foreigner who does not understand one word of what is spoken to you. Very often the Russian troublemaker will give in to the hopelessness of the language situation and after just a few minutes you will be allowed to pass on. This may not be politically correct advice to give, but it is very well tested and it works!

Always remember that when you deal with foreign police, you must walk the fine line between asserting your rights and respecting the fact that they represent the law of the land. Though illegally demanding money from you, a corrupt cop can still find ways to legally put you in jail!

As **Birgitte Bang Nielsen** noted, tackling corruption will take everyone's efforts. In that regard, **Dmitry Budanov's** contribution ends with mitigating measures international businesses can put in place.

CORRUPTION AND INTERNATIONAL BUSINESS IN RUSSIA: A PREDICTION BASED ON IN-DEPTH ANALYSIS

DMITRY BUDANOV

ASIS INTERNATIONAL RUSSIA CHAPTER CHAIR (HTTP://WWW. ASISRUSSIA.RU). REPRINTING AND MODIFICATIONS MADE BY PERMISSION. SEE "CORRUPTION AND INTERNATIONAL BUSINESS IN RUSSIA" DMITRY BUDANOV, SASMA. JULY 2010. HTTP://SAS-MA.ORG/ENG/EDITION-JULY-2010/228-CORRUPTION-AND-INTERNATIONAL-BUSINESS-IN-RUSSIA-DMITRY-BUDANOV

Corruption in Russia, just as the vast majority of other modern matters and trends, has deep historical roots, which require some explanation. This is a brief summary of corruption in Russia.

In ancient Russia corruption was divided into two types—obtaining unjust advantages for the lawful acts ("recompense") or unlawful acts ("covetousness"). Corruption was an absolutely legal type of activity for Russian officials until the eighteenth century: They did not receive any salary; therefore they lived on the so-called "feeding" or, in other words, they took bribes for a living. In 1715, accepting any form of bribes was announced a grave offense, while the government started paying a salary to its officials. In the meantime, the reign of Peter the Great witnessed bureaucracy expanding incredibly. Salary was paid from time to time and the corrupt practices actually remained the only source of income for the low- and mid-level officials. After the death of Peter the Great, the "feeding" system was reestablished and only Catherine II returned official salaries. However, the switchover to paper money and a number of other political and economic factors still contributed to the growth of corruption.

After the revolution in Soviet Russia, the criminal code of 1922 punished bribery by execution. Later in the twentieth century, the corruption issue was not open to public debate until the mid 1980s. There were two main reasons: first, political considerations, and second, the level of bribery and other types of corruption practices in Soviet times proved to be considerably smaller than during "perestroika" and in the following years.

The early 1980s were marked by a handful of high-profile anti-corruption cases. This trend has been ongoing. The bottom line—we are currently in a situation where at least 50% of the Russian population does not consider corruption a crime and has personal experience in giving forced bribes (according to a survey of the All-Russia Public Opinion Research Center in 2006). Many federal high-ranking officials, by using their political weight, system imperfections, and absence of any real political will demonstrated by the Russian leadership in fighting corruption, do not even bother to comply with the drastic anti-corruption measures, which the government announces on a regular basis.

Some "corruption stabilization" in the last decade in Russia as stated by the world ratings of Transparency International (corruption perception index, 2.4 in 1999 vs. 2.2 in 2009) in fact led to the ever-growing amount of criminal cases against bribery and corruption.

More recently the world financial crisis contributed to the global growth of corruption by more than 9%. Furthermore, Russia still does not have any considerably efficient anti-bribery mechanisms and policies. It is obvious that corruption practices cannot be suppressed by punitive actions alone, while Russian "democracy" is not mature enough to have a "helicopter view" of the entire picture.

However, the purpose of this contribution is not only to raise the "corruption outrage" matter once again. The ultimate objective is to briefly describe the dynamics of change in the attitude of the large multinational businesses in Russia toward such corruption practices and try to find the reasons why they take place.

A representative of the U.S. nonprofit TRACE International, which consults large multinationals on how to handle corruption, at the meeting held in Moscow recommended large foreign businesses to "reconsider their position in Russia" and added that she is "more optimistic about [the business climate in] Nigeria than Russia."[*]

The business community has often noted that, from the viewpoint of corruption, countries such as Nigeria, Brazil, China, or India look more appealing. Why?

My personal opinion, which is based on my 18-year working experience in commercial security and risk management in the best interests of large international companies in Russia and other former Soviet Union (FSU) countries (as an external advisor and a company employee), is that return on investment and competitive advantage for these companies have largely reduced lately compared to the business-related risks. That is, the business rate of return has decreased due to several objective and subjective reasons. While the business environment has become more structured and organized, some business risks remain pretty much the same throughout the years and the cost of their mitigation is growing.

I would say the time, peaking in the late 1980s and early 1990s, when foreign business consciously chose to face very high risks by investing into Russia and thus receiving excess revenues, has already gone by or is going by as we speak.

---

[*] *The Moscow Times*, March 16, 2010, "Corruption Too Much for Western Companies."

While corruption has historically played a big role, I forecast that international businesses operating in Russia will witness decline in corruption affecting them. What do I base my prediction on? I cite several reasons (not in priority order):

- There is an increase in qualification and appreciation of the labor force at virtually all levels and across all industries. For example, the next generation of the low- and mid-level managers, who are graduating from universities right now and/or have already started their working careers, is absolutely competitive with their contemporaries in Europe and the United States. The number of professional and highly paid top managers is growing exponentially. Similar processes are taking place in the production sphere. The competitive environment, growing trade union movement, general statistical improvement of the material wealth of the Russian urban population, gradual improvement of the legal framework, one and a half generations of youth that grew up in the new environment of corporate relations, vast educational opportunities, and many other factors have drastically altered the situation in the labor market in the last 15 to 20 years.
- The competitive environment has changed significantly: Russian businesses are becoming more mature, diversified, and competitive, which of course affects the cost of assets across virtually all the categories without any exception. Meanwhile, there is an obvious growth of some industrial giants, and above all in the energy sector, as well as natural resources development, banking activities, etc.—the interests of which have long gone beyond the Russian borders. It is also necessary to mention that there are many "young" foreign businesses in the market, which due to their sizes and "appetite" react to any changes in the business environment more actively and promote their business solutions more aggressively and uncommonly compared to the large multinationals.
- The growth of Russia's political weight abroad is accompanied by the political stabilization in the domestic market. This and some other measures and events led to the formation of a more organized business environment, which is substantially different from the chaos that reigned in Russia in the early 1990s.

This is not the full list of recent trends; nevertheless they are the most common.

It is also necessary to mention two things that I personally witnessed several times: First, some large multinationals justify their unprofessional business practices, ineffective talent retention policy, poorly adapted marketing solutions, lack of reliable financial forecasting, inability to understand the complexity of the local environment, unacceptable losses, and so forth. They tend to blame chaotic market trends, political instability, high percentage of the infringement production, and so on, and so on, and … corruption. This gets them off the hook for acknowledging their contribution to illegal activities.

Second, there are many examples in which large international companies state today that they are ready to leave the Russian market due to existing corruption issues. Yet the 1990s ensured their "soft" breakthrough into the Russian market and receipt of the immediate competitive advantage by having accepted "the rules of the game." Put otherwise, they contributed to the growth of corruption and sometimes organized crime by paying monthly rewards for so-called protection. As a rule, such companies are sooner or later caught in the spotlight of corruption scandals.

But there are many other examples too. Typically, they concern those companies that came to Russia to stay for a long while and are involved in regular reinvestment of the money they earn. They are socially responsible not only in the annual reports for the external auditors but in practice spend much effort and money in search of the creative solutions, which allow them to avoid traps of the Russian "corruption" for years on end.

In the near future, we may see that success for foreign businesses in Russia will largely depend on:

- Understanding and accepting those changes, which have taken place in this country in recent years
- How clearly the risk identification models are built and used
- Employment of the qualified managers, who are ready and able to look for the legitimate solutions to difficult situations that the business faces
- How strictly the business not only declares observance of but actually observes the laws of this country in practice

We also cannot underestimate the importance of adequate internal control systems, which prevent internal corruption and contribute to healthy corporate structure and environment. Preventive measures aimed at increasing loyalty and corporate responsibility for the company's personnel will be by no means unimportant in tackling corruption in Russia. Companies need to make sure that employees follow anti-corruption measures, as this will undoubtedly minimize the risks considerably.

For further reading about corruption, a lot depends on your particular interests. The cartoon "Say No to Corruption! Follow the 10 Commandments!" on the I Paid A Bribe website is for anyone traveling or moving to a destination that struggles under corruption: Its usefulness derives from a humored approach and quick overview.[180] The Serious Fraud Office's "Corruption Indicators" article is an excellent resource because it gives practical samples that could apply to both your private and/or professional life.[181]

If corruption will affect your work life, then the Business Anti-Corruption Portal is an excellent resource covering country profiles, tools, e-learning, and resources:

It would probably also be useful for NGO managers, too.[182] The World Bank's "Governance & Anti-Corruption" website is filled with links that could be worth exploring.[183] And, of course, Transparency International has tools, resources, and news on their website.[184]

For other types of readings, on the Internet there are a range of resources from reports such as "Fraud and Corporate Governance: Changing Paradigm in India" by Ernst & Young for specific business interests[185] to "Corruption in the NGO World: What It Is and How to Tackle It" by the *Humanitarian Exchange Magazine* for how it broadly affects a sector.[186]

2.17   WELL-BEING: STRESS MANAGEMENT

Simply being an international traveler can add to your stress levels. But not all stress is bad. **Sian Kelly's** contribution explains the symptoms of different types of stressors and what you and your organization can do to prevent stress from becoming a negative strain on you and your productivity.

STRESS: POSITIVE, NEGATIVE, AND WHAT TO DO

SIAN KELLY

HEALTH, SAFETY, AND WELL-BEING CONSULTANT AND EXECUTIVE COACH. DIRECTOR, CALM-CONSULTING (HTTP://WWW.CALM-CONSULTING.COM)

Stress is normal. It is the body's natural reaction to a physical or emotional challenge. Stress can be positive in activating a person's body and mind. In small doses, stress helps you to stay focused, energetic, and alert. But when stress becomes overwhelming it can damage your health, mood, productivity, relationships, and can impact on your abilities to keep safe and secure.

Travelers and expatriates need to be aware of underlying factors that contribute to stress when starting a new assignment and whether a factor affects you positively or negatively. Factors such as adjusting to changes in the new environment, being away from family and friends, working with new people in a different culture, long-haul traveling, being in different time zones, and so forth all contribute to a basic level of stress that normally decreases after the first few weeks of a new assignment depending on your ability to adapt.

Everyone experiences stress differently but there are some common warning signs and symptoms that we need to recognize in order to reduce its harmful effects. Some of the most common signs or symptoms of stress include:

- *Physical symptoms*: over-tiredness, diarrhea, constipation, headaches, abdominal and back pains, sleeping disorders, appetite changes
- *Emotional signs*: anxiety, frustration, guilt, mood swings, undue pessimism or optimism, irritability, crying spells, nightmares, apathy, depression

- *Mental signs*: forgetfulness, poor concentration, poor job performance, negative attitude, loss of creativity and motivation, boredom, negative self-talk, paranoid thoughts
- *Relational signs*: feeling isolated, resentful or intolerant of others, loneliness, marriage problems, nagging, social withdrawal, antisocial behavior
- *Behavioral changes*: increased alcohol, drug, and/or tobacco use, change in eating habits or sexual behavior, increase in risky behavior, hyperactivity, avoidance of situations, cynical attitudes
- *Collapse of belief systems*: feeling of emptiness, doubt in religious beliefs, feeling unforgiving, looking for magical solutions, loss of purpose of life, needing to prove self-worth, cynicism about life

A person does not need to display all of these, but if the person or you notice a few signs then it could indicate that coping techniques and stress management strategies need implementing.

There are different types of stressors that you should be aware of, but preventative self-care measures can help you avoid and cope with stress in its various forms.

CUMULATIVE STRESS

Other factors such as a chaotic and reactive work environment, assimilating new information under tight deadlines, and experiencing communication difficulties due to personality and cultural differences can also build up over time to cause cumulative stress. Personal reactions may be intensified if one is feeling isolated from family and other social support networks, facing moral and ethical dilemmas, or experiencing travel difficulties and/or sleep deprivation. A sequence of relatively mild events can create high stress levels if not dealt with effectively on an ongoing basis and may develop into professional exhaustion, known as burnout. Burnout is an exhaustion of normal stress coping mechanisms.

BURNOUT

When stress accumulates over a long period of time, a point can be reached where you feel you can't take any more. You may feel physically, emotionally, and mentally exhausted. People will not suddenly burn out, however, since it is a gradual process that occurs over a period of time. By addressing any physical, emotional, and behavioral warning signs or symptoms of stress at an early stage, burnout can be prevented. Ignoring, denying, or neglecting warning signs, however, can lead to a state of burnout.

TRAUMATIC STRESS

Traumatic stress disrupts one's sense of control, as a result of a critical incident in which a person is threatened with serious harm or death. Examples of critical incidents include car accidents, robbery and muggings, assaults, witnessing extreme suffering/death, being within range of gunfire, bombings, kidnapping, carjacking, and experiencing a natural disaster.

After a traumatic event or critical incident, strong reactions may arise from thoughts of what might have happened. Reactions during the first hours may include shock, disbelief, feelings of being overwhelmed, confusion, difficulty in making decisions, and physical reactions such as nausea, dizziness, intense fatigue, muscle tremors, and sleeping difficulties. All these reactions are normal.

In some rare cases, a pathological condition called posttraumatic stress disorder (PTSD) may develop months or even years later. Support from a mental health specialist will be required.

WHAT YOU CAN DO

Recognize that feelings of distress in yourself and others are legitimate. They are not signs of personal weakness or a lack of professionalism. For your own care and maintenance, take personal responsibility for noticing signs and symptoms that your coping mechanisms are heading toward overload. Ensure you get support to deal with symptoms of stress. Identify and tackle the cause of the stress.

SELF-CARE STRATEGIES

Know yourself:

- Your resources.
- Your limits.
- Your personal warning signs and stress reactions.
- Use physical exercise, music, rest, breathing, and relaxation to reduce tension.
- Monitor intake of coffee, alcohol, and nicotine.
- Share, communicate, be clear:
  - have a support network in place so that stressful events can be talked through. Similarly, find someone to share your doubts, fears, and disappointments with.
  - express your needs (to your line manager, company psychologist)
  - say no (e.g., to unreasonable work demands).

In a team, the following group reactions may be the effect of excessive stress:

- Anger toward managers' lack of initiative
- Clique formation (inner and outer circle) and conflict between groups
- High turnover of personnel
- Negative attitude toward workplace
- Critical attitudes toward colleagues
- Scapegoat mentality

Support each other:

- Show that you care for your colleagues and listen to them.
- Avoid criticizing or playing down their remarks.

- Be alert to changes in behavior and propose action if necessary (e.g., take a long weekend off).
- In case of security incidents, take time to talk and share emotions.

Stress busting tips:

- Whenever possible, respect normal working hours.
- Avoid working on weekends.
- Allow sufficient time for rest, relief, and relationships.
- Eat well-balanced meals at regular times.
- Avoid excessive alcohol.
- Keep your body fit. Do things that you enjoy.

MANAGEMENT'S ROLE

If your role is to manage others, you can play a vital part in the prevention of cumulative stress by maintaining a healthy working environment. You can serve as a healthy role model; create opportunities for staff to speak about tensions and communication problems, facilitate extracurricular activities such as sports, and organize social events. If you notice negative trends, give the person affected an opportunity to rest and talk about the causes of his or her stress. Depending on the seriousness of the situation, you may need to seek professional advice and assistance.

If you manage others, ensure you can recognize the early signs of cumulative stress and burnout. Be aware of the importance of adequate support and action. Top management should look into ways of reducing stress coming from inside the organization.

Sian Kelly recommends that you "know yourself" in terms of your resources and limitations. To help you achieve that, you can consider using the battery model, as described in the next contribution, or similar models.

BATTERY MODEL TO BALANCE THE NEGATIVE STRAINS AND POSITIVE GAINS OF EXPATRIATE LIVING

TANYA SPENCER

GLOBAL TRAVEL SECURITY AND CRISIS MANAGEMENT SPECIALIST, TRAININGSOLUTIONS (HTTP://WWW.TRAININGSOLUTIONS.DK)

The "battery model" can be used to help you balance the negative strains and positive gains of daily life as an international traveler. On the positive side, look at all the things that give you or replace your energy. And conversely, what on the negative side drains you. For example, you might be the sporty type at home but while abroad you might decide that you neither have the time nor the opportunity. However, after several weeks on the road or multiple trips abroad, you might feel that it is harder to gather the energy to meet all your work demands. By using the battery model, you might discover that it is quite important for you to exercise, and based on that, you could decide to pack a yoga mat, elastic exercise band, or simply promise yourself to do your sit-ups and push-ups every morning.

If you are interested in reading more about stress management in general or any specific aspects of it such as things you can do at your workplace, the Internet is awash with resources. To recommend a few, the article "Stress Management: How to Reduce, Prevent, and Cope with Stress" on the HelpGuide.org website lays out a comprehensive overview with plenty of practical advice.[187] For instance, in a text box, advice for dealing with stressful situations can be summed up by the four A's. Either "Change the situation": Avoid or alter the stressor. Or "Change your reaction": Adapt or accept the stressor. Similarly, the "Stress Management" article on MedicineNet.com is a comprehensive, fact-filled resource with plenty of links.[188] The website StressManagementTips.com is filled with practical exercises and tips that you can easily integrate into your daily regime.[189] As for practical tips, the *Reader's Digest* article "37 Stress Management Tips: Find Your Own Escape Route with Our Easy Stress Management Tips" is not only comprehensive but has useful links.[190]

If you want to set aside time for considered reflection, a good resource is the bundle of workbooks available through the McGraw-Hill Higher Education (MHHE) website on such related topics as "General Wellness," "Stress Management," "Psychological and Spiritual Wellness," and "Personal Safety."[191] Another easy-to-use resource is the "Stress Management Worksheets" by Inner Health Studio.[192] In addition, many of the websites listed in the corresponding section in **Chapter 1 (see Section 1.17)** also have resources about stress and managing it proactively.

Especially since your stressors and responses are so individual, based on your unique set of circumstances including your upbringing, cultural heritage, trials and errors, and support systems, then it is advisable that you seek stress management advice and tips from sources that are most relevant for you.

All said, the human construction of mind, body, and soul is set up in such a way that a lot can be done with simply breathing deeply—the expanding-your-belly, letting-your-whole-body-slowly-relax-and-"hold-it," before gradually-deflating-your-belly, preferably with your eyes closed repeated ten times or more, kind. But, even if your circumstances do not allow all that, just concentrating on your breathing when calm is required can often ease tensions and put you in a better position to make the "right" decisions and actions. Furthermore, regularly breathing deeply can decrease your stress levels. As a free and easy resource, concentrated breathing is a tool that you can utilize anywhere, at any time.

2.18   WORTH KNOWING, WHILE TRAVELING: CHAPTER 2 SUMMARY

Hopefully, as a reader, you highlighted, took note, or acted upon suggestions that are relevant to you and modified other tips to suit your circumstances. Accordingly, the chapter's key points will differ from reader to reader, so the summary offered here of the three points for each section can be used to "jog your memory." How do these points compare with the ones you identified?

2.1 Understanding the Potential Risks While Traveling

- While risks do exist, billions of people live in and millions of people travel safely in every location, everyday, so your task is to establish the facts about the likelihood of facing a particular threat.
- With facts in hand, you can then ask yourself, are the risks acceptable? Even if your answer is "yes," you can always consider what else can you do to further mitigate the risks.
- You should aim to have the right levels of knowledge about the threats, context, and current situation; possess security and cultural awareness skills; maintain an attitude that respects others while requiring respect for you; and behave in ways that mitigate risks.

2.2 Personal Considerations

- Supplement your understanding of potential threats by getting answers to such questions as: Who and what are affected? Where? What type of incident? Who did it? What weapon? When?
- To help you avoid violence, particularly sexually oriented threats, maintain positive self-worth, radiate self-confidence, be aware, register your reaction, take a stand, act, and create distance.
- Think about likely scenarios and prepare yourself accordingly.

2.3 Implementing Situational Awareness

- To better read the environment, be cognizant of what you normally observe and what else you should be noticing, given your threat and contextual assessments for your location.
- Actively hone your skill set that helps you identify the buildup of potentially insecure situations.
- If you want to use your mobile as a tool in an insecure situation, such as walking from the train station to your accommodations, then have it call-ready, in your hand though out of sight, and note that talking on the phone can represent both a distraction for you and a target for criminals.

2.4 Preparedness

- Weigh the practical and security implications of situational updates and current information.

- Decide on which basic precautions apply and how they should be modified to suit the local conditions.
- Have confidence in your preparedness so that you can concentrate on getting the most of every trip.

2.5 Organizational Considerations

- Recognize the different vulnerabilities of local and international staff and implement appropriate remedies for safeguarding them.
- Organizational policies, procedures, and preparations have to be operable before an incident.
- Good leadership is needed for good security management, which in turn is needed for good international operations.

2.6 Political Considerations

- Understand political considerations to create more options and make better decisions: In other words, use these insights to expand the safe space you can maneuver in.
- Always think how the circumstances might affect you and adjust accordingly.
- Compare your personal strengths and weaknesses, and external opportunities and threats (SWOT) in light of the information that you gathered from the PEST (politics, economics, sociocultural, technological) model: Use any insights to update your mitigation measures.

2.7 Cultural Considerations

- Use your cultural insights to prevent misunderstandings and to properly handle potentially volatile situations.
- Pick a cultural framework, model, or any combination thereof that makes sense to you and fits your realities.
- To deescalate interpersonal conflicts, try actively listening to the person, highlighting agreements and making clear points while maintaining a respectful attitude and an attitude that demands respect.

2.8 Medical Considerations

- Most of the diseases that travelers catch when overseas are waterborne or water-related: Accordingly, hydration and sanitation are two of the most essential areas where you should make an effort to prevent aches and pains.
- You are responsible for maintaining as high a standard as possible for your own health and well-being, including allowing yourself time to adjust to the changes traveling brings.
- When you get back from a prolonged trip, a medical check-up is advisable.

2.9 Insurance

- It is possible to buy a new policy or extend your existing one while you are abroad but it is worth knowing that not all insurance companies offer policies for after a trip has started.
- Most insurance companies do allow for extensions but they may set limits on how many times this can be done.
- Obtaining proper coverage before a trip is still the best option.

2.10 Personal Belongings and Documents

- From the time you leave home and throughout your journeys, carry a closely guarded "secret stash" of reserve money, identity papers (originals or copies), and details for key contacts.
- Know how many bags you are carrying and recount them regularly whenever you are in transit: And it is worth emphasizing, the more valuable it is to you, the closer you should keep it to your person.
- Consider not using obvious laptop bags or the like for your mobile devices.

2.11 Information Security: Identity Theft and Industrial Espionage

- Be aware of the relevant variations of IT threats and emerging trends (worldwide, regionally, and locally).
- Do not assume others will not be curious or mischievous if they find your lost mobile device: Do be vigilant about safeguarding data and entry points into systems.
- When you travel as a company representative you need to always be alert to threats against your organization's information: Even on vacation you need to think about how much information and what information you are willing to tell to inquiring strangers.

2.12 Communication Equipment and Procedures

- In these modern times, you need to protect your devices, data, and apps.
- At the very least, use the devices' locking mechanisms and securely lock away devices that you are not carrying with you.
- All your mobile devices should be scanned, formatted, reset, and backed up before connecting to your home or office network.

2.13 Airports and Airlines

- Threats from thieves and terrorists are the highest in the entry and exit halls of airports so move out of these areas as quickly as possible.
- Remove any cash from your wallet before you place it in the tray and know what you placed on the conveyor belt so you can retrieve all of your possessions.
- Be polite and cooperative with passport control officials and security checkpoint personnel because they literally have your ticket to travel in their hands.

2.14 Transportation

- Realize that often security cameras in bus and train stations are not monitored "in real time" so they can give a false sense of safety since help may not be on its way when you hope for it.
- Remove any interior and exterior signs of your vehicle being a rental car and choose a model that blends in.
- Casually but purposefully scan your surroundings and the inside of your vehicle as you approach it, lock your car doors once you are inside, and use your seatbelt while driving are all basic precautions you can take anywhere in the world.

2.15 Accommodation

- Exercise a degree of caution when giving out private information in public spaces: For instance, if your room number is spoken too loudly by the clerk and people might have heard it, have the receptionist assign you a new room.
- When you initially view your room, security criteria you can use include: Making sure that it is between the third and sixth floors, faces the hotel's inner courtyard, is close to the elevator/stairs but away from emergency exits, has adequate locks and physical security features, and has a working phone.
- Take a couple of minutes to run through a few realistic scenarios and decide on your action plan: At a minimum locate the exits as soon as you arrive and plan not to use the elevators in cases of fire or unknown threat.

2.16 Crime and Corruption

- When you are about to use a cash machine/ATM, follow basic precautions such as looking around as you approach the machine and at least once during your transaction, wiggling parts of the machine to make sure a scanning device has not been attached, and opting for your credit card since these tend to have better protection guarantees than debit cards.
- If you do experience street crime, it will be helpful to report details about the place, transportation, and people: For people, try to note age, body build, clothing, distinguishing marks, elevation (how tall), face, and gait (walk).
- If you are confronted with corrupt police, some options available to you include asking for and writing down their badges and names, not giving them your documents before you have verified that they are police, getting receipts for everything you hand over, and insisting upon having a translator if required. And, of course, you should avoid leaving busy areas with police.

2.17 Well-Being: Stress Management

- Not all stress is bad: Stress can be positive and help you to stay focused, energetic and alert, but when stress becomes overwhelming it can damage your health, mood, productivity, relationships, and impact your ability to keep safe and secure.
- Maintain healthy habits, as well as know your own resources, limits, personal warning signs, and stress reactions.
- Common warning signs that indicate a person is stressed include sleeping disorders, poor concentration, loneliness, increased alcohol, drug, and/or tobacco use, and cynicism.

All this is to say, there is a lot you can do while traveling to continuously ensure that you a have safe, secure, healthy, and enjoyable trip: It is just a question of which measures best suit you and your upcoming travel realities.

REFERENCES

1. "2011 Quality of Living Worldwide City Rankings," Mercer Consulting. November 2011. http://www.mercer.com/qualityoflivingpr#personal-safety.
2. "2011 'Extremely Turbulent' for Business Travelers," Anne Freedman, Risk and Insurance. January 30, 2012. http://www.riskandinsurance.com/story.jsp?storyId=5333 44807&topic=Main.
3. "The World's Most Dangerous Cities," Robert Wenzel, *Economic Policy Journal*. May 25, 2012. http://lewrockwell.com/wenzel/wenzel181.html.
4. "Colorado's Dark Night," *The Economist*. July 28, 2012.
5. "Global Study on Homicide," UNODC. 2011. http://www.unodc.org/documents/data-and-analysis/statistics/Homicide/Global_study_on_homicide_Key_findings.pdf.
6. "Murder Most Foul: A Global Picture of Homicide Rates," *The Economist*. October 6, 2011. http://www.economist.com/blogs/dailychart/2011/10/homicide-rates.
7. "San Pedro Sula, La Ciudad Más Violenta Del Mundo; Juárez, La Segunda," Seguridad, Justicia y Paz. January 11, 2012. http://www.seguridadjusticiaypaz.org.mx/sala-de-prensa/541-san-pedro-sula-la-ciudad-mas-violenta-del-mundo-juarez-la-segunda.
8. "How Safe Is Mexico for Tourists?," Daniel Schwartz, CBC News. January 6, 2012. http://www.cbc.ca/news/world/story/2012/01/06/f-mexico-q-a-walter-mckay.html.
9. "Street Crime Stats Not Included in State Department Travel Warnings," Tisha Thompson and Rick Yarborough, NBC Washington. May 24, 2012. http://www.nbcwashington.com/news/local/Street-Crime-Stats-Not-Included-in-State-Department-Warnings-153284895.html.
10. "How Many Americans Die Abroad Each Year," The Jetpacker. June 24, 2010. http://thejetpacker.com/how-many-americans-die-abroad-each-year.
11. "Aid Worker Fatalities Pages," Kevin Tommer, Patronus Analytical. ND. http://www.patronusanalytical.com/aid%20worker%20fatalities/fatalities%20main%20page.html.
12. "Advanced Search 2000–2010," Global Terrorism Database. October 21, 2012. http://www.start.umd.edu/gtd/search/Results.aspx?start_yearonly=2000&end_yearonly=2010&start_year=&start_month=&start_day=&end_year=&end_month=&end_day=&asmSelect0=&asmSelect1=&dtp2=all&success=yes&casualties_type=b&casualties_max.
13. "How Scared of Terrorism Should You Be?," Robert Bailey, Reason.com. September 6, 2011. http://reason.com/archives/2011/09/06/how-scared-of-terrorism-should.
14. "Sexual Assault: An Overview and Implications for Counselling Support," Pablo A. Fernandez, *Australasian Medical Journal* (Online). September 18, 2011. http://www.readperiodicals.com/201109/2532894531.html#ixzz27iKzSQSW.
15. "Rape in India: The Real Role of the Police and Where Lies the Truth?," W-Women Globally. January 29, 2011. http://www.wwomenglobally.com/rape-in-india-the-real-role-of-the-police-and-where-lies-the-truth.
16. "The National Intimate Partner and Sexual Violence Survey: 2010 Summary Report," Michele C. Black, Kathleen C. Basile, Matthew J. Breiding, Sharon G. Smith, Mikel L. Walters, Melissa T. Merrick, Jieru Chen, and Mark R. Stevens, Centers for Disease Control and Prevention. November 2011. http://www.cdc.gov/violenceprevention/nisvs.
17. "Crime Statistics in South Africa," South Africa News. January 23, 2012. http://southafricanews.wordpress.com/2012/01/23/crime-statistics-in-south-africa.
18. "Annual Kidnap Review 2011," Special Contingency Risks LTD. 2011. http://www.scr-ltd.co.uk.
19. Ibid.
20. "Taliban Gaining More Resources from Kidnapping," Declan Walsh, *The New York Times*. February 19, 2012. http://www.nytimes.com/2012/02/20/world/asia/pakistani-taliban-turn-to-kidnapping-to-finance-operations.html?pagewanted=all&_r=0.

21. "The Human Face of Piracy: Pakistan's Response," Christian Bueger, Piracy Studies. March 12, 2012. http://piracy-studies.org.

22. "Kidnap for Ransom in the Asia-Pacific Region," ASI Global. 2012. http://www. asiglobalresponse.com/downloads/Asia%20paper.pdf.

23. "Hijack Claims Are Down," Lisa Steyn, Mail & Guardian. July 13, 2012. http://mg.co. za/article/2012-07-13-hijacking-claims-are-down.

24. "Sydney the Carjacking Capital of Australia," Clementine Cuneo, *Daily Telegraph.* March 9, 2011. http://www.dailytelegraph.com.au/sydney-the-carjacking-capital-of-aust/story-fn6b3v4f-1226017949706-.

25. "Timeline of the Jyllands-Posten Muhammad Cartoons Controversy," Wikipedia. October 20, 2012. http://en.wikipedia.org/wiki/Timeline_of_the_Jyllands-Posten_Muhammad_cartoons_controversy. "Danish Cartoon Controversy," Patricia Cohen, *The New York Times.* August 12, 2009. http://topics.nytimes.com/topics/reference/timestopics/subjects/d/danish_cartoon_controversy/index.html.

26. "Arab Spring: An Interactive Timeline of Middle East Protests," Garry Blight, Sheila Pulham, and Paul Torpey, *Guardian.* January 5, 2012. http://www.guardian.co.uk/world/interactive/2011/mar/22/middle-east-protest-interactive-timeline.

27. "Occupy Movement," Wikipedia. Updated version, October 19, 2012. http://en.wikipedia. org/wiki/Occupy_movement.

28. Ibid.

29. "Water or Gold? Locals across South America Protest Multinational Mining Projects," Chrystelle Barbier and Christine Legrand, *Le Monde.* March 11, 2012. http://www. worldcrunch.com/water-or-gold-locals-across-south-america-protest-multinational-mining-projects/4823.

30. "Money Can't Buy Me Love," *The Economist.* June 16, 2012.

31. "Protests and Demonstrations in China: The Tensions and Methods Behind," Jeffrey Hays, Facts and Details. Updated version, March 2012. http://factsanddetails.com/ china.php?itemid=305&catid=8&subcatid=49.

32. "German Companies Cite Cost of Espionage, Sueddeutsche Says," Joseph de Weck, Bloomberg. April 23, 2012. http://mobile.bloomberg.com/news/2012-04-23/ german-companies-cite-cost-of-espionage-sueddeutsche-says?category=.

33. "Identity Theft Victim Statistics," IdentityTheft.info. ND. http://www.identitytheft.info/ victims.aspx.

34. "Identity Theft Facts," Squidoo. ND. http://www.squidoo.com/identity-theft-facts.

35. "Travelers at High Risk of Identity Theft, Experts Say," Nancy Trejos, USA Today Travel. December 12, 2011. http://travel.usatoday.com/news/story/2011-12-12/Travelers-at-high-risk-of-identify-theft-experts-say/51841144/1-.

36. "How Much Does Identity Theft Cost?," Jolie O'Dell, Mashable. January 29, 2011. http://mashable.com/2011/01/29/identity-theft-infographic.

37. "Identity Theft Facts," Squidoo. ND. http://www.squidoo.com/identity-theft-facts.

38. "Credant Survey Finds Travelers Left Behind More Than 8,000 Mobile Devices at Top U.S. Airports," Credant Technologies. July 3, 2012. http://www.credant.com/news-a-events/press-releases/295-credant-survey-finds-travelers-left-mobile-devices-at-airports.html.

39. "What Security? MoD Has 287 Computers Stolen (Or Lost) in Last 18 Months," Chris Slack, Mail Online. November 25, 2011. http://www.dailymail.co.uk/news/ article-2065856/Ministry-Defence-280-laptops-stolen-18-months.html.

40. "Lost Cellphones Added Up Fast in 2011," Roger Yu, *USA Today.* March 23, 2012. http://www.usatoday.com/tech/news/story/2012-03-22/lost-phones/53707448/1.

41. "The Symantec Smartphone Honey Stick Project," Scott Wright, Symantec Corporation. 2012. http://www.symantec.com/about/news/resources/press_kits/detail. jsp?pkid=symantec-smartphone-honey-stick-project.

42. "The 'Lost' Cell Phone Project, and the Dark Things It Says about Us," Bob Sullivan, MSN Digtallife Today. March 8, 2012. http://digitallife.today.msnbc.msn.com/_news/2012/03/08/10595092-exclusive-the-lost-cell-phone-project-and-the-dark-things-it-says-about-us?lite.

43. "Duty of Care and Travel Risk Management Global Benchmark Study," Dr. Lisbeth Claus, International SOS. 2011. http://www.internationalsos.com/dutyofcare.

44. "Top Ten Countries with Highest Reported Crime Rates," Maps of the World. 2012. http://www.mapsofworld.com/world-top-ten/countries-with-highest-reported-crime-rates.html.

45. "Corruption," UNODC. ND. http://www.unodc.org/unodc/en/data-and-analysis/statistics/corruption.html.

46. "Corruption in Business: Power to Destroy Firms," Bizshifts. January 3, 2011. http://bizshifts-trends.com/2011/01/03/corruption-in-business-power-to-destroy-firms.

47. "Impact of Corruption on Indian Businesses: Survey," Viral Dholakia, Trak.in. March 15, 2012. http://trak.in/tags/business/2011/03/15/impact-of-corruption-on-indian-businesses-survey.

48. "Fraud and Corporate Governance: Changing Paradigm in India," Ernst & Young. 2012. http://www.ey.com/IN/en/Services/Assurance/Fraud-Investigation---Dispute-Services/Fraud-and-corporate-governance-Changing-paradigm-in-India.

49. "Danger Zones! Worldwide Deaths from Natural Disasters," Home Owners Insurance. April 12, 2010. http://www.homeownersinsurance.org/danger-zones.

50. "Global Food Crisis: Sector Results Profile," World Bank. 2012. http://go.worldbank.org/QJPC2BEFA0.

51. "The World Is Closer to a Food Crisis Than Most People Realize," Lester R. Brown, Guardian. July 24, 2012. http://www.guardian.co.uk/environment/2012/jul/24/world-food-crisis-closer.

52. "The Coming Food Crisis: Blame Ethanol?," William Pentland, Forbes. July 28, 2012. http://www.forbes.com/sites/williampentland/2012/07/28/the-coming-food-crisis-blame-ethanol.

53. http://www.aidworkersecurity.org.

54. "Location of Attacks (1997–2011)," The Aid Workers Security Database. Updated version, July 25, 2012. https://aidworkersecurity.org/incidents/report/location.

55. "Comparing Urban and Rural Security Incidents," Christina Wille and Larissa Fast, Insecurity Insight. 2010. http://www.insecurityinsight.org/files/Security%20Facts%201%20Urban%20Rural.pdf.

56. "10 Safety Tips for Seniors Using Public Transportation," Sharon O'Brien, About.com Senior Living. ND. http://seniorliving.about.com/od/travelsmart/a/publictransport.htm.

57. "Train Travel Safety," Nancy Parode, About.com Senior Travel. ND. http://seniortravel.about.com/od/traintravel/qt/Train-Travel-Safety.htm.

58. http://www.lonelyplanet.com/thorntree/forum.jspa?forumID=35.

59. http://globetrottergirls.com/category/lgbt.

60. http://mygaytravelguide.com.

61. "Why You Can't Bulletpoint Gay Travel," Waegook Tom. July 11, 2012. http://www.waegook-tom.com/lgbt/stereotype-gay-travel.

62. "Kids Airport Diversion Guide," Cheapflights.com. ND. http://www.cheapflights.com/travel/kids-airport-diversion-guide.

63. "Preventing Abductions," Steven Dowshen, MD, Kids Health. February 2009. http://kidshealth.org/parent/firstaid_safe/outdoor/abductions.html#.

64. "Tip Sheet: Crowd Safety," We Just Got Back. ND. http://www.wejustgotback.com/default.aspx?mod=tips_safety.

65. "Preventing Abductions," Steven Dowshen, MD, Kids Health. February 2009. http://kidshealth.org/parent/firstaid_safe/outdoor/abductions.html#.

66. "Situational Awareness: How Everyday Citizens Can Help Make a Nation Safe," Scott Steward, Stratfor. August 11, 2011. http://www.stratfor.com/weekly/20110810-situational-awareness-how-everyday-citizens-help-make-nation-safe.
67. "Color Codes of Awareness," Self Defense Resource.com. ND. http://www.self-defenseresource.com/general/articles/awareness-color-codes.php.
68. "BRIC Benchmarking: Research Uncovers the Top Threats & Coping Strategies," Myles Druckman, Dialogues on Duty of Care. August 9, 2012. http://dialoguesondutyofcare.com/2012/08/bric-benchmarking-research-uncovers-top-threats-strategies.
69. Ibid.
70. "Lloyd's Risk Index, 2011," The Economist Intelligence Unit, Lloyd's. 2011. http://www.lloyds.com/~/media/Files/News%20and%20Insight/360%20Risk%20Insight/Lloyds_Risk_Index_2011.pdf-Lloyd's.
71. "10 Tips for Active Listening," Barbara Bray, Rethinking Learning. January 10, 2012. http://barbarabray.net/2012/01/10/10-tips-for-active-listening.
72. "10 Tips for Effective & Active Listening Skills," Susie Michelle Cortright, Power to Change Student. ND. http://powertochange.com/students/people/listen.
73. http://www.worldnomad.com.
74. "Can You Buy Travel Insurance after Your Vacation Has Begun?," Travel Insurance Review. ND. http://www.travelinsurancereview.net/2010/01/20/can-you-buy-travel-insurance-after-your-vacation-has-begun.
75. "Mobile Wallet Pickpocket Risks Low," Liau Yun Qing, ZD Net Asia. November 28, 2011. http://www.zdnetasia.com/mobile-wallet-pickpocketing-risks-low-62303041.htm.
76. "Travelers Forget Everything from Passports to False Teeth," Gary Stoller, USA Today Travel. November 9, 2011. http://travel.usatoday.com/news/story/2011-11-08/Travelers-forget-everything-from-passports-to-false-teeth/51124844/1.
77. "The Fallacy of Remote Wiping," Ryan Naraine and Thomas Porter, ZD Net. July 12, 2012. http://www.zdnet.com/the-fallacy-of-remote-wiping-7000000611.
78. "80% of Olympic Sites Are Scams," Emil Protalinski, ZD Net. August 3, 2012. http://www.zdnet.com/80-of-olympic-sites-are-scams-7000002124.
79. "Travelers at High Risk of Identity Theft, Experts Say," Nancy Trejos, USA Today Travel. December 12, 2011. http://travel.usatoday.com/news/story/2011-12-12/Travelers-at-high-risk-of-identify-theft-experts-say/51841144/1-.
80. "The 'Lost' Cell Phone Project, and the Dark Things It Says About Us," Bob Sullivan, MSN Digtallife Today. March 8, 2012. http://digitallife.today.msnbc.msn.com/_news/2012/03/08/10595092-exclusive-the-lost-cell-phone-project-and-the-dark-things-it-says-about-us?lite.
81. Ibid.
82. "The Symantec Smartphone Honey Stick Project," Scott Wright, Symantec Corporation. 2012. http://www.symantec.com/about/news/resources/press_kits/detail.jsp?pkid=symantec-smartphone-honey-stick-project.
83. "Data Security: Most Finders of Lost Smartphones Are Snoops," Ashlee Vance, Bloomberg Businessweek. March 8, 2012. http://www.businessweek.com/articles/2012-03-08/data-security-most-finders-of-lost-smartphones-are-snoops.
84. "Hush… It's a Honey Trap," Indrani Rajkhowa Banerjee, *The Times of India.* March 17, 2011. http://articles.timesofindia.indiatimes.com/2011-03-17/people/28248711_1_madhuri-gupta-traps-honey.
85. "The History of the Honey Trap," Phillip Knightley, Foreign Policy. March 12, 2010. http://www.foreignpolicy.com/articles/2010/03/12/the_history_of_the_honey_trap?print=yes&hidecomments=yes&page=full.
86. "Preventing Digital Identity Theft," Greg Rodgers, About.com Asia Travel. October 6, 2011. http://goasia.about.com/b/2011/10/07/preventing-digital-identity-theft.htm.

87. "Internet Cafe Security in Asia," Greg Rodgers, About.com Asia Travel. ND. http://goasia.about.com/od/Planning/a/Internet-Cafe-Security.htm.

88. "Safe Travels for You and Your Data," Riva Richmond, *The New York Times*. February 17, 2010. http://www.nytimes.com/2010/02/18/technology/personaltech/18basics.html?_r=1&scp=7&sq=laptop%20and%20theft&st=cse.

89. "Preventing Digital Identity Theft," Greg Rodgers, About.com Asia Travel. October 6, 2011. http://goasia.about.com/b/2011/10/07/preventing-digital-identity-theft.htm.

90. "Safe Travels for You and Your Data," Riva Richmond, *The New York Times*. February 17, 2010. http://www.nytimes.com/2010/02/18/technology/personaltech/18basics.html?_r=1&scp=7&sq=laptop%20and%20theft&st=cse.

91. "Travelers at High Risk of Identity Theft, Experts Say," Nancy Trejos, USA Today Travel. December 12, 2011. http://travel.usatoday.com/news/story/2011-12-12/Travelers-at-high-risk-of-identify-theft-experts-say/51841144/1-.

92. "5 Essential Mobile Security Tips," Robert Lemos, *Information Week*. September 9, 2011. http://www.informationweek.com/news/security/mobile/231601091.

93. Ibid.

94. "iPad Data Protection: 5 Insights to Secure Your Data," Kensington. July 23, 2012. http://clicksafe.kensington.com/laptop-security-blog/bid/85502/iPad-data-protection-5-insights-to-secure-your-data.

95. "Paperclips Pose Security Threat to iPhones," Rosa Golijan, NBC News Technology. February 21, 2012. http://www.technolog.msnbc.msn.com/technology/technolog/paperclips-pose-security-threat-iphones-157719.

96. "The Cost of Stolen Laptops," David Storm, Kensington Infographic. February 14, 2012. http://www.readwriteweb.com/mobile/2012/02/infographic-the-cost-of-stolen.php.

97. "Report: Most People Don't Rush to Lock Devices with Passwords," Rosa Golijan, NBC News Technology. March 2, 2012. http://www.technolog.msnbc.msn.com/technology/technolog/report-most-people-dont-rush-lock-devices-passwords-295899.

98. "Laptop Theft Statistics," Kensington ClickSafe. August 10, 2011. http://www.slideshare.net/ClickSafelocks/laptop-theft-statistics.

99. "Smartphone Boom Raises Identity Theft Fear," Elmer W. Cagape, Asian Correspondent. April 16, 2012. http://asiancorrespondent.com/80549/scary-consequences-for-losing-smartphones.

100. "Lost Cellphones Added Up Fast in 2011," Roger Yu, USA Today Tech. March 23, 2012. http://www.usatoday.com/tech/news/story/2012-03-22/lost-phones/53707448/1.

101. Ibid.

102. "Credant Surveys San Francisco Hotels and Finds Thousands of Mobile Devices Are Lost and Unclaimed by Business Travelers and Consumers," Credant Technologies. February 27, 2012. http://www.credant.com/news-a-events/press-releases/275-credant-surveys-san-francisco-hotels.html.

103. "2nd Annual Airport Survey," Credant Technologies. 2012. http://www.credant.com/resources/tools.html.

104. "Mobile Devices at Risk of Theft during London Olympics: Report," Nathan Eddy, eWeek. July 28, 2012. http://www.eweek.com/c/a/Mobile-and-Wireless/Mobile-Devices-at-Risk-of-Theft-During-London-Olympics-Report-377645.

105. Ibid.

106. "Lost Laptops Costs $1.8 Billion per Year," Matthew J. Schwartz, *Information Week*. April 21, 2011. http://www.informationweek.com/news/security/mobile/229402043.

107. "Tech//404 Data Loss Cost Calculator," Allied World. ND. http://www.tech-404.com/calculator.html.

108. "The Billion Dollar Lost Laptop Problem: A Benchmark Study of U.S. Organizations," Ponemon Institute, Intel. October 31, 2010. http://www.intel.com/content/www/us/en/enterprise-security/enterprise-security-the-billion-dollar-lost-laptop-problem-paper.html.

109. "Security Breaches Are on the Rise, but Preventable," Druva. August 15, 2012. http://www.druva.com/blog/2012/08/15/security-breaches-are-on-the-rise-but-preventable.

110. "The Cost of Stolen Laptops," David Storm, Kensington Infographic. February 14, 2012. http://www.readwriteweb.com/mobile/2012/02/infographic-the-cost-of-stolen.php.

111. Ibid.

112. "Airport/ Airline Safety," Safe Traveler. ND. http://www.safetraveler.com/Airport_Airline_Safety.html.

113. "4 Ways to Protect Your Stuff at Airport Security," Genevieve Shaw Brown, ABC News Travel. April 22, 2012. http://abcnews.go.com/blogs/lifestyle/2012/04/4-ways-to-protect-your-stuff-at-airport-security.

114. "Airport/Airline Safety," Safe Traveler. ND. http://www.safetraveler.com/Airport_Airline_Safety.html.

115. http://www.ihatetaxis.com.

116. "Stranger Danger Safety Tips for Walkers," Wendy Bumgardner, About.com Walking. Updated version, April 6, 2012. http://walking.about.com/cs/med/a/strangerdanger.htm.

117. "How to Walk Safely," Wendy Bumgardner, About.com Walking. Updated version, August 28, 2012. http://walking.about.com/cs/safety/ht/htsafewalking.htm.

118. "Basic Safety for All Travelers." ASIRT. ND. http://www.asirt.org/KnowBeforeYouGo/LeisureTravel/SafetyTipsforEveryone/tabid/230/Default.aspx.

119. "How to Stay Safe on Public Transportation," Sheila C. Wilkinson, eHow. ND. http://www.ehow.com/how_4466156_stay-safe-public-transportation.html.

120. "Tips for Your Safety while Riding Public Transportation," Donna Biasi, Streetdirectory.com Singapore Guide. ND. http://www.streetdirectory.com/travel_guide/215921/travel_tips/tips_for_your_safety_while_riding_public_transportation.html.

121. "10 Safety Tips for Seniors Using Public Transportation," About.com Senior Living. ND. http://seniorliving.about.com/od/travelsmart/a/publictransport.htm.

122. "China: Shanghai Taxi Gang Preys on Tourists," Larry Habegger, World Travel Watch. March 12, 2008. http://www.worldtravelwatch.com/08/03/china-shanghai-taxi-gang-preys-on-tourists-unusual-hostage-incident-in-xian.html.

123. http://www.riskline.com.

124. "Airport Taxi Scams and How to Avoid Them," Price of Travel. November 5, 2010. http://www.priceoftravel.com/575/airport-taxi-scams-and-how-to-avoid-them.

125. "7 Common Taxi Scams—and 7 Steps to Beat Them," Scambusters. ND. http://www.scambusters.org/taxi.html.

126. "Travel Security—Rental Cars, What to Check For," TrainingSolutions. January 11, 2011. http://www.trainingsolutions.dk/?page_id=11.

127. "Car Rental Tips," Travel Sense. ND. http://www.travelsense.org/tips/carrentaltips.cfm.

128. "Road Crash Statistics," Association for Safe International Road Travel. ND. http://www.asirt.org/KnowBeforeYouGo/RoadSafetyFacts/RoadCrashStatistics/tabid/213/Default.aspx.

129. "Duty of Care and Travel Risk Management Global Benchmark Study," Dr. Lisbeth Claus, International SOS. 2011. http://www.internationalsos.com/dutyofcare.

130. "Coping with a Car Crash Abroad," Damian Tysdal, Travel Insurance Review. ND. http://www.travelinsurancereview.net/2012/07/23/coping-with-a-car-crash-abroad.

131. "Random Checkpoint," Wikipedia. Updated version, October 23, 2012. http://en.wikipedia.org/wiki/Random_checkpoint.

132. "Security Checkpoint," Wikipedia. Updated version, June 27, 2012. http://en.wikipedia.org/wiki/Military_checkpoint.

133. *Safety First: A Safety and Security Handbook for Aid Workers*. Shaun Bickley, International Save the Children Alliance. 2010. http://www.eisf.eu/resources/library/SafetyFirst2010.pdf.

134. "Mental Preparation," No Nonsense Self Defense. ND. http://www.nononsenseselfdefense. com/mental_preparation.htm.

135. "Travel Safety: Tips And Information," BugBog. ND. http://www.bugbog.com/travel_ safety/travel_safety.html#barcelona.

136. "Travel Safety: Advice and Information 2," BugBog. ND. http://www.bugbog.com/ travel_safety/travel_safety_2.html.

137. "How Pickpockets Work," Tom Harris, How Stuff Works. ND. http://money.howstuff-works.com/pickpocket.htm.

138. "Common Scams," Jeff Starck, TruSys Institute. March 23, 2012. http://www.slide-share.net/jeffstarck/common-travel-scams.

139. "Tips for Business Travelers to Nigeria," Passports USA. ND. http://www.passportsusa. com/travel/tips/brochures/brochures_2113.html.

140. "Beware China's 'Honeytrap' Spies," *The Week*. February 3, 2011. http://theweek.com/ article/index/211717/beware-chinas-honeytrap-spies.

141. "How Scams Work," ScamWatch. ND. http://www.scamwatch.gov.au/content/index. phtml/tag/HowScamsWork.

142. "Common Scams," Jeff Starck, TruSys Institute. March 23, 2012. http://www.slide-share.net/jeffstarck/common-travel-scams.

143. "Reverse PIN Technology and Your Safety," Tom Murse, About.com US Government Info. April 13, 2011. http://usgovinfo.about.com/od/censusandstatistics/a/Why-Reverse-PIN-Is-Not-in-Use.htm.

144. "Hackers Tech: Credit Card Skimming," Jason Collazo, *Business Insider*. October 29, 2011. http://articles.businessinsider.com/2011-10-29/tech/30332949_1_credit-card-bank-card-card-reader#ixzz1yS8SkkQW.

145. "Card Skimming," SCAMwatch. ND. http://www.scamwatch.gov.au/content/index.phtml/ tag/CardSkimming.

146. "Hackers Tech: Credit Card Skimming," Jason Collazo, *Business Insider*. October 29, 2011. http://articles.businessinsider.com/2011-10-29/tech/30332949_1_credit-card-bank-card-card-reader#ixzz1yS8SkkQW.

147. Ibid.

148. "Credit Card Skimming Affects One in Five ATM Users," UniBul. October 12, 2010. http:// blog.unibulmerchantservices.com/credit-card-skimming-affects-one-in-five-atm-users.

149. "Credit Card Skim Scams Net $170 Million," Janet Fife-Yeomans, *Daily Telegraph*. April 15, 2011. http://www.dailytelegraph.com.au/archive/national-old/ credit-card-skim-scams-net-170-million/story-e6freuzr-1226039359854.

150. Ibid.

151. "Threat of Credit Card 'Skimming' Rises during the Holidays," Justine Griffin, *Sun Sentinel*. December 18, 2011. http://articles.sun-sentinel.com/2011-12-18/business/ fl-skimming-credit-card-threat-20111218_1_card-numbers-credit-card-credit-and-debit.

152. "Taking a Trip to the ATM? Beware of 'Skimmers,'" Federal Bureau of Investigation (FBI). July 14, 2011. http://www.fbi.gov/news/stories/2011/july/atm_071411.

153. "Skimming the Cash out of Your Account," Laura Bruce, Bankrate.com. October 4, 2002. http://www.bankrate.com/finance/checking/skimming-the-cash-out-of-your-account-1.aspx.

154. "7 Popular Cities to Watch for Credit Card Skimming Scams," Mark Brown, BillShrink. May 27, 2009. http://www.billshrink.com/blog/3685/popular-cities-credit-card-skimming-scams.

155. "Why That mp3 Player Is Stealing Your Identity with Skimming," SCAMwatch. ND. http://www.spamlawT.com/identity-theft-skimming.

156. "2012: Year of the Skimmer," Tracy Kitten, Bank Info Security. January 18, 2012. http:// www.bankinfosecurity.com/2012-year-skimmer-a-4417/op-1.

157. "Credit Card Skimming: How Thieves Can Steal Your Card Info without You Knowing It," Jamey Heary, NetworkWorld.com. October 1, 2008. http://www.networkworld.com/community/node/33210?page=0%2C0.

158. "Keep Your Credit Cards Safe from Skimmers," Robert Vamosi, *PCWorld*. December 8, 2010. http://www.pcworld.com/article/212969/keep_your_credit_cards_safe_from_skimmers.html.

159. "Hackers Tech: Credit Card Skimming," Jason Collazo, *Business Insider*. October 29, 2011. http://articles.businessinsider.com/2011-10-29/tech/30332949_1_credit-card-bank-card-card-reader#ixzz1yS8SkkQW.

160. "How Credit Card Skimming Works," LaToya Irby, About.com Credit, Debt Management. ND. http://credit.about.com/od/privacyconcerns/a/credit-card-skimming.htm.

161. "Card Skimming," SCAMwatch. ND. http://www.scamwatch.gov.au/content/index.phtml/tag/CardSkimming.

162. "Five Stages to Violent Crime," No Nonsense Self Defense. ND. http://www.nononsense-selfdefense.com/five_stages.html.

163. "Freeze Response," No Nonsense Self Defense. ND. http://www.nononsenseselfde-fense.com/freeze-response.htm.

164. "Fact Sheet—If Your Wallet or Handbag Is Stolen," Protect Your Financial Identity. ND. http://www.protectfinancialid.org.au/Your-wallet-or-handbag-checklist/default.aspx.

165. "What Was in Your Wallet?," CreditCards.com. ND. http://www.creditcards.com/down-loads/what_was_in_your_wallet.pdf.

166. "Your Wallet Recovery Kit," Melody Warnick and Juan Rodriguez, CreditCards.com. October 11, 2011. http://www.creditcards.com/credit-card-news/credit-card-wallet-recovery-kit-1282.php.

167. "My Wallet Was Stolen: 4 Lessons Learned," Candice Lee Jones, Kiplinger. November 9, 2009. http://www.kiplinger.com/features/archives/my-wallet-was-stolen-4-lessons-learned.html.

168. Ibid.

169. "What to Do If You Lost Your Wallet," CreditCards.com. ND. http://www.creditcards.com/downloads/what_to_do_if_you_lost_your_wallet.pdf.

170. "Fact Sheet: Immediate Steps," Protect Your Financial Identity. ND. http://www.protect-financialid.org.au/Immediate-steps/default.aspx.

171. "Stolen Purse, Lost Wallet? What to Do, Step By Step," Identity Theft Labs. http://www.identitytheftlabs.com/stolen-wallet-purse.

172. "How to Protect Data after Laptop Theft," Jennifer Saranow Schultz, *The New York Times*. October 12, 2010. http://bucks.blogs.nytimes.com/2010/10/13/how-to-protect-data-after-laptop-theft.

173. "Corruption Costs Us R30bn a Year," Sapa, Times Live. March 12, 2012. http://www.timeslive.co.za/politics/2012/03/31/corruption-costs-us-r30bn-a-year-acdp.

174. "A New Type of Scam," Baobab. March 29, 2012. http://www.economist.com/blogs/baobab/2012/03/nigerian-corruption.

175. "Corruption Costs Indonesia $238 M in 2011," Ezra Sihite, Jakarta Globe. January 30, 2012. http://www.thejakartaglobe.com/home/corruption-costs-indonesia-238m-in-2011/494558.

176. "Watch GPS: How Corrupt Is China?," Fareed Zakaria GPS, CNN. April 27, 2012. http://globalpublicsquare.blogs.cnn.com/2012/04/27/watch-gps-how-corrupt-is-china.

177. "An Analysis of India's Pathetic 95th Rank in the Corruption Index and Its Far Reaching Social Impact!," Prof. Arindam Chaudhuri, Business and Economy. February 2, 2012. http://www.businessandeconomy.org/02022012/editordesk.asp?sid=6721&pageno=2.

178. "Corruption Perception Index 2011," Transparency International. 2011. http://cpi.transparency.org/cpi2011/results.

179. "Corruption Indicators," Serious Fraud Office. ND. http://www.sfo.gov.uk/bribery--corruption/corruption-indicators.aspx.
180. "Say No to Corruption! Follow the 10 Commandments!," I Paid A Bribe. ND. http://www.ipaidabribe.com/blog/say-no-corruption-follow-10-commandments.
181. "Corruption Indicators," Serious Fraud Office. ND. http://www.sfo.gov.uk/bribery--corruption/corruption-indicators.aspx.
182. http://www.business-anti-corruption.com/?L=0.
183. "Governance & Anti-Corruption," World Bank. ND. http://www.worldbank.org/wbi/governance.
184. http://www.transparency.org.
185. "Fraud and Corporate Governance: Changing Paradigm in India," Ernst & Young. 2012. http://www.ey.com/IN/en/Services/Assurance/Fraud-Investigation---Dispute-Services/Fraud-and-corporate-governance-Changing-paradigm-in-India.
186. "Corruption in the NGO World: What It Is and How to Tackle It," Jerome Larche, *Humanitarian Exchange Magazine*. October 2011, Issue 52. http://www.odihpn.org/humanitarian-exchange-magazine/issue-52/corruption-in-the-ngo-world-what-it-is-and-how-to-tackle-it.
187. "Stress Management: How to Reduce, Prevent, and Cope with Stress," Melinda Smith, MA and Robert Segal, MA, HelpGuide.org. Updated version, July 2012. http://www.helpguide.org/mental/stress_management_relief_coping.htm.
188. "Stress Management," Melissa Conrad Stöppler, MD, MedicineNet.com. August 24, 2011. http://www.medicinenet.com/stress_management_techniques/article.htm.
189. http://www.stressmanagementtips.com.
190. "37 Stress Management Tips: Find Your Own Escape Route with Our Easy Stress Management Tips," Michael Castleman, Reader's Digest. ND. http://www.rd.com/health/wellness/37-stress-management-tips.
191. "Wellness Worksheets," McGraw Hill Higher Education. 2004. http://www.mhhe.com/socscience/hhp/wellness.
192. "Stress Management Worksheets," Inner Health Studio. ND. http://www.innerhealthstudio.com/stress-management-worksheets.html.

3 Extreme Risks

To help you mitigate extreme risks, this chapter draws on authoritative facts, statistics, definitions, and top tips to give you insights into such questions as:

- Which of your "normal" security measures addresses high risks **(see Section 3.1)**?
- What are the indications that someone could be observing you for criminal purposes **(see Section 3.2)**?
- How can you mitigate kidnapping risks **(see Section 3.3)**?
- Could myths, assumptions, and fears potentially blindside you to the risk of sexual violence **(see Section 3.4)**?
- If carjackings are a threat, what can you do **(see Section 3.5)**?
- How can you avoid getting caught up in a demonstration of civic unrest **(see Section 3.6)**?
- How much time you do have to safely evacuate a crashed airplane **(see Section 3.7)**?
- What should your first response be in the event of a traffic accident **(see Section 3.8)**?
- How likely is terrorism **(see Section 3.9)**?
- What are the key points you should keep in mind to prevent extreme risks and react in life-saving ways **(see Section 3.10)**?

Although this chapter provides "best practice" advice, it has to be underlined that your security depends on the unique interplay between you and your environment: In other words, to realistically mitigate extreme risks, your security measures need to address the threats and suit you. As a businessperson, you might need to be knowledgeable about identifying surveillance operations if you are traveling to Russia, whereas if you are a humanitarian aid worker in Rwanda, then it is particularly vital that you have basic first aid skills because serious traffic accidents are a real risk. Accordingly, you are encouraged to personalize your approach to managing travel risks. With that aim, this chapter recommends flexible frameworks, models, and tools that you can customize for your travel realities.

"The world is full of risks, but opportunities come to those who know how to manage them": Although kidnapping, sexual violence, and terrorism are examples of extreme risks, these can be managed proactively so that you know how to prevent being a victim of them and how to react in life-saving ways in a worst-case scenario.

3.1 PREVENTING AND REACTING TO EXTREME RISKS

Preventing and reacting in life-saving ways to extreme risks such as demonstrations in Abidjan, sexual assault in Barcelona, kidnapping in Caracas, or bombing in Damascus involves utilizing the same knowledge, skills, attitudes, and behaviors needed to proactively implement the **Risk Management Framework (RMF)**. Decipher the likelihood of a risk by analyzing the threats in the environment **(RMF 1)** and your vulnerabilities to them **(RMF 2)**, creating options that realistically address the threats **(RMF 3)**, monitoring and adjusting accordingly **(RMF 4)**, and having confidence in your security precautions and reactions **(RMF 5)**.

The extreme risks covered in this chapter are **Surveillance (see Section 3.2)**, **Kidnapping (see Section 3.3)**, **Sexual Violence (see Section 3.4)**, **Carjacking (see Section 3.5)**, **Demonstrations and Riots (see Section 3.6)**, **Plane Crash (see Section 3.7)**, **Medical Emergencies (see Section 3.8)**, and **Terrorist Attacks (see Section 3.9)**. For the subjects of kidnappings, sexual violence, carjackings, and civic unrest, **Understanding the Potential Risks while Traveling (see Section 2.1)** relays more facts and statistics.

Risks to your personal or organizational data can also be considered an extreme risk, given the high stakes that can be involved: You can refer to the sections on **Personal Belongings and Documents (see Sections 1.10 and 2.10)**, **Information Security (see Sections 1.11 and 2.11)**, and **Communication Equipment and Procedures (see Sections 1.12 and 2.12)**. The discussions about violent crime and after a crime in the **Crime and Corruption** section **(see Section 2.16)** can be useful supplementary reading to assist you with comprehensively addressing the risks that might apply to you in this section. For instance, by understanding the key aspects that make up violent crime, perhaps you can better avoid becoming a kidnap victim. Or by noting the identifying aspects of the carjackers or their vehicle, perhaps you can help the police catch the criminals who attempted to take your car.

On the preventative side, building up your security awareness could include reading the contributions **"Being Your Own Bodyguard" (see Section 1.3)**, **"Psychological Techniques That Prevent Violence" (see Section 2.2.3)**, **"States of Awareness: The Cooper Color Codes" (see Section 2.3)**, or **"Get into Your Peak State to Get Away" (see Section 2.3)**. Also, a lot of insights can come from reading extreme risk sections that may not seemingly be directly related to you: Yet, if you had, for example, knowledge of anti-surveillance techniques as part of your security toolkit, this could be useful against a kidnapping, an act of sexual violence, or a carjacking.

3.1.1 LIFE IS FULL OF RISKS, BUT OPPORTUNITIES COME TO THOSE WHO MANAGE THEM

For any destination that generally presents high risks or specific risks for you, the following contribution offers a list of "to do's" that could support your efforts to remain safe and secure wherever and however you travel: You will probably notice that the suggestions in the next contribution are in line with the expert advice and tips for any location. In other words, "prior proper planning prevents problems and poor performance," even if you are heading for risky environments.

IF TRAVELING TO AFGHANISTAN: ADVICE FOR ALL HIGH-RISK DESTINATIONS

ANDREAS POPPIUS

SECURITY CONSULTANT, ADVENTURE TRAVELER, AND FORMER SENIOR SECURITY OFFICER/SWEDISH EMBASSY KABUL, AFGHANISTAN (HTTP://WWW.U3KOMPETENS.SE)

If you are planning to travel to Afghanistan, first of all, I must say don't. But if you are going anyway, there are a few things to consider. Of course you can make a trip to Afghanistan somewhat safe—most of the people going in and out of the country survive.

I spent a year and some as a senior security officer at the Swedish embassy in Kabul and I saw many of the things people shouldn't do and the results of their many wrong assumptions. I will list here some of the things you need to know if you choose to travel to a war torn country such as this. The list claims in no way to be a complete guide to safe travel in Afghanistan—but it will provide you with some basic points.

- Make sure it is worth it!
- Check your country's consular support—if you have a consular representative in Afghanistan, they will most likely have a very limited ability to support astray travelers. You will be on your own.
- Check your insurance company's travel insurance policy. They will probably have an article stating that if you choose to travel to countries like this, the insurance will not cover anything. You are on your own again.
- Check the safest way in and out of the country—during 2010, the European Aviation Safety Agency revoked all Afghan-based airline permits to travel into and out of Europe due to several severe violations of aviation safety regulations. Several domestic flights also have concerning safety issues.
- Check how to travel safely between the airports and your destination. Sometimes low-key travel is the safest way to travel—but then you need to know enough phrases in Dari to manage. But remember that an armored vehicle is only bulletproof to a certain extent.
- Report to the embassy. Even if the embassy has a limited consular service, you may be able to meet other countrymen and discuss safety and security issues as well as have a good time.
- Check your travel routes in the country. Avoid high-risk areas such as embassies, military installations, and ministries. If traveling back and forth between destinations, you should alternate your routes.
- Make sure that you have established the necessary contacts in the country to get the latest safety and security information. Lots of security companies sell this kind of information—check that the information they provide is relevant to you and reflects your realities.

- Use a grab-bag with the most necessary things (e.g., medical supplies; copies of documents such as passport, visas, tickets, etc.; money; water; satellite phone; and some energy bars). Keep it with you at all time. Keep passport, visas, ID cards, money, tickets, and such on your person at all times.
- Check your lodging. One of the safest hotels in Kabul, Hotel Serena, is also a target itself due to all the guests and its location in the immediate vicinity of the presidential palace—yet another popular target for the insurgents. Make sure that you are familiar with the hotel's emergency plan.
- Make sure that someone always knows where you are going, which route you will travel, and when you are supposed to be back—even if no one can offer you direct support, it will ease later efforts to aid you if people know where and when you traveled—you may just have had a flat tire!
- And remember, if/when something bad happens, no matter how great the consular support your embassy provides and how generous your travel insurance is, you still have to survive long enough to be able to benefit from all of that!

Andreas Poppius's first point about "Make sure it is worth it!" ties into the concept of "acceptable levels of risks," which is essential for you to review before embarking on a trip to a potentially dangerous location or engaging in risky activities. In your considerations, you are basically assessing if the risks are worth the potential benefits. Even though, or perhaps because, parts of the Middle East are heading toward democracy, there exist potential outbreaks of violent civic unrest, or murder cloaked as unrest. But that does not mean you should avoid being awed by the pyramids if that is what you want to do. If circumstances allow you to go, seriously weigh all the factors: To help make sure that the risks are at an acceptable level, do things like learn the local scams and cons, take heed of the advice in the **Demonstrations and Riots** section **(see Section 3.6)**, and always have two "exit plans" for all the situations you might find yourself in—applied to relevant aspects such as your accommodation, transportation, and marketplaces.

On the other hand, if the risks are unbearably high for any reason, do not go or expose yourself to the threat. Let's say you booked a flight with an airline with a somewhat bad reputation for service and mishaps, but its departure is hours before the better airline, so you could avoid traveling to the airport at night. Do not step on board your scheduled flight if suddenly your intuition or "gut feeling" alerts you. You do not need to proceed to the tarmac only to see the maintenance crew still working on the engine to decide that the level of acceptable risk is too high for that set of circumstances.

This decision will cost you time and money, and maybe even inconvenience: And you might question the integrity of that decision in hindsight, if nothing happened. However, on balance, you made the right decision based on probability of a crash given the company's track record combined with your survival instincts. In such situations, your aim is not to make "perfect" decisions but well-informed decisions given the realities of the circumstances, and, as always, to have, create, and be aware of the best available options in a situation. Hopefully, you charged your mobile phone and have relevant contact numbers in it so that you can call your travel agent to see if they can make alternative arrangements while you wait in the long line of the better airline's service desk, for instance **(see Sections 1.12 and 2.13)**.

3.2 SURVEILLANCE

All crimes involve surveillance to one degree or another. A bag-grabbing street criminal will scan the public square for distracted persons, maybe observing you for a few seconds or minutes before snatching your belongings. A gang of kidnappers might take months to first stalk you on the Internet and then physically shadow your moves to map out when you are most vulnerable before snatching you. Generally, the more complicated the crime, the more time (and resources) a criminal will use on planning and preparation.

If you are selected for surveillance, then the perpetrators will employ physical and/or technical means. Physical methods basically involve other persons tracing your movements and activities. An example could be watching your home in order to rob it—a stationary method. Or a mobile method could entail following you. A stationary operation is usually hard to spot if the perpetrators are able to blend in or have an excusable presence. Technical methods use electronic devices to follow your movements, eavesdrop on your conversations, or find out about your activities. For example, a skilled information technology (IT) criminal can remotely switch the audio and visual functions on your IT device **(see Sections 1.11 and 2.11)**. Even for the unskilled, the Internet provides opportunity to buy smaller and cheaper surveillance equipment and to watch instructions on YouTube.

This section focuses on physical surveillance, with an emphasis on the buildup to a serious crime. As for technological methods and gadgetry, they are expansive and growing areas. Some mitigating measures are covered in the **Information Security** sections **(see Sections 1.11 and 2.11)**: However, if you have identified IT surveillance as a threat **(see Section 1.1.1)** before you traveled or suspect something while abroad, then you should seek specialist advice. Since countersurveillance measures and equipment often have legal ramifications, it is further recommended that you review those measures with a legal advisor.

3.2.1 Know How to Read the Signposts and Indicators

When thinking about physical surveillance, you should suspend your assumptions about what the perpetrators will look like. They could be an individual or large rotating team; men or women; elderly or children; smartly dressed or in smelly rags, and the list goes on to include walking or using a vehicle, and so forth. Since many people assume women, elderly, and children are less threatening, they are often used as operatives, particularly women. A woman walking a dog on her own or even kissing her "husband" is not perceived as dangerous. Operatives use our assumptions against us to monitor us or get close enough to plant an electronic device.

Because physical operations are time consuming and resource intensive, they are expensive. Thus, a cheaper way to run a physical surveillance is to use a smaller team who then changes their appearance with clothes, props, hair/headwear, vehicles, and so forth. This works to your advantage because it gives you a better chance to notice that you have repeatedly seen the same persons, if you can see past their theater tricks.

Indicators are signposts alerting you to the possibility that someone is observing you. Some are clear signals of danger while others are nuanced and professional. In some circumstances, you will want to react right away. But, often, it is reasonable to be alert and cautious while on the lookout for additional indicators. However, it could be only a matter of a short time before the perpetrators spring their operation, a factor you do not control, so you certainly do not want to wait too long before you implement extra security measures. It is one of those "better to be safe than sorry" situations, and by implementing better measures you might be able to thwart an attempted crime. At this point, it certainly does not hurt to seek specialist advice and at least inform your organization's security department.

If you believe for any reason that you could be under observation for criminal intentions, then trust your instincts and look for indicators such as:

- Persons paying too much attention to you or your surroundings. If they are inexperienced, they might "give themselves away" through their nervous, suspicious behavior. However, a well-resourced professional team will not be that obvious. If you suspect that someone is watching you, your best option is to stay in or get to public places, and look for other indicators.
- Persons displaying either of two extreme forms of physical contact. Either someone aims to make contact with you (i.e., social engineering, **see Section 2.11**, and befriending scams, **see Section 2.16**) or your belongings (i.e., industrial espionage, **see Section 1.11**). Or they might go out of their way to avoid making any contact, such as suddenly turning around if you look their way or crossing the street if you walk in their direction. This type of low-profile perpetrator would rather keep you within visual range by following after you, sitting near you, or parking close by. You can use your situational awareness to notice the suspected person's behavior reflected in a shop window as you casually stop to browse. Or use your mobile to naturally disguise that you are looking around while you talk.
- Persons who behave oddly, such as being hesitant to enter the building you just went into or quickly leaving the cafe just after you. Other normal yet odd behavior includes often checking the time, taking notes, or wearing clothes, shoes, or headgear that seems "out of place."
- Perpetrators, if working in a team, need to keep in contact with each other, so look for mobiles and ear-sets. Admittedly, this is not the strongest indicator in modern societies but it supplements the overall picture you are trying to sketch out.
- A person or vehicle appearing to be signaling someone.
- As the perpetrators need to plan and execute the operation, you may see the same persons and/or vehicles repeatedly in the vicinity.
- A vehicle parked for extended periods at a good observation point with several people in it. That said, professionals would typically avoid that

FIGURE 3.1   Courtesy of Peter Steudtner/www.panphotos.org.

indicator or neutralize it by having at least one woman in the observation team. The vehicle and/or the persons inside can change.

- Sometimes weather conditions will affect where the vehicle is parked, such as in a shady spot when it is hot and sunny. Obviously, when it is sunny most drivers would opt to park in the shade so this is not an indicator in itself: But combined with other signposts, such as sneaking a peek in the car as you walk by because a couple has been parked there three days in a row and noticing pieces of clothes that you have seen elsewhere or some other hint or "gut feeling," then it is time to boost your security measures and seek specialist assistance.
- Mail you were expecting didn't arrive. Suspicious packages.
- Of course, if the perpetrators are pointing a camera in your direction, especially if it corresponds with suspicious behavior, then that's a clear indicator. But technological advances give criminals plenty of options for capturing your image in less obvious ways. Illegal cameras over ATMs used to film people's PIN codes are a form of surveillance for criminal gain **(see Section 2.16)**.

(Figure 3.1).

A critical area, yet overlooked per definition, is the category of "Extraordinary yet apparently normal incidents," such as:

- A fire alarm.
- Your housekeeper noticing someone ruffling through your trash.
- Someone asking to use your phone after his or her car broke down.
- Someone calls but claims it is the wrong number, especially if it happens more than once.
- Unannounced repairs (or another excuse to be there) in the vicinity of your home or job. Or a request to access these places (e.g., book sellers, religious groups, insurance).

By definition these incidents are uneventful, so they should not "ring any alarm bells" for you. But if you have any reason to believe that any singular event indicates criminal intentions, or any combination of events occurs, then it is time to strengthen your security measures. For example, last Monday, there was an unexplained fire alarm at the center where you volunteer as their accountant once a week. Then Thursday evening, a night when your family is out of the house with various sporting activities, a wrong number call woke you from your sickbed. By Friday morning, you should talk with your spouse and housekeeper about indicators they may have noticed and should be aware of, and let them know that you will get more advice from the company's security department during the day. Luckily you raised this topic, because your housekeeper mentions that recently she has often seen a car drive off soon after you leave the house. The sequence of these types of "normal" events strongly suggests that they could have been orchestrated for purposes of gathering information. With alarm bells ringing, you should seek specialist advice.

A key point to remember is that "the surveillance phase is the only time during which a potential victim has an opportunity to truly influence the outcome of a criminal act" as Richard Wright points out in *Kidnap for Ransom: Resolving the Unthinkable*.[1]

3.2.2   Know How to Prevent and React

If, before your trip or at any point during it, your threat **(see Section 1.1.1)** and vulnerability analyses **(see Section 1.2)** reveal that surveillance is a realistic risk (remember to think broadly because you may not necessarily be the direct target but the determining factors could be external ones such as who you associate with or where you go), then you should take extra care to plan and implement the appropriate level of security measures. If you have reason to be suspicious, then it is not the time to engage in a bit of "007, James Bond" counter-spying on those who are spying on you when there is a real threat. Instead, be informed about "best available solutions" to tackle "worst-case scenarios." The earlier you start that process, the more preventative and reactive options you will have. Preventative options include being:

- Aware of general and context-specific indicators.
- Unpredictable by adding variety to your daily and weekly routines.
- Aware regarding limiting private information about you in public places and information given to others—apply the "need to know" concept to restrict the number and type of people who know details about your schedule and plans.
- Extra careful at vulnerable points—at your office, at certain places were traffic is always jammed, and other locations where it is easy to predict that you will be there and can be easily grabbed.
- Prepared with an exit plan or a plan for reaching safety.

Regarding being unpredictable, it can be a challenge to significantly vary your routines while living or working abroad because there are job and family obligations at set times. If you have children who need to be transported to and from school, then to add variety to your schedule, you could arrange for others to assist with the task. However, if for some reason you are concerned that your children might also be at risk of surveillance as a consequence of being associated with you, then it will be a challenge to do anything about the times they are delivered and picked up. If your risk levels have reached this point, you are certainly recommended to seek specialist advice.

It should be highlighted that a schedule in which on every Monday you go to the gym, but you feel secure because you added variety by going there at a different time every Wednesday, and for when you go running on Thursdays you alter the times, but only by half and hour, is too predictable: If there is a real threat, then this type of scheduling is a vulnerability that leaves you unnecessarily exposed. Be unpredictable, do the unexpected, and certainly always radiate that you are a security-aware person.

It is important to note that depending on the nature of the potential crime, it could be risky to expose the surveillance operation. Thus, you should be cautious before doing so: You should preferably seek advice and support beforehand. The same holds true for suspected technical surveillance operations. If you happen to read the "How to Detect Surveillance and Shadowing: Parts I and II" article, you will notice that it is written for countersurveillance professionals and it lists many things that should not be undertaken by individual travelers. Even though such resources might give you insights, aiding you with being a security-aware traveler, in potential cases of serious crimes you are strongly advised to seek assistance.

Of course, in a situation in which a gang of street kids is scoping you out in a public square in Addis Abba or Zagreb, then you probably want to make it clear to them that you are aware of their tricks. Generally speaking, and there definitely are exceptions, non-targeted, un-/semi-professional surveillance operations should be exposed as early as possible—when the criminal is still assessing targets and conditions. However, in cases where you are the direct target and the potential perpetrators are, for example, a part of the government, competitors, or professional criminals, then it could put you at greater risk to expose the operation alone. Hence, you should seek assistance.

Specialist advice can be provided by various sources. The main categories are authorities (e.g., police, embassy), organizations (e.g., your company, NGO), and external experts (e.g., in the local situation, countersurveillance). There are a multitude of pluses and minuses for each category, depending on the situation and your resources.

3.2.3 Know How to React if Followed by a Vehicle While Driving

When people follow you, it is often to learn about you so they can commit a crime in the near future. A preventative measure you can take is to learn to recognize setups and scams—your knowledge of the local context will support this (see Section 1.1.2). Similarly, to be better prepared for most scenarios, you can implement the guidelines on safer driving (see Section 2.14) such as keeping your car in gear when you are waiting at stoplights or other times when you stop in traffic, and using your rearview mirrors to be alert about what is going on around you.

While it is generally unlikely, it could arise that you are suspicious that you are being followed. Then it would be useful to know what to do:

- Stay calm and create options for yourself.
- Make an unexpected move—suddenly turn, accelerate, signal one direction and turn to the other, or pull up to a safe place. If possible, do this naturally

while continuing to observe the reactions of the suspicious car. Cars that tailgate you, particularly through turns, U-turns, roundabouts, or red lights, warrant your concern.

- Block the visual line between you and the perpetrators—try to get other cars to obscure your moves.
- Draw attention—flash your lights or honk the horn.
- Get help—safely use your mobile and your easily accessible important local contact numbers.
- Do not return to your accommodation—you do not want to increase your vulnerabilities. Going to the police is the obvious choice, though in some circumstances this may not be your best first option.
- Try to remember details—vehicle model, license plate, place, time, and people. You can use the "A, B, C, D, E, F, G" model in the discussion of what to do after a crime in the **Crime and Corruption** section **(see Section 2.16)** as a guideline.
- If your car has been disabled, then you should open your window only a small amount to talk with people who want to help you, and try to call for assistance. Of course, this will depend on if you took the precautionary steps of inserting key contact details into your mobile and making sure it is charged at all times.

For further reading, an excellent, one-stop resource, and one of the main sources for the list of indicators, is the article "How to Detect Surveillance and Shadowing: Parts I and II" available on the Victoriya Security Agency website.[2] To learn more about classic surveillance methods, see the articles "What to Do When You Believe You're Being Followed" on the *Road and Travel* magazine website,[3] "Stranger Danger Tips for Walkers 2: If You Think You Are Being Followed" available on the About.com Walking website,[4] "Protection for You and Your Car" on the Corporate Travel Safety website,[5] and "How to Lose Someone when Being Followed" by eHow.[6] The Stratfor article "The Kaspersky Kidnapping—Lessons Learned" is an example of how criminals are combining modern IT methods with traditional ones.[7] The *Huffington Post*'s "How to Disappear: 9 Ways to Avoid the Creepy Surveillance Systems All Around You" photo-article contains advice for those who are truly concerned about being under surveillance in public.[8] The eHow articles "Home Counter Surveillance Tips and Help"[9] and "How to Detect the Use of Surveillance Equipment"[10] relate some common electronic methods that you should be aware of.

3.3 KIDNAPPING

Kidnapping is a murky world, and sensational media coverage of kidnappings makes it difficult to distinguish fact from fiction. Take the case of Mexico City. The depth and breadth of kidnapping are well covered in the international media. This is probably because the city is consistently the kidnapping capital of the world, so the threat is real. But that Phoenix, Arizona, in the United States is also a "hot spot," ranked second in 2010, was not widely reported outside of the United States. While kidnappings in Latin American countries are a serious threat, the region is no longer the world leader—the Asia and Pacific region was in 2011. Control Risks' "Risk Map 2012" compared 2003 figures with 2011's:

- 65% in 2003: 24% in 2011, for Latin America
- 19%: 39%, for Asia and the Pacific
- 6%: 1%, for the United States, Canada, and Caribbean
- 5%: 35%, for Africa and the Middle East
- 5%: 1%, for Europe[11]

This section sheds light on the worldwide facts and statistics, followed by what motivates the perpetrators, how they operate, which mitigating steps you can take at each phase of a kidnapping, what you can expect if taken, and last but most important, how you can prevent this crime from happening to you.

3.3.1 BASICS: FACTS, STATS, AND DEFINITIONS

One of the hardest facts to establish is the actual number of kidnappings worldwide, simply because it is like an iceberg (or hippo) in water, you only see a small fraction at the top while the greatest volume lies underneath the surface. Or, in the case of kidnappings, it goes unreported. *The Independent* 2010 newspaper article entitled "The £1 Billion Hostage Trade: How Kidnapping Became a Global Industry" proclaimed 12,000 people are taken hostage each year,[12] whereas the 2011 article "Kidnap for Ransom: A Fateful Growth Industry" available on the *Insurance Journal* website puts the annual worldwide figures between 12,500 and 25,000.[13] But if the estimates are correct for Mexico City, for example, then the 60 express kidnappings and 49 kidnap for ransom cases that are believed to occur each day, as reported in the "Annual Kidnap Review 2011" by Special Contingency Risks,[14] means that there are nearly 40,000 cases per year. For both the Mexico example and in general, experts calculate about 90% of cases go unreported.

There are multiple reasons for the scarcity of reliable numbers. One of the main causes is that when a family gets that terrible call with instructions *not* to contact the police, they do as they are told. For them, there is the here-and-now fear for the well-being of the victim but also fear of any future retaliation. There is the additional complication that, unfortunately, police forces in many countries are inflicted with corruption and ineffectiveness so they are not the helping hand they should be. Once the crime is reported, governments can leave their fingerprint on the information by interpreting, packaging, and in some cases hiding data. Part of the problem is that kidnapping means different things to different people who include different variables. For instance, the Chinese government includes the kidnapping of women and children in their figures whereas many governments categorize these crimes under specific issues such as sex trafficking or parental custody battles. These two categories are by far the most prevalent forms of illegal, forcible abductions of human beings against their will.

For the purposes of this book, express kidnapping, kidnapping for ransom (K&R), and virtual kidnapping are three forms of the crime that affect travelers and will be highlighted. However, to indicate the broad scope of kidnapping threats, though admittedly not specifically addressed in this book, the list includes the following.

Piracy is a form of kidnapping that affects thousands of travelers, albeit mainly the crew of international companies shipping wares around the world, but as international headline news attests, some tourists are also taken captive. This ancient crime in need of modern international solutions is beyond the scope of this book. However, if you are considering a seafaring vacation, then the "Travel Security—Piracy Expert's Advice on Safer Coastal Holidays" video available on the TrainingSolutions website gives expert advice on mitigating the risks.[15] Tiger kidnapping is a form of extortion where someone is kidnapped and pressure is put on a third party to commit a crime to gain the release of the victim: For instance, in Belgium there have been several cases in which bankers were forced to hand over company assets or data because a family member was taken. If you are at risk of this type of kidnapping, then you should seek specialist advice. Detention by officials in which the legality of the detention is questionable can also be considered a form of kidnapping, but such terminology is politically weighted and should be handled appropriately.

Though the terms "express" and "ATM" kidnappings are currently used interchangeably, in the past, these terms had different meanings. Previously, some experts used the term "express kidnapping" to describe a short kidnap for ransom (K&R) case in which the victim was often beaten up to put pressure on the payees to pay greater amounts, quickly. Yet, the kidnappers wanted to avoid lengthy negotiations because they would have to care for the victim without getting caught, making it different from traditional K&R cases. ATM kidnappings pertain to victims being held for the purpose of forcing the victim to withdraw the maximum allowable amount of money from ATMs. These typically last "just" a few hours up to a few days and the criminals explicitly do not want others involved. In Mexico City, for example, kidnappers pose as taxi drivers or police officers, often in areas frequented by wealthy people. These opportunistic criminals usually earn around MXN 20,000 ($1,800) for a few hours' work.[16] There are local variations, of course: for example, in some Caribbean countries victims are not taken to the ATM but to their homes in order to rob them.[17] With the past definitions, an ATM kidnapping could not have been an express kidnapping because it does not involve negotiating a speedy release, but an express kidnapping could have both ATM and K&R elements.

Over time, the terms "express" and "ATM kidnapping" have come to mean kidnappings for the purpose of cash withdrawals within a short duration. These often involve violence or the threat of violence but they rarely entail the death of the victim, though it does happen. To help you avoid crimes near or at ATMs, you can read the relevant advice in the **Crime and Corruption** section **(see Section 2.16)**. Of course, any advice should be modified to suit the local variations to minimize your exposure to the threat.

K&R is a longer-term process involving the negotiation of ransom demands: Be it political for, say, exchange of the release of certain ideological prisoners or simply lots of money. It is a psychological thriller, but unlike the movies a life is at stake and time ticks slowly for weeks, months, and sometimes years. A myriad of issues are at play:

- Who leads the negotiations—family, organization, external consultants, police, embassy, etc.?

- Who else should be informed—friends, colleagues, media?
- How do you get proof of life without ending up receiving the victim's finger?
- When should you actually say "yes" to a settlement?

And the list goes on. Meanwhile, if you are the victim, you are probably wondering if *any* action is being taken.

A virtual kidnapping does not actually involve a kidnapping: The "victim" is safe somewhere while the family is conned into believing the person has been abducted and thus willing to pay for his or her release. Typically the "victim" has been under surveillance **(see Section 3.2)**, so the perpetrators know he or she is in a movie, for example, and will have mobile devices turned off. This type of kidnapping is quickly becoming a "hot" trend worldwide because it offers high benefits for the perpetrators in terms of handsome ransoms yet there are few costs like the risks associated with actually keeping someone hostage: So, in the criminal mindset, a few well-spent hours can have good returns for their investment. In Singapore, for example, there were 44 reported cases in 2011 that paid out $250,000 compared to 9 that paid $98,000 in 2010.[18] These are still relatively small numbers compared to the estimated $9 million that all forms of scams are believed to cost Singaporeans: The result has been the government's enacting a new Organized Crime Act, in hopes to curb these worrying costs to society.[19]

Even though the prospect of being kidnapped is scary, survival rates are quite good. Experts, speaking "off the record," estimate for 2010 and 2011:

- 68–75% of kidnappings worldwide end with the release of the victim
- 18–20% are rescued
- 2–4% escape
- 5–8% are killed or die

All said, about 92–95% of kidnapping victims survive. Of those killed, about 60% die during the rescue operation, making it the most dangerous part of the crisis. Oddly enough, there is a positive point in this sad statistic: If you learn how to behave during a rescue attempt, you can greatly improve your chances of surviving. Other lethal dangers are during the initial phases when the kidnappers are nervous and then later on when the effects of the overall conditions, especially sanitation and access to medicines/medical care, can wear down a person. In that regard, the best advice is to maintain your well-being as much as possible.

Probably because express kidnappings are widespread, it is estimated that three quarters of kidnappings end within a week. Even most longer-term kidnappings "only" last about a month; about 2% of worldwide kidnappings continue past three months.

Is kidnapping a realistic threat that you need to be concerned about? To find the answer to this critical question, your starting point is to do a threat analysis **(see Section 1.1.1)** that integrates specific points related to kidnappings, followed by your individualized vulnerability assessment **(see Section 1.2)**. If the threat is indicated for any reason, such as generally high occurrence rates, or specifically high rates in areas you will be frequenting, and/or vulnerabilities that place you in the threat's crosshairs such as being directly targeted in revenge for a soured business deal, then you should seek specialist advice and support.

In your threat analysis, you will look at where kidnappings occur: This should be done on the macro and micro levels. For the macro level, you can ask which regions and countries? For the micro level, you can ask at which locations are you vulnerable?

The top 10 countries for kidnappings, according to the "Annual Kidnap Review 2011" by Special Contingency Risks LTD are:

1. Nigeria
2. Pakistan
3. Afghanistan
4. Mexico
5. Venezuela
6. India
7. Iraq
8. Philippines
9. Honduras
10. Brazil[20]

Unless otherwise stated, the following figures and facts for each of the top 10 countries are from the "Annual Kidnap Review 2011" by Special Contingency Risks LTD.[21] The information is categorized by region. For some years, most business travelers rarely ventured to destinations on such a list. But, the economic realities of recent years have resulted in increasing interest in these locations. That said, NGOs have been operating in countries with the medium/high risk of kidnapping for decades because of their work in conflict zones, natural disasters, or a dangerous mix called a complex emergency.

Kidnapping for ransom is a growing threat in Africa—34% of the world's cases occurred there in 2011. According to the NBC News article "Kidnappings by Militant Groups Increase in North Africa" from October 2012 that cites David Cohen, U.S. undersecretary for terrorism and financial intelligence, in the past decade militant groups received an estimated $120 million in ransoms and, particularly for the Sahel region, K&R is deemed an "urgent threat."[22] The "K&R Bulletin" of October 2012 by JLT Specialty Limited notes that for the African continent the top affected sectors for the period January 2011–August 2012 were:

- 19% NGO
- 17% oil industry
- 8% medical and construction
- 6% media[23]

With nearly a quarter of all recorded cases, Nigeria is the current "kidnapping capital." Criminal gangs dominate the market, responsible for 97% of the cases in 2010. Besides local politicians, oil and construction workers (local and foreign) and their families are the main targets. As the editorial "Nigeria as a Fast-Rising Kidnap Capital?—Politics—Nairaland" posted on the Nairaland Forum in October 2012 laments:

When the potential for quick money with relatively lower risk became apparent, kidnapping soon blossomed into a "lucrative business."

With that realisation also came a change in approach, the targets shifting from foreigners to practically anybody—the rich, the poor, government officials, private individuals, professionals, octogenarians and toddlers; no discrimination.[24]

According to the 2010 article "The £1 Billion Hostage Trade: How Kidnapping Became a Global Industry" by *The Independent*, the "going rate" for a Nigerian hostage is about \$30,000 and for foreigners the rate is \$200,000—kidnappers call unprotected foreigners "walking gold."[25]

Comparing 2011's figures with 2010's, Afghanistan has unfortunately moved up three positions: Kidnap for ransom cases went up 33% in the first half of 2011. Similarly, in Pakistan, the number of reported incidents rose by 28% in the first half of 2011; however, this comes after reduced levels in 2010. For both countries, criminal gangs, intent on financial gain, carried out some incidents. But it was the Taliban and other militant groups who drove the numbers up. Both countries suffer from political and economic instability, thus many kidnappings are motivated by political and/or financial gains. Another significant factor is the low number of police and the prevalence of corruption within the police force. These are the prominent factors that create the "perfect storm" of conditions for the crime to flourish. In Pakistan, the crime affects the whole society but wealthy locals and foreigners are particularly sought.

In India, the social, political, and economic factors of ethnic tensions, inadequate policing, and significant income disparities, amongst other reasons, join forces to create the right conditions for kidnapping to be a widespread crime. Organized gangs, or opportunistic criminals motivated by financial gain are the usual culprits. Though some politically motivated kidnappings do occur, these typically target local businesses and mining operations. In the Philippines, the crime is often politically motivated with financial gain being mixed in. It is a widespread crime but the epicenter is the southern island of Mandanao where militant groups operate.

As **Vivi Hannibal's** contribution points out, "Kidnapping levels have risen steadily in the Middle East, although this region still only accounts for 7% of the global total, with Iraq making up 55% of that." The type of political and/or religious motivation of the extremist militants often means the victims do not survive. In Iraq, criminal gangs, increasingly composed of former militants, inflict great violence and target society's vulnerable, Iraqi women and children. These gangs are motivated by financial gains. Headline news attests to the fact that the political and security vacuum, social strife, and resentment of the occupation are unique factors for Iraq: Or are they? Are any of these factors in your context assessment (**see Section 1.1.2**) and situational analysis (**see Section 1.1.3**) and if so, to what extent?

Daily, there are an estimated 60 express kidnappings and 49 longer-term kidnappings in Mexico City, but underreporting makes it impossible to accurately state. As for other countries, corrupt police is a key ingredient for kidnappings to be a growth industry. The perpetrators can be opportunistic individuals, small groups of well-armed thugs, or professional criminal gangs. Foreigners are usually targeted for express kidnappings more than kidnap for ransom.

A quite disturbing trend to be particularly aware of if you are planning a trip to Mexico is victims are being killed at alarmingly high rates. For the first four months of 2012, according to the April–May 2012 "Global K&R Watch" by ASI Global, 46.4% of kidnappings ended with the victim's death.[26] For the same period in 2011, the figure was 17.1%. One possible explanation could be that the perpetrators do not want a witness to identify them to the police. The report does note that statistics are "notoriously unreliable" and unclear.

Compared to the rest of the region, kidnappings in Venezuela tend not to be violent, partially because much of the expertise comes from Colombian guerilla members who were ideologically motivated. During 2010–2011, the average ransom demand was $350,00 while the average settlement was $250,000. The main targets are dependents, because of the emotional pressure they can apply on the family, and businesspeople, because they can generate large sums of money via their networks. Foreigners can be targeted for express kidnappings. In Brazil, the capital São Paulo is the main center for kidnappings. As wealthy residents took more assertive security measures, the crime began to shift toward increasingly affecting a wide berth of middle class locals from students to businesspersons.

Kidnapping in Honduras has had an up and down curve in recent years. The government crackdown of 2001–2006 saw declining figures, but from 2007 the numbers climbed up after the criminal gangs reorganized. However, there was the problem that new gangs had established themselves, causing the conditions for gang feuds, which in turn, fuel the high murder rates (see Section 2.1). The gangs target wealthy nationals as well as foreign nationals, with the majority of these coming from the Latin American region.

As with other threats, the likelihood that you will experience a kidnapping depends on who you are, what you do, and where you do it; in other words, factors that you should include in your vulnerability assessment (see Section 1.2). Generally, as a tourist you will not be kidnapped, unless you engage in risky behavior in high-risk places: This could range from trekking in Colombia to using an ATM at night, alone in contested areas of Indonesia. As a businessperson, your chances of being kidnapped may increase because of your wealth (or appearance of wealth in an impoverished country) or due to factors related to your work such as a key stakeholder perceiving a threat stemming from your company/sector. As for NGOs, many have operations in locations where kidnapping is a general risk and/or direct threat because of the type of work they do, negative perceptions of them, and so forth. In general, local staff members bear the brunt of incidents. This is all to say that insights gained from your vulnerability analysis are essential.

A crucial aspect of your vulnerability analysis is to be aware of where kidnappings typically occur and compare that with your potential exposure at those places. For example, between 20% and 30% of victims are taken from either their work or school. How can you decrease you and your children's vulnerabilities? As for figures regarding victims taken from their homes, the expert figures vary quite a bit, from less than 20% to double that. Still, that leaves about half taken while they were in transit: Thus, during times of transportation, you are quite vulnerable. What is the best local advice for your situation? And which insights from other areas can you modify and apply in order to further booster your mitigating measures?

Another telling list of kidnapping "hot spots" is the "Kidnap Brief," available from the AKE Group website, because it specifically focuses on incidents affecting foreigners. In the fourth quarter report for 2011, the monthly figures for abducted foreigners were:

1. Mexico: ~10
2. Venezuela: 3
3. Afghanistan/Pakistan: 3–4
4. Colombia: 2–3
5. Somali waters: 13
6. Gulf of Guinea waters: 8
7. Philippines: 2
8. Sahel region: 2
9. Somalia/Kenya: 2
10. Iraq: 1
11. Democratic Republic of Congo: 0–1
12. Nigeria: 0–1
13. Sudan/South Sudan: 0–1
14. Yemen: 0–1[27]

When this list is compared with the top 10 countries for kidnappings in the "Annual Kidnap Review 2011," a few notable points are evident. First of all, piracy is a significant threat to foreigners. Secondly, Nigeria, Iraq, and Honduras do not pose a significant kidnapping threat to foreigners, which is generally speaking, of course, because the picture would be different if you worked for one of the resource extraction industries. Colombia is more dangerous for foreigners than is indicated on the list by Special Contingency Risks, LTD. That said, it does normally feature in the top 10. And, lastly, the remaining countries have more or less the same placements on each list.

3.3.2 Motivation: The "Why's" and How These Affect You

Kidnapping is a complicated crime driven by various factors, but the basic motives are:

- Political—Italian journalist kidnapped to achieve the political aim of getting Italy to pull its troops out of Iraq.
- Religious—South Korean NGO workers kidnapped to stop Christian groups from conducting religious activities in Afghanistan.
- Criminal/financial—Express kidnappings raise quick money with few risks.
- Minors—A divorced parent snatches his or her child from school because he or she lost visitation rights.
- Sex trade/financial—Young women are promised a better life through work or marital opportunities abroad but instead are enslaved for the financial benefit of an individual or gang.

For the purposes of this book, the focus is on the first three because these affect travelers. That said, children are made to travel in international custody battles and women are certainly forced into the international sex trade, but these are beyond the scope of this book. It should be noted that the illegal abduction of women and children are the two categories that victimize the most people.

The kidnappers' motivation often determines the outcome of the crisis. In Yemen, you can be "lucky" if your captors are simply using you as a tool to resolve a local dispute since they tend to adhere to the Islamic tradition of treating guests kindly, even if the negotiations take a while. However, you can definitely be "unlucky" if you have either been taken by a criminal gang who sells their human assets to militants or are directly captured by militants. Then the end result might be your execution because they hope this will boost their political/religious objectives. The kidnapping landscape has changed since 2008 when militant groups started to use Yemen to regroup, according to the August 2011 "Monthly Kidnap News" by Control Risks on the behalf of Hiscox. To quote the report, "Although tribesmen have been responsible for most of the kidnaps recorded between 1999 and 2011, the migration of jihadists to the country has heightened the risk of kidnapping, especially for foreign nationals."[28]

Be aware that certain combinations of motivations can be more lethal: It is easy to think of Iraq's cocktail. But it could also be the destiny of countries transformed by, say, politics but still weakened by religious conflicts, economic downfall, and/or heavily militarized society.

Generally speaking, financial motivation plays a decisive factor in most kidnappings: But the type of financial gain is a critical variable. For instance, in Mexico it is estimated that 90% of kidnappings are related to the drug trade and very few victims survive the ordeal.[29] A drug cartel may gladly take a ransom from the victim's family but they will still kill the person to achieve a greater financial goal. If you are not involved in the drug trade or have any associations with it (even unwittingly), then you generally should be more concerned with kidnappings that have more modest financial stakes like withdrawing a few thousand dollars over a 36-hour period.

Your understanding of the perpetrator's motivations can add to your insights into how to react if you are captured. Take an easy example, but one that regularly affects travelers, of being taken while using a cash point/ATM for the criminal purpose of stealing as much of your cash as they can in the hours or days they hold you. If you are taken, then know that even though they may physically and mentally abuse you, your chances for surviving are quite good if you can keep your composure and follow instructions. However, if you are kidnapped by militants who particularly detest your nationality and to verify that to the world they will film your execution, then you may seriously consider escaping—it might get you killed, but the torture and threats by your captors clearly show you will probably die by their hands anyway. This is an extreme example, but the contrast with the ATM case highlights that having the right type of information will aid you with making the best decisions. Travel risk management is about creating the "best available options" even in the "worst-case scenario."

3.3.3 Stages: What Is Happening and Your Response Options

Every kidnapping is different. Table 3.1 charts a general outline of the typical stages and your response options.

TABLE 3.1

Typical Stages and Your Response Options

Kidnap Stage	Your Response Options
Planning and surveillance	• Vary the times, routes, etc., of your daily routine. • Look like a hard target by radiating self-confidence in your security management. • Report your suspicions of being monitored and follow up to make sure additional security measures are taken.
Attack	• Make a commotion. • Escape if it does not endanger you or others—even if they have a gun, it will be harder to hit you if are moving in a crooked line. • Try to remember details about the vehicle, place, and persons (see Section 2.16).
Transport	• Regain your composure and stay calm. • Avoid eye contact and be low-key. • Follow rules.
Captivity	• Maintain your dignity, win their respect, get them to see you as a human being. • Set goals and keep up hope. • Maintain your mental and physical health. • Understand your captors without being naïve. • Accept that your fellow hostages may have different reactions, but be willing to quickly react if their behavior endangers others.
Release	• Stay low since bullets will be flying in all directions. • Raise your hands, if possible, to show you are unarmed. • Expect to be poorly treated until your identity is confirmed.

3.3.4 CAPTIVITY: WHAT TO EXPECT

The only thing that you can expect is the unexpected. The kidnappers will deliberately confuse you in order to gain control over the situation. They might do this by using some combination of:

- Physical restraint: handcuffs, mouth gag
- Sensory deprivation: solitary confinement, blindfolding
- Threatening: interrogations, frightening animals
- Medical- and health-related abuse: inadequate sanitation, insufficient food
- Mental abuse: lies, mock execution
- Physical abuse: sexual assault, torture
- Verbal abuse: death threats, threats to family
- Indoctrination: brainwashing, propaganda

Through these methods, the perpetrators maintain control over you. About 40% of victims are released unharmed, thus 60% are harmed in some way but the extent varies case by case.[30]

Deprivation and degradation are parts of the horrible tales that K&R survivors later relay. A wealth of emotions could further wear you down, if you do not deal with them. An excerpt from Richard Wright's book *Kidnap for Ransom: Resolving the Unthinkable* underscores some of the emotions felt by survivors.

Kidnap victims report extreme feelings of frustration; many express a feeling of utter helplessness at not being able to positively resolve the situation. The need to depend on the kidnappers for communication, news and movement fosters feelings of impotence, particularly among those accustomed to making decisions and acting immediately.

Kidnappers also like to play with a victim's expectations and hopes of returning home. Some are very professional and keep the hostage informed as to the progress of the negotiations. Many gratuitously create false expectations, only to dash the hostage's hopes repeatedly. This also is a method of enhancing control over the victim and may be one of the cruelest measures of all.[31]

To pick one quote from the book's many survivor stories:

I had been held for over two months. My captors liked to tell me at least once a week that, "tomorrow, you are going home." The first few times, I really got my hopes up and was crushed when nothing happened. I finally stopped believing that I would ever get out of there. The day before I was released they told me the same thing, but this time they made me scrub the entire room where I had been held. They told me that I had to do this to make things ready for the "next guest." Since they had never done that I was pretty sure that they were either going to kill me like they had threatened to do so many times, or let me go. Fortunately, it was the latter.[32]

Throughout your ordeal, your only task is to keep your humanity by maintaining your physical, mental, and spiritual health, as much as the circumstances allow. Challenge yourself, keep goals, and eat. The *USA Today* article "Hope in Captivity: How Kidnapped Journalists Coped" quotes Mr. Micah Garen, a freelance American filmmaker who was held in Iraq: "You force yourself to remain positive, calm, and focused,"[33] and Mr. Roland Madura, a French sound engineer, held in the Philippines: "It's in difficult situations like that you discover you actually can hold on." Remember, worldwide more than 90% of kidnap victims actually survive the ordeal. If you need vital medicines, demand that you be allowed to take them.

Keeping your humanity also deals with your interactions with your captors. Show them that you are a human being by providing just enough information about you to make you a person in their eyes but taking extreme care not to give any private or sensitive information. Be respectful and open but remember to be cautious in regards to what you say about sensitive subjects and to be aware of their biases and attempts to indoctrinate you.

It is the task of your family, friends, organization, government, and often the media to secure your release. Never get involved in your own negotiations! Professional kidnappers will find a way to manipulate you like a puppet. You can tell the kidnappers who to contact and stop there. Your contribution to your release should have happened in your pre-trip preparations and ongoing travel risk management. For example, your travel plan and communication procedures **(see Section 1.12)** would alert others to your disappearance, as would a note on your hotel bed or telling the bed and breakfast owners when they can expect your return **(see Section 2.15)**. This is valuable information for K&R specialists because it will give them insights into where you might be and who might have taken you so they can start building up likely scenarios that will guide them in their strategy to gain your release **(see Section 2.5)**.

Interviews with kidnapped survivors show that they often worry about daily things such as: Does their spouse have access to bank accounts and insurance policies, and is there a good person from the company to talk to? They contemplate their will/testament of assets and the financial well-being of their family. They wish that someone is caring for their loved ones. If you are exposed to the threat of kidnappings, then you should consider organizing these practical aspects before traveling to risky places. In the worst case of being kidnapped, you will know you have these in order, leaving you to focus on being a survivor.

While reading **"Kidnap for Ransom: Get a Helping Hand"** below, notice how key aspects of the threat and vulnerability assessments are covered: For the threat, where is it most likely? What motivates the perpetrators? Which methods do they use? How do they operate? As for vulnerabilities, who is targeted—directly or indirectly? How might the victim's own motivations blind them to the threat? When are victims most exposed? Which factors affect the victim's chances of surviving the ordeal? Of course, the purpose of these types of questions is to give you insights into your own situation. Ultimately, it is about having relevant preventative measures in place such as attending a specialized course and appropriate contingencies such as insurance coverage.

KIDNAP FOR RANSOM: GET A HELPING HAND

VIVI HANNIBAL

*BUSINESS DIRECTOR, SPECIAL CONTINGENCY
RISKS (HTTP://WWW.SCR-LTD.CO.UK)*

Special Contingency Risks, part of Willis Group Holdings (NYSE: WSH), is a leading risk management adviser and insurance broker in the field of kidnap and ransom risks. Too often, I deal with clients who seek high risk insurance after an incident has happened. Such ordeals are a heavy burden on individuals and organizations: the fact is economic kidnapping and extortion is one of the fastest-growing industries in the world. There are more than 30,000 incidents globally and over $500 million is paid in ransom demands every year, according to estimates, although accurate statistics are impossible to obtain as many cases go unreported.

Looking at the reported figures for 2011, Nigeria finished the year as the highest risk country, followed by Pakistan, Afghanistan, and Mexico. Latin America, while still experiencing high numbers of cases, is not the global hotspot it once was, with Colombia falling out of the "top 10" for the first time since this analysis began. South Asia remains a high risk area in terms of kidnapping for ransom. Kidnapping levels have risen steadily in the Middle East, although this region still only accounts for 7% of the global total, with Iraq making up 55% of that.

Some industry sectors are more at risk than others either due to a perception of wealth and the corresponding perceived availability of funds or due to the fact that they work in isolated and exposed environments, where they can be easily identified. High on the list are extractive and energy industries, shipping, and NGOs. As the global race for resources heats up, with China and India's rapid expansion fuelling demand for natural resources, investment in mineral-rich countries that have previously been deemed high risk is now considered attractive. Those working in extractive industries are considered targets not least because of the remote locations of work sites but sometimes also due to resentment from local communities at perceived profiteering at the expense of indigenous people and land. This risk is compounded by a perception of wealth for those connected to large companies operating in this sector and the value of the product in which they deal.

Most kidnappers tend to follow a similar sequence of events, from choice of victim to final release. It is possible to try to avoid becoming a victim if you understand these events. While each kidnap is different, there are usually common features, such as the way a target is selected. You have to ask yourself, what factors would make you a target? Outsiders' perception of wealth, high-profile business activities, and media appearances could be some of the factors that make you stick out as a potential kidnap target. Nearly all kidnap victims admit afterward that in the time leading up to their kidnap they noticed something unusual. This could be strangers observing their office/home, unexplained phone calls, or odd signs of nervousness in a trusted employee.

As the illustrative cases below show, kidnaps can occur at any time: on routine journeys, close to the home, at illegal roadblocks, or in the areas where workers are carrying out their day-to-day business. A large number of abductions happen in the morning where the daily routine tends to be at its most predictable with travel from home to office, school, or another regular location.

ILLUSTRATIVE CASES

Finland, February 2012

Two Finnish men were held in custody in Estonia on suspicion of making preparations for taking a hostage for ransom. The leading prosecutor said that the men, who were arrested in September, were planning to abduct the son of a Finnish banker in hopes of a large ransom payout. Police said that the kidnapping was supposed to take place in Finland, but the arrested men were recruiting Estonians for the implementation of the crime.

Argentina, February 2012

A businessman was kidnapped by three people in Buenos Aires in the early hours of February 7, 2012. He was intercepted as he was driving. The kidnappers took him to a number of ATMs to take money out of his bank account and beat him. They then called his wife and demanded a ransom of cash and electrical goods. The victim was released following payment of

10,000 pesos (US$2,400). The kidnappers also took his car. According to press reports, 200 cases of express kidnapping occur every year in Buenos Aires.

Yemen, November 2011

Gunmen kidnapped a female French aid worker and two Yemeni nationals, a driver and a translator, while they were travelling near Msaimeer (Lahij province) on November 22, 2011. The victims were seized from an International Committee of the Red Cross (ICRC) vehicle. A Yemeni security official claimed that the kidnappers were militants affiliated with the Southern Movement and were demanding the release of prisoners who were arrested by Yemeni authorities on November 21 in Aden (Aden province). The victims were released unharmed on November 24, though it was not clear if a ransom was made or any concessions were made to secure their release.

Ireland, August 2011

The female partner and teenage son of a security van driver were the victims of a tiger kidnap in Belfast on August 17, 2011. At 6 p.m., two masked and armed men forced their way into the home of the driver. The woman and teenager were abducted. The gang issued concise instructions to the driver and stayed for no more than an hour at the house. They told the man to go to work as normal and then hand over the cash later in the day. It was made very clear to them that their lives would be in danger if the instructions were not followed. The man handed over the money on August 18. The hostages had been locked in a shed in Castleblayney and were found by Gardai that same evening with pillow cases over their heads. The gang members had set fire to the van used to transport them and the blaze was spotted by someone in the area who contacted the Gardai. It was thought up to 10 men were involved in the tiger kidnapping gang.

It is clearly important for organizations to mitigate risks and to assess the threat against employees. Personal security relies on constant awareness of the surroundings and the need to exercise care and common sense at all times. It is the responsibility of every individual to take simple and sensible precautions to enhance his or her personal safety. Regularly, failure to follow these predetermined guidelines leads to very serious security situations, including kidnapping. If an incident does occur, organizations need to be ready to respond effectively to a crisis. While some organizations have extensive security and risk management resources in-house, few security departments have handled sensitive and time-consuming kidnapping, extortion, or political detention incidents.

Incidents can be very short in nature or run over years. But more often than not they leave a lasting impact on the affected persons and organization. In a kidnap situation the victims are at risk throughout the ordeal: from the moment of abduction itself, to the hand-over of the hostage, and during any intervention by the security forces. Often, it is at the moment of intervention that victims are most at risk.

There are various providers who offer training in what is known as Hostile Environment Training (HEAT) in which participants are taught skills and techniques that may assist in dealing with a kidnapping event.

When a kidnap event occurs, usually the kidnappers will either contact the victim's family or company to let them know what they want. This contact can be hours, days, or even weeks later. They will probably claim to have the victim, make demands, and almost certainly say that they will harm the victim if the police or other law enforcement authorities are informed of the kidnap.

Helpfully, strategic negotiation assistance is available via specialist companies, and through thorough planning and training it is possible for organizations to significantly mitigate both the risk of kidnapping and also to reduce the effects of kidnapping if it does arise.

The financial and management implications of such kidnap and extortions and the subsequent potential litigation issues give rise to a need for appropriate preventative and incident management advice. Many organizations therefore choose, where permitted by law, to transfer aspects of the financial risk and to seek preventative risk management advice and solutions through a kidnap and ransom insurance program.

A key differentiator between available kidnap and extortion insurance products is the quality of crisis response consultants that the insurers provide following an incident. The expertise of these advisors varies, particularly in terms of resourcing, skills, and experience. Having access to the "right" advisors may not only impact the outcome of an incident, but also any subsequent liability.

Happily, statistics show that the majority of all kidnap cases are resolved via a negotiated safe release of the victim.

If you have survived a kidnapping, regardless of the length of the event or extent of the abuse, you should expect unexpected psychological and physical responses in the aftermath of your ordeal. You ought to immediately seek professional support, as should your family and perhaps certain colleagues, if resources afford this kind of extended care. And, if you do not like the first professional you deal with, find another: It is your healing process. It can be done but it is not advisable to go through all the aftereffects without some professional support. As soon as you can, you need to map out your healing process so that you know how to cope when reactions surface and so that you can inform those around you about how they can best support you: Opt for an expert who guides you through your process. Every person is different so you may need to have one session, ten sessions, or more. At the other extreme, not dealing with these issues potentially allows them to fester, and they tend to rear their ugly heads at times when you least want them **(see Section 1.17)**. In other words, you are potentially creating dangerous vulnerabilities of varying temperaments waiting to be triggered. What could set one of these off—a daily interaction with someone close to you or the same pre-kidnap conditions on a future trip three years after your release?

3.3.5 PREVENTION: HOW NOT TO BECOME A VICTIM

The best strategy for preventing kidnapping is to layer your security management, drawing upon the most suitable combination of mitigating measures. When in country, consider applying these slightly mundane yet generally effective preventative tips:

- Maintain a low profile.
- Do not display anything that is attractive to criminals and shows your wealth.
- Neither display nor publicly discuss sensitive information about yourself, your activities, your employer, etc.
- Minimize the money, credit cards, and personal information that you risk losing.
- Be alert in general and especially in high-value or highly contentious places.
- Be selective about the type of transportation you use and consider the safest options.
- Vary your daily routine **(see Section 3.2)**.
- Make sure that your family members and others close to you follow these measures.
- Make risky behavior safer.
- Trust that you can safely deal with the threat of kidnapping—first aim to be a part of the millions of people who never experience this crime, and if you face it then be part of vast majority who survive it.

Of course, any local specific advice supersedes these generic points. But, usually it is some combination that best safeguards you.

Your pre-trip research and continuous monitoring of the situation will alert you to the threat of kidnapping. A critical question you need to ask yourself is: Is this within my level of acceptable risks? This can be an uncomfortable question to ask especially when you have certain obligations to meet, but if kidnapping is a threat then you need to have your "long security lights" on. If you do not feel comfortable with the risk, then do not go: The "Duty of Care and Travel Risk Management Global Benchmark Study" states that 44% of the 628 surveyed companies have "'refuse to work' policies for risky assignments."[34] If you feel it is a manageable threat or a threat worth facing because of your work, if you are a journalist, for instance, then ask further questions:

- What knowledge, skills, tools, and resources do you need to help you reduce your vulnerabilities and increase your capacities?
- How can you prevent kidnappings and react in life-saving ways? Which measures are you willing or not willing to take—how do these in total affect the risk levels?

To find answers to these questions, you can start by using the same **Risk Management Framework** that has been illustrated throughout this book.

- Be informed **(RMF 1 and 2)**: What, if any, types of kidnappings are common? When? Where? How? Who are the targets?

- Consider the likelihood (**RMF 1 and 2**): What about you, your activities, your employer, etc., could put you in danger?
- Take control (**RMF 3 and 4**): What options are available to you? What preventative measures best address the realities? Does updated information require adjusting your security measures? Before you are in danger, how can you proactively create the "best options" in "worst-case scenarios"?
- Maintain control (**RMF 5**): How can you best prepare yourself to handle a kidnapping? What can you say to yourself to get you through this crisis? What do you want to say to others during moments of crisis? What do you need to focus on to get safely out of danger?

To read more about the topic, Richard Wright's *Kidnap for Ransom: Resolving the Unthinkable*[35] is a recommended book. On the Internet, a good resource is "Kidnapping for Ransom: A Fateful International Growth Industry."[36] The "Kidnapping and Hostage Survival Guidelines," though written for staff of the U.S. Department of Agriculture, has good advice for travelers.[37] The article "11 Surprising Insights about Being Kidnapped" on the 11 Points blog is an interesting read.[38] The open resources available on the ASI Global website provide insightful, realistic analysis of the facts, which can help you to prevent becoming a victim.[39]

3.4   SEXUAL VIOLENCE

To define sexual violence, the "Australian Crime: Facts & Figures" report uses the Australian Bureau of Statistics (ABS) definition:

a physical assault of a sexual nature, directed toward another person who:

- Does not give consent, or
- Gives consent as a result of intimidation or fraud; or
- Is legally deemed incapable of giving consent because of youth or incapacity.[40]

The article "Sexual Assault—Reducing the Risk" on the Washington, DC Metropolitan Police Department's website explains, "A sexual assault is about power, anger, and control. It is an act of violence and an attempt to degrade someone using sex as a weapon. Above all, sexual assault is a crime. Sexual assaults can happen to anyone."[41]

According to the BBC News article "Sweden's Rape Rate Under the Spotlight," which cites information from Amnesty International, Sweden has one of the highest rates of sexual assault in the world, with 63 incidents per 100,000 in 2010: figures that are twice the numbers for the United Kingdom or United States and 30 times those for India, hence it is dangerous place for this type of crime.[42] In comparison, Hong Kong and Mongolia reported zero cases in 2010.

But is Sweden that dangerous? One of the issues that make official figures notoriously difficult to compare is the fact that government agencies have different recording habits and policies on inclusions/exclusions. Another issue is the public's reporting habits. According to the BBC News article, the Swedish numbers are greatly affected by the fact that officials separately record each incident inflicted upon a victim, whereas many countries count that as a single report. In addition, after two decades of public debates, there is a higher level of awareness, a great deal of encouragement and willingness to report, and improved police handling of cases: These are due to a shift in attitudes toward this crime.

The Federal Bureau of Investigation (FBI) reported 84,767 forcible rapes in the United States for 2010, but the report has some important exclusions: For instance, it does not include any cases from Chicago.[43] Not because rapes did not occur there, but because the city refused to discard cases that did not fit the federal definition, which it deemed too narrow. As a result, none of Chicago's nearly 1,400 cases were counted. Similarly, other cities had their numbers shaved off in the FBI's report.

As noted in the **Understanding the Potential Risks while Traveling** section **(see Section 2.1)**, 2010–2011 figures for South Africa show that a sexual offense occurs every seven minutes: However, doubts are cast on these because in 2009 several police stations were known to have substantially reduced crime statistics in order to win a large government bonus.[44]

Despite the zero reported incidents in places like Hong Kong, sexual assault happens in every country, mainly between people who know each other, and affects all ages and both genders, though women are predominantly assaulted. Even though it is a widespread threat, it is underreported in many countries because it is stigmatized and there exists a "blame the victim" attitude. It is estimated that fewer than 50% of rapes are reported.[45]

As with any other risk, it is crucial to be realistically aware of the threat's likelihood **(see Section 1.1.1)** and your vulnerabilities **(see Section 1.2)** in order to mitigate the risk. As with other threats, it is the perpetrator who commits the crime. Therefore, it is impossible for you to negate the risk completely. For example, a survey found that 84% of the college men who had committed rape did not consider it as such[46]: Evidently, a lot more awareness raising has to be done before rape is no longer a threat. But you can focus on proactively managing the aspects that are within your control. Especially because sexual assault is a sensitive subject, you should not allow yourself to be blindsided by myths, assumptions, or fears. Accordingly, this section relies on facts, statistics, expert advice, and real stories from travelers to assist you with preventing this crime and reacting to it.

The following contribution exemplifies how a managed and proactive approach to the threat of sexual violence is the best way to safeguard all staff.

TO INCLUDE "SEXUAL VIOLENCE" OR NOT IN A PAKISTANI WORKSHOP? SHOCKING REVELATIONS MEANT I HAD TO BUCK CULTURAL NORMS AND SPECIAL SENSITIVITIES

TANYA SPENCER

GLOBAL TRAVEL SECURITY AND CRISIS MANAGEMENT SPECIALIST, TRAININGSOLUTIONS (HTTP://WWW.TRAININGSOLUTIONS.DK)

Some years ago, when I conducted my first security management workshop in Pakistan, my new employer had recently decided sexual violence would be a core topic in every NGO workshop, mainly to push awareness. But my client in Pakistan discretely insisted the subject should only be offered to the three female participants as a separate evening session. The agenda had already been distributed to the nearly 40 participants before the workshop, so I had to explain the new arrangement and I exchanged it for a new topic in the week-long course.

Interestingly and fairly quickly, several male participants asked me to present the subject. They requested it because, as managers, they were responsible for all their staff. And many shockingly revealed that male rape did occur, especially by police and security forces as a form of torture. NGO work exposed their male staff to this type of threat. I convinced my client on behalf of the participants to include the topic and rearranged the schedule, with the group attending a very early morning session on the last day. My employer in the United Kingdom later said they had never before experienced such candor from Pakistani participants. For me, it was an eye-opening experience because it was a good example of how presenting a managed approach to security can shed light on normally taboo subjects.

While it is generally difficult to gather statistical facts about sexual assaults on men, rapes of men are reported in 5% of the cases in the United States.[47] Worldwide, an estimated 13% of females and 3% of males have been sexually assaulted, according to the *Australasian Medical Journal* (Online) article "Sexual Assault: An Overview and Implications for Counselling Support" from 2011.[48]

The highly recommended and comprehensive article "Sexual Assault" on the Southern Illinois University website reports that in only 20% of the cases is the perpetrator a stranger and an overwhelming 80% know the offender in the United States.[49] The statistics from "Australian Crime: Facts & Figures" show similar statistics: 30% were a family member, 43% knew their victim but were not related, and 21% were complete strangers for cases reported in 2010.[50] The fact that 60% of sexual assaults in Australia occur in private dwellings and 6% were categorized as "other residential" compared to 7% on the street/footpath and 3% during transportation reinforces the fact "stranger danger" attacks are a less common threat than when two people are in some way associated with each other.

Specifically regarding attacks of women in public spaces, the article "Serious Safety Tips for Women" provides numerous practical insights based on interviews with rapists:

- They prefer targeting women with hair that is easy to grab such as long hair, braids, or a ponytail.
- They look for targets who are distracted by talking on their mobile phone, searching their purse, or the like.
- Most attacks occurred between 5:00 and 8:30 a.m.

- The top three places for abducting a woman for the purposes of raping her later or assaulting her at the location were grocery store parking lots, office parking lots/garages, and public restrooms.
- Because getting caught for rape with a weapon means significantly longer jail terms in the United States, only 2% used a weapon to commit the crime.[51]

The following contribution provides preventative and reactive advice for both "stranger dangers" and threats from known persons. Many of the practical tips apply to all travelers, especially in the subjects of accommodation, transportation, and social interactions. The advice on supporting a survivor of an attempted or successful assault is good to know in order not to revictimize a survivor.

While reading the contribution, you can also refer to relevant sections to supplement the proffered advice: For example, the sections on situational awareness (**see Sections 1.3 and 2.3**), cultural considerations (**see Sections 1.7 and 2.7**), transportation (**see Sections 1.14 and 2.14**), and accommodation (**see Sections 1.15 and 2.15**). Particularly **Chris Poole's** contribution on psychological self-defense (**see Section 2.2.3**) and **Tom Givens'** contribution about reading the environment (**see Section 2.3**), as well as the discussion about violent crime in the **Crime and Corruption** section (**see Section 2.16**) could be useful further readings. Of course, the **Women Travelers** sections (**see Sections 1.2.3 and 2.2.3**) are directly related to female readers.

SEXUAL ASSAULT: PREVENTING AND RESPONDING AS AN INTERNATIONAL TRAVELER

SARAH MARTIN

CONSULTANT AND SPECIALIST ON PREVENTION AND RESPONSE TO GENDER-BASED VIOLENCE (HTTPS:// SITES.GOOGLE.COM/SITE/SMARTINDC/)

In general, women traveling in foreign countries have the same security concerns as men: Crime does not discriminate and having your hotel room burgled, wallet stolen, or being taken advantage of by a scam can happen to men and women. Therefore, many security measures are the same for men and women. But a woman traveling alone can be seen as vulnerable—particularly to sexual assault.

This section has been written with women in mind, but men may find that these safety measures are applicable to their own security awareness efforts, as men can also be victims of rape or sexual assault. It has been compiled by reviewing the security manuals of World Vision, Care, and Refugees International. Other resources include the Médecins Sans Frontières "Guidelines for Medical and Psycho-social Care of Rape Survivors," interviews with women travelers on human rights, humanitarian action, and international business, and from my experiences traveling in more than 50 countries and specializing in strengthening gender-based violence (GBV) prevention and response in humanitarian settings.

While an understanding and awareness of sexual assault can help you avoid dangerous situations, it is not always possible to prevent rape. Sexual assault is a violent crime and the onus of stopping sexual assault should be with the perpetrator, not the survivor. With this in mind, however, women are sometimes placed in danger while traveling and there are ways to mitigate some of your vulnerabilities. The following tips and ideas have been compiled to help travelers take precautions against sexual assault and respond if attacked. There are also suggestions on how to support colleagues if they are sexually assaulted while traveling.

Rape myths suggest that women are raped by strangers lurking in dark alleys. While this can happen, women are much more likely to be attacked by someone familiar to them—a coworker, a driver, or a friend. Particularly while traveling, it makes sense to be extra cautious about socializing with men that you don't know. Most men are unlikely to sexually assault women and women should not avoid all social engagements while traveling. But you should be aware that there have been cases of miscommunication between the sexes and of predatory men using tactics to take advantage of women travelers.

STRANGER DANGERS

To prevent "stranger dangers," you should follow the appropriate advice in this book, including the primary advice of looking and acting confident, being alert, and using your common sense. Some additional general tips, specifically for women travelers though probably applicable to men too, are below.

OVERALL TIPS

- Practice situational awareness. Try practicing "soft vision" so your focus is not only on one point and your peripheral vision is turned on. It allows you to react faster if someone approaches you from the side. It's also good for staying tuned into the vibes in a room, so if other people are getting nervous you pick up on it right away.
- Consider taking a self-defense course in your own country. They will teach you many good tips on general safety that are applicable to every country. Note: Many countries prohibit the importation of mace or pepper spray. If you use this against your attacker, you may be charged with criminal assault yourself. Find out before you travel.
- Learn a few words or phrases in the local language so that you can deter an offender or signal your need for help (i.e., "police" or "fire"). Studies have shown that people are more likely to respond to "fire" than they are to "rape."
- Avoid using an iPod or plugging anything into your ears that might make you less vigilant. This is especially true if you are walking

home alone late at night, as you will not be able to hear anyone approaching you.
- Consider putting maps on your smartphone so you look as if you are checking messages rather than looking at a map if you get lost. However, conspicuous use of a smartphone in a crime-ridden area may draw attention.

This is all in addition to the usual security precautions such as avoiding walking in dark alleys, parks, or similarly desolate places at night; using trusted taxi drivers/companies instead of hailing one from the street; and checking the quality of your hotel door's bolts and chain.

ACCOMMODATION

- Avoid full names on luggage tags. Use your first initial and avoid Ms. or Mrs. Some con men will read your name off your baggage tags and attempt to strike up a conversation with you by calling out your first name. They may also use this information to call your hotel to get more information on you.
- Keep the door to your room open when a male staff member is in with you. Male hotel staff are often solicited for sex so may offer their "services" to you. Be firm about turning them down and if they are harassing you, report them to hotel management. If you are in a chain hotel, be sure to report to the management headquarters rather than just the local manager. It also helps to check Tripadvisor.com or other travel websites to see if other solo travelers have reported problems.
- Maintain friendly relations with female staff in the hotel. They may be able to provide support to you if male staff are sexually harassing you.
- For long-term housing, consider sharing a residence with another woman or living in a group home or apartment.
- Carry "Blu-Tak" with you when traveling. It is very useful for making sure curtains close all the way (hair clips can also work for this purpose). It can also be used to put up newspapers or cloth over a window that has no coverings to prevent peeping toms.
- Always wear pajamas or a nightgown that you could run into the streets in. Sleeping naked or in a revealing nightgown might make you think twice before running out of your hotel room in case of an assault.

In Delhi, India, I was staying in a 3-star hotel with a "push button" lock and a chain on the door. Late at night, my colleague came over to share some documents with me and when she left, I forgot to re-chain the door. At 6 a.m., I awoke to a hotel employee entering with no knock and no call of "housekeeping." He ran out when I shouted. I ran down to the front desk to complain and they defended the employee. The male desk attendant began to shout at me and when I asked to file a complaint with the manager, I was ignored. Lesson learned: always make sure your door is locked and hotel staff cannot open it from the outside.

Consider bringing a door wedge to place under the door to delay an intruder from getting the door open. Some women suggest bringing a travel lock or a bicycle chain lock to secure doors. Make sure the bolts work or change rooms. While this applies to all travelers, experience shows that women are particularly vulnerable in their accommodation and by following the basic precautions, they have avoided attempts by men to enter their room.

TAXIS AND HIRED DRIVERS

- Always look at the ID tag of your taxi driver. Check that the ID tag of your taxi driver matches that of the driver. Don't be afraid to get another cab if not.
- Be extremely vigilant if your taxi has central locking. You may be locked in without your permission.
- Some women put the identification number of a taxi driver in their mobile phones or take a photo of the driver/photo ID when they get into cabs to make it easier to report any problems.
- Try to travel with another person in the cab if you have been drinking so the taxi driver doesn't take advantage of your impaired state.
- Use a driver you trust—establish a business relationship with a regular "Taxi Guy"—ask your colleagues for a reference for one. Don't become overly "familiar" with your driver. In many cultures, men think that familiarity is an advance and feel free to approach you.
- Stand in a lighted and populated area if you're waiting for your driver to arrive at night. A common mistake that many women make is to wait at their "usual" spot even if it is dark and there are no people around.

DRIVING ALONE

- Do a defensive driving course if you are going to the field or a place with bad roads/drivers. You should know how to drive in sand, mud, etc., so you avoid getting stuck. It always helps to be able to drive yourself so you are not vulnerable if something happens to the driver.
- Know how to change a tire so you don't spend hours on the side of the road. Make sure your car is equipped properly with spares and all necessary tools.
- If driving at night in a dangerous city or a badly lit area, see if you can drive in a convoy with friends. Always know your route, especially when driving at night.

- Insist that your car have "anti-smash and grab" windows, particularly in countries where carjacking and violent robberies are common.
- Have your mobile phone (or radio) and your keys out as you walk to your car, whether you are parked in a parking lot or on the street. You don't want to be digging in your bag standing in front of your car door. Keep your mobile phone easily accessible so you don't have to fumble in your purse looking for it.
- Don't be afraid to ask someone to accompany you to your car at night. Make sure this is someone you can trust.

AVOIDING UNWANTED MALE ATTENTION

- Consider your attire. Women's dress can be a major issue in some developing countries. In some countries, it is considered provocative to show your legs, in others your shoulders, and in others your hair. In some Islamic countries, women cover themselves from head to toe to avoid unwanted attention. When in doubt, the best option is to dress like a local—see what your female counterparts are wearing. Learn the local dress code as soon as you arrive; buy appropriate clothing locally if necessary. While opinions differ on wearing headscarves, it is useful to dress respectfully of local customs. Covering will not prevent sexual assault (as women from that country who dress modestly are also sexually assaulted) but will help avoid unwanted or lewd attention, and other harassment by local men. Unfortunately, many men in developing countries believe the rumor that Western women are "easy" or that women in bars alone are prostitutes. By not drawing further attention to yourself, you can avoid unwanted advances.
- Consider wearing a wedding ring or wearing one of your rings on the traditional "wedding ring" finger. Especially in conservative countries, a married woman is viewed as the property of another man and therefore off limits. Single women can be considered "available" for all sexual contact. In crime-prone areas, make sure it doesn't look too expensive so it doesn't become a target!
- Avoid prolonged eye contact with men. Prolonged eye contact with a man is an invitation to flirt. In some developing countries or some societies, any eye contact at all may be considered carte blanche to approach you. Eye contact also may be considered disrespectful in some countries and may invite aggressive behavior from strangers. Wearing sunglasses can help reduce unwanted eye contact. Talk with local women to learn the rules.
- Bring a book or computer to restaurants or hotel bars when dining alone so as to discourage unwanted male attention (although a computer may draw attention to you as "rich" in some places and make you a target for crime). Sit at a table for one rather than at the bar.

Politely but firmly (and if necessary, loudly) state that you do not wish to be disturbed if another diner is aggressively soliciting you. If you leave the dining room, linger in the lobby near the front desk before going to your room to ensure you are not being followed or ask a member of the hotel staff to accompany you to your room.

In 2003, I learned the hard way that a woman sitting alone at a bar is an open invitation to sexual advances. In Gisenyi, Rwanda, I was sitting at the bar in my hotel eating a bowl of spaghetti bolognese and a man sat beside me ignoring all of my attempts to be curt and signaling him to leave me alone. Finally, I paid my bill and stood up to leave. He grabbed my wrist strongly and said he would accompany me to my room. I loudly said, "I am not interested in you. Leave me alone and do not touch me." Luckily this embarrassed him and he dropped my hand. I then asked the front desk clerk to walk me to my room. However, I felt nervous for the rest of my stay and ate my dinners in my room after that. Now I usually take a table instead of sitting at the bar and that discourages most unwanted advances.

DANGERS FROM "FRIENDS"

While avoiding stranger dangers is relatively easy to do, dangers from friends, associates, and colleagues can be more of a challenge because these are men in your daily life, and for the vast majority of them, they present no danger to you. "Sophie's" story can show how even "fun" coworkers can be a threat.

"Sophie"

One of the problems we have is stressed-out aid workers going out dancing and drinking after a long hard day. The women want to dance and have fun but some men don't know how to stop at no. I had a friend who had to come into my room and stay with me for the night because her supervisor kept calling her on the phone and knocking on her door all night trying to have sex with her. She felt like it was her fault because she had danced with him that night, but because he was married, she thought it was safe.

Every woman has the right to go to dinner with friends, wear what she likes, and act in the way that she chooses and not be raped. However, when traveling in a culture that is foreign to you, an ounce of caution can help improve your safety and maintain your security. Potential perpetrators don't wear badges announcing their intentions, so be cautious, even with friends.

SOCIAL SITUATIONS

- Exercise caution when meeting someone you don't know well. An evening date with a group of people at a public place is far safer than an evening alone with a new acquaintance. If you are going out alone, be sure to make sure someone knows where you are going and when you expect to return. Make an appointment to check in with a friend or security if unsure about the person you are meeting. You can also tell your date that you have a security curfew and must check in with the security officer.

- Speak up! Communicate your wishes clearly. Be sure to make male acquaintances know that you are meeting for business or friendship purposes. Do not invite business acquaintances to your hotel room; ask them to wait in the lobby while you go up to the room.
- Assert yourself. Insist on being treated with respect and remind the acquaintance of what is unacceptable in your own culture.
- Be cautious when accepting food or drink from strangers in restaurants or bars. There have been many reported cases of women being drugged and sexually assaulted by men who buy them drinks in bars. Rohypnol (the brand name of flunitrazepam), or "roofie," is a benzodiazapine, a prescription pill similar to Valium that can be ground up and mixed into a drink by someone who wishes to rob or sexually assault you. It causes sedation, a feeling of extreme intoxication, and amnesia. The drug's amnesiac effect lasts at least eight hours and most people have no memory of events while under the drug's influence. The following rohypnol advice is quoted from the article "Rohypnol or Roofies—How to Avoid Date Rape Drugs":

- Roofies may have a bitter taste when dissolved in alcohol; be alert to a strange taste in your drink.
- When placed in a light-colored drink, the newer roofies will turn the beverage blue. If your water and tonic turns blue, dump it and become especially alert; someone has tried to drug you. The older roofies won't change the color of your drink.
- If you suddenly feel unusually drunk after just a small amount of alcohol, quickly ask for help (preferably not from the strange man next to you at the bar who may have given you the roofie)—you might have just a few minutes of alert behavior left to you.
- Don't drink anything you did not open yourself or that you didn't see being opened or poured.
- Don't accept a drink from someone you don't know unless you see it being opened or poured by a bartender.
- Always watch your drink at parties and bars. If you leave your drink unattended, get a fresh one to be on the safe side."*

---

* Kathleen Crislip, "Rohypnol or Roofies—How to Avoid Date Rape Drugs." About.com Student Travel. ND. http://studenttravel.about.com/od/springbreak/a/roofies.htm.

Most female travelers probably have read similar advice about protecting their drinks (and food) while out. An example from Carol, an international development worker, shows that a bartender can also be part of the threat scene. In this case, it would have been better to heed the forewarning about the reputation of the establishment and avoid it.

Carol

In East Timor, there was a nightclub that was notorious for women being drugged and sexually assaulted. Everybody knew it was a problem so they kept their drinks close. However, a friend of mine was drugged and made it home safely. She reported it to the owners who were aware of the problem and trying to investigate to see if it was anyone who worked with them. Another friend woke up next to a man she knew the next morning who treated her very rudely. She had no memory of going home with him or even flirting with him. We suspected it was a bartender and that men would bribe him to drug women they found attractive.

SEXUAL HARASSMENT AT THE WORKPLACE

Many security manuals focus on the issue of assault by a stranger. Unfortunately, sexual harassment by coworkers in the field is also a problem. Studies have shown that women are more likely to be sexually assaulted by someone that they are acquainted with than by a stranger. Seemingly mild-mannered colleagues can become sexually aggressive when out of their normal world. Spending long hours in bars or hotels socializing with female colleagues can cause them to throw caution to the wind and act in ways they might never consider in their home country. Alcohol can exacerbate this problem.

Many companies have a sexual harassment policy but still employees are often intimidated or afraid to react because of fear of not being taken seriously or because of the difference in authority between the aggressor and the employee. In my line of work, as a specialist on gender-based violence, I've heard too many stories like Julia's.

Julia

In one of my first volunteering abroad experiences, I met another foreign woman in a cafe and we were chatting about our jobs working for charities. She eventually disclosed that a colleague in the organization that she worked for had sexually assaulted her. She felt like she could do very little because of his position, the importance of their work and her fear of disrupting it, and a host of other reasons. So she was telling this stranger (me) in a cafe rather than reporting it to her office.

Read up on your company's sexual harassment policy. If they do not have one, demand that human resources create one! Many organizations have insufficient sexual assault policies that provide very little support for the survivor and are designed by insurance agencies to protect the organization. Women should read these policies before traveling and know what support they can get from their organization if a colleague or someone outside the organization sexually assaults them. This is Lina's advice, vowing to never again accept a superior brushing aside sexual harassment.

Lina

I was sexually harassed by a colleague, repeatedly, during one of my early field assignments. Our boss would insist that we go into the field together—sometimes this meant lengthy car rides, with ample opportunity for him to put his hand on my leg, proposition me, or ask me, "Do you know how beautiful you are?" As I was in my early twenties and new to international work, I hesitated before complaining to the boss. When I did, I should have been better prepared. I didn't know if the organization had a sexual harassment policy. I should have checked. He said that because I am from that part of the world, I should know how the men are. "Do you expect him to admit to it?" he asked me. "It would be like nailing Jell-O to the wall." I'll never forget his response—and never accept that as an answer again.

If you find yourself in a similar situation, the best advice is to:

- Tell your colleague firmly and clearly that his actions are making you uncomfortable and you consider it to be sexual harassment (or that he is in violation of your company's sexual harassment policies). If possible, put this in writing so you have proof for management.
- Maintain professional boundaries with colleagues and limit alcohol consumption, if necessary. While socializing can be a fun and sometimes necessary part of your travel, having clear boundaries can stop any potential miscommunication.
- Do not be afraid to report problems to your superiors. Do it early. Keep a written log.

WHAT TO DO IF SEXUALLY HARASSED, PHYSICALLY THREATENED, OR ATTACKED

There is no single right or wrong way to respond to an attack and each situation is different. Only you can decide whether or not to resist your attacker. You can try to talk your way out of it, give in to the demands made of you, shout for help, flee, or fight. Note: Never risk your life or safety for material possessions—your principal objective in any assault is to survive with as little harm as possible.

SEXUAL HARASSMENT
- Ignore the advance. If a man is trying to get a reaction and finds he cannot, he may stop.

- Confront him. If you politely ask, "Were you speaking to me?" the annoying party may feel embarrassed, especially if his actions were based on fear or insecurity.
- Get help. Do not try to cope alone.
- Say no. If you're being groped or touched inappropriately in a crowd, know how to say, "Leave me alone!" or "Do not touch me!" loudly in the local language. Learn how to shout "police" or "fire" to draw attention.
- Find a local woman or group of women to help you if you are being pressured or followed by a strange man. In many countries, women will gather around someone being harassed and denounce the man publicly.

PHYSICAL OR SEXUAL ASSAULT

- Do not hesitate to call attention to yourself if you are in danger: scream, shout, run, or sound the horn of your vehicle. Dress in ways that do not limit your movements (long tight skirts or very high heels).
- If you think you're going to be raped, some women travelers have suggested making yourself as physically unpleasant as possible by pretending to vomit. Others have suggested trying to kick or strike the attacker's genitals although it may encourage further violence from the assailant or an arrest for assault in some countries where women have few rights.
- Shout "FIRE!" or "POLICE!" in the local language, as unfortunately, studies have shown that people are reluctant to be involved in rape and may not intervene if you shout "RAPE!"
- Some travelers recommended carrying a whistle as this will draw attention to you and discourage the perpetrator.

IF YOU'VE BEEN SEXUALLY ASSAULTED OR RAPED

It's not your fault. Remember: Nothing that you have done has caused you to be raped and you may not have been able to prevent it. Social stigma and dangerous myths still remain (in all countries) and the people whose job it is to assist or support you in this situation may not. You have the right to pursue the treatment you need and the right not to report the rape if that is what you wish to do.

In a foreign land, the social services that you expect from your home country may not be available. Most legal systems are woefully unsupportive of rape survivors. You can seek in-country support for accessing services and guidance on appropriate approaches to authorities. Your embassy can send assistance in some cases or in recommending an embassy-approved medical practitioner. If in a humanitarian setting, some NGOs such as Médecins Sans Frontières or the International Rescue Committee can provide support and medical care as they are situated to provide services to rape survivors.

Most medical organizations should have postexposure prophylaxis for HIV prevention.

You can seek help if you are the victim of this crime of violence. You are in control of what happens next. Seeking medical care from local providers or reporting to the police may not be a prudent option but the choice is yours. Local colleagues can offer some advice on this matter as they will be familiar with the reputation of local hospitals, police departments, and other services.

MEDICAL CARE

There are many steps you can take to protect yourself from unwanted pregnancy, HIV/AIDS infection, and sexually transmitted infections. These actions are time sensitive. Find medical help immediately. You can insist on having female medical personnel present—although lack of certified trained female practitioners is a problem in many countries. You can also ask for a female nurse to be with you during the medical exam. Many countries have mandatory reporting laws and the physician is required to report the assault to the police. In all cases, you should insist on medical attention first as many of the steps outlined below are time sensitive.

If medical care is not available, there are some actions you can take yourself to protect yourself from unwanted pregnancy or HIV infection.

- Within 72 hours of a sexual assault, in order to reduce risk of HIV infection, you can take postexposure prophylaxis (PEP), an antiretroviral. Ideally, the PEP should be administered within 4 hours of the attack. PEP is administered for 28 days and can have some rather severe side effects so should be administered by a medical professional who can provide counseling to help you. Many health care agencies have PEP available for accidental needle sticks or assaults on their employees. If the hospital near you does not carry it, approach medical officers in embassies or large corporations.
- Within 5 days (or 120 hours), you can receive emergency contraception to prevent pregnancy. Emergency contraception is usually a heavy dose of oral contraception (available in many pharmacies as "the morning after pill" or the "La pilule du lendemain" in French or "La píldora del día despúes" in Spanish). If you don't have access to "emergency contraception" but have access to oral contraceptives (birth control pills) check and see if you can put together 1.5 mg of levonorgestrel. This pill should be taken as soon as possible. The longer you wait, the less effective it becomes.
- If you do not get your period within 21 days, you should seek out further medical care. Some female travelers carry emergency contraceptive pills with them in remote areas in order to be able to prevent pregnancy in case of rape.
- You should get a tetanus shot if there has been broken skin.

- Sexually transmitted infection (STI) treatments: You may be at risk for transmission of hepatitis B, chlamydia, gonorrhea, syphilis, or chancroid. Seek medical attention as soon as possible to be treated for these illnesses.

LEGAL RESPONSE: TO REPORT OR NOT?

If you are assaulted, you must decide whether or not to report the crime. If you report the crime, in most cases the police will want to question you about the circumstances of the event, and in most countries, will likely demand a hospital examination. Most developing countries are not well-trained or supported in providing services to rape survivors. You might find that you are subjected to unnecessary medical investigations, responsible for providing proof of the rape, and treated with judgment and lack of empathy. Reporting sexual assault is encouraged in order to punish the perpetrator and prevent attacks on other women, but it is a personal matter for you to decide whether or not you wish to pursue legal action. In some countries, the treatment by the legal system may further traumatize you and not lead to prosecution, so decide for yourself what you wish to do and do not allow anyone to pressure you.

GETTING SUPPORT FROM YOUR EMPLOYER

Do not be afraid to ask work for some time off—use sick leave or personal leave since it is not vacation time. You are entitled to recovery from these incidents: Your agency should support (and possibly fund) this. Ask human resources about identifying counselors or therapists who can be available to you (either in your home office or via phone if you choose to stay in the field). It's important to ask about how much counseling your agency will pay for. Many survivors find that they need to talk in confidence to someone to deal with trauma around the event—someone who is not related to the workplace.

SUPPORTING A COLLEAGUE WHO HAS BEEN
SEXUALLY ASSAULTED OR RAPED

In some cases, you may be traveling with someone who has been raped. This causes a lot of anxiety and fear as people may be afraid to "do the wrong thing" or further traumatize the survivor. It is important for survivors to know that they went through abnormal events and that their emotional reaction to those events is normal. Guilty feelings may appear; therefore, it is important to communicate explicitly that sexual violence is not the fault of the survivor. There are many myths, false beliefs, and misconceptions around sexual violence. Many cultures blame the victim for the sexual assault. If the individual expresses feelings of shame or guilt, be sure to address them directly. Give a clear message that sexual violence is never the fault of the survivor: The crime is the fault of the perpetrator.

There are ways that you can help your colleague recover from this criminal act. As rape is an extremely disempowering experience, your focus should be on trying to empower the survivor in all areas possible, restoring her ability to feel that she has control over her body (by asking consent before each action— calling the police, informing your office, hugging or touching her, etc.) and reducing further victimization by avoiding diminishing her control over the situation (not talking about her without her consent) or making decisions for her. Do not pressure the survivor to make decisions she is not comfortable with. In general:

- Be respectful.
- Maintain confidentiality.
- Be non-judgmental.
- Be consistent.
- Be patient.
- Be empathetic.
- Allow the person to cry.
- Avoid "why" questions.
- Don't force the person to talk if she does not want to.
- Don't criticize the survivor's choices.
- Support survivors in their choice to leave the situation or continue working if they desire it.

Supplementing the advice about "date rape" given in **Sarah Martin's** contribution is a quote from the article "Sexual Assault" on the Southern Illinois University's website about such drugs as ketamine, GHB, and Rohypnol:

- **Date rape drugs are being used to sedate potential rape victims.** These drugs are odorless, colorless, and tasteless and go by names such as Rohypnol, ruffies, ketamine, GHB, and Forget Pill. These drugs alone or mixed with alcohol can cause people to lose their ability to fight back and remember events. *But also realize that non-alcoholic drinks and water can also be drugged.* These drugs dissolve quickly and invisibly into liquids and cause rapid and severe intoxication, dramatically reducing inhibitions and inducing memory loss.
- **Symptoms of date rape drugs can include** feeling overly intoxicated, dizziness, memory loss, nausea or breathing difficulties. If you think you, or a friend, has been drugged—get medical attention IMMEDIATELY. These drugs can be fatal. Most rape victims don't report the rape within twenty-four hours. Some of these drugs can be out of your system in six hours. This makes proving that they were drugged and raped very difficult.
- **It just takes a second to slip a drug into your drink.** Never leave any drink unattended, even for a few seconds. If you do, lose it and get a fresh one. Do not drink from communal punch bowls, cups, bottles, or cans. Only take drinks from servers or bartenders; do not let another person handle your drink before you drink it. Watch out for your friends; if they start to act

unusually intoxicated, dizzy, or nauseous, get them to the emergency room right away.

- **Ketamine**, also known as Special K, is a fast-acting general anesthetic approved for veterinary uses and can be administered in liquid, tablet, or powder form. The effects of the drug usually last for up to an hour, but a person can take 48 hours to fully recover.
- **GHB**, which is short for gamma-hydroxybutyrate, is mostly administered as a clear liquid and is illegal in the United States. The drug's effects usually last about eight hours and can cause the central nervous system to shut down when mixed with alcohol.
- **Rohypnol** often is used as a tablet dropped into drinks because it dissolves so quickly. The effects of the drug can begin within 15 minutes and last up to four hours.[52]*

It is important to underline that *anyone* can be drugged using these or other locally available drugs, as in the contribution **"'Friends' with Criminal Intentions Make Dangerous Tea in Kenya" (see Section 2.16.3)**. Drugs are often employed in a honey trap scam **(see Section 2.11)** in which men are the most likely prey so that compromising pictures can be used for blackmail or to access data and systems on mobile devices, for example. If your vulnerability analysis **(see Section 1.2)** warns you about potential exposure to this risk, then proactively manage it by being aware of the indicators and knowing how to reduce your risks. The About.com Teen Advice article "Date Rape Drugs: Date Rape Drugs Explained and De-Mystified" is recommended because it comprehensively deals with the subject and has a plethora of links to additional resources.[53] For example, one of the links is to the Drink Safe Technologies website, which sells coasters and kits to test drinks.[54]

For further reading, the article "Sexual Assault" available on the Southern Illinois University's website is quite comprehensive: In addition to the excellent preventative and reactive advice, it also covers many aspects including legal issues and medical advice, so it stands out as a highly recommended, "one-stop" resource.[55] A shorter article "Sexual Assault—Reducing the Risk" by the Metropolitan Police Department provides a useful overview of the key points.[56] The No Nonsense Self Defense website has an extensive set of resources in their "Rape Hub": For example, the "How to Avoid Rape" article could be useful reading.[57] However, be forewarned, the article states: "if you have just arrived on this page through a search engine—that you go get yourself a cup of coffee, come back to the computer, go to the Rape Hub and be prepared to spend the next few hours reading. It's that big of a subject." Throughout all their articles, there are plenty of hyperlinked key words that lead the reader to further reading. Similarly, the websites of the National Sexual Violence Resource Center[58] and PreventConnect[59] each have a multitude of resources on offer. The "Serious Safety Tips for Women" article on the Women Travel Tips website describes a few easy-to-use self-defense moves in the event of an attack.[60] The article "Surviving a Rape or Sexual Assault while Travelling" on the Female Traveller website offers advice on aftercare issues.[61]

---

* Reprinting and modifications made by permission. Copyright © 2012 Department of Public Safety at Southern Illinois University Carbondale.

3.5 CARJACKINGS

The Australian Institute of Criminology conducted research on carjackings in the United States, United Kingdom, South Africa, and Australia, and in 2009 produced the report "Carjacking in Australia: Recording Issues and Future Directions" that found that the media had overrepresented the rare cases that involved weapons and violence.[62] For carjackers, cars are literally vehicles to achieve something else: Reselling the cars or parts was one of the top motivations. Using cars to perpetrate other crimes such as robbery or simply going joy riding were other motivators. From the criminal's perspective, carjackings are risky, especially when they use violence: But if they can obtain both the car and keys, then the car is a more valuable commodity to them, regardless of whether they intend to make money or have fun.

If carjackings (also known as "hijackings" in many parts of the world) are a potential threat at your next destination, then the general places you should be particularly alert include:

- Congested traffic
- Intersections
- High crime areas
- Parking lots, residential driveways, and gates
- Isolated roads and areas
- Pick-up and drop-off points, such as at schools
- When people test drive a car you are selling

According to the book *Staying Safe*, carjackings typically occur at or near:

- Airports, bus terminals, train stations, and the like: 40%
- Home or friend's home: 25%
- Commercial places and parking lots: 20%[63]

Ploys used to carjack you include bumping your car from behind, pretending or creating a problem with your car so you will pull over, putting an obstacle such as a fallen bicyclist or tree trunk in your path, and acting as fake police. The greater the likelihood that you might face a carjacking, the more time and effort you should invest in learning about the local variations including typical locations, times, means (trick, con, weapon), and targeted vehicles.

The importance of having some insights into the local variations needs to be highlighted: For example, normally it is "best practice" to drive to a populated place, which on the road often means a gas station. But in Kenya, a "trap" is often prearranged at the next gas station, so after you discover a tire is flat (cut discretely at the last intersection) or someone bumps you, you pull into the gas station unaware of the eventual danger. In other words, if you have not adjusted the generic advice to the local situation you might end up increasing your vulnerabilities.

To avoid becoming a victim, follow the relevant advice in the **Transportation** sections **(see Sections 1.14 and 2.14)**. If the circumstances seem like the buildup of a carjacking based on the examples in this book or local cases you found out about, take appropriate evasive actions. For example, if two young men at a desolate intersection bump your car, then it is better to drive to the nearest police station than to pull over.

Regarding devices and services that stop the engine or track the vehicle, in many places, criminals know about these and will immediately ask you about them.

3.5.1 SURVIVING A CARJACKING

Everyone in the vehicle should briefed and preferably drilled in avoidance and response measures if carjackings are a realistic threat in your environment. General advice includes:

- Avoid eye contact, as it can be interpreted as aggression on your part. Keep your eyes lowered or maintained at the mouth/nose region of the speaker.
- Give up your car without hesitation.
- Stay calm and follow instructions quickly.
- Do not make any sudden moves and keep your hands up, ideally at chest level.
- Point to your seatbelt just before releasing it; otherwise this move could be tragically misread and appear as though you might be reaching for a gun.
- Leave the keys in the ignition, the car in neutral and running. You want them to take the vehicle as soon as possible, before the crime escalates into kidnapping or sexual assault.
- Unlock the door, get out of the car, and keep your eyes down and hands up.
- If there are children in the car, inform the criminals but otherwise keep quiet. In some circumstances, you may consider taking the keys with you until you obtain your children but any such actions should depend on how you evaluate the situation.
- If the perpetrator demands that you drive, you can consider crashing the car in an area that will draw attention. However, this can be risky in many ways.
- Report the incident to the police and, on some occasions, your organization.

As for further reading, the two best resources in terms of being comprehensive yet concise are "Preventing Hijacking" by the South African Police Service[64] and "Carjacking—Don't Be a Victim" by the U.S. Department of State.[65] The "How to Avoid Carjacking" article on the Corporate Travel Safety website offers basic preventative and reactive advice.[66] The WikiHow article "How to Avoid Being Carjacked"[67] provides similar advice but with the addition of photos. Two interesting articles, with juxtaposing angles, are "Confessions of a Car Hijacker"[68] and "Car Hijack Victim's Nightmare—What It Feels Like to Have Your Precious Life in the Hands of Someone Else"[69]—both available on the Sowetan Live website.

3.6 DEMONSTRATIONS AND RIOTS

As an international traveler, you can be "at the wrong place at the wrong time" and accidentally get caught up in a demonstration, protest, or riot: The contribution **"It's No One, It's the Mob: Meeting an Angry Demonstration during a Family Diving Vacation in Sri Lanka"** attests to this. But there are ways to proactively avoid civil unrest while you are traveling and to react in life-saving ways if tensions erupt: This section covers both to help you keep safe.

The international media tend to headline a few vocal or political demonstrations, but there is less reporting on local occurrences of civil unrest. This skews the picture and hides the fact that protests are common events. Every day, for instance, there are approximately 500 protests in China[70]—how many of these have you heard about? Statistics from the 2011 "Duty of Care and Travel Risk Management Global Benchmark Study" of the 628 surveyed companies indicate how widespread protests are: 60% of the Global 500 enterprises recorded that staff had experienced civil unrest, 56% of large companies with 10,000+ employees, 48% of medium sized companies, and 35% of small companies of less than 1,000 staff members.[71] And, for the somewhat ambiguous category of "Lawlessness," the respective numbers were 40%, 39%, 29%, and 24%.

To mitigate the risk, start by drawing upon your context **(see Section 1.1.2)** and situational **(see Section 1.1.3)** analyses to answer such questions as:

- When are significant dates: Historical (e.g., lost battles), political (e.g., elections), religious (e.g., processions), etc.? Review, for example, Red 24's event calendar in their "Threat Forecast 2013."[72]
- Why are these significant? To whom? And whom is the resentment directed toward?
- Where are contentious locations?
- What are the tensions: Social (e.g., inequality), economic (e.g., unemployment), cultural (e.g., ban on certain clothing), etc.?
- How have tensions manifested in the past? Potentially in the future?

Answering these types of questions will give you insights into potential triggers that could ignite into unrest. Most protesters are peaceful but there can be agitators within the crowd, and actors external to it can aggravate the situation, making the event unpredictable. Therefore, you are advised to avoid protests and demonstrations, especially because as a foreign visitor, you may not have the legal right to be present, potentially resulting in the police targeting you for arrest. If it is your job to be "in the middle" of a protest because you are a journalist or medic, for instance, then your organization should give you extra security measures such as a "buddy system" and special clothing or markings.

The next contribution is a prime example of the "butterfly effect"—when a butterfly flaps its wings and the chain reaction results in a major storm on the other side of the world. Quick thinking helped **Jerome** and his Danish-looking wife and child from being swept away in a blaze of angry feelings about the "Mohammed cartoons": Without his good reactions, his family's vacation could have ended very differently.

IT'S NO ONE, IT'S THE MOB: MEETING AN ANGRY DEMONSTRATION DURING A FAMILY DIVING VACATION IN SRI LANKA

JEROME

FREQUENT BUSINESS TRAVELER AND DIVER. RETAIL, MANUFACTURING, AND CUSTOMER GOODS INDUSTRY

We were in a shoe shop in Galle, Sri Lanka, and it was a quiet day. When we heard gunshots and shouting, I peeped outside and saw a mob coming down the street. All the men wore the local distinctive traditional Muslim outfit and some waved burning Danish flags. It seemed like thousands had joined an anti-Denmark demonstration against the "Mohammed cartoons." I turned inside the shop and told my blond, blue-eyed wife what was happening and asked her and my daughter to stay quiet in the back of the shop. I could see her freeze in an expression of fear that I never saw in her before. She looked into my eyes and mumbled, "But, I'm Finnish, not Danish." Fear made her cling to rationale even though it rarely feeds truly fearful situations. I knew the power of the mob would ignore that frail nuance of my wife's nationality. The danger in such a situation is that it's no one, it's the mob.

I had my wife and daughter hide in the back while I stood in the entrance of the shop. For me, the unknown was scarier and I wanted to monitor the situation. I didn't feel threatened because of my brown skin color and I was wearing a sarong and a t-shirt—I dressed like a local. Together with the shop owner, I watched the angry mob shout its way past.

If a demonstration, protest, or riot might occur at your next destination, then basic precautions include:

- Keeping yourself informed using an array of sources.
- Avoiding contentious locations.
- Avoiding clothing that could associate you with one side or another, for instance, a red shirt that shows you support the opposition or khaki military pants that identify you with the military.

As part of your ongoing monitoring, look for potential triggers such as a visit by a dignitary, death of a leader, cultural offenses, university student's rallying issues, or economic downturn. The issue that ignites civil unrest can be local, regional, or international. The *Globe and Mail* article "Food Riots: What Creates the Anger?" is an interesting piece about the political and psychological factors that drive people to riot over price hikes even when the food item is not a substantial part of their diet.[73] Similarly, the article "Protests and Demonstrations in China: The Tensions and Methods Behind" on the Facts and Details blog,[74] as referred to in the **Understanding the Potential Risks while Traveling** section **(see Section 2.1)**, gives an in-depth assessment of the underlying issues: This could be of interest if you want to explore issues related to the PESTLIED model of political, economic, social, technological, legal, international, environmental, and demographic root causes **(see Section 1.6)** or as part of your preparations for your next trip to China.

You should have a strategy for how you might cope if unrest is likely: How can you escape from places where you might be exposed to a protest? Is it better to travel in a vehicle with your organization's logo or by other means? Your strategy has to be based on a realistic understanding of the threat **(see Section 1.1.1)**. If there is civil unrest, how likely is it to turn violent or even affect you? How have the authorities responded in the past? What are the current political, economic, social, technological, and environmental factors **(see Section 1.6)** that potentially could tip peaceful demonstrations into violence? As with any applicable threat, your understanding of your vulnerabilities in terms of who you are, what you do, and how you do it **(see Section 1.2)** will help you actualize realistic security measures. The next contribution is about getting away from a demonstration.

THOUGH CHALLENGED, WE GOT AWAY FROM AN ANGRY CROWD IN SERBIA

TANYA SPENCER
GLOBAL TRAVEL SECURITY AND CRISIS MANAGEMENT SPECIALIST, TRAININGSOLUTIONS (HTTP://WWW.TRAININGSOLUTIONS.DK)

Some years ago, when I was a conflict resolution trainer and human rights monitor in Kosovo, I happened to be in Belgrade when anti-American sentiments boiled over. On the bus ride from Pristina, the radio announced American air bombings in Bosnia and I understood enough Serbian and could see the change in atmosphere that I knew trouble was brewing. The following evening, when my friend and I got out from a movie, we heard loud chanting and instantly started to run away. The only problem was we were handicapped in several ways: My friend had mobility challenges and used a walking cane because he was a polio survivor, but he had the advantages of knowing the area and language well and he could pass as a Yugoslav. All his advantages were my challenges but I could run faster than him. Arm in arm, we got away. But, given our line of work, we knew the troubles would just land on our desk.

The following contribution goes over the international legal framework that allows for peaceful demonstrations and offers advice on how to react if you get caught up in a protest.

AVOID DEMONSTRATIONS BUT IF YOU GET CAUGHT UP IN ONE, HERE'S HOW TO BEHAVE

JOCHEN RIEGG

PROTECTION OFFICER, HUMAN RIGHTS MONITORING NGO

Around the world, the use of force by security forces is a common practice to break up demonstrations, while international standards enshrine the freedoms of association and expression. See, for example:

- Right to freedom of association: Article 21 of the "International Covenant on Civil and Political Rights" permits the right to peaceful assembly.
- Right to freedom of expression: Article 19 of the "Universal Declaration of Human Rights" states that "everyone has the right to freedom of opinion and expression." (On freedom of expression, see also: Article 9 of the African Charter, Article 13 of the American Convention, Article 10 of the European Convention.)

In many countries, the government imposes restrictions on these rights. This is mainly justified by the interest of restoring public order. However, the UN declaration as well as the "International Covenant on Civil and Political Rights" prohibit the force of firearms with two exceptions:

- During illegal/unlawful but nonviolent assemblies, the security forces should restrict the use of force to the minimum extent necessary but can use force and firearms if other means have been exhausted.
- During violent assemblies, the security forces are not prohibited by international law to use firearms. However, less dangerous means should be enforced before making use of firearms.

In addition to the risks posed by security forces, demonstrators can also turn violent and easily equip themselves with ad-hoc weapons, such as stones. For most of the demonstrations that I have monitored, the majority of people do not have violent intentions—they are there as nonviolent, peaceful protestors (though that doesn't exclude them from being loud). But any number of things can trigger a violent escalation of events, such as strong feelings whipped up by the rally speakers, aggressive or violent policing, or a few radical agitators or agent provocateurs.

All in all, most travelers and even expatriates living abroad for extended periods should generally avoid demonstrations, especially when you don't fully understand the political, social, and economic context. Having a better understanding of the context will at least help you decide if it will be a peaceful assembly (and remain so).

To avoid demonstrations, keep yourself informed using local newspapers, or ask taxi drivers, because they are usually the first ones to know if any protests will go on. If you do get caught in a demonstration, then:

- Make sure that you are not seen as part of the demonstrators (keep a distance, do not start any action that can be misinterpreted).
- Look for escape routes (no small alleys but open streets).
- Do not take pictures since this can be perceived as a provocation.

In many countries, the police use tear gas to stop demonstrations. In such a case, take a little towel or scarf soaked in vinegar and put it in front of your nose and mouth, whereas water should be used to clean your eyes. If you hear the shooting of rubber bullets or live bullets, immediately lie down on the ground (do not stand up) and wait until it is over.

If you are suddenly confronted with a protest, the best advice is to follow your common sense, and:

- Keep calm.
- Do not run, as this attracts attention, so walk instead.
- Find shelter but take care not to "go from the frying pan into the fire" by selecting the safest option given the circumstances. Let's say you are standing in front of an American restaurant that has a guard at the door and next to it is a local shop: If the loud crowd is ranting anti-American slogans, then you best opt for the local shop. But if your context analysis has shown you that interreligious tensions can boil over into looting and fire bombing, then head for the restaurant instead of the local shop.
- Try to inform others of your situation, again with caution. Be safe first and then think about communicating with others.
- If confronted by an angry crowd, remain calm and comply with demands.
- If you are in a car and see a riot but cannot safely leave the area, remain in the car with the doors locked and keep calm.
- If your car is attacked and you are forced out of the car, try to leave the car and the area. At this point, your hope is that they will focus on the vehicle.
- If you are in a building, lock up and shield windows. Have at least two exit routes.
- If your building is besieged, seek to negotiate with one or two of their representatives. Do not leave your safe haven and avoid making promises.

If it is your job to take photographs of the demonstrations (Figure 3.2), then some basic advice includes:

- Carry identification with you.
- Carry a charged mobile phone. Preferably take two phones, each using a different service provider.

FIGURE 3.2   Courtesy of Peter Steudtner/www.panphotos.org.

- Carry enough money to be able to take transportation away from the dem-onstration, but be aware that the demonstrators might also use public trans-portation, which will make the authorities target these.
- Wear heavy clothing even if there is warm weather to protect against flying projectiles and tear gas. Bring extra clothes in case your primary set gets contaminated with tear gas or wet from water cannons.
- Bring (and wear before the trouble starts) latex gloves to protect against pepper spray.
- Bring something to protect your head if possible.
- Wear practical shoes.
- Carry water for thirst and to rinse eyes if tear gas is used.
- If possible, carry swimming goggles to protect your eyes from projectiles and tear gas if the situation escalates in that direction. Alternatively, smear-ing toothpaste under your eyes (not above because it will run into your eyes) can also combat some of the chemical affects on your eyes. Absolutely do not rub your skin, especially your eyes and nose, if you have come in con-tact with chemicals.
- Avoid wearing oil-based skin products such as sunscreen because these help tear gas to cling to your skin.
- Do not wear contact lenses because chemicals can become trapped under them.
- Bring several plastic bags each with a piece of cloth soaked in vinegar or lemon juice to filter air through a homemade gas mask.
- Prepare a spray bottle filled with a solution of water and antacid medi-cine like Tums, Pepto-Bismol, or Alka-Seltzer (baking soda/bicarbonate of soda also works)—use the spray on your face to decontaminate any tear gas chemicals on you.

- Consider bringing sugar candy for quick energy boosts but not chocolate if it is a warm climate.
- Be aware that large crowds move like water currents so the middle is faster than the sides—use this to strategically place yourself given your circumstances and goals.
- If tear gas is used in your vicinity, then before moving away, take a second to check out the direction of the wind and go in the opposite direction if possible. Tear gas is heavier than air so move to higher ground for fresh air and do not go into tunnels and underground stations.
- If there is shooting, then stay low.
- If there is both shooting and tear gas, then staying low will help keep you alive but the chemicals will contaminate you.
- *Always* have an exit plan and a "Plan B." And have an idea where safe places are.

To be honest, you have fewer options available to you if you are in the vicinity of a demonstration. So your best option is to be informed about the trigger issues as this enables you to avoid demonstrations, protests, and riots.

A good resource for further reading about how to prevent and react to situations of civil unrest is *Safety First* by the International Save the Children Alliance.[75] The WikiHow article "How to Survive a Riot" is recommended because it concisely and practically deals with the subject[76]: The article draws upon information from the book *How to Avoid Being Killed in a War Zone*.[77] The article "Violent Protest Tactical Guide—Defense Essentials" is interesting because it gives advice based on first-hand experience from the Egyptian uprising in 2011.[78] Another WikiHow article entitled "How to Deal with Riot Control Agents" is useful if there is a risk that chemical agents will be used.[79]

3.7 PLANE CRASH

The first 90 seconds after a crash is considered the "golden time" according to the airline industry.[80] To increase your chances of surviving a crash, the BBC News article "How to Survive a Plane Crash" recommends that you consider:

- The life and death decisions you should make during the evacuation.
- Statistically where you should sit to increase your chances of surviving.
- How to survive the moment of impact.
- What to do if there is a fire onboard.[81]

This section deals with the essentials of surviving a plane crash, using the four points from the BBC News article as a framework for the advice.

The Aviation Safety Network's (ASN) Aviation Safety Database is updated weekly and has been compiling worldwide occurrences since 1921.[82] The total figures, as of March 26, 2013, were:

- Accidents—13,626
- Criminal occurrences (excluding hijackings)—696

- Hijackings—1,042
- Other occurrence—795
- Unknown occurrence—516
- **Total**—16,675

To put these figures in perspective, the worldwide chance that you will be involved in a plane crash is 1 in 9 million[83] and for the United States the chance is 1 in 14 million.[84] Furthermore, the overall survival rate is about 95%, up from 90% just a few years ago.[85] The industry averages 1 accident, of varying severity, for every 1.2 million flights.[86] In comparison, the likelihood that you will be a car accident is 1 in 19,000.[87] As **Patrick Kane** emphasized in his contributions, **"Reduce Air Travel Risks before You Go" (see Section 1.13)** and **"Travel Security at Airports and on the Aircraft" (see Section 2.13)**, air travel is relatively safe.

From a travel risk management perspective, it makes sense to take a few basic contingency measures in case you experience the rare event of a crash or emergency landing. But, generally speaking, during the course of your air travels you are more likely to experience delays or lose your luggage than crash. Statistics from the 2011 "Duty of Care and Travel Risk Management Global Benchmark Study" of 628 companies with headquarters in 50 countries are revealing: 76% of small companies (less than 1,000 staff) experienced travel delays, 52% lost luggage, and 2% experienced airline catastrophes. Compared with Global 500 enterprises, the respective percentages were: 85%, 68%, and 12%.[88] Therefore, packing wisely, as recommended in the **Personal Belongings and Documents** section **(see Section 1.10)**, will help you mitigate the most likely inconveniences associated with air travel.

3.7.1 Prepare for "Best Available Decisions" before a "Worst-Case Scenario"

To increase your ability to react in the "golden time" of 90 seconds, you can take a few easy contingency measures that could save your life in the worst-case scenario of a plane crash. Having these in place better enables you to make the "best available decisions," hence improving your chances of surviving. Some experts assess that about a third of the deaths from air traffic accidents were because people did not know what to do and did not take action.[89]

- To start, you need to know where the nearest two exits are. Before take-off, walk to at least one of the exits while touching the seats and counting them.
- After sitting down, formulate a plan, look over the safety guidelines, and pay attention to the preflight instructions … again. Because 80% of accidents happen during take-off or landing, it is recommended that you are alert for the first three minutes and the last eight minutes of the flight.[90]
- It is worth practicing your seat buckle: Panic can cause you to fumble with the unfamiliar mechanisms, whereas practicing can speed up your reaction time. Being mentally and physically prepared helps you keep calm. Interviews with more than 1,900 crash survivors found that many said they

lost valuable time trying to undo their buckle in the same way as the seat-belts in their cars.[91] The best way to wear your seat buckle is to keep it firmly over your pelvis instead of your stomach: This reduces the likelihood of internal injuries because bone is stronger than flesh, and for every centi-meter of slack in the belt the G-force impact is tripled.[92]

- If traveling with your family, you and your spouse or traveling companions should decide who will assist which child so that if there is an incident, you can quickly spring into action. A tip that could save the life of your infant is to get a seat and use an appropriate child restraint system: This is because, in the unlikely event of a crash, an infant traveling in your lap has a greater chance of being killed during the impact.[93]

Even before you head for the airport, a simple measure you can take is to wear clothes that are comfortable, preferably not synthetic materials, and dress in layers. Dressing like this improves your mobility and reduces fire risks, and layers help against flying debris during a crash and keep you warm while you wait for rescuers. While it is unlikely that you will be involved in a crash, it is likely that you will be more comfortable dressing this way even for uneventful flights.

3.7.2 CHOOSE THE SAFEST SEAT, OR CAN YOU?

A study that is still the most comprehensive and most cited as of 2013 is the 2007 study by *Popular Mechanics* of crashes in the United States over a 36-year period. It found that the first 15% of the craft (i.e., business/first class) had sur-vival rates of 49%, the over-wing section had 56% rates, and the rear of the plane had rates of 69%: In other words, people sitting in the rear had a 40% better chance of surviving compared to those in the first rows.[94] The article "Safest Seat on a Plane: PM Investigates How to Survive a Crash" on the *Popular Mechanics* website has a diagram of airplane seating with the corresponding statistics.[95] Another study by the U.S. Federal Aviation Administration in 2005 concluded that because no two crashes are alike there were no safest seats.[96] This is sup-ported by many experts who point to the large number of variables that are criti-cal factors in a crash.

The MSN Travel article entitled "How to Survive a Plane Crash" notes that sit-ting within five rows of an exit greatly improves your chances of survival, and an aisle seat has better survival rates than window seats.[97] However, since you are more likely to experience turbulence on your flights than a crash, it might be useful to know that the rows over the wing are the most reinforced area and so can reduce some of the wobbling sensations. Furthermore, in such situations, items falling from the overhead cabins is a realistic risk more than crashing so you may choose a seat based on these considerations.

3.7.3 SURVIVE THE INITIAL IMPACT

To survive the impact "the important thing is to get your upper torso down as much as possible," recommends Tom Barth, an expert on surviving impacts of crashes in the BBC News article.[98] For the best bracing positions, check the safety guidelines for every plane you fly on. Generally, you need to remove any sharp object (e.g., a pen) from near your body, if time allows it. You need make sure they are placed where they cannot become potentially deadly projectiles. You should not tuck your legs under your seat because that increases the chances of your breaking your legs below the knees. Similarly, lacing your fingers can result in more injuries than just placing your hands on the back of your head—if there is a pillow nearby, use this to protect your head. Keep your elbows close to your head. Remain in the brace position until you hear instructions: This is because there might be additional bounces or other dangers after the initial impact.

3.7.4 EXPECT A FIRE AND GET OUT

In the harrowing seconds after a crash you must *act*! Assume that there will be a fire and react accordingly. You cannot wait to find out: Toxic smoke can quickly kill you. Here are seven easy things to remember to save your life in case of a fire, and in general after a plane crash:

1. Keep calm.
2. Stay low.
3. Orientate yourself—in some cases, down might be up.
4. Leave your belongings.
5. Count your way out and avoid pushing.
6. Listen for instructions.
7. Get away from the crash site. But stay close enough to be easily found for rescue (at least 500 feet [150 meters]).

Specifically regarding emergency water landings, the main additional advice is to not inflate your life vest before you are at the exit, ready to disembark. By inflating it too early, you could risk getting trapped in the aircraft if the plane starts to submerge.

Regarding the event that oxygen masks are dropped down, it is imperative that you immediately put it on and, as the airline's preflight safety instructions inform passengers, you need to put yours on first and tug the line before assisting anyone, even your child. That is because you only have about 30–60 seconds before you will lose consciousness if you are flying at 35,000 feet (10,000 meters).[99]

To proactively manage air travel risks, you can think over ways to reduce the probability of facing particular risks such as choosing airlines with a good safety record and direct flights **(see Section 1.13)**, and reduce the impact by following the advice in this section such as knowing two exits and the brace position. After that, have peace of mind that air travel is safe. One study found that if you flew on a random flight in the United States once a day, where the chances of dying in an airplane accident are 1 in 14 million, it would take 38,000 years before you died in a crash.[100] While some frequent flyers might feel like they have racked up that many years of air travel, the calculation does show how rare the risk of dying in a plane crash is for the average traveler.

For further reading, of the five articles with the same title "How to Survive a Plane Crash," the versions by MSN Travel[101] and How Stuff Works[102] are slightly more informative than the CNN.com Business Traveler version[103]: And though seemingly outdated, as it stems from 2006, the BBC News article is the source for many other Internet resources.[104] That said, the WikiHow version stands out because it both describes and illustrates 11 key pieces of advice from clothing to exiting, plus it includes extra tips and links.[105]

3.8   MEDICAL EMERGENCIES

While the **Medical Considerations** sections **(see Sections 1.8 and 2.8)** in the first two chapters focus on mitigating measures to deal with common health issues that many travelers face, this section covers the basic advice you can draw upon during a medical emergency. However, it is important to emphasize that "there is no substitute for proper training," as **Catherine Plumridge** notes in the next contribution.

FIRST AID KNOWLEDGE SAVES LIVES: WHAT TO DO AT THE SCENE OF A CAR ACCIDENT AND OTHER MEDICAL EMERGENCIES

CATHERINE PLUMRIDGE

DIRECTOR, HUMANITRAIN. FORMER NURSE (CRITICAL CARE AND TROPICAL MEDICINE), FORMER BRITISH ARMY OFFICER, AND HAS WORKED FOR SEVERAL NGOS, ICRC, AND THE UN (HTTP://WWW.HUMANITRAIN.COM)

First aid knowledge can be invaluable in a situation where health services are substandard or otherwise hard to access. Before departure, go to a first aid course, take an appropriate first aid kit, and do some research on the location and level of health facilities. All these will contribute to reducing the impact of a medical emergency should you find yourself in a first aid incident.

Knowing your environment and the types of hazards that pose a threat is vital in avoiding them and to informed decision making. This also applies to medical incidents. For example, if it is known that in a certain area, thieves create a pretend accident in order to trick other road users into stopping and getting out of their vehicles, then it is advisable to not stop but to use any effective means of communication to report to the authorities. Prior knowledge and good judgment are essential, even if you are a skilled first aid responder.

Always check to see if the overall situation is safe for you to respond. Never put yourself at risk of becoming another victim. Look over the scene for any hazards to you and the casualty. Keep checking. In a stressful situation, your arc of awareness is drastically reduced. That is your ability to register both visually and aurally what is happening both in front of you as well as outside of your peripheral vision. When this is reduced, you may not notice, for example, a crowd becoming angry and posing a threat to you. Be aware of hazards such as an unstable vehicle or damaged infrastructure, leaking pipes, downed electrical lines, sources of ignition for fire, and/or hostile bystanders. Should there be any deterioration in the mood of the crowd, or the presentation of any other new threat, rapid withdrawal may be the only option available.

In the case of road accidents, every year even skilled, trained, and well-equipped emergency responders are killed on the road. In many countries road safety is of a very poor standard and accidents are common. Therefore, if you determine that it is safe to stop and assist at an accident, make sure that you take every possible precaution to protect yourself. Oncoming traffic is the biggest threat. Make sure you are wearing a high visibility vest, in a lit area if it is nighttime, and that your vehicle has put some warning out for other road users.

REMEMBER: BE SAFE

- S   Safety, security, sending for help.
- A   Assessment, what has happened?
- F   Find casualties and free anyone trapped.
- E   Examine and treat in order of priority.

Your first aid kit should be in the cabin of the vehicle but properly secured so that it does not become a harmful projectile in the event of an accident. The recommended contents of a first aid kit are covered in Table 3.2.

Communicate to the authorities and to your organization any accident or incident. Inform them of your position or location, provide a brief summary of the event, when it happened, the number of people injured, and any support

---

TABLE 3.2
First Aid Kit Contents

1. Conforming stretch gauze × 2 packets	12. Tape × 1
2. Sterile swabs × 5 packets	13. Ribbon gauze × 1
3. Combat tourniquet × 1	14. Sterile trauma dressing/Israeli
4. Foil blanket × 2	bandage 4″ × 2″ and 6″ × 1″
5. Gloves × 5 pairs	15. QuikClot gauze × 1
6. Cling film × 1	16. Bolin Chest Seal × 1
7. High-visibility vest × 4	17. Face protection shields × 2
8. Scissors × 1	18. Condoms × 2
9. Head torch × 1	19. Puritabs × 1 strip
10. Light sticks × 5	20. Matches × 1 box
11. Triangular bandage × 4	

Top tip: Put gloves in your rucksack, glove compartment, office, and residence.

needed. The whole situation may not be clear but give whatever information you have.

If there is more than one person in your party, one person can assess the scene and the injuries and give instructions to others if possible. Ensure that any responder is wearing gloves to prevent cross-infection. As a foreigner, there may be a weight of expectation on you and your group to attend to the situation.

Assess all of the casualties for response and signs of life. Tap on both shoulders and ask the victim(s) to open their eyes. Check breathing. Be aware that this might be perceived as a crime or culturally inappropriate—you should explain your actions to any observers and, perhaps, ask one person to explain it again if the crowd is agitated. Place your head close to the victim's chest, looking in the direction of his or her feet. Look to see if the chest is rising and falling, listen for breath sounds, and feel for any breath on your cheek. Maintain this for 10 seconds. Anyone screaming, while they may be seriously injured, is breathing so look to the others. Any unconscious casualties should have their airway opened by tilting their head back slightly and lifting up their chin to prevent airway obstruction. If you think that someone may have sustained a spinal injury, it is essential not to move them unless their airway is obstructed. In that case, their jaw bone can be moved forward (like a bulldog's bottom teeth protruding over its top teeth). This is a question of putting life over limb.

DANGER CRABC

Attend to the most injured victims first. At Humanitrain, we use the "Danger CRABC" model to help people to remember what to do (see Figure 3.3).

C - Catastrophic bleeding
R - Response
A - Airway
B - Breathing
C - Circulation

FIGURE 3.3 Danger CRABC.

Check for <u>DANGER</u>.

- **<u>C</u>**   Deal with catastrophic bleeding first. (See the explanation for tourniquets and bleeding.)
- **<u>R</u>**   Check for response by tapping both shoulders and speaking to the casualty, asking him to open his eyes.
- **<u>A</u>**   Airway, open the airway by tilting the head back and lifting the chin.
- **<u>B</u>**   Breathing, look down the chest with an ear close to the casualty's mouth. Look for the chest to rise and fall; listen for breath sounds and try to feel breath on your cheek.
- **<u>C</u>**   Circulation, look for any further bleeding and for signs of life.

DEAL WITH CATASTROPHIC BLEEDING FIRST

Use a tourniquet:

- If bleeding is massive (flowing blood, pumping artery "gusher/fountain") not controlled with pressure
- If casualty must be moved
- If in a combat situation—under fire or in other danger

A tourniquet should be 5 cm (2 in.) thick. Remember that it cannot be placed over a joint and that a pad should be placed underneath it. The tourniquet must be tight enough to stop the blood flow. This is very painful and the victim should be warned about that. A tourniquet should remain bandaged but not covered (by a blanket or clothes). A "T" should be written on the forehead and a note of the time that it was applied should be made on the bandage or arm of the victim. If you are able to control the bleeding or move to safety to have a better look at the wound within fifteen minutes, then the tourniquet can be loosened. If the wound continues to bleed, tighten the tourniquet again and do not keep undoing and redoing it.

RAPID TRAUMA SURVEY: RESPONSE, AIRWAY, BREATHING, CONTROL BLEEDING

In a critical situation, quick decisions and actions can make the difference between life and death. The rapid trauma survey checks the response, airway, and breathing, and controls any bleeding.

If there is penetrating trauma to the chest, then this immediately calls for the partial sealing of a sucking chest wound using a "three-sided" plastic dressing with tape on the top and the sides but leaving the bottom open. If the casualty has sustained a flail chest (through blunt force trauma from either a fall or, for example, not wearing a seatbelt and having a car accident) this manifests itself with severe pain when breathing and having part of the ribs that are not moving with the rest of the rib cage (paradoxical breathing). The stabilization of a flail chest is done with a high arm sling, with a pad over the affected area and another band around the chest over the sling and under the armpit of the unaffected side. For impaled objects, first stop any bleeding with pressure, and then stabilize it by building up dressings around the wound and keeping the object still.

Starting from the head, moving to the neck, the chest, the abdomen, the lower extremities, and the upper extremities, assess the body for the following: deformities, contusions, abrasions, puncture, perforations, burns, tenderness, lacerations, and swelling.

Remember that bleeding is the most common cause of hypovolemic shock. Massive hemorrhage takes precedence over the airway.

BREATHING AND AIRWAY

If a casualty is unresponsive and not breathing, then cardiac compressions should begin:

- With palms flat against each other and straight, locked arms, only the heel of the hand should be flat in the center of the chest between the nipples. Push down hard so the chest wall goes in 5 cm (2 in.).
- Press 30 times at a rate of 120 per minute. Or put more simply, think of the beat to the Bee Gees "Stayin' Alive" song and you will do it well.

Next, if you are willing and able, do rescue breaths. For adults, we assume that when they collapsed, they had sufficient oxygen in their lungs. For children, we assume the opposite and give rescue breaths first. This also applies to drowning situations.

- The head should be in position from opening the airway, but if not, do a head tilt, chin lift again.
- If you have a face-shield, use it. Put your lips round the casualty's mouth, making a seal, and blow your breath into their mouth for two seconds and then lift your mouth away. You should be able to see the chest rise and fall. Repeat the breath again.
- Then go straight back to compressions.

CONTROL BLEEDING

Your aim is to *stop the bleeding*. Remember:

- S   Sit or lay the casualty down.
- E   Examine the wound very quickly.

- <u>E</u>   Elevate the wound.
- <u>P</u>   Pressure on the wound.

If the wound bleeds through the first dressing, keep the pressure on and apply another one tightly around the area. Do not remove the first one. Put on 3–4 dressings if necessary.

If the bleeding does not come into the category of a "gusher" or "fountain," but the bleeding will not stop, indirect pressure points can be pressed by the casualty or responder. Have the casualty make a fist on the uninjured side and place this under the armpit of the injured side, pulling their arm across sufficiently to put pressure into the armpit. For the groin, use your foot, knee, or fist to put pressure on the femoral artery in the groin, on the affected side.

For a traumatic amputation, first stop the bleeding and then:

- Apply dressing.
- Elevate.
- Tourniquet if needed.
- Rinse amputated part, but don't delay evacuation especially if there is no chance of its being sown back on.
- Wrap in saline gauze.
- Put in plastic bag.
- Keep cool.

MECHANISMS OF INJURY

Understanding what has taken place (blast, fall, blunt or penetrating trauma, burns, gunshot) is key to treatment and evacuation in an appropriate and timely manner. The mechanisms of injury relate to the amount of force, length of time force was applied, and the areas of the body injured.

FRACTURES

Check for tenderness, instability, and crepitus. Pain, loss of power, unnatural movement, swelling, and deformity are also signs of fractures. This could indicate a fractured bone. Stabilize the affected area of any fracture below the elbow using a low arm sling. For any fracture above the elbow, including the collarbone, the humerus, or a dislocation of the collarbone, use a high arm sling.

For a leg fracture, stabilize with a splint on both sides of the broken leg, or use the good leg as a splint. Keep shoes or boots on as the feet held together are more stable. Remember to pad between the knees and the elbows and any area where the splint comes into contact with the leg.

When checking the head, look for blood and secretions (especially straw-colored fluid, which is cerebral spinal fluid that usually surrounds the spinal cord and brain) in the ear, nose, or mouth. Presence of either indicates a serious injury.

Assess for cyanosis (blue lips, extremities). Inspect and palpate the chest. Listen for equal breath sounds. Check for entry or exit wounds. Inspect the pelvis, assessing for stability and priapism (this is a perpetual penile erection, indicating spinal injury). When looking at extremities, check for a pulse and motor and sensory function.

SPINAL INJURY

While only 1.4% of conflict injuries involve the spine, road traffic accidents, bomb blasts, head trauma, any deceleration trauma, falls, and assault can also cause spinal injury. The neck must be immobilized well and immediately. This can be done by keeping the casualty's head and neck still by kneeling down with the head between the rescuer's knees. The casualty should be log-rolled in order to evaluate their back during the rapid trauma survey only if severe bleeding is suspected. If evacuated, it must be on a hard board, well strapped down for transfer. But a good rule of the thumb is that if you suspect spinal injury, then do *not* move the casualty unless absolutely necessary.

BURNS

The following will impact the severity of a burn:

- <u>S</u>   Size—the bigger it is, the worse it is.
- <u>C</u>   Cause—fat is worse than vapor, for example, as the tissue "cooks."
- <u>A</u>   Age—the elderly and babies cannot cope with fluid loss or infection well.
- <u>L</u>   Location—face, hands, joints, and genitals fare worse.
- <u>D</u>   Depth—first, second, and third degree.

To estimate the size of a burn, imagine that your hand represents 1% of the casualty's body. Put your hand over the burnt area but not touching it to estimate the size of the area.

Your actions:

- Cool with cool water for 15 minutes, which is vital to stop the burn from getting worse.
- Remove any constricting clothes or jewelry.
- Dress with cling film or damp cloth, cover with a plastic bag, and evacuate immediately.

It is vital for anyone who has breathed in hot air or fumes to be evacuated, as a medical emergency such as swelling of the airway does not always manifest itself straight away. Look inside the mouth for soot-like particles. Even if you don't see that, you must evacuate the victim straight away as he or she may need support to keep the airway open.

EVACUATION

It is essential that a proper assessment by qualified medical personnel is made as soon as possible. Reassurance and making the casualty as comfortable as possible is key to maintaining their status. If you are able to make radio or telephone contact with a medic, do so and describe the casualty's condition. If you are able to position them well, this can aid pain relief. If you are permitted to give oral fluids, give oral rehydration solution. Make sure that the casualty is accompanied, has their travel documents, insurance information, and next of kin contact numbers. Ensure that everyone who needs to know the status of the casualty is informed.

SUMMARY

First aid is usually a part of personal security courses, but even if your organization has not sent you to one, first aid courses are easy to find. Most Red Cross National Societies run them relatively cheaply, but other organizations are also committed to providing this training, both commercially and not for profit. While the advice above outlines the basics, first aid skills can only be taught in person and need to be practiced. There is no substitute for proper training.

In a medical emergency, it is ethically correct to respond but only if you are safe and it is within your abilities. But it is important to realize that there could be legal or social consequences for responding or not responding, depending on the circumstances. Your understanding of the context can be a resource to you (**see Section 1.1**).

At Qualsafe.com, you can purchase first aid books such as "Emergency First Aid Made Easy" or "Pediatric First Aid Made Easy"—this series is recommended because of its clear explanations and visual aids.[106] At http://www.bbc.co.uk/health, the subject of first aid is well covered as well as other health and medical issues.[107] At http://www.humanitarian.com you can purchase a "talking trauma kit" that is equipped with first aid supplies, and an audio box that explains the procedures can be ordered in any language.[108]

3.9   TERRORIST ATTACKS

Terrorism is an emotive topic: Everything about it, from its definition to the responses to it, is disputed. But there is some agreement on the follow key criteria, as listed in the Wikipedia article "Terrorism," citing the 2006 book *Inside Terrorism* by Bruce Hoffman:

- Ineluctably political in aims and motives.
- Violent, or equally important, threatens violence.
- Designed to have far-reaching psychological repercussions beyond the immediate victim or target.

- Conducted by an organization with an identifiable chain of command or conspiratorial cell structure (whose members wear no uniform or identifying insignia).
- Perpetrated by a subnational group or nonstate entity.[109]

The U.S. National Counterterrorism Center (NCTC) "2011 Report on Terrorism" uses the definition of "premeditated, politically motivated violence perpetrated against noncombatant targets by sub-national groups or clandestine agents."[110] It is important to note that this definition excludes state-sponsored terrorism, which is one of the disputed issues. Also, it is not clear if it includes the terror a "lone-wolf" or single person can inflict in a shooting spree of work colleagues in the United States or political targets in Norway, as examples. While the definition is in dispute, it is safe to say that terrorism affects normal people in many ways—car bombings, kidnappings, assignations, grenade attacks, and so forth.

Terrorism is disempowering: That is not part of official definitions but it is essentially its aim. This book is about empowerment with the aim of helping you to have a peace of mind so that you concentrate on the task at hand while abroad. With that as an objective, this section establishes some key facts that can help you with your threat **(see Section 1.1.1)** and vulnerability **(see Section 1.2)** analyses. It then concentrates on providing you with advice you can use to mitigate the risk of terrorism.

By following your common sense and the expert advice provided here, you can do a lot to avoid terrorist acts and react in life-saving ways during an incident. Frankly speaking, however, it is impossible to negate the risk completely: A perpetrator who is crafty, motivated, and lucky enough will succeed. To counter that, this section is about boosting your security knowledge, skills, attitudes, and behavior so that you succeed in steering clear of harm's way.

3.9.1 ANALYSIS AIDS AVOIDANCE

Millions of people travel to all corners of the globe every day and never experience a terrorist attack. Yet, terrorism weighs heavily in the concerns of many travelers. Therefore, it is important to establish the likelihood. Nairobi and New York each face terrorist threats but the situations and probabilities are very different. To get facts about the likelihood, one of the best resources available on the Internet is the Global Terrorism Database: It collects of all types of recorded incidents and dates back to 1970.[111] Of the 104,689 incidents from 1970 until 2011, the five regions with the highest attack rates were:

1. Middle East/North Africa: 20,712 incidents.
2. South Asia: 19,885.
3. South America: 17,867.
4. Western Europe: 14,930.
5. Central America/Caribbean: 10,566.[112]

From 1970 until 2011, the number of incidents peaked in the early 1990s with more than 5,000 incidents and again from 2007 onward with just over 4,500 recorded successful or attempted attacks each year.

FIGURE 3.4   Courtesy of Peter Steudtner/www.panphotos.org.

To narrow the search period from 2000–2010 and the target groups, businesses were affected by 3,292 incidents, 343 targeted NGOs, and 132 were directed toward tourists.[113] As a comparison, for all types of successful and attempted attacks there were 29,820 incidents worldwide in the same period (Figure 3.4).

Explosive bombs are the preferred tactic of terrorists. Figures from the Global Terrorism Database clearly show that out of 104,689 incidents from 1970–2011, 51,081 were attributed to explosive bombs/dynamite, while the next highest was firearms with 39,002 incidents.[114] There is a steep drop to the next highest categories of unknown at 13,932 and incendiary at 8,803. Similarly, the NCTC figures for 2011 are telling:

- 6,354 deaths attributed to 3,747 IED attacks
- 5,585 fatalities due to 3,713 firearm incidents.
- 4,732 deaths resulting from 3,541 explosions.[115]

Almost anything can be made into a bomb: These are known as improvised explosive devices (IEDs) and vehicle improvised explosive devices (VIEDs). During the Nepali civil war, antigovernment banners were arranged to explode if anyone attempted to untie them. During Sri Lanka's civil war, a big threat was from suicide bombers on motorcycles. The "Shoe Bomber" was luckily a failed attempt to detonate explosives on a transatlantic flight, but it does indicate the creativity that terrorists are willing to deploy.

The 2011 "Duty of Care and Travel Risk Management Global Benchmark Study" of 628 companies by International SOS revealed that 40% of Global 500 enterprises recorded that their staff had experienced terrorism, while only 10% of small companies with fewer than 1,000 employees listed the same.[116] It should be noted that the study uses a narrower term for the category of terrorism than the Global Terrorism Database, which includes all types of tactics (e.g., kidnapping, murder) used by terrorists.

FIGURE 3.5   Courtesy of Peter Steudtner/www.panphotos.org.

According to the NCTC "2011 Report on Terrorism," civilians bear the brunt of deaths due to terrorism at 51% of the more than 12,000 fatalities in 2011, but this figure is down from its high of 64% in 2007 (the NCTC has been recording incidents since 2004).[117] For 2011, the report cites 358 deaths in the business category (Figure 3.5).

Civilians suffer so many fatalities simply because the perpetrators choose targets that will inflict maximum damage. The NCTC's 2011 report shows that the top two facilities that were attacked were transportation means and infrastructure (27%) and public spaces like markets, religious sites, and schools (21%).[118] The number of attacks on public places has steadily stepped down from its 2007 high of 4,121 to 2,186 in 2011.

The next contribution shows a trend of terrorists selecting hotels to achieve their goals and get media attention. By choosing hotels, the terrorists reveal increasing sophistication in their methods because the casualties are a certain type of people (i.e., foreign, well-off, and perhaps engaging in immoral activities according to the perpetrators), so the civic backlash after the attack tends to be greatly reduced.

"WHY ATTACK LIONS WHEN THERE ARE SO MANY SHEEP": TERRORISTS ATTACKS ON HOTELS

JOHN J. STRAUCHS

SECURITY DESIGN CONSULTANT AT STRAUCHS, LLC WHO HAS WORKED IN SAUDI ARABIA, KUWAIT, JORDAN, SINGAPORE, HONG KONG, VIETNAM, GREECE, VENEZUELA, AND COLOMBIA, AMONGST OTHERS (HTTP://WWW.STRAUCHS-LLC.COM)

The trend in recent years has been a steep increase in attacks against "soft targets," including hotels and resorts. It's as a PLO leader once stated in an interview many years ago, "why attack lions when there are so many sheep?" In the period 2000–2009, there have been at least 62 attacks against hotels in 20 different countries. Some of the major attacks were:

- 2005, three hotels in Amman, Jordan (Grand Hyatt, Radisson SAS, and Days Inn)
- 2005, resort in Sharm el-Sheikh, Egypt
- 2008, hotels in Kabul, Afghanistan (Serena Hotel), Islamabad, Pakistan (JW Marriott), and Mumbai, India (Oberoi Trident and Taj Mahal Palace hotels)
- 2009, hotels in Peshawar, Pakistan (Pearl Continental Hotel), and Jakarta, Indonesia (JW Marriott and Ritz-Carlton hotels)
- 2010, hotels in Baghdad, Iraq, and Mogadishu, Somalia
- 2011, the Intercontinental Hotel in Kabul, Afghanistan

Not only is there a trend toward attacking soft targets but also the tactics and weapons used are ominous. In many of these attacks, the weapons have included automatic rifles and military explosives. IEDs and/or VIEDs were used in all of the attacks.

Several of these incidents involved the terrorists directly attacking the security forces at the hotel. Most of the incidents involved at least 5 attackers—Mumbai had 10. In three of these cases, the terrorists used disguises, such as wearing police or security uniforms, and smuggled in materials prior to the assault.

Clearly, terrorism is a potential threat for travelers, but how does it compare to other risks? As cited in the **Understanding the Potential Risks while Traveling** section **(see Section 2.1)**, the article "How Scared of Terrorism Should You Be?" contextualizes the risk from terrorism by comparing it to daily risks for Americans such as "dying in a car accident of 1 in 19,000; drowning in a bathtub at 1 in 800,000; dying in a building fire at 1 in 99,000; or being struck by lightning at 1 in 5,500,000."[119] The article goes on to note that in the period from 2005–2010, the likelihood of an American dying in a terrorist attack was 1 in 20 million.

Of course, you are encouraged to do a more detailed and nuanced assessment of the likelihood for your upcoming destinations. Get answers to questions such as: Has there been a terrorist threat in the past, recently, or is there a possibility of one in the near future **(see Section 1.1.1)**? Who are the likely perpetrators and what is known about their objectives and tactics? At which locations or situations is the danger greatest? What issues could possibly trigger an attack such as contentious anniversaries, elections, or religious festivals **(see Sections 1.1.3 and 3.2)**? The threat level should dictate the amount of time, effort, and resources you allocate to this. In other words, let the realities determine your actions.

To minimize your personal risk to terrorism, you can use your vulnerability analysis **(see Section 1.2)** as a tool to chisel out a safe space for you while you are traveling. What about who you are could increase the likelihood that you might be caught up in a terrorist attack—indirectly and particularly directly targeted? Could what others think you represent be a potential factor, namely, your national, religious, or work affiliation? For example, over the past five years Muslims have suffered between 82 and 97% of the deaths related to terrorist acts.[120] Could what you do tilt your chances of being affected by terrorism? Visiting family in Israel, trekking in the Philippines, or being involved in operations in any of the world's "hot spots" could increase your exposure to the risk. And could the way you conduct your activities be a potential source of vulnerability? Are you a predictable target (**see Section 3.2**)? Is too much information about your activities publicly available on the Internet (**see Section 1.11**)? All in all, this is a very personal process, but if the threat is likely, then investing some time, effort, and resources can help you not be a victim of terrorism.

3.9.2 Life-Saving Reactions during an Actual Attack, but Prevention Is Still Best

In many countries, there are "if you see it, report it" or similar campaigns where the population is asked to be aware of, avoid, and report unattended luggage, packages, and other suspicious things or activities. But what else can you do? A general rule of thumb is to stay at least 500 meters (1,600 feet) from governmental, diplomatic, and other potential targets. You can use this "rule" when planning your accommodation before your travel and deciding on which routes you are willing to take while you are in the country. Beyond that, you should find out about the local variations.

Regardless if you are at a hotel, in an office building, on a train, or wherever you might be, you should know how to exit. Make it a habit to quickly note the exit points and how to get there. Most of us will never experience a major catastrophe, but if a bomb explodes, then your chances of survival are greatly increased by having this basic knowledge.

The next contribution draws upon a real-life case to illustrate the "best practice" advice for surviving a bomb attack.

THE DO'S AND DON'TS FOR INCREASING YOUR CHANCES OF SURVIVING A BOMB ATTACK

TANYA SPENCER

GLOBAL TRAVEL SECURITY AND CRISIS MANAGEMENT SPECIALIST, TRAININGSOLUTIONS (HTTP://WWW.TRAININGSOLUTIONS.DK)

One of the times that I was in London, the building I was in was suddenly evacuated. The meeting point:

- Was across the street: Good because it put distance between us and the major train station that was on the next street.

- In front of us was an open space: Also good because the power of the blast would have an open outlet to release its energy.
- Behind us were buildings with large glass window: Not so good because I couldn't trust that all the windows had bomb-blast film on them.
- We were next to an unattended parked van: No way. Move away! Soft targets (i.e., our group) who were secure were now standing next to a potential bomb.

Seeing the van set off my internal survivor alarms: I told one of the conference organizers that I was not going to stand next to an unattended parked van. I suggested that she have the group meet me a block away, toward more open spaces. I literally was walking and talking at the same time as to not lose valuable time.

The embarrassing thing is that it was a forum of security experts and trainers—we were all used to working in very dangerous places and yet the rest of the group let their guard down while in London. They remained near the unattended park van, just under loads of windows. We later found out that it was only a fire that was quickly extinguished. But at the time of the building evacuation, we didn't have any specific information so all I knew was that the Madrid bombings had recently occurred and the United Kingdom government was also a member of the "coalition of the willing" during the Iraq war. As it turned out, there was a terrorist attack targeting the transportation system in London the following year.

People shouldn't go around feeling paranoid, but if you experience any "red flags," internal survivor alarms, or whatever, then take responsibility for your security. Practical advice that can potentially save your life during a bomb scenario includes:

Do not:

- Stand near vans, other large vehicles, large trashcans, etc.
- Pick up an explosive device. It is best to quickly turn away from it and lie down. If there is better shelter nearby then you can crawl (not walk) to that. In theory, you can kick the device away but you don't know how long you have before it explodes. By picking the device up, you increase the blast arc, which will result in more deaths. In other words, you stand a chance of being killed and helping the terrorists kill more people.
- Use the same gathering/emergency meeting point twice, if the organization is contentious and the point can be observed.

Do:

- Trust your instincts and act accordingly.
- Stay calm.
- Consider your options and value life over assets.
- Put distance between you and any potential targets or containers.

- Get solid things (wall, buildings) between you and the potential target. Hiding behind a vehicle is less than ideal because it can become a secondary incendiary device, but in some situations it may be the only option available given the time pressure to react quickly. In such circumstances, then choose the front of the car because the motor is the densest part of the vehicle.
- Stay away from glass. Under the right conditions, glass as secondary shrapnel can kill more people than the explosive device.
- Stay low, preferably lying on the ground but making sure your chest is slightly raised from it and your face is tilted to one side so your head is resting on one hand while the other hand covers the exposed ear, and cross your legs at your ankles. These measures help reduce the impact of the explosive. Even if you can't adopt this position, still stay low. Think of your vital organs having a red bull's-eye on them; you need to get that bull's-eye as low as possible to avoid shrapnel.
- Continuously monitor and adjust to your situation.
- Listen to information provided by authorities or other reputable sources. But still be cautious because there can be secondary attacks, crossfire, and sadly, as the "lone-wolf" massacre in Norway in 2011 in which the terrorist tricked his victims into believing he was a police officer shows, terrorists use disguises and manipulation to achieve their goals.
- Have your hands up when you step away from your shelter and expect to be treated harshly by security forces until they can confirm your identity. Never run toward the security forces, unless explicitly instructed to. At this point, only you know you are an innocent bystander—to them you are a potential threat.

In a bombing situation, there are all kinds of factors such as type of bomb (i.e., grenade or VIED) and the surroundings (i.e., hard surfaces and glass found in urban settings, or soft surfaces typically found in rural areas) that will determine the explosive power of the bomb. In my workshops, I tell my participants that these factors are beyond their control. Instead, they are advised to concentrate on things within their control, mainly getting down as quickly as possible.

Generally speaking, though with the caveat that there are plenty of extenuating circumstances, the average kill zone for a grenade has a radius of 5 meters (16 feet), the casualty-inducing radius is 15 meters (50 feet), and shrapnel/fragments can travel to about 230 meters (755 feet). Technically, you can be within these distances and still survive or have minimal injuries, so a lot depends on the circumstances including having a bit of luck.

Since a terrorist incident can also involve shooting, lethal when used by either the terrorists or emergency response teams, you should basically follow the advice for a bombing situation. Namely, quickly get down and remain so until you are certain the danger has cleared.

After looking at tactics, you can look at specific locations that might be vulnerable. Since transportation, both means and infrastructure, is the preferred target of terrorists, the next contribution provides expert advice on mitigating that risk.

SURVIVING A TERRORIST ATTACK ON PUBLIC TRANSPORTATION

ANDREW TAYLOR-GAMMON
INTERNATIONAL SECURITY AND CRISIS MANAGEMENT SPECIALIST

The chance of being caught up in an act of terrorism whilst going about your day-to-day business on public transportation is small—very small. The threat may increase depending on your geographical location, but essentially you would have to be very, very unlucky to get caught up in an attack.

But it can happen.

The bombings of the London Underground in 2005 and the attacks on the Madrid rail system in 2004 underline that attacks can, and do, happen anywhere in the world. In the highly unlikely event that you are caught up in an attack, however, it helps to have some idea of how to respond.

UNDERSTAND THE SITUATION

The vast majority of attacks on public transportation historically have involved the use of an explosive device, be it carried by a suicide bomber or a package left behind for timed or remote detonation.

Armed assaults on board are far less common, while firearm attacks external to the vehicle (such as that against the Togolese national football team bus in Angola in 2010) require a degree of control of the surrounding environment that can be hard for the attackers to create—depending on the political stability of the country. If you get caught up in an attack, it is therefore likely to be an explosion. The chance that it will be solely (or followed up by) an armed assault is more remote.

DECIDE TO STAY OR GO

The most important action in the immediate aftermath of an attack generally revolves around the choice to stay or move. Understanding the potential threat will help you make a positive and informed decision on the best action to take. The need to act quickly and calmly will mean that you are not aiming for "perfect" decisions and actions—that's more for Hollywood than real life.

After an explosion, the environment is likely to be thick with dust and fumes that pose a secondary threat to your health. There is additionally a risk of fire caused by the blast. In such a scenario and provided that it is safe to do so, the prudent course of action is to move away from the vehicle upwind from the smoke and fumes generated by the event (covering your nose and mouth), to a location that you assess to be safe.

Unlike buildings, public modes of transportation by their very nature offer few places in which to effectively hide from an armed assault. If the vehicle is attacked by external perpetrators, it is imperative that the vehicle keeps moving away from the assault and that passengers get low and out of sight, avoiding the windows. The choice to retaliate against an active shooter should be informed by the situation and where possible be a last resort.

STAY CALM

In the aftermath of an attack, the location of the event will largely determine how long it takes the first responders to arrive on scene. During this period, some important decisions need to be made, and to be able to do so, it is important to remain calm. Those who remain in control of their emotions can help to reverse any trend for panic in others by offering reassurance and direction, which in turn can reduce further injury.

Once it is safe to do so, you should contact the emergency services to inform them of the event and then set about helping others with injuries if you have the necessary skills or find others who do. Having a prior basic knowledge of first aid will make you more confident in helping those in immediate peril (e.g., those at risk of bleeding out).

MAKE YOURSELF KNOWN

On arrival, the first responders will be looking to assess the situation and identify whether an ongoing threat exists. In order to aid the appraisal, make sure that your hands are empty and visible and that you follow any instructions promptly.

Following your extraction from the attack site, it is important that the emergency services have your personal details before you leave the area. According to a UK Home Office report[*] following the 2005 London bombings, a quarter of people who experience a traumatic event go on to develop posttraumatic stress disorder, often manifesting itself over the long term after an event. In order to ensure that the police can contact you for further details of the attack and so that other agencies can assist you with additional support services, provide your details to ensure that you are taken into account and kept informed.

---

[*] UK Home Office, "Addressing Lessons from the Emergency Response to the 7 July 2005 London Bombings," 2006, http://www.london.gov.uk/sites/default/files/london-prepared/homeoffice_lessonslearned.pdf.

SUMMARY

The chance of being caught up in an act of terrorism whilst going about your day-to-day business on public transport is small. By seeking to understand the situation, staying calm, and making positive decisions on the actions you take, however, you can optimize your chances of surviving the event.

If you are in a building during a terrorist attack, you should follow the sample procedures as recommended by **Andrew Taylor-Gammon**. In addition, be aware not to light a match, as there might be gas leaks. If there is smoke, get on your hands and knees and crawl from place to place. Use the back of your hand to touch things—there are potentially high temperatures. Unless there are people directly behind you, close any doors to help contain the fire/smoke.

If you followed the advice offered in this book such as carrying a "secret stash" (having a little money, a credit card, and important numbers hidden away) and perhaps even carrying a few vital resources on you such as a whistle and flashlight **(see Section 1.10)**, then you should be in a better position to react in the aftermath of an attack. Being able to call upon your resources will help you cope with the situation.

You can use the **Risk Management Framework** to be informed about the threats in the environment **(RMF 1)**, take steps to reduce your vulnerabilities and increase your capacities **(RMF 2)**, proactively create safe options for yourself **(RMF 3)**, continuously monitor the situation **(RMF 4)**, and have confidence in your preventive measures and ability to react in life-saving ways if the worst should happen **(RMF 5)**. Similarly, your organization needs to do the same. Notice how the Lloyd's/IISS 2007 report "Terrorism in Asia: What Does It Mean for Business?" uses elements of the **RMF**:

1. Like most regions around the globe Southeast Asia is no stranger to terrorism. However, there is no such thing as a uniform global threat—the regional threat is unique and complex and your response must recognize that.
2. Analysis of incidents to date identifies a number of common themes which can help companies to manage risk.
3. Business needs to get better at gathering information from the right sources and using it to guide strategy and operations.
4. Corporate response to terrorism risk essentially involves the strengthening of existing resilience mechanisms, but needs a positive mindset toward security.[121]

These four recommendations generally apply to other parts of the world as well, especially the point that every place is unique.

For further reading about grenades, the article "How Grenades Work" available on the How Stuff Works website is an excellent resource in terms of the clear descriptions, videos, and graphics, plus there are links to related topics and quizzes.[122]

Regarding IEDs, the Wikipedia article "Improvised Explosive Device" is a detailed resource.[123] However, it is important to point out that while it might be interesting to know how a grenade or bomb might look and how it functions, in an actual bombing situation, you should only be concerned with safeguarding your life.

3.10 WORTH KNOWING, EXTREME RISKS: CHAPTER 3 SUMMARY

Hopefully, as a reader, you highlighted, took note, or acted upon suggestions that are relevant to you and modified other tips to suit your circumstances. Accordingly, the chapter's key points will differ from reader to reader, so the summary offered here of the three points for each section can be used to "jog your memory." How do these points compare with the ones you identified?

3.1 Preventing and Reacting to Extreme Risks

- Even extreme risks can be mitigated using the **Risk Management Framework**.
- High-risk locations warrant extra attention on transportation and accommodation issues.
- Before heading for a high-risk destination or engaging in risky activities, ask yourself if, after all your preventative and contingency measures are eventually in place, is the residual level of risk acceptable: If you have remaining concerns or gaps, then proactively take steps to better safeguard yourself.

3.2 Surveillance

- Be aware of indicators that you might be under surveillance, such as persons displaying two extreme forms of physical contact—either someone aims to make contact with you, your belongings, or space by manipulating the encounter, or they might go out of their way to avoid you—for example, suddenly turning around if you look their way or crossing the street if you walk in their direction.
- If you suspect that you are being followed while driving, then make an unexpected move such as signaling one direction yet turning to the other, or pull up to a safe place: Aim to behave naturally while continuously observing the reactions of the suspicious car.
- Be unpredictable, do the unexpected, and remember to vary your daily and weekly routines sufficiently to add an element of uncertainty: In other words, avoid being an easy target.

3.3 Kidnapping

- The basic motives driving the kidnapping industry are political, religious, criminal/financial, minors, sex trade/financial. Your insights into the motivations of potential perpetrators will aid you with avoiding this crime and reacting if you are captured.
- The five stages of a kidnapping are planning and surveillance, attack, transport, captivity, and release. If kidnapping is a threat you might face, then you should map out your possible options and actions at each stage.
- Know that between 92 and 95% of kidnap victims survive the ordeal.

3.4 Sexual Violence

- Worldwide, an estimated 13% of females and 3% of males have been sexually assaulted: This crime can victimize anyone under the "right" set of circumstances.
- Be aware of how to avoid being drugged by, for instance, keeping your drink in your hands in a social drinking situation and being able to identify the indicators that your drink has potentially been tampered with if it briefly turns blue.
- If someone you know has been sexually assaulted or got away from an attempt, then be aware of how not to revictimize the person by, amongst other things, helping the survivor feel empowered to make decisions and take actions that helps with her/his coping and recovery.

3.5 Carjacking

- Ploys used to carjack you include bumping your car from behind, pretending there is or creating a problem with your car so you will pull over, putting an obstacle such as a fallen bicyclist or tree trunk in your path, and acting as fake police: Be aware of local variations.
- General places you should be particularly alert include: Congested traffic, intersections, parking lots, residential driveways and gates, and pick-up and drop-off points such as schools and work places.
- Learn reactive tips that could increase the chances of your surviving a carjacking, such as not making any sudden moves, keeping your hands up, quickly getting out of the car but still indicating your next move, and leaving the keys in the ignition with the car in neutral and running: You want them to take the vehicle as soon as possible, before the crime escalates into kidnapping, sexual assault, or murder.

3.6 Demonstrations and Riots

- If a demonstration, protest, or riot might occur at your next destination, then basic precautions include following the news, keeping informed using an array of sources, and avoiding contentious locations. As part of your ongoing monitoring, look for potential triggers such as a visit by a dignitary, death of a leader, cultural offenses, grievances of university students, or price hikes.
- While most protests are peaceful, the situation can be unpredictable so you should avoid potential episodes of civic unrest.
- If faced with an angry crowd, the best advice is the most obvious: Stay calm, seek shelter, and comply with their demands if directly confronted; with any luck, they are after assets and not people.

3.7 Plane Crash

- The first 90 seconds after a crash is considered the "golden time" in which you must react to increase your chances of surviving an air traffic accident.
- After sitting down, formulate a plan by knowing where the nearest two exits are, practicing your seat buckle, looking over the safety guidelines, and paying attention to the preflight instructions: Taking a few minutes before

takeoff can help you mitigate the increased risks during the early stages of the flight, and similarly being alert during the landing stages can reduce risks.
- In the event of a crash, expect secondary shocks so remain in your brace position until you hear instructions. From then on, it is important you react quickly: You should stay calm, keep low, leave your belongings, count your way out, listen for further instructions, and get at least 150 meters (500 feet) from the site.

3.8 Medical Emergencies
- Carry an appropriate first aid kit for your travels and know what is in it.
- At the scene of a traffic accident, first it is crucial that you assess if it is safe to stop and assist by making sure that you take every possible precaution to protect yourself: Oncoming traffic is the biggest threat, but angry crowds are a serious risk in some locations or circumstances.
- Attend to the most injured casualties first: Check for danger, next look for catastrophic bleeding, response, airway, breathing, and circulation.

3.9 Terrorist Attacks
- While it is impossible to negate the risk from terrorism completely, you can assess the likelihood, create options for yourself, and continuously adjust to the situation so that you succeed in steering clear from harm's way.
- In a bombing situation, your first actions should be getting down and staying clear of glass.
- If you are on public transportation during a terrorist attack, then quickly decide if it is safer to exit, potentially toward additional threats, or stay in place, where there is little shelter and the potential for fire and toxic fumes: There is no generic advice for such a situation. You will have to depend on your ability to make informed decisions, common sense, and luck.

All this is to say, there is a lot you can do to ensure that you have a safe, secure, healthy, and enjoyable trip, even if extreme risks exist: It is just a question of which measures best suit you and your upcoming travel realities.

REFERENCES

1. *Kidnap for Ransom: Resolving the Unthinkable*. Richard Wright, Boca Raton, FL: CRC Press. 2009.
2. "How to Detect Surveillance and Shadowing: Parts I and II," Victoriya Security Agency. ND. http://www.victoriya-security.ru/eng/consultation.php?id=18 and http://www.victoriya-security.ru/eng/consultation.php?id=19.
3. "What to Do when You Believe You're Being Followed," Sandy Esslinger, *Road and Travel* magazine. N/D. http://www.roadandtravel.com/safetyandsecurity/beingfollowed.html.
4. "Stranger Danger Tips for Walkers 2: If You Think You Are Being Followed," Wendy Bumgardner/ About.com Walking. April 06, 2012. http://walking.about.com/cs/med/a/strangerdanger_2.htm?p=1.
5. "Protection for You and Your Car," Detective Kevin Coffey, Corporate Travel Safety. ND. http://www.kevincoffey.com/driving/protection_for_you_and_your_car.htm.

6. "How to Lose Someone When Being Followed," eHow. ND. http://www.ehow.com/how_2258687_lose-someone-being-followed.html.

7. "The Kaspersky Kidnapping—Lessons Learned," Scott Stewart, Stratfor. April 28, 2011. http://www.stratfor.com/weekly/20110427-kaspersky-kidnapping-lessons-learned.

8. "How to Disappear: 9 Ways to Avoid the Creepy Surveillance Systems All Around You," Betsy Isaacson, *Huffington Post*. September 18, 2012. http://www.huffingtonpost.com/2012/09/18/how-to-disappear-avoid-surveillance_n_1872419.html.

9. "Home Counter Surveillance Tips and Help," Brian Westover, eHow. ND. http://www.ehow.com/way_5598055_home-counter-surveillance-tips.html.

10. "How to Detect the Use of Surveillance Equipment," Noel Lawrence, eHow. ND. http://www.ehow.com/how_5907277_detect-use-surveillance-equipment.html.

11. "Risk Map 2012," Control Risks. 2012. http://www.controlrisks.com/OurThinking/CRsDocumentDownload/RiskMap_2012_report.pdf.

12. "The £1 Billion Hostage Trade: How Kidnapping Became a Global Industry," Esme McAvoy and David Randall, *The Independent*. October 17, 2010. http://www.independent.co.uk/news/world/politics/the-1-billion-hostage-trade-2108947.html.

13. "Kidnap for Ransom: A Fateful Growth Industry," Frank Zuccarello, *Insurance Journal*. June 20, 2011. http://www.insurancejournal.com/magazines/features/2011/06/20/202864.htm.

14. "Annual Kidnap Review 2011," Special Contingency Risks LTD. 2011. http://www.scr-ltd.co.uk.

15. "Travel Security—Piracy Expert's Advice on Safer Coastal Holidays," TrainingSolutions. August 20, 2011. http://www.trainingsolutions.dk/?page_id=11.

16. "Annual Kidnap Review 2011," Special Contingency Risks LTD. 2011. http://www.scr-ltd.co.uk.

17. Ibid.

18. "Kidnap for Ransom in the Asia-Pacific Region," ASI Global. 2012. http://www.asiglobalresponse.com/downloads/Asia%20paper.pdf.

19. Ibid.

20. "Annual Kidnap Review 2011," Special Contingency Risks LTD. 2011. http://www.scr-ltd.co.uk.

21. Ibid.

22. "Kidnappings by Militant Groups Increase in North Africa," NBC News, Associated Press and Reuters. October 2, 2012. http://worldnews.nbcnews.com/_news/2012/10/02/14189474-kidnappings-by-militant-groups-increase-in-north-africa?lite.

23. "K&R Bulletin: Africa," JLT Specialty Limited. October 2012. http://www.jltgroup.com/content/UK/risk_and_insurance/Newsletter/265861_KR_Bulletin_Africa_Final_1.pdf.

24. "Nigeria as a Fast-Rising Kidnap Capital?—Politics—Nairaland," Tony Spike, Nairaland Forum. October 19, 2012. http://www.nairaland.com/1078891/nigeria-fast-rising-kidnap-capital.

25. "The £1 Billion Hostage Trade: How Kidnapping Became a Global Industry," Esme McAvoy and David Randall, *The Independent*. October 17, 2010. http://www.independent.co.uk/news/world/politics/the-1-billion-hostage-trade-2108947.html.

26. "Global K&R Watch," ASI Global, Travelers Insurance. April–May 2012. http://www.asiglobalresponse.com/kidnap-and-ransom-watch.aspx.

27. "Kidnap Brief," AKE Group. Q4 2011. http://www.akegroup.com.

28. "Monthly Kidnap News," Control Risks, Hiscox. August 2011, issue 66. http://www.hiscox.co.uk/search/?q=monthly%20kidnap%20news.

29. "The Psychology of Kidnapping and Abduction," David V. Dafinoiu, Security and Intelligence. July 15, 2011. http://securityandintelligence.wordpress.com/2011/07/15/the-psychology-of-kidnapping-and-abduction.

30. Kidnap for Ransom: A Fateful Growth Industry," Frank Zuccarello, *Insurance Journal*. June 20, 2011. http://www.insurancejournal.com/magazines/features/2011/06/20/202864.htm.

31. *Kidnap for Ransom: Resolving the Unthinkable*. Richard Wright, Boca Raton, FL: CRC Press. 2009.

32. Ibid.

33. "Hope in Captivity: How Kidnapped Journalists Coped," Peter Ford, *USA Today*. January 26, 2006. http://usatoday30.usatoday.com/news/world/2006-01-26-journalists-in-captivity_x.htm.

34. "Duty of Care and Travel Risk Management Global Benchmark Study," Dr. Lisbeth Claus, International SOS. 2011. http://www.internationalsos.com/dutyofcare.

35. *Kidnap for Ransom: Resolving the Unthinkable*. Richard Wright, Boca Raton, FL: CRC Press. 2009.

36. "Kidnap for Ransom: A Fateful Growth Industry," Frank Zuccarello, *Insurance Journal*. June 20, 2011. http://www.insurancejournal.com/magazines/features/2011/06/20/202864.htm.

37. "Kidnapping and Hostage Survival Guidelines," United States Department of Agriculture. ND. http://www.dm.usda.gov/ocpm/Security%20Guide/T5terror/Kidnap.htm.

38. "11 Surprising Insights about Being Kidnapped," Sam Greenspan, 11 Points. August 16, 2011. http://www.11points.com/Interviews/11_Surprising_Insights_About_Being_Kidnapped.

39. http://www.asiglobalresponse.com.

40. "Australian Crime: Facts & Figures 2011," Australian Institute of Criminology. 2012. http://www.aic.gov.au.

41. "Sexual Assault—Reducing the Risk," Metropolitan Police Department. ND. http://mpdc.dc.gov/node/208022.

42. "Sweden's Rape Rate Under the Spotlight," Ruth Alexander, BBC News. September 14, 2012. http://www.bbc.co.uk/news/magazine-19592372.

43. "U.S. to Expand Its Definition of Rape in Statistics," Charlie Savage, *The New York Times*. January 6, 2012. http://www.nytimes.com/2012/01/07/us/politics/federal-crime-statistics-to-expand-rape-definition.html.

44. "Crime Statistics in South Africa," *South Africa News*. January 23, 2012. http://southafricanews.wordpress.com/2012/01/23/crime-statistics-in-south-africa.

45. "Sexual Assault," Southern Illinois University. Updated version, September 19, 2012. http://www.dps.siu.edu/cp_sexual_assault.htm.

46. Ibid.

47. Ibid.

48. "Sexual Assault: An Overview and Implications for Counselling Support," Pablo A. Fernandez, *Australasian Medical Journal* (Online). September 18, 2011. http://www.readperiodicals.com/201109/2532894531.html#ixzz27iKzSQSW.

49. "Sexual Assault," Southern Illinois University. Updated version, September 19, 2012. http://www.dps.siu.edu/cp_sexual_assault.htm.

50. "Australian Crime: Facts & Figures 2011," Australian Institute of Criminology. 2012. http://www.aic.gov.au.

51. "Serious Safety Tips for Women," Marybeth Bond, Women Travel Tips. ND. http://www.womentraveltips.com/tips5.shtml.

52. "Sexual Assault," Southern Illinois University. Updated version, September 19, 2012. http://www.dps.siu.edu/cp_sexual_assault.htm.

53. "Date Rape Drugs: Date Rape Drugs Explained and De-Mystified," About.com Teen Advice. ND. http://teenadvice.about.com/library/weekly/aa062502a.htm.

54. http://www.drinksafetech.com.

55. "Sexual Assault," Southern Illinois University. Updated version, September 19, 2012. http://www.dps.siu.edu/cp_sexual_assault.htm.

56. "Sexual Assault—Reducing the Risk," Metropolitan Police Department. ND. http://mpdc.dc.gov/node/208022.

57. "How to Avoid Rape," No Nonsense Self Defense. ND. http://www.nononsenseselfdefense.com/avoid_rape.htm.

58. http://www.nsvrc.org.

59. http://preventconnect.org.

60. "Serious Safety Tips for Women," Marybeth Bond, Women Travel Tips. ND. http://www.womentraveltips.com/tips5.shtml.

61. "Surviving a Rape or Sexual Assault while Travelling," Beth Morrisey, Female Traveller. September 21, 2010. http://www.femaletraveller.co.uk/surviving-rape-sexual-assault-while-travelling.html.

62. "Carjacking in Australia: Recording Issues and Future Directions," Lisa Jane Young, Charles Sturt, Dr. Maria Borzycki, Australian Institute of Criminology. Updated version, July 13, 2009. http://www.aic.gov.au/publications/current%20series/tandi/341-360/tandi351/view%20paper.aspx.

63. *Staying Safe*. Juval Aviv and William P. Kucewicz, New York: HarperCollins. 2004.

64. "Preventing Hijacking," South African Police Service. ND. http://www.saps.gov.za/crime_prevention/safety_tips/car_hijacking.htm.

65. "Carjacking—Don't Be A Victim," U.S Department of State. August 2002. http://www.state.gov/m/ds/rls/rpt/19782.htm.

66. "How to Avoid Carjacking," Detective Kevin Coffey, Corporate Travel Safety. ND. http://www.kevincoffey.com/driving/how_to_avoid_carjacking.htm.

67. "How to Avoid Being Carjacked," WikiHow. Updated version, October 25, 2012. http://www.wikihow.com/Avoid-Being-Carjacked.

68. "Confessions of a Car Hijacker," Vuyi Jabavu, *Sowetan Live*. October 13, 2011. http://www.sowetanlive.co.za/news/2011/10/13/confessions-of-a-car-hijacker.

69. "Car Hijack Victim's Nightmare—What It Feels Like to Have Your Precious Life in the Hands of Someone Else," Vusi Masango, *Sowetan Live*. November 17, 2011. http://www.sowetanlive.co.za/news/2011/11/17/car-hijack-victim-s-nightmare---what-it-feels-like-to-have-your-precious-life-in-the-hands-of-someone-else.

70. "Money Can't Buy Me Love," *The Economist*. June 16, 2012.

71. "Duty of Care and Travel Risk Management Global Benchmark Study," Dr. Lisbeth Claus, International SOS. 2011. http://www.internationalsos.com/dutyofcare.

72. "Threat Forecast 2013," Red 24. 2013. http://www.red24.com/threat_forecast/threat_forecast_2013.php.

73. "Food Riots: What Creates the Anger?," Jessica Leeder, *The Globe and Mail*. February 1, 2011. http://www.theglobeandmail.com/news/world/food-riots-what-creates-the-anger/article564412.

74. "Protests and Demonstrations in China: The Tensions and Methods Behind," Jeffrey Hays, Facts and Details. Updated version, March 2012. http://factsanddetails.com/china.php?itemid=305&catid=8&subcatid=49.

75. *Safety First: A Safety and Security Handbook for Aid Workers*. Shaun Bickley, International Save the Children Alliance. 2010.

76. "How to Survive a Riot," WikiHow. Updated version, August 20, 2012. http://www.wikihow.com/Survive-a-Riot.

77. *How to Avoid Being Killed in a War Zone*. Rosie Garthwaite, New York: Bloomsbury. 2011.

78. "Violent Protest Tactical Guide—Defense Essentials," Amr Bassiouny, Amrbassiouny. November 22, 2011. http://abassiouny.wordpress.com/2011/11/22/violent-protest-tactical-guide-defence-essentials.

79. "How to Deal with Riot Control Agents," WikiHow. Updated version, March 14, 2012. http://www.wikihow.com/Deal-With-Riot-Control-Agents.

80. "How to Survive a Plane Crash," Charles W. Bryant, How Stuff Works. January 28, 2008. http://adventure.howstuffworks.com/how-to-survive-a-plane-crash.htm.

81. "How to Survive a Plane Crash," Milla Harrison, BBC News. October 3, 2006. http://news.bbc.co.uk/2/hi/uk_news/magazine/5402342.stm.

82. http://aviation-safety.net/database.

83. "How to Survive a Plane Crash," WikiHow. Updated version, August 16, 2012. http://www.wikihow.com/Survive-a-Plane-Crash#_note-0.

84. "Plane Crashed on Purpose to Help People Survive," Jim Avila, ABC News. May 1, 2012. http://abcnews.go.com/blogs/technology/2012/05/scientists-use-experimental-plane-crash-to-analyze-survivability-rates.

85. "How to Survive a Plane Crash," WikiHow. Updated version, August 16, 2012. http://www.wikihow.com/Survive-a-Plane-Crash#_note-0.

86. "How to Survive a Plane Crash," Emma Clarke, CNN. March 20, 2009. http://edition.cnn.com/2009/TRAVEL/03/04/survive.airplane.accident/index.html#cnnSTCText.

87. "How Scared of Terrorism Should You Be?," Robert Bailey, Reason.com. September 6, 2011. http://reason.com/archives/2011/09/06/how-scared-of-terrorism-should.

88. "Duty of Care and Travel Risk Management Global Benchmark Study," Dr. Lisbeth Claus, International SOS. 2011. http://www.internationalsos.com/dutyofcare.

89. "How to Survive a Plane Crash," Rachel Burge, MSN Travel. November 15, 2011. http://travel.uk.msn.com/travel-advice/how-to-survive-a-plane-crash.

90. Ibid.

91. Ibid.

92. "How to Survive a Plane Crash," WikiHow. Updated version, August 16, 2012. http://www.wikihow.com/Survive-a-Plane-Crash#_note-0.

93. *The Complete Flier's Handbook: The Essential Guide to Successful Air Travel.* Brian Clegg, London: Pan Macmillan. 2002.

94. "Safest Seat on a Plane: PM Investigates How to Survive a Crash," David Nooland, *Popular Mechanics.* July 18, 2007. http://www.popularmechanics.com/technology/aviation/safety/4219452.

95. Ibid.

96. "How to Survive a Plane Crash," Charles W. Bryant, How Stuff Works.

97. "How to Survive a Plane Crash," Rachel Burge, MSN Travel.

98. "How to Survive a Plane Crash," Milla Harrison, BBC News.

99. "How to Survive a Plane Crash," Rachel Burge, MSN Travel.

100. "Plane Crashed on Purpose to Help People Survive," Jim Avila, ABC News.

101. "How to Survive a Plane Crash," Rachel Burge, MSN Travel.

102. "How to Survive a Plane Crash," Charles W. Bryant, How Stuff Works.

103. "How to Survive a Plane Crash," Emma Clarke, CNN.

104. "How to Survive a Plane Crash," Milla Harrison, BBC News.

105. "How to Survive a Plane Crash," WikiHow.

106. http://www.qualsafe.com/fabooks.html.

107. http://www.bbc.co.uk/health.

108. http://humanitrain.com/talking-trauma-kit.html.

109. "Terrorism," Wikipedia. Updated version, September 13, 2012. http://en.wikipedia.org/wiki/Terrorism.

110. "2011 Report on Terrorism," National Counterterrorism Center. March 12, 2012. http://www.nctc.gov/docs/2011_NCTC_Annual_Report_Final.pdf.

111. http://www.start.umd.edu/gtd.

112. "1970–2011, Advanced Search: Region," Global Terrorism Database. November 3, 2012. http://www.start.umd.edu/gtd/search/Results.aspx?charttype=bar&chart=regions& casualties_type=&casualties_max=.

113. "2000–2010, Advanced Search: Incidents," Global Terrorism Database. November 3, 2012. http://www.start.umd.edu/gtd/search/Results.aspx?charttype=pie&chart=target& casualties_type=b&casualties_max=&start_yearonly=2000&end_yearonly=2010&dtp2=all.

114. "1970–2011, Advanced Search: Weapon Type," Global Terrorism Database. November 3, 2012. http://www.start.umd.edu/gtd/search/Results.aspx?charttype=bar&chart= weapon&casualties_type=b&casualties_max=&dtp2=all.

115. "2011 Report on Terrorism," National Counterterrorism Center. March 12, 2012. http:// www.nctc.gov/docs/2011_NCTC_Annual_Report_Final.pdf.

116. "Duty of Care and Travel Risk Management Global Benchmark Study," Dr. Lisbeth Claus, International SOS. 2011. http://www.internationalsos.com/dutyofcare.

117. "2011 Report on Terrorism," National Counterterrorism Center. March 12, 2012. http:// www.nctc.gov/docs/2011_NCTC_Annual_Report_Final.pdf.

118. Ibid.

119. "How Scared of Terrorism Should You Be?," Robert Bailey, Reason.com. September 6, 2011. http://reason.com/archives/2011/09/06/how-scared-of-terrorism-should.

120. "2011 Report on Terrorism," National Counterterrorism Center. March 12, 2012. http:// www.nctc.gov/docs/2011_NCTC_Annual_Report_Final.pdf.

121. "Terrorism in Asia: What Does It Mean for Business?," Lloyd's, IISS. 2007. http://www.lloyds.com/Search?as_sitesearch=www.lloyds.com/~/media/ Lloyds&q=goods+in+transit.

122. "How Grenades Work," Tom Harris, How Stuff Works. ND. http://science.howstuffworks. com/grenade.htm.

123. "Improvised Explosive Device," Wikipedia. Updated version, October 30, 2012. http:// en.wikipedia.org/wiki/Improvised_explosive_device.

Further Reading and Resources

To support you in being an informed traveler, this section categorizes the further reading and resources into subject areas. The * next to an item means the resource is recommended.

GENERAL PREPARATION: THREAT, CONTEXT, AND SITUATIONAL ASSESSMENTS

*http://www.about.com.
*http://www.ihatetaxis.com.
*http://www.smartraveller.gov.au.
*http://www.streetdirectory.com/travel_guide/singapore.
*http://www.voyage.gc.ca.
*http://www.wikitravel.org.
http://www.aljazeera.com.
http://www.asigroup.com.
http://www.baidu.com.
http://www.bbc.co.uk.
http://www.cnn.com.
http://www.controlrisks.com.
http://www.english.ctrip.com.
http://www.fco.gov.uk.
http://www.osac.org.
http://www.riskline.com.
http://www.sina.com.
http://www.worldtravelwatch.com.
*"Interactive Charts," Lloyd's. ND. http://www.lloyds.com/news-and-insight/risk-insight/lloyds-risk-index/infographics.
**"Risk Map 2013," Control Risks. 2013. http://www.controlrisks.com/Oversized%20assets/RiskMap_2013_REPORT.pdf.
*"Threat Forecast 2013," Red 24. 2013.http://www.red24.com/threat_forecast/threat_forecast_2013.php.
"2011 'Extremely Turbulent' for Business Travelers," Anne Freedman, Risk and Insurance. January 30, 2012. http://www.riskandinsurance.com/story.jsp?storyId=533344807&topic=Main.
"2011 Quality of Living Worldwide City Rankings," Mercer Consulting. November 2011. http://www.mercer.com/qualityoflivingpr#personal-safety.
"How Many Americans Die Abroad Each Year," The Jetpacker. June 24, 2010. http://thejetpacker.com/how-many-americans-die-abroad-each-year.
"Lloyd's Risk Index, 2011," *The Economist* Intelligence Unit, Lloyd's. 2011 http://www.lloyds.com/~/media/Files/News%20and%20Insight/360%20Risk%20Insight/Lloyds_Risk_Index_2011.pdf—Lloyd's.
"The World's Most Dangerous Cities," Robert Wenzel, *Economic Policy Journal*. May 25, 2012. http://lewrockwell.com/wenzel/wenzel181.html.

PERSONAL PREPARATIONS, PLANNING, AND PACKING

http://www.realmenrealstyle.com.

*"Documents, Info, Policies and Advice," Arlene Fleming, About.com Air Travel. ND. http://airtravel.about.com/od/beforeyougo/u/Docs.htm.

*"How to Choose Travel Clothing," REI. ND. http://www.rei.com/learn/expert-advice/travel-clothing.html#top.

*"Traveller's Checklist," Foreign Affairs and International Trade Canada. ND. http://www.voyage.gc.ca/preparation_information/checklist_sommaire-eng.asp.

*"Travel Plan," TrainingSolutions. ND. http://www.trainingsolutions.dk.

*"Travel Wise Checklist," TrainingSolutions. ND. http://www.trainingsolutions.dk.

*"What Should I Wear, Where?," Journeywoman. ND. http://www.journeywoman.com/ccc/default.html.

"5 Tips for Those Who Are Considering Becoming an Expatriate," Donald Saunders, Streetdirectory.com Singapore Guide. ND. http://www.streetdirectory.com/travel_guide/211705/travel_tips/5_tips_for_those_who_are_considering_becoming_an_expatriate.html.

"Best Apps and Websites for Travelers," Tom Samilijan, NBC News Travel Kit. September 20, 2012. http://www.nbcnews.com/travel/travelkit/best-apps-websites-travelers-1B6002828.

"Moving Tips: 12 Amazing Tips to Facilitate Relocation," Abhishek Aqarwal, Streetdirectory.com Singapore Guide. ND. http://www.streetdirectory.com/travel_guide/215930/travel_tips/moving_tips___12_amazing_tips_to_facilitate_relocation.html.

BUSINESS TRAVELERS

*http://www.economist.com/blogs/gulliver.

http://www.businesstraveller.com.

http://www.edition.cnn.com/CNNI/Programs/business.traveller/archive/index.html.

http://www.executivetravelmagazine.com.

*"Safety and Security for the Business Professional Traveling Abroad," Federal Bureau of Investigations. ND. http://www.fbi.gov/about-us/investigate/counterintelligence/business-brochure.

"James Bond as Business Traveler: Hotels Worthy of 007," Chestnut, Mark, Orbitz. October 2, 2012. http://www.orbitz.com/blog/2012/10/james-bond-as-business-traveler-hotels-worthy-of-007.

"5 Business Travel Threats for 2013," Tony Ridley. ND. http://tony-ridley.com/risk-management/5-top-business-travel-threats-2013-travel-risk-management.

NONGOVERNMENTAL ORGANIZATION (NGO) TRAVELERS

*http://www.aidworkers.net.

*http://www.aidworkersecurity.org.

*http://www.allindiary.org.

*"Comparing Urban and Rural Security Incidents," Christina Wille and Larissa Fast, Insecurity Insight. 2010. http://www.insecurityinsight.org/files/Security%20Facts%201%20Urban%20Rural.pdf.

*Generic Security Guide for Humanitarian Organizations. ECHO. 2004. http://www.aidworkers.net/?q=node/809.

*Good Practice Review 8: Operational Security Management in Violent Environments. Humanitarian Practice Network, Overseas Development Institute. Updated version, December 2010. http://www.alnap.org/pool/files/gpr-8-new.pdf.

*"Heat Map," The Aid Worker Security Database. ND. https://aidworkersecurity.org/incidents/report/map.

New Protection Manual for Human Rights Defenders. Enrique Eguren and Marie Caraj, Protection International. 2009. http://www.protectiononline.org.

Safety First: A Safety and Security Handbook for Aid Workers. Shaun Bickley, International Save the Children Alliance. 2010. http://www.eisf.eu/resources/library/SafetyFirst2010.pdf.

"Aid Worker Fatalities Pages," Kevin Tommer, Patronus Analytical. ND. http://www.patronusanalytical.com/aid%20worker%20fatalities/fatalities%20main%20page.html.

"Attacks and Interference Heighten Humanitarian Risks," Tim Witcher, AFP. April 12, 2011. http://www.google.com/hostednews/afp/article/ALeqM5iP2NK5Bq6s9HrVrLVQ8smi_bndeQ?docId=CNG.339fc2df9b43da9680cd9933ecbd37aa.191.

"Location of Attacks (1997–2011)," The Aid Workers Security Database. Updated version, July 25, 2012. https://aidworkersecurity.org/incidents/report/location.

Staying Alive: Safety and Security Guidelines for Humanitarian Volunteers in Conflict Areas. David Lloyd Roberts, International Committee of the Red Cross. 2006. http://www.icrc.org/eng/resources/documents/publication/p0717.htm.

To Stay and Deliver: Good Practice for Humanitarians in Complex Security Environments. United Nations. 2011. http://www.unhcr.org/refworld/type,RESEARCH,,,4d9039e32,0.html.

WOMEN TRAVELERS

*http://www.journeywoman.com.

http://gutsytraveler.com.

http://www.safetravel4women.com.

*"Her Own Way: A Woman's Safe-Travel Guide," Foreign Affairs and International Trade Canada. 2011. http://www.voyage.gc.ca/publications/woman-guide_voyager-feminin-eng.

"Female Business Travel—Is Your Employer Keeping You Safe Abroad?," International SOS. July 19, 2012. http://www.internationalsos.com/en/pressreleases_6571.htm.

"Serious Safety Tips for Women," Marybeth Bond, Women Travel Tips. ND. http://www.womentraveltips.com/tips5.shtml.

"Women Travel Statistics Explained by Travel Expert," Marybeth Bond. ND. http://gutsytraveler.com/women-travel-statistics-2.

TRAVELERS WITH DISABILITIES

http://www.able-travel.com.

http://www.disabledtravelersguide.com.

http://www.e-bility.com.

http://www.lonelyplanet.com/thorntree/forum.jspa?forumID=38.

*"Disabled Travelers," Foreign and Commonwealth Office. Updated version, September 19, 2011. http://www.fco.gov.uk/en/travel-and-living-abroad/your-trip/disabled-travellers#.

"Air Travel with Mobility Devices or Mobility Aids: Airlines and Wheelchairs, Walkers, Canes," Arlene Fleming, About.com Air Travel. ND. http://airtravel.about.com/od/accessableairtravel/tp/advicewheelchair.htm.

"Travelling with Disability," Natalie Ippolito, Streetdirectory.com Singapore Guide. ND. http://www.streetdirectory.com/travel_guide/215847/travel_tips/travelling_with_disability.html.

ELDERLY TRAVELERS

*http://seniortravel.about.com.

http://www.50plusinfobus.com.

http://www.senioryears.com/travel.html.

*"Safe and Healthy Travels for Senior Citizens," Centers for Disease Control and Prevention. Updated version, April 2, 2012. http://www.cdc.gov/Features/SeniorTravel.

*"Smart Traveller," Department of Foreign Affairs and Trade. November 2011. http://www.smartraveller.gov.au/tips/travelling-seniors.pdf.

"10 Safety Tips for Seniors Using Public Transportation," Sharon O'Brien, About.com Senior Living. ND. http://seniorliving.about.com/od/travelsmart/a/publictransport.htm.

"Over 65's Travel Insurance," Travel Insurance Guide.org.uk. ND. http://www.travelinsuranceguide.org.uk/over-50.html.

"Seniors—Air Travel Tips and Advice," Arlene Fleming, About.com Air Travel. ND. http://airtravel.about.com/od/travelindustrynews/tp/seniorstips.htm.

"Train Travel Safety," Nancy Parode, About.com Senior Travel. ND. http://seniortravel.about.com/od/traintravel/qt/Train-Travel-Safety.htm.

HOMOSEXUAL, BISEXUAL, AND TRANSGENDER TRAVELERS

*http://www.ilga.org.

http://www.globetrottergirls.com/category/lgbt.

http://www.lonelyplanet.com/thorntree/forum.jspa?forumID=35.

http://www.mygaytravelguide.com.

*"Homosexual, Bisexual, and Transgender Travel—FAQ" Foreign Affairs and International Trade Canada. ND. http://www.voyage.gc.ca/faq/homosexuality_homosexualite-eng.

*"LGBT Travellers," Foreign and Commonwealth Office. Updated version, October 11, 2010. http://www.fco.gov.uk/en/travel-and-living-abroad/your-trip/LGBT-travellers.

"Security—Information and Tips," Gays on Tour. Updated March 30, 2011. http://www.gaysontour.com/index.php?page=254&lang=en.

"Travel Tips," Queer Trip. ND. http://www.queertrip.com/travel.php.

"Why You Can't Bulletpoint Gay Travel," Waegook Tom. July 11, 2012. http://www.waegook-tom.com/lgbt/stereotype-gay-travel.

TRAVELING FAMILIES

*"6 Safety Tips for Traveling Abroad with Kids," Jason Brink, The Flipkey Blog. November 11, 2011. http://www.flipkey.com/blog/2011/11/11/6-safety-tips-for-traveling-abroad-with-kids.

*"Children and Flying Fears," Children's National Medical Center. ND. http://www.childrensnational.org.

*"Keep Kids Safe," Transport Canada. ND. http://www.tc.gc.ca/eng/roadsafety/safedrivers-childsafety-car-time-stages-1083.htm.

*"Tip Sheet: Crowd Safety," We Just Got Back. ND. http://www.wejustgotback.com/default.aspx?mod=tips_safety.

*"Traveling Abroad with Kids," Lori Morris, Parents. ND. http://www.parents.com/fun/vacation/international/checklist-traveling-abroad-with-kids/?page=1.

"Child Safety Tips" Alvin Eden, MD, and Elizabeth Eden, MD. 2006. http://tlc.howstuffworks.com/family/kids-safety-tips2.htm.

"Child Travel Consent," LawDepot.com. ND. http://www.lawdepot.com/contracts/child-travel-consent.

"Choose with Care: A Parent's Guide to Choosing Child Safe Organisations," Child Wise. 2004. http://www.crin.org/resources/infodetail.asp?ID=4790.

"Flying with Children," Sharon. Updated version, March 2011. http://flyingwithchildren1.
blogspot.dk.

"Kids Airport Diversion Guide," Cheapflights.com. ND. http://www.cheapflights.com/travel/
kids-airport-diversion-guide.

"Preventing Abductions," Steven Dowshen, MD, Kids Health. February 2009. http://kidshealth.
org/parent/firstaid_safe/outdoor/abductions.html#.

"Single Parent Travel," Jamie Jefferson, Streetdirectory Singapore Guide. ND. http://www.
streetdirectory.com/travel_guide/215976/travel_tips/single_parent_travel.html.

"Travelling with Children," Foreign Affairs and International Trade Canada. ND. http://www.
voyage.gc.ca/publications/children_enfants-eng.

RELIGIOUS TRAVELERS

*http://www.crescentrating.com.

http://www.flyertalk.com/forum/religious-travelers-604.

http://www.independenttraveler.com.

"12+1 Tips to Safeguard Your Salaat While Traveling," Fazal Bahardeen, Crescentrating.
Updated version, August 15, 2012. http://www.crescentrating.com/en/muslim-guides/
travel-tips-etiquettes/item/1859-safeguard-salaath-prayers-while-traveling.html.

"Defining Faith-Focused Security," David Dose, Safe Travel Solutions. April 11, 2011.
http://safetravelsolutions.org/home/index.php?option=com_content&view=article
&id=207:defining-faith-focused-security-&catid=41:training-articles&Itemid=211.

ACCOMMODATIONS

*http://www.tripadvisor.com.

http://www.lonelyplanet.com/thorntree.

"Business Travelers, Avoid These Rooms," Jill Becker, CNN. July 9, 2012. http://edition.cnn.
com/2012/07/09/travel/hotel-rooms-avoid/index.html.

"Hotel Room Safety," Jonathon E. Stewart, About.com Hotels & Resorts. ND. http://video.
about.com/hotels/Hotel-Room-Safety.htm.

"Hotel Security Tips for Small Business Travelers," Paul Davis, Business Know How. ND.
http://www.businessknowhow.com/security/hotelsafety.htm.

"Marybeth Speaks about Travel Safety on CNN News. Gutsy Traveler. ND. http://www.
gutsytraveler.com/hotel-security-2.

ACTIVE LISTENING SKILLS

"10 Tips for Active Listening," Barbara Bray, Rethinking Learning. January 10, 2012. http://
barbarabray.net/2012/01/10/10-tips-for-active-listening.

"10 Tips for Effective & Active Listening Skills," Susie Michelle Cortright, Power to Change
Student. ND. http://powertochange.com/students/people/listen.

AIR TRAVEL

*http://www.seatguru.com.

http://www.airlinequality.com.

http://www.aviation-safety.net/database.

http://www.ec.europa.eu/transport/air-ban/doc/list_en.pdf.

http://www.planecrashinfo.com.

*"How to Survive a Plane Crash," Charles W. Bryant, How Stuff Works. January 28, 2008. http://adventure.howstuffworks.com/how-to-survive-a-plane-crash.htm.

*"How to Survive a Plane Crash," Rachel Burge, MSN Travel. November 15, 2011. http://travel.uk.msn.com/travel-advice/how-to-survive-a-plane-crash.

*"How to Survive a Plane Crash," WikiHow. Updated version, August 16, 2012. http://www.wikihow.com/Survive-a-Plane-Crash#_note-0.

"4 Ways to Protect Your Stuff at Airport Security," Genevieve Shaw Brown, ABC News Travel. April 22, 2012. http://abcnews.go.com/blogs/lifestyle/2012/04/4-ways-to-protect-your-stuff-at-airport-security.

"Airline Accident Rates," About.com Air Travel. ND. http://airtravel.about.com/gi/o.htm?zi=1/XJ&zTi=1&sdn=airtravel&cdn=travel&tm=13&f=20&su=p284.13.342.ip_&tt=13&bt=1&bts=0&zu=http%3A//www.planecrashinfo.com/rates.htm.

"Airline Safety: Tips for Business Travelers," Greig Waddell, About.com Business Travel. ND. http://businesstravel.about.com/od/healthsafety/tp/airline_safety_businesstravel.htm.

"Airport/Airline Safety," Safe Traveler. ND. http://www.safetraveler.com/Airport_Airline_Safety.html.

The Complete Flier's Handbook: The Essential Guide to Successful Air Travel. Brian Clegg, London: Pan Macmillan. 2002.

"How to Choose Your Airplane Seat: 5 Tips for Getting the Seat You Want," Greig Waddell, About.com Business Travel. ND. http://businesstravel.about.com/od/airlines/tp/choose_your_airplane_seat.htm.

"How to Survive a Plane Crash," Emma Clarke, CNN. March 20, 2009. http://edition.cnn.com/2009/TRAVEL/03/04/survive.airplane.accident/index.html#cnnSTCText.

"How to Survive a Plane Crash," Milla Harrison, BBC News. October 3, 2006. http://www.news.bbc.co.uk/2/hi/uk_news/magazine/5402342.stm.

"Know Your Rights when Traveling," American Civil Liberties Union. ND. http://www.aclu.org/technology-and-liberty/know-your-rights-when-traveling.

"Plane Crashed on Purpose to Help People Survive," Jim Avila, ABC News. May 1, 2012. http://abcnews.go.com/blogs/technology/2012/05/scientists-use-experimental-plane-crash-to-analyze-survivability-rates.

"The Safest Airplanes in the World—World's Safest Airplanes," Arlene Fleming, About.com Air Travel. ND. http://airtravel.about.com/od/safetysecurity/qt/safestairplane.htm.

"Safest Seat on a Plane: PM Investigates How to Survive a Crash," David Nooland, *Popular Mechanics*. July 18, 2007. http://www.popularmechanics.com/technology/aviation/safety/4219452.

"Travelers Forget Everything from Passports to False Teeth," Gary Stoller, USA Today Travel. November 9, 2011. http://travel.usatoday.com/news/story/2011-11-08/Travelers-forget-everything-from-passports-to-false-teeth/51124844/1.

CORRUPTION

*http://www.business-anti-corruption.com/?L=0.

*http://www.transparency.org.

*"Corruption Indicators," Serious Fraud Office. ND. http://www.sfo.gov.uk/bribery--corruption/corruption-indicators.aspx.

*"Corruption Perception Index 2011," Transparency International. 2011. http://cpi.transparency.org/cpi2011/results.

*"Fraud and Corporate Governance: Changing Paradigm in India," Ernst & Young. 2012. http://www.ey.com/IN/en/Services/Assurance/Fraud-Investigation---Dispute-Services/Fraud-and-corporate-governance-Changing-paradigm-in-India.

*"Governance & Anti-Corruption," World Bank. ND. http://www.worldbank.org/wbi/governance.

*"Say No to Corruption! Follow the 10 Commandments!" I Paid a Bribe. ND. http://www.ipaidabribe.com/blog/say-no-corruption-follow-10-commandments.

"A New Type of Scam," Baobab. March 29, 2012. http://www.economist.com/blogs/baobab/2012/03/nigerian-corruption.

"An Analysis of India's Pathetic 95th Rank in the Corruption Index and Its Far Reaching Social Impact!" Arindam Chaudhuri/*Business and Economy*. February 2, 2012. http://www.businessandeconomy.org/02022012/editordesk.asp?sid=6721&pageno=2.

"Corruption," UNODC. ND. http://www.unodc.org/unodc/en/data-and-analysis/statistics/corruption.html.

"Corruption and International Business in Russia," Dmitry Budanov, SASMA. July 2010. http://sas-ma.org/eng/edition-july-2010/228-corruption-and-international-business-in-russia-dmitry-budanov.

"Corruption Costs Indonesia $238m in 2011," Ezra Sihite, *Jakarta Globe*. January 30, 2012. http://www.thejakartaglobe.com/home/corruption-costs-indonesia-238m-in-2011/494558.

"Corruption Costs Us R30bn a Year," Sapa, *Times Live*. March 12, 2012. http://www.timeslive.co.za/politics/2012/03/31/corruption-costs-us-r30bn-a-year-acdp.

"Corruption in Business: Power to Destroy Firms," Bizshifts. January 3, 2011. http://bizshifts-trends.com/2011/01/03/corruption-in-business-power-to-destroy-firms.

"Corruption in the NGO World: What It Is and How to Tackle It," Jerome Larche, Humanitarian Exchange Magazine. October 2011, Issue 52. http://www.odihpn.org/humanitarian-exchange-magazine/issue-52/corruption-in-the-ngo-world-what-it-is-and-how-to-tackle-it.

"Corruption Too Much for Western Companies," *The Moscow Times*, March 16, 2010.

"Impact of Corruption on Indian Businesses: Survey," Viral Dholakia, Trak.in. March 15, 2012. http://trak.in/tags/business/2011/03/15/impact-of-corruption-on-indian-businesses-survey.

"Statement on the Adoption by the General Assembly of the United Nations Convention Against Corruption," The Secretary General (Kofi Annan). October 31, 2003. http://www.unodc.org/unodc/en/treaties/CAC/background/secretary-general-speech.html.

"Watch GPS: How Corrupt Is China?" Fareed Zakaria GPS, CNN. April 27, 2012. http://globalpublicsquare.blogs.cnn.com/2012/04/27/watch-gps-how-corrupt-is-china.

CREDIT CARDS SKIMMING AND ATMS

*"Credit Card Skimming: How Thieves Can Steal Your Card Info without You Knowing It," Jamey Heary, NetworkWorld.com. October 1, 2008. http://www.networkworld.com/community/node/33210?page=0%2C0.

"2012: Year of the Skimmer: Fraud Losses to Increase; Mag-Stripe Vulnerabilities to Blame," Tracy Kitten, Bank Info Security. January 18, 2012. http://www.bankinfosecurity.com/2012-year-skimmer-a-4417/op-1.

"7 Popular Cities to Watch for Credit Card Skimming Scams," Mark Brown, BillShrink. May 27, 2009. http://www.billshrink.com/blog/3685/popular-cities-credit-card-skimming-scams.

"Card Skimming," SCAMwatch. ND. http://www.scamwatch.gov.au/content/index.phtml/tag/CardSkimming.

"Credit Card Skim Scams Net $170 Million," Janet Fife-Yeomans, *Daily Telegraph*. April 15, 2011. http://www.dailytelegraph.com.au/archive/national-old/credit-card-skim-scams-net-170-million/story-e6freuzr-1226039359854.

"Credit Card Skimming Affects One in Five ATM Users," UniBul. October 12, 2010. http://blog.unibulmerchantservices.com/credit-card-skimming-affects-one-in-five-atm-users.

"Hackers Tech: Credit Card Skimming," Jason Collazo, Business Insider. October 29, 2011. http://articles.businessinsider.com/2011-10-29/tech/30332949_1_credit-card-bank-card-card-reader#ixzz1yS8SkkQW.

"How Credit Card Skimming Works," LaToya Irby, About.com Credit/Debt Management. ND. http://credit.about.com/od/privacyconcerns/a/credit-card-skimming.htm.

"Keep Your Credit Cards Safe from Skimmers," Robert Vamosi, PCWorld. December 8, 2010. http://www.pcworld.com/article/212969/keep_your_credit_cards_safe_from_skimmers.html.

"Reverse PIN Technology and Your Safety," Tom Murse, About.com US Government Info. April 13, 2011. http://usgovinfo.about.com/od/censusandstatistics/a/Why-Reverse-PIN-Is-Not-in-Use.htm.

"Skimming the Cash Out of Your Account," Laura Bruce, Bankrate.com. October 4, 2002. http://www.bankrate.com/system/util/print.aspx?p=/finance/checking/skimming-the-cash-out-of-your-account-1.aspx#ixzz1ycRJCafl.

"Taking a Trip to the ATM? Beware of 'Skimmers'," Federal Bureau of Investigation (FBI). July 14, 2011. http://www.fbi.gov/news/stories/2011/july/atm_071411.

"Threat of Credit Card 'Skimming' Rises during the Holidays," Justine Griffin, *Sun Sentinel*. December 18, 2011. http://articles.sun-sentinel.com/2011-12-18/business/fl-skimming-credit-card-threat-20111218_1_card-numbers-credit-card-credit-and-debit.

"Why That mp3 Player Is Stealing Your Identity with Skimming," SCAMwatch. ND. http://www.spamlawT.com/identity-theft-skimming.

CRIME: STREET AND VIOLENT

*"How Pickpockets Work," Tom Harris, How Stuff Works. ND. http://money.howstuffworks.com/pickpocket.htm.

"Australian Crime: Facts & Figures 2011," Australian Institute of Criminology. 2012. http://www.aic.gov.au.

"Colorado's Dark Night," *The Economist*. July 28, 2012.

"Crime Statistics in South Africa," *South Africa News*. January 23, 2012. http://southafricanews.wordpress.com/2012/01/23/crime-statistics-in-south-africa.

"Five Stages to Violent Crime," No Nonsense Self Defense. ND. http://www.nononsenseselfdefense.com/five_stages.html.

"Freeze Response," No Nonsense Self Defense. ND. http://www.nononsenseselfdefense.com/freeze-response.htm.

"Global Study on Homicide," UNODC. 2011. http://www.unodc.org/documents/data-and-analysis/statistics/Homicide/Global_study_on_homicide_Key_findings.pdf.

"How Safe Is Mexico for Tourists?," Daniel Schwartz, CBC News. January 6, 2012. http://www.cbc.ca/news/world/story/2012/01/06/f-mexico-q-a-walter-mckay.html.

"Mental Preparation," No Nonsense Self Defense. ND. http://www.nononsenseselfdefense.com/mental_preparation.htm.

"Murder Most Foul: A Global Picture of Homicide Rates," *The Economist*. October 6, 2011. http://www.economist.com/blogs/dailychart/2011/10/homicide-rates.

"San Pedro Sula, La Ciudad Más Violenta Del Mundo; Juárez, La Segunda," Seguridad, Justicia y Paz. January 11, 2012. http://www.seguridadjusticiaypaz.org.mx/sala-de-prensa/541-san-pedro-sula-la-ciudad-mas-violenta-del-mundo-juarez-la-segunda.

"Street Crime Stats Not Included in State Department Travel Warnings." Tisha Thompson and Rick Yarborough, NBC Washington. May 24, 2012. http://www.nbcwashington.com/news/local/Street-Crime-Stats-Not-Included-in-State-Department-Warnings-153284895.html.

"Top Ten Countries with Highest Reported Crime Rates," Maps of the World. 2012. http://www.mapsofworld.com/world-top-ten/countries-with-highest-reported-crime-rates.html.

"Travel Safety: Advice and Information 2," BugBog. ND. http://www.bugbog.com/travel_
      safety/travel_safety_2.html.
"Travel Safety: Tips and Information," BugBog. ND. http://www.bugbog.com/travel_safety/
      travel_safety.html#barcelona.

CULTURAL CONSIDERATIONS

http://www.geert-hofstede.com.
Cultures and Organizations: Software of the Mind. Geert Hofstede, Gert Jan Hofstede, and
      Michael Minkov. New York: McGraw-Hill. 2010.
Do's and Taboos around the World. Roger E. Axtell. 1993. White Plains, NY: The Parker
      Pen Company.
Understanding Global Cultures. Martin J. Gannon and Rajnandini Pillai. 2012. Thousand
      Oaks, CA: Sage Publications.
When Cultures Collide: Leading across Cultures. Richard D. Lewis. 2006. Boston, MA:
      Nicholas Brealey Publishing.

DATE RAPE DRUGS

*http://www.drinksafetech.com.
*"Date Rape Drugs: Date Rape Drugs Explained and De-Mystified," About.com Teen Advice.
      ND. http://teenadvice.about.com/library/weekly/aa062502a.htm.
"Rohypnol or Roofies—How to Avoid Date Rape Drugs," Kathleen Crislip, About.com
      Student Travel. ND. http://studenttravel.about.com/od/springbreak/a/roofies.htm.

DEMONSTRATIONS AND CIVIL UNREST

*"How to Deal with Riot Control Agents," WikiHow. Updated version, March 14, 2012. http://
      www.wikihow.com/Deal-With-Riot-Control-Agents.
*"How to Survive a Riot," WikiHow. Updated version, August 20, 2012. http://www.wikihow.
      com/Survive-a-Riot.
"Arab Spring: An Interactive Timeline of Middle East Protests," Garry Blight, Sheila Pulham,
      and Paul Torpey, *Guardian.* January 5, 2012. http://www.guardian.co.uk/world/
      interactive/2011/mar/22/middle-east-protest-interactive-timeline.
"Danish Cartoon Controversy," Patricia Cohen, *The New York Times.* August 12, 2009. http://
      topics.nytimes.com/topics/reference/timestopics/subjects/d/danish_cartoon_controversy/
      index.html.
"Food Riots: What Creates the Anger?" Jessica Leeder, *The Globe and Mail.* February 1,
      2011. http://www.theglobeandmail.com/news/world/food-riots-what-creates-the-anger/
      article564412.
How to Avoid Being Killed in a War Zone. Rosie Garthwaite, New York: Bloomsbury. 2011.
"Money Can't Buy Me Love," *The Economist.* June 16, 2012.
"Occupy Movement," Wikipedia. Updated version, October 19, 2012. http://en.wikipedia.org/
      wiki/Occupy_movement.
"Protests and Demonstrations in China: The Tensions and Methods Behind," Jeffrey Hays,
      Facts and Details. Updated version, March 2012. http://factsanddetails.com/china.php?
      itemid=305&catid=8&subcatid=49.
"Timeline of the Jyllands-Posten Muhammad Cartoons Controversy," Wikipedia.
      October 20, 2012. http://en.wikipedia.org/wiki/Timeline_of_the_Jyllands-Posten_
      Muhammad_cartoons_controversy.

"Violent Protest Tactical Guide—Defense Essentials," Amr Bassiouny, Amrbassiouny. November 22, 2011. http://abassiouny.wordpress.com/2011/11/22/violent-protest-tactical-guide-defence-essentials.

"Water or Gold? Locals across South America Protest Multinational Mining Projects," Chrystelle Barbier and Christine Legrand, *Le Monde*. March 11, 2012. http://www.worldcrunch.com/water-or-gold-locals-across-south-america-protest-multinational-mining-projects/4823.

DUTY OF CARE/DUTY OF LOYALTY

*http://www.dialoguesondutyofcare.com.

*http://www.internationalsos.com/dutyofcare.

*http://travelriskmanagementsolutions.com/duty-of-care.

*"Duty of Care and Travel Risk Management Global Benchmark Study," Dr. Lisbeth Claus, International SOS. 2011. http://www.internationalsos.com/dutyofcare.

"BRIC Benchmarking: Research Uncovers the Top Threats & Coping Strategies," Myles Druckman, MD/Dialogues on Duty of Care. August 9, 2012. http://dialoguesondutyofcare.com/2012/08/bric-benchmarking-research-uncovers-top-threats-strategies.

"C'est La Vie? A Step-by-Step Guide to Building a Travel Risk Management Program," Advito. 2009. http://www.advito.com.

"Corporate Travel Safety," Jim Glab, *Executive Travel Magazine*. March/April 2012. http://www.executivetravelmagazine.com/articles/corporate-travel-safety.

"Lloyd's Risk Index, 2011," Lloyd's, The Economist Intelligence Unit. 2011. http://www.lloyds.com/~/media/Files/News%20and%20Insight/360%20Risk%20Insight/Lloyds_Risk_Index_2011.pdf.

HOME SECURITY

*"15 Steps You Can Take to Prevent Home Burglary," Scambusters. ND. http://www.scam-busters.org/homeburglary.html.

*"Home Security," Crime Doctor. ND. http://www.crimedoctor.com/home.htm.

*"Home Security Tips," How Stuff Works. ND. http://home.howstuffworks.com/home-improvement/household-safety/security/home-security-tips.htm.

*"Protecting Your Home," ADT India. ND. http://www.adt.in/en/index.aspx?page=Protect.

HONEY TRAPS, SOCIAL ENGINEERING, SCAMS, AND PSYCHOLOGICAL TRICKS

*"How Scams Work," ScamWatch. ND. http://www.scamwatch.gov.au/content/index.phtml/tag/HowScamsWork.

"9 Dirty Tricks: Social Engineers' Favorite Pick-Up Lines" Joan Goodchild, CSO. February 16, 2009. http://www.csoonline.com/article/print/480589.

"Beware China's 'Honeytrap' Spies," *The Week*. February 3, 2011. http://theweek.com/article/index/211717/beware-chinas-honeytrap-spies.

"Common Scams," Jeff Starck, TruSys Institute. March 23, 2012. http://www.slideshare.net/jeffstarck/common-travel-scams.

"Hush … It's a Honey Trap," Indrani Rajkhowa Banerjee, *The Times of India*. March 17, 2011. http://articles.timesofindia.indiatimes.com/2011-03-17/people/28248711_1_madhuri-gupta-traps-honey.

"The History of the Honey Trap," Phillip Knightley, Foreign Policy. March 12, 2010. http://www.foreignpolicy.com/articles/2010/03/12/the_history_of_the_honey_trap?print=yes&hidecomments=yes&page=full.

"Tips for Business Travelers to Nigeria," Passports USA. ND. http://www.passportsusa.com/travel/tips/brochures/brochures_2113.html.

IMPROVISED EXPLOSIVE DEVICES (IEDS), LANDMINES, AND GRENADES

*"How Grenades Work," Tom Harris, How Stuff Works. ND. http://science.howstuffworks.com/grenade.htm.

*"Improvised Explosive Device," Wikipedia. Updated version, October 30, 2012. http://en.wikipedia.org/wiki/Improvised_explosive_device.

*"Landmine Awareness," CAT-UXO. 2012. http://itunes.apple.com/us/app/id515291377?mt=8.

INDUSTRIAL ESPIONAGE

http://www.cybersafe.my/guidelines.html.

http://www.infosecawareness.in/downloads.

"2012 Global State of Information Security Survey," PriceWaterhouse Cooper, *CIO Magazine*, and *CSO Magazine*. October 2012. http://www.pwc.com/gx/en/information-security-survey/index.jhtml.

"10 Most Notorious Acts of Corporate Espionage," Business Pundit. April 25, 2011. http://www.businesspundit.com/10-most-notorious-acts-of-corporate-espionage.

"Corporate Espionage on the Rise in India," Shilpa Phadnis and Mini Joseph Tejaswi, *The Economic Times*. September 24, 2010. http://articles.economictimes.indiatimes.com/2010-09-24/news/27571489_1_detective-agencies-corporate-espionage-requests.

"German Companies Cite Cost of Espionage, Sueddeutsche Says" Joseph de Weck, *Bloomberg*. April 23, 2012. http://mobile.bloomberg.com/news/2012-04-23/german-companies-cite-cost-of-espionage-sueddeutsche-says?category=.

"How to Detect and Stop Corporate Espionage," Michael Podszywalow, Continuity Central. December 2, 2011. http://www.continuitycentral.com/feature0938.html.

"UK Cyber Crime Costs £27bn a Year—Government Report," BBC. February 17, 2011. http://www.bbc.co.uk/news/uk-politics-12492309.

"U.S. Calls Out China and Russia for Cyber Espionage Costing Billions," Fox News. November 3, 2011. http://www.foxnews.com/politics/2011/11/03/us-calls-out-china-and-russia-for-cyber-espionage-costing-billions/#ixzz1yJqVa8LG.

INFORMATION SECURITY, IDENTITY THEFT, AND SOCIAL MEDIA

*http://www.trmg.biz/publications/the-a-to-z-guides.

http://www.identitytheft.info.

http://www.idtheftcenter.org.

*"How Identity Theft Works," Lee Ann Obringer, How Stuff Works. ND. http://www.howstuffworks.com/identity-theft.htm.

*"Identity Theft," Scamwatch. ND. http://www.scamwatch.gov.au/content/index.phtml/tag/identitytheft.

*"Safe Travels for You and Your Data," Riva Richmond, *New York Times*. February 17, 2010. http://www.nytimes.com/2010/02/18/technology/personaltech/18basics.html?_r=1&scp=7&sq=laptop%20and%20theft&st=cse.

*"Tech//404 Data Loss Cost Calculator," Allied World. ND. http://www.tech-404.com/calculator.html.

"15 Social Media Scams," Joan Goodchild, CSO. June 20, 2012. http://www.csoonline.com/slideshow/detail/52935/15-social-media-scams?source=csointcpt_ss#slide1.

"80% of Olympic Sites Are Scams," Emil Protalinski, ZD Net. August 3, 2012. http://www.zdnet.com/80-of-olympic-sites-are-scams-7000002124.

"Data Security: Most Finders of Lost Smartphones Are Snoops," Ashlee Vance, *Bloomberg Businessweek*. March 8, 2012. http://www.businessweek.com/articles/2012-03-08/data-security-most-finders-of-lost-smartphones-are-snoops.

"Digital Criminal Report 2010," Legal & General. 2010. http://www.legalandgeneral.com/_resources/pdfs/insurance/digital-criminal-2.pdf.

"The Fallacy of Remote Wiping," Ryan Naraine and Thomas Porter, ZD Net. July 12, 2012. http://www.zdnet.com/the-fallacy-of-remote-wiping-7000000611.

"How Much Does Identity Theft Cost? (Infographic)," Jolie O'Dell, Mashable. January 29, 2011. http://mashable.com/2011/01/29/identity-theft-infographic.

"Identity Theft Facts," Squidoo. ND. http://www.squidoo.com/identity-theft-facts.

"Identity Theft Victim Statistics," Identity Theft.info. ND. http://www.identitytheft.info/victims.aspx.

"Internet Cafe Security in Asia," Greg Rodgers, About.com Asia Travel. ND. http://goasia.about.com/od/Planning/a/Internet-Cafe-Security.htm.

"The 'Lost' Cell Phone Project, and the Dark Things It Says about Us," Bob Sullivan, MSN Digtallife Today. March 8, 2012. http://digitallife.today.msnbc.msn.com/_news/2012/03/08/10595092-exclusive-the-lost-cell-phone-project-and-the-dark-things-it-says-about-us?lite.

"Preventing Digital Identity Theft," Greg Rodgers, About.com Asia Travel. October 6, 2011. http://goasia.about.com/b/2011/10/07/preventing-digital-identity-theft.htm.

"The Socialbot Network: When Bots Socialize for Fame and Money," Yazan Boshmaf, Ildar Muslukhov, Konstantin Beznosov, and Matei Ripeanu, University of British Columbia. 2011. http://lersse-dl.ece.ubc.ca/record/264/files/ACSAC_2011.pdf.

"The Symantec Smartphone Honey Stick Project," Scott Wright, Symantec Corporation. 2012. http://www.symantec.com/about/news/resources/press_kits/detail.jsp?pkid=symantec-smartphone-honey-stick-project.

"Three New Ways to Protect Your Identity in 2012," Justine Rivero, *Forbes*. January 3, 2012. http://www.forbes.com/sites/moneywisewomen/2012/01/03/three-new-ways-to-protect-your-identity-in-2012.

"Travelers at High Risk of Identity Theft, Experts Say," Nancy Trejos, USA Today Travel. December 12, 2011. http://travel.usatoday.com/news/story/2011-12-12/Travelers-at-high-risk-of-identify-theft-experts-say/51841144/1-.

"What It's Like to Steal Someone's Identity," Joan Goodchild, CSO. November 18, 2010. http://www.csoonline.com/article/637763/what-it-s-like-to-steal-someone-s-identity.

INFORMATION SECURITY: RECOVERY STEPS FOR LOST OR STOLEN DATA

*"Fact Sheet—If Your Wallet or Handbag Is Stolen," Protect Your Financial Identity. ND. http://www.protectfinancialid.org.au/Your-wallet-or-handbag-checklist/default.aspx.

*"Fact Sheet: Immediate Steps," Protect Your Financial Identity. ND. http://www.protectfinancialid.org.au/Immediate-steps/default.aspx.

*"How to Protect Data after Laptop Theft," Jennifer Saranow Schultz, *The New York Times*. October 12, 2010. http://bucks.blogs.nytimes.com/2010/10/13/how-to-protect-data-after-laptop-theft.

*"Stolen Purse, Lost Wallet? What to Do, Step by Step," Identity Theft Labs. ND. http://www.identitytheftlabs.com/stolen-wallet-purse.

*"What Was in Your Wallet?" CreditCards.com. ND. http://www.creditcards.com/downloads/what_was_in_your_wallet.pdf.

*"Your Wallet Recovery Kit," Melody Warnick and Juan Rodriguez, CreditCards.com. October 11, 2011. http://www.creditcards.com/credit-card-news/credit-card-wallet-recovery-kit-1282.php.

"My Wallet Was Stolen: 4 Lessons Learned," Candice Lee Jones, Kiplinger. November 9, 2009. http://www.kiplinger.com/features/archives/my-wallet-was-stolen-4-lessons-learned.html.

"What to Do If You Lost Your Wallet," CreditCards.com. ND. http://www.creditcards.com/downloads/what_to_do_if_you_lost_your_wallet.pdf.

INSURANCE

*http://www.travelinsurancereview.net.

"Can You Buy Travel Insurance after Your Vacation Has Begun?," Travel Insurance Review. ND. http://www.travelinsurancereview.net/2010/01/20/can-you-buy-travel-insurance-after-your-vacation-has-begun.

"Five 'Loopholes' and How to Avoid Them," Travel Insurance Review. ND. http://www.travelinsurancereview.net/small-print.

"Four Steps after You Purchase Travel Insurance," Travel Insurance Review. ND. http://www.travelinsurancereview.net/after-purchase.

"How to Select a Plan Based on Your Needs," Travel Insurance Review. ND. http://www.travelinsurancereview.net/selecting-a-plan.

"Top 10 Questions Every Traveler Asks," Travel Insurance Review. ND. http://www.travelinsurancereview.net/questions.

"Top Ten Tips," Travel Insurance Guide. ND. http://www.travelinsuranceguide.org.uk/top-10-tips.html.

KIDNAPPINGS

*http://www.asiglobalresponse.com.

*"Annual Kidnap Review 2011," Special Contingency Risks LTD. 2011. http://www.scr-ltd.co.uk.

*Kidnap for Ransom: Resolving the Unthinkable. Richard Wright, Boca Raton, FL: CRC Press. 2009.

*"Kidnapping and Hostage Survival Guidelines," United States Department of Agriculture. ND. http://www.dm.usda.gov/ocpm/Security%20Guide/T5terror/Kidnap.htm.

*"Kidnapping for Ransom: A Fateful International Growth Industry," Frank Zuccarello, Insurance Journal. June 20, 2011. http://www.insurancejournal.com/magazines/features/2011/06/20/202864.htm.

*"Travel Security—Piracy Expert's Advice on Safer Coastal Holidays," TrainingSolutions. August 20, 2011. http://www.trainingsolutions.dk/?page_id=11.

"The £1 Billion Hostage Trade: How Kidnapping Became a Global Industry," Esme McAvoy and David Randall, The Independent. October 17, 2010. http://www.independent.co.uk/news/world/politics/the-1-billion-hostage-trade-2108947.html.

"11 Surprising Insights about Being Kidnapped," Sam Greenspan, 11 Points. August 16, 2011. http://www.11points.com/Interviews/11_Surprising_Insights_About_Being_Kidnapped.

"Global K&R Watch," ASI Global, Travelers Insurance. April-May 2012. http://www.asiglobalresponse.com/kidnap-and-ransom-watch.aspx.

"Hope in Captivity: How Kidnapped Journalists Coped," Peter Ford, USA Today. January 26, 2006. http://usatoday30.usatoday.com/news/world/2006-01-26-journalists-in-captivity_x.htm.

"The Human Face of Piracy: Pakistan's Response," Christian Bueger, Piracy Studies. March 12, 2012. http://piracy-studies.org.

"K&R Bulletin: Africa," JLT Specialty Limited. October 2012. http://www.jltgroup.com/content/UK/risk_and_insurance/Newsletter/265861_KR_Bulletin_Africa_Final_1.pdf.

"Kidnap for Ransom in the Asia-Pacific Region," ASI Global. 2012. http://www.asiglobalresponse.com/downloads/Asia%20paper.pdf.

"Kidnappings by Militant Groups Increase in North Africa," NBC News, Associated Press, and Reuters. October 2, 2012. http://worldnews.nbcnews.com/_news/2012/10/02/14189474-kidnappings-by-militant-groups-increase-in-north-africa?lite.

"Monthly Kidnap News," Control Risks, Hiscox. August 2011, issue 66. http://www.hiscox.co.uk/search/?q=monthly%20kidnap%20news.

"Nigeria as a Fast-Rising Kidnap Capital?—Politics—Nairaland," Tony Spike, Nairaland Forum. October 19, 2012. http://www.nairaland.com/1078891/nigeria-fast-rising-kidnap-capital.

"The Psychology of Kidnapping and Abduction," David V. Dafinoiu, Security and Intelligence. July 15, 2011. http://securityandintelligence.wordpress.com/2011/07/15/the-psychology-of-kidnapping-and-abduction.

"Taliban Gaining More Resources from Kidnapping," Declan Walsh, *The New York Times*. February 19, 2012. http://www.nytimes.com/2012/02/20/world/asia/pakistani-taliban-turn-to-kidnapping-to-finance-operations.html?pagewanted=all&_r=0.

MEDICAL CONSIDERATIONS AND FIRST AID

*http://www.bbc.co.uk/health.

*http://www.cdc.gov.

*http://www.humanitrain.com/talking-trauma-kit.html.

*http://www.qualsafe.com/fabooks.html.

*"First Aid in the A-Z Situations," Government of India. ND. http://www.healthy-india.org/first-aid/knowledge-of-first-aid-may-help-in-the-a-z-of-situations.html.

*"Health and Travel," Safe Travel New Zealand Government. ND. http://www.safetravel.govt.nz/beforeugo/health.shtml.

*"Well on Your Way: A Canadian's Guide to Healthy Travel Abroad," Public Health Agency of Canada. ND. http://www.phac-aspc.gc.ca/tmp-pmv/well-way_bon-depart-eng.php.

"International Drug Names Database," Drugs.com. ND. http://www.drugs.com/international.

"Staying Healthy Abroad," Christopher R. Cox, *Travel and Leisure*. July 2006. http://www.travelandleisure.com/articles/staying-healthy-abroad.

MOBILE DEVICES: LAPTOPS, PHONES, AND TABLETS

*http://www.onguardonline.gov/topics/secure-your-computer.

*"5 Essential Mobile Security Tips," Robert Lemos, *Information Week*. September 9, 2011. http://www.informationweek.com/news/security/mobile/231601091.

*"iPad Data Protection: 5 Insights to Secure Your Data," *Kensington*. July 23, 2012. http://clicksafe.kensington.com/laptop-security-blog/bid/85502/iPad-data-protection-5-insights-to-secure-your-data.

*"Laptop Security for Aid Workers," SaferAccess. January 2008. http://www.eisf.eu/resources/item/?d=1656.

*"Travel Light in the Age of Digital Thievery," Nicole Perlroth, *New York Times*. February 10, 2012. http://www.nytimes.com/2012/02/11/technology/electronic-security-a-worry-in-an-age-of-digital-espionage.html?_r=1.

"2nd Annual Airport Survey," Credant Technologies. 2012. http://www.credant.com/resources/tools.html.

"The Billion Dollar Lost Laptop Problem a Benchmark Study of U.S. Organizations," Ponemon Institute, Intel. October 31, 2010. http://www.intel.com/content/www/us/en/enterprise-security/enterprise-security-the-billion-dollar-lost-laptop-problem-paper.html.

"The Cost of Stolen Laptops," David Storm, Kensington Infographic. February 14, 2012. http://www.readwriteweb.com/mobile/2012/02/infographic-the-cost-of-stolen.php.

"Credant Survey Finds Travelers Left Behind More Than 8,000 Mobile Devices at Top U.S. Airports," Credant Technologies. July 3, 2012. http://www.credant.com/news-a-events/press-releases/295-credant-survey-finds-travelers-left-mobile-devices-at-airports.html.

"Credant Surveys San Francisco Hotels and Finds Thousands of Mobile Devices Are Lost and Unclaimed by Business Travelers and Consumers," Credant Technologies. February 27, 2012. http://www.credant.com/news-a-events/press-releases/275-credant-surveys-san-francisco-hotels.html.

"Laptop Theft Statistics," Kensington ClickSafe. August 10, 2011. http://www.slideshare.net/ClickSafelocks/laptop-theft-statistics.

"Lost Cellphones Added Up Fast in 2011," Roger Yu, USA Today Tech. March 23, 2012. http://www.usatoday.com/tech/news/story/2012-03-22/lost-phones/53707448/1.

"Lost Laptops Costs $1.8 Billion Per Year," Matthew J. Schwartz, *Information Week*. April 21, 2011. http://www.informationweek.com/news/security/mobile/229402043.

"Mobile Devices at Risk of Theft during London Olympics: Report," Nathan Eddy, eWeek. July 28, 2012. http://www.eweek.com/c/a/Mobile-and-Wireless/Mobile-Devices-at-Risk-of-Theft-During-London-Olympics-Report-377645.

"Paperclips Pose Security Threat to iPhones," Rosa Golijan, NBC News Technology. February 21, 2012. http://www.technolog.msnbc.msn.com/technology/technolog/paperclips-pose-security-threat-iphones-157719.

"Report: Most People Don't Rush to Lock Devices with Passwords," Rosa Golijan, NBC News Technology. March 2, 2012. http://www.technolog.msnbc.msn.com/technology/technolog/report-most-people-dont-rush-lock-devices-passwords-295899.

"Security Breaches Are on the Rise, but Preventable," Druva. August 15, 2012. http://www.druva.com/blog/2012/08/15/security-breaches-are-on-the-rise-but-preventable.

"Smartphone Boom Raises Identity Theft Fear," Elmer W. Cagape, Asian Correspondent. April 16, 2012. http://asiancorrespondent.com/80549/scary-consequences-for-losing-smartphones.

"What Security? MoD Has 287 Computers Stolen (or Lost) in Last 18 Months," Chris Slack, Mail Online. November 25, 2011. http://www.dailymail.co.uk/news/article-2065856/Ministry-Defence-280-laptops-stolen-18-months.html.

MONEY MATTERS

*http://www.compareprepaid.co.uk.

*"ATM Locations and Lost and Stolen Cards," I Hate Taxis. ND. http://www.ihatetaxis.com/advice/atm-locations-and-damaged-cards.

*"Wallet Safety Tips," CreditCards.com. ND. http://www.creditcards.com/downloads/wallet_safety_tips.pdf.

"Mobile Wallet Pickpocket Risks Low," Liau Yun Qing, ZD Net Asia. November 28, 2011. http://www.zdnetasia.com/mobile-wallet-pickpocketing-risks-low-62303041.htm.

NATURAL DISASTERS

"The Coming Food Crisis: Blame Ethanol?," William Pentland, *Forbes*. July 28, 2012. http://www.forbes.com/sites/williampentland/2012/07/28/the-coming-food-crisis-blame-ethanol.

"Danger Zones! Worldwide Deaths from Natural Disasters," Home Owners Insurance. April 12, 2010. http://www.homeownersinsurance.org/danger-zones.

"Global Food Crisis: Sector Results Profile," World Bank. 2012. http://go.worldbank.org/QJPC2BEFA0.

"The World Is Closer to a Food Crisis Than Most People Realize," Lester R. Brown, *Guardian*. July 24, 2012. http://www. guardian.co.uk/environment/2012/jul/24/world-food-crisis-closer.

POLITICAL CONSIDERATIONS

*"PEST Analysis," Mindtools. ND. http://www.mindtools.com/pages/article/newTMC_09.htm.

*"World Bank's Worldwide Governance Indicators (WGI) Project," World Bank. ND. http://info.worldbank.org/governance/wgi/index.asp.

"Mapping Political Context: A Toolkit for Civil Society Organizations," Robert Nash, Alan Hudson, Cecilia Lottrell, Overseas Development Institute. July 2006. http://www.odi.org.uk.

"PEST Analysis," Quick MBA. ND. http://www.quickmba.com/strategy/pest.

SEXUAL VIOLENCE AND HARASSMENT

*http://www.nsvrc.org.

http://www.preventconnect.org.

*"Sexual Assault," Southern Illinois University. Updated version, September 19, 2012. http://www.dps.siu.edu/cp_sexual_assault.htm.

*"Sexual Assault—Reducing the Risk," Metropolitan Police Department. ND. http://mpdc.dc.gov/node/208022.

*"Surviving a Rape or Sexual Assault while Travelling," Beth Morrisey, Female Traveller. September 21, 2010. http://www.femaletraveller.co.uk/surviving-rape-sexual-assault-while-travelling.html.

"How to Avoid Rape," Nonsense Self Defense. ND. http://www.nononsenseselfdefense.com/avoid_rape.htm.

"The National Intimate Partner and Sexual Violence Survey: 2010 Summary Report," Michele C. Black, Kathleen C. Basile, Matthew J. Breiding, Sharon G. Smith, Mikel L. Walters, Melissa T. Merrick, Jieru Chen, and Mark R. Stevens, Centers for Disease Control and Prevention. November 2011. http://www.cdc.gov/violenceprevention/nisvs.

Psy kisk selvforsvar for kvinder: nedsæt din risiko for krænkelser og vold (Psychological Self Defense for Women: Reduce Your Chances of Experiencing Harassment and Violence), Chris Poole, 2012, self published.

"Rape in India: The Real Role of the Police and Where Lies the Truth?," W-Women Globally. January 29, 2011. http://www.wwomenglobally.com/rape-in-india-the-real-role-of-the-police-and-where-lies-the-truth.

Risk Reduction Interventions to Prevent Sexual Victimization in College Women. Lindsey M. Orchowski. Athens: Ohio University, 2006.

"Sexual Assault: An Overview and Implications for Counselling Support," Pablo A. Fernandez, *Australasian Medical Journal* (Online). September 18, 2011. http://www.readperiodicals.com/201109/2532894531.html#ixzz27iKzSQSW.

Stopping Rape: Successful Survival Strategies. Pauline B. Bart and Patricia H. O'Brian. Oxford: Pergamon Press, 1985.

"Sweden's Rape Rate under the Spotlight," Ruth Alexander, BBC News. September 14, 2012. http://www.bbc.co.uk/news/magazine-19592372.

"U.S. to Expand Its Definition of Rape in Statistics," Charlie Savage, *The New York Times*. January 6, 2012. http://www.nytimes.com/2012/01/07/us/politics/federal-crime-statistics-to-expand-rape-definition.html.

SITUATIONAL AWARENESS

*"Pyramid for Personal Safety," No Nonsense Self Defense. ND. http://www.nononsenseselfdefense.com/pyramid.html.

*"Situation Awareness," Wikipedia. Updated version, September 23, 2012. http://en.wikipedia.org/wiki/Situation_awareness.

*"Situational Awareness: How Everyday Citizens Can Help Make a Nation Safe," Scott Steward, Stratfor. August 11, 2011. http://www.stratfor.com/weekly/20110810-situational-awareness-how-everyday-citizens-help-make-nation-safe.

The Bodyguard's Bible—The Definitive Guide to Close Protection. James Brown, BEM. 2007. Bible Publications.

"Color Codes of Awareness," Self Defense Resource.com. ND. http://www.selfdefenseresource.com/general/articles/awareness-color-codes.php.

"Got Situational Awareness?," Joe Lavelle. ND. http://thepeakmind.com/dealing-with-setbacks/got-situational-awareness.

"Situational Awareness Exercises," Defensive Carry.com. ND. http://www.defensivecarry.com/forum/defensive-carry-tactical-training/110323-situational-awareness-exercises.html.

SURVEILLANCE

*"How to Detect Surveillance and Shadowing: Parts I and II," Victoriya Security Agency. ND. http://www.victoriya-security.ru/eng/consultation.php?id=18 and http://www.victoriya-security.ru/eng/consultation.php?id=19.

*"How to Lose Someone when Being Followed," eHow. ND. http://www.ehow.com/how_2258687_lose-someone-being-followed.html.

"Home Counter Surveillance Tips and Help," Brian Westover, eHow. ND. http://www.ehow.com/way_5598055_home-counter-surveillance-tips.html.

"How to Detect the Use of Surveillance Equipment," Noel Lawrence, eHow. ND. http://www.ehow.com/how_5907277_detect-use-surveillance-equipment.html.

"How to Disappear: 9 Ways to Avoid the Creepy Surveillance Systems All Around You," Betsy Isaacson, *Huffington Post*. September 18, 2012. http://www.huffingtonpost.com/2012/09/18/how-to-disappear-avoid-surveillance_n_1872419.html.

"The Kaspersky Kidnapping—Lessons Learned," Scott Stewart, Stratfor. April 28, 2011. http://www.stratfor.com/weekly/20110427-kaspersky-kidnapping-lessons-learned.

"Stranger Danger Tips for Walkers 2: If You Think You Are Being Followed," Wendy Bumgardner, About.com Walking. April 6, 2012. http://walking.about.com/cs/med/a/strangerdanger_2.htm?p=1.

"What to Do when You Believe You're Being Followed," Sandy Esslinger, *Road and Travel Magazine*. ND. http://www.roadandtravel.com/safetyandsecurity/beingfollowed.html.

TERRORISM

*http://www.start.umd.edu/gtd.

"1970–2011, Advanced Search: Region," Global Terrorism Database. November 3, 2012. http://www.start.umd.edu/gtd/search/Results.aspx?charttype=bar&chart=regions&casualties_type=&casualties_max=.

"1970–2011, Advanced Search: Weapon Type," Global Terrorism Database. November 3, 2012. http://www.start.umd.edu/gtd/search/Results.aspx?charttype=bar&chart=weapon&casualties_type=b&casualties_max=&dtp2=all.

"2000–2010, Advanced Search: Casualties," Global Terrorism Database. October 21, 2012. http://www.start.umd.edu/gtd/search/Results.aspx?start_yearonly=2000&end_yearonly=2010&start_year=&start_month=&start_day=&end_year=&end_month=&end_day=&asmSelect0=&asmSelect1=&dtp2=all&success=yes&casualties_type=b&casualties_max.

"2000–2010, Advanced Search: Incidents," Global Terrorism Database. November 3, 2012. http://www.start.umd.edu/gtd/search/Results.aspx?charttype=pie&chart=target&casualties_type=b&casualties_max=&start_yearonly=2000&end_yearonly=2010&dtp2=all.

"2011 Report on Terrorism," National Counterterrorism Center. March 12, 2012. http://www.nctc.gov/docs/2011_NCTC_Annual_Report_Final.pdf.

"Addressing Lessons from the Emergency Response to the 7 July 2005 London Bombings," UK Home Office, 2006. http://www.london.gov.uk/sites/default/files/london-prepared/homeoffice_lessonslearned.pdf.

"How Scared of Terrorism Should You Be?," Robert Bailey, Reason.com. September 6, 2011. http://reason.com/archives/2011/09/06/how-scared-of-terrorism-should.

"Terrorism," Wikipedia. Updated version, September 13, 2012. http://en.wikipedia.org/wiki/Terrorism.

"Terrorism in Asia: What Does It Mean for Business?," Lloyd's, IISS. 2007. http://www.lloyds.com/Search?as_sitesearch=www.lloyds.com/~/media/Lloyds&q=goods+in+transit.

TRANSPORTATION: DRIVING AND RENTAL VEHICLES

*"Basic Safety for All Travelers," ASIRT. ND. http://www.asirt.org/KnowBeforeYouGo/LeisureTravel/SafetyTipsforEveryone/tabid/230/Default.aspx.

*"Car Rental Tips," Travel Sense. ND. http://www.travelsense.org/tips/carrentaltips.cfm.

*"Travel Security—Rental Cars, What to Check For," TrainingSolutions. January 11, 2011. http://www.trainingsolutions.dk/?page_id=11.

"Protection for You and Your Car," Detective Kevin Coffey, Corporate Travel Safety. ND. http://www.kevincoffey.com/driving/protection_for_you_and_your_car.htm.

TRANSPORTATION: PUBLIC TRANSPORTATION AND WALKING

"How to Stay Safe on Public Transportation," Sheila C. Wilkinson, eHow. ND. http://www.ehow.com/how_4466156_stay-safe-public-transportation.html.

"How to Walk Safely," Wendy Bumgardner, About.com Walking. Updated version, August 28, 2012. http://walking.about.com/cs/safety/ht/htsafewalking.htm.

"Stranger Danger Safety Tips for Walkers," Wendy Bumgardner, About.com Walking. Updated version, April 6, 2012. http://walking.about.com/cs/med/a/strangerdanger.htm.

"Tips for Your Safety while Riding Public Transportation," Donna Biasi, Streetdirectory.com Singapore Guide. ND. http://www.streetdirectory.com/travel_guide/215921/travel_tips/tips_for_your_safety_while_riding_public_transportation.html.

TRANSPORTATION: TAXIS

*"7 Common Taxi Scams—And 7 Steps to Beat Them," Scambusters. ND. http://www.scambusters.org/taxi.html.

*"Airport Taxi Scams and How to Avoid Them," Price of Travel. November 5, 2010. http://www.priceoftravel.com/575/airport-taxi-scams-and-how-to-avoid-them.

"China: Shanghai Taxi Gang Preys on Tourists," Larry Habegger, World Travel Watch. March 12, 2008. http://www.worldtravelwatch.com/08/03/china-shanghai-taxi-gang-preys-on-tourists-unusual-hostage-incident-in-xian.html.

"Getting Around in China—Taking a Taxi," Sara Naumann, About.com China Travel. ND. http://gochina.about.com/od/tripplanning/p/Taxi_China.htm.

"San Francisco Taxi Tips," Ingrid Taylar, About.com San Francisco. ND. http://sanfrancisco.about.com/od/gettingaroun1/qt/sftaxitips.htm.

TRANSPORTATION HAZARDS: ACCIDENTS

*"Coping with a Car Crash Abroad," Damian Tysdal, Travel Insurance Review. ND. http://www.travelinsurancereview.net/2012/07/23/coping-with-a-car-crash-abroad.

"Global Status Report on Road Safety 2013," World Health Organization. 2013. http://www.who.int/violence_injury_prevention/road_safety_status/2013/en/index.html.

"Road Crash Statistics," Association for Safe International Road Travel. ND. http://www.asirt.org/KnowBeforeYouGo/RoadSafetyFacts/RoadCrashStatistics/tabid/213/Default.aspx.

TRANSPORTATION HAZARDS: CARJACKING/HIJACKING

*"Carjacking—Don't Be a Victim," U.S. Department of State. August 2002. http://www.state.gov/m/ds/rls/rpt/19782.htm.

*"Preventing Hijacking," South African Police Service. ND. http://www.saps.gov.za/crime_prevention/safety_tips/car_hijacking.htm.

"Car Hijack Victim's Nightmare—What It Feels Like to Have Your Precious Life in the Hands of Someone Else," Vusi Masango, Sowetan Live. November 17, 2011. http://www.sowetanlive.co.za/news/2011/11/17/car-hijack-victim-s-nightmare---what-it-feels-like-to-have-your-precious-life-in-the-hands-of-someone-else.

"Carjacking in Australia: Recording Issues and Future Directions," Lisa Jane Young, Charles Sturt, Dr. Maria Borzycki, Australian Institute of Criminology. Updated version, July 13, 2009. http://www.aic.gov.au/publications/current%20series/tandi/341-360/tandi351/view%20paper.aspx.

"Confessions of a Car Hijacker," Vuyi Jabavu, Sowetan Live. October 13, 2011. http://www.sowetanlive.co.za/news/2011/10/13/confessions-of-a-car-hijacker.

"Hijack Claims Are Down," Lisa Steyn, *Mail & Guardian*. July 13, 2012. http://mg.co.za/article/2012-07-13-hijacking-claims-are-down.

"How to Avoid Being Carjacked," WikiHow. Updated version, October 25, 2012. http://www.wikihow.com/Avoid-Being-Carjacked.

"How to Avoid Carjacking," Detective Kevin Coffey, Corporate Travel Safety. ND. http://www.kevincoffey.com/driving/how_to_avoid_carjacking.htm.

Staying Safe. Juval Aviv and William P. Kucewicz, New York: HarperCollins. 2004.

"Sydney the Carjacking Capital of Australia," Clementine Cuneo, *Daily Telegraph*. March 9, 2011. http://www.dailytelegraph.com.au/sydney-the-carjacking-capital-of-aust/story-fn6b3v4f-1226017949706-.

TRANSPORTATION HAZARDS: CHECKPOINTS

"Random Checkpoint," Wikipedia. Updated version, October 23, 2012. http://en.wikipedia.org/wiki/Random_checkpoint.

"Security Checkpoint," Wikipedia. Updated version, June 27, 2012. http://en.wikipedia.org/wiki/Military_checkpoint.

WELL-BEING, STRESS, AND FEAR

*http://www.stressmanagementtips.com.

*"37 Stress Management Tips: Find Your Own Escape Route with Our Easy Stress Management Tips," Michael Castleman, *Reader's Digest*. ND. http://www.rd.com/health/wellness/37-stress-management-tips.

*"Stress Management," Melissa Conrad Stöppler, MD, MedicineNet.com. August 24, 2011. http://www.medicinenet.com/stress_management_techniques/article.htm.

*"Stress Management: How to Reduce, Prevent, and Cope with Stress," Melinda Smith, MA, and Robert Segal, MA, HelpGuide.org. Updated version, July 2012. http://www.helpguide.org/mental/stress_management_relief_coping.htm.

*"Stress Management Worksheets," Inner Health Studio. ND. http://www.innerhealthstudio.com/stress-management-worksheets.html.

*"Understanding Feelings of Insecurity," Dr. Donald Bosch, Headington Institute. May 2012. http://headington-institute.net/wp/?p=750.

*"Wellness Worksheets," McGraw Hill Higher Education. 2004. http://www.mhhe.com/socscience/hhp/wellness.

"Fear Management vs Danger Management," No Nonsense Self Defense. ND. http://www.nononsenseselfdefense.com/FEARvsDANGER.html.

"How to Manage Yourself during a Critical Incident," Dr. Donald Bosch, Headington Institute. ND. http://www.youtube.com/watch?v=9QI7CSUO-Rg&feature=youtu.be.

"Travel Psychology 101," Michael Brein. ND. http://www.michaelbrein.com/travel-psychology-101.html.

Index